BATH OF STEEL

THE ERASURE AND REGENERATION OF MARGINALISED PSYCHOLOGIES

DR. DEAN WHITTINGTON

authorHOUSE®

AuthorHouse™
1663 Liberty Drive
Bloomington, IN 47403
www.authorhouse.com
Phone: 1-800-839-8640

Published by AuthorHouse   01/11/2012

ISBN: 978-1-4678-8365-8 (sc)
ISBN: 978-1-4678-8367-2 (hc)
ISBN: 978-1-4678-8366-5 (ebk)

CONTENTS

"But beyond the idea that it was good for medicine, many doctors believed that war was good for the men who fought in it. In a nation beset by "nervous crisis," plagued by fears of degeneration, epidemics of neurasthenia, and unchecked traumatic neurosis, war emerged as a nervous cure all, a collective "nerve corrective." Like the naive poet sons of the European bourgeoisie, doctors and social critics alike expressed longing for what Franz Marc called "war's purifying fire." Psychiatrists valorized "the mighty healing power of the iron bath (Stahlbad) . . .

Paul Lerner (2003) P46 "Hysterical Men,"

"Insanity in individuals is something rare—but in groups, parties, nations and epochs, it is the rule."

Nietzsche F. (1886) N156 "Beyond Good and Evil,"

Dedicated to those without emotional shelter

ACKNOWLEDGEMENTS

I would like to thank Nick, Alan, Patsy and Anthony plus everyone in the hostel who gave their support over the years. I would also like to say thanks to Dr. Chris Maddox and Laishan for their direction. Further thanks to Tony, Natalie, Rei, Julie and Kay for belief. I would also express my gratitude to Don, Daniel, Ritchie and Jason for their special insights as I have finally incorporated some of them and Paola for pointing me in the right direction.

I would also like to Kate White editor of the attachment journal for providing the impetus to write the book, Mike Shiner and Jean Grove for their help over the years. I would also like to highlight the role of the Adlerian Society in keeping a beacon alight and for Robin in igniting a future with his psychologically informed revolution. Also thanks to Elinor for her assistance. Also not forgetting my wife who supported me over the months this book was put together.

CHAPTER 1
INTRODUCTION

This book outlines how a series of fundamental policy errors distorted the treatment of substance use, homelessness and psychological health, creating a paradigm paralysis. Treatment was based on a series of miscalculations that halted the social, psychological, regeneration of people, during an era of economic abundance. Vast resources were poured into a bureaucratic infrastructure, producing a paucity of outcome results. This becomes particularly acute when investigated for any social psychological, regenerative return in the substance use field. An issue ongoing issue since the National Drugs Strategy was launched in the UK in 1998. The focus has always been on reducing crime as the remit was passed onto the National Treatment Agency (NTA) in 2001. They focused on greater access into drug treatment aiming to retain people, and then satiate their opiate levels with state sponsored opioids. State intervention was undertaken to stop substance users from committing crimes to buy heroin. This became the treatment mantra and the eventual rationale for the state intervention. Harm reduction seemingly halted HIV through providing needles, citric acid, spoons and condoms, as clean works and protected sex stopped people from passing the Aids virus. This appeared to be a successful strategy but strangely failed to stem the rise of Hepatitis C.

Social psychological recovery was erased as a discussion item during this era. It was then written out as a treatment outcome. The idea of recovery and shifting to a positive lifestyle was quietly dropped. I will argue this erasure has engendered systemic failure and is still negatively conceived and enacted.

Treatment agencies were ostensibly commissioned to provide harm reduction or crime reduction services. Mixtures of private, voluntary sector and National Health Service (NHS) services were commissioned by 149 Drug Alcohol Action Teams (DAAT). The NTA provided the guidelines for initiating and commissioning treatment. It was then monitored by a central monitoring team who oversaw 9 regions with a number of regional officers who each monitor a number of County, Unitary Authority or Metropolitan Authority Drug and Alcohol Action Teams (DAAT's). Within the DAAT's are council officers; the data collection officer, the DAAT leader, the young people's co-ordinator, the shared care worker, the service user rep, the admin and the various researchers. A huge tier of bureaucrats formed as a hierarchical pyramid, building themselves on the shoulders of the front line worker in differing managerial tiers. Each treatment agency had its own internal chain of command. There were perhaps three of four agencies in each London Borough. Treatment delivery was wholly centralised and bureaucratised as treatment agencies were reduced to functionaries who delivered systemised, routinised, interventions, overseen by a vast bureaucratic army of council officials, police officers, civil servants and health officials. This vast bureaucracy cascaded edicts onto the practitioner, regulating their practical interventions. This thwarted innovation, as the research evidence emanating out of addictions psychiatry was essentially flawed, based on a complete erasure of understanding the impact of childhood and adult trauma.

The homeless sector meanwhile was overseen by Council officials who viewed homelessness as another service that could be commissioned and decommissioned according to cost. There was no sense of social psychological regeneration of homeless people.

These systems were based upon a philosophical and psychological perception of two essential groups, the socially included and the socially excluded, those who belong and those who do not. I will be analysing the genealogy of this outlook and the case histories I draw upon will be used to overturn the normative research stereotypes.

This book challenges the fundamental belief system systems underpinning the government interventions, perceiving them as, at best, blinkered ideological viewpoints that sucked in financial resources for no appreciable gain. In undertaking a genealogy of system formation, it becomes apparent they were based on various scientific concepts. These were incorporated into crime reduction/criminology and addiction/psychiatry. Satiating young people with the short term panacea of Methadone became a long term strategy, with no thought of any social psychological regeneration. In stark contrast to this nihilism, I will provide an alternative view based on transformation. This is derived from Individual Psychotherapy. This view is also based on Praxis, an immersion within the everyday lives of people on the margins. This entails I stand opposed to the social scientists who observe from a distance. The fundamental difference being I had clinical supervision to look at the resonances that emerged when working with the homeless. This stands distinctly opposed to the social science methodology of objectification, studying people as objects. This entails no self introspection on self prejudice and self construction to ascertain whether the "knowledge" produced, is simply an autobiographical projection, disguised as objective social knowledge. It also fails to explore the internal meanings of those who are deemed the "other" (Sartre 1943).

I will outline how these various theoretical and practical assumptions of the NTA prohibited psychological change from occurring en masse, in the mainstream funded treatment services. I will then draw on the case histories, to portray an alternative paradigm, missed by the overemphasis on "Crime Reduction," "addiction" and the various CBT techniques the NTA has passed, as appropriate for intervention. I will also challenge the philosophical assumptions built around these terminologies. Significant problems have arisen from a lack of psychological, theoretical, conceptualisation of the dominant emotional resonances. The policy makers lacked any insights from individual psychology (Adler 1927, 1931, 1956, 2004). Their interventions were based on significant scientific errors that focused on genetics, addiction, crime management and this shaped their intervention techniques. Nihilism has been the result. The template based on addiction has ignored any sense of personal history.

Moreover there is no proof of an addiction gene, the mu opioids reception gene polymorphism (A118G) claimed to be the addiction receptor is primarily linked to stress, (MCCaul M, Yang , Reynolds J, Gotjen D, Lee S, Ali A, 2002) rather than "drug addiction." There is however a strong belief an addiction gene exists, derived from the study of the Mu receptor site. This belief has created a significant policy error, as it has entailed the emotional lives of those who have chronic substance use issues, being eradicated from any policy discussion or academic debate. The Social Sciences and the Psychiatric addictions experts have never defined their philosophies explicitly in the UK as genetic. This encompasses the work of the National Addiction Centre at King's College, including the architects of the TOPS forms Dr. John Marsden and Dr. Michael Farrell (2007) and the Social Sciences work of Kamlesh Patel (Patel K. and Wibberley C. 2002). The theoretical vacuum these scientists have created has led to a theoretical malaise that weighs heavily upon the current treatment system.

In the UK the conceptual understanding of trauma and self medication has been eradicated. Numerous departments exist to study "addictions" but there is no department that studies "self medication." Yet in the USA through the work of Substance Abuse and Mental Health Services (SAMHSA), trauma and substance use are seen as irretrievably linked. There have been numerous links made between cocaine use and trauma by Brady, et al (2001), addiction and trauma have been studied by Evans, K. and Sullivan, J. M. (1995). The links between violence and trauma have been made explicit since the early 1990's in the work of Herman, J. (1992). The relationship between alcohol use and trauma is documented in a British article by Moncrieff, J. et al (1996). Najavitis (2002) produced a manual that showed how to work with substance use and trauma. Another article by Rice, C. et al (2001) looks at the self reports of physical, sexual an emotional abuse and the relationship to alcoholism.

These studies raise numerous questions on why trauma erasure occurred. Drawing on Foucault (1998), it appears science colonised everyday life as a discourse erasing the emotions. It installed a new "faith" of objectification, with a claim to be "value free." There is no independent evidence to verify the various claims, and the resulting research has built its foundations on empirical sand. It has constructed fantastical worlds, formulated on trauma erasure.

This scientific colonisation leads discipline and punishment and the medical model, both linked to market economies to provide substance use, mental health and homeless services. In drawing on various research reports and case histories I will highlight how this impacted on the ground, thwarting psychological regeneration.

I will show how these philosophical errors rested upon ungrounded assumptions, based on the emotional shutdown of the authors and the numerous miscalculations that resulted. These assumptions became embedded within the national policy, influencing how it was administered. This culminated in constraining the emotional growth of the people who needed the support from treatment services, to climb out of an abyss.

Then I will highlight new ways of working, based on various psychotherapeutic models drawn from a substance use agency I built (1989-2005), the ideas gleaned from a homeless hostel I worked within (2007-2011), and the resonant effect with the ideas of Julian Le Grand (2011) in the 21st century. This will involve building on the work of Attachment Theory (Bowlby 1984, 1969, 1973, 1980), Self Medication (Khantzian 1985, 1995, 1999 2010) and Individual Psychology (1956, 2004). The ideas within this book are gleaned from Praxis (1970), the combination of action and reflection. The evidence is based on the resonances emanating from numerous case histories, illuminating the emotional realities of people who exist on the margins, undertaken over the years.

The key to transformation is belief, and this arises from the work of Alfred Adler (1927, 1931, 1956, 2004) and Viktor Frankl's (1952, 1959) ideas derived from "Individual Psychology," and "Existential Psychology," both drawing on Friedrich Nietzsche (1895).

"If we possess our why of life we can put up with any how."

Nietzsche F. (1895) N12 "Twilight of the Idols,"

One remit of therapy is to create a meaning (Frankl V. 1952, 1959) and an engagement with the world, a will to live. This provides a purpose that negates meaninglessness, Stirner (1844) and Nietzsche (1878, 1889, 1882, 1895, 1968) both identified these forms residing within nihilism. This arises from a collapse in the belief that religion and science can transform the world. A purpose is formed from self belief, harnessing emotions, thereby creating an emotional nexus that sustains belief. The basis of a social network rests upon becoming an emotional being. This entails making external connections from an internal desire to reach outwardly.

The works of Stirner (1844) and Nietzsche (1878, 1889, 1882, 1895, 1968) challenged the certainty of social facts. These authors highlight the transitory nature of "belief." Beliefs collapse and fade away, but what remains are the emotional resonances of being human. This creates life, and its antithesis; meaninglessness, the nothingness (Sartre 1943) that is glimpsed when people die, relationships dissolve and people lose contact with their social networks. It leaves a deep and enduring loss, as the huge trapdoor opens, to show a soundless universe where all elaborate certainties tumble into this silent abyss.

"Let us beware of saying there are laws in nature; There are only necessities, there is nobody who commands, nobody who obeys, nobody who trespasses.

Nietzsche F. (1882) N109 "The Gay Science,"

Constraining the ideas of emotional growth and the dynamic of moving forward have been the nihilistic ideas that deny change and harness people to ideologies that denigrate transformation. These, as Stirner (1844) points out, are "wheels in the head." Societies are constrained as much by belief systems, as they are by objects. I will highlight how these belief systems have constrained social regeneration. Science can either be transformative or be used to promote meaninglessness. This quote highlights the nature of relativism hidden within the mantle of science.

"Ultimately, man finds in things nothing but what he himself has imported into them: the finding is called Science.

Nietzsche F. (1968) N606 "Will to Power,"

Science is seen as rational. It is used to discover knowledge that exists independently of people. Nietzsche asks another set of questions. Is science merely the reflection of the prejudices of scientists? Is Science just another "will to power?"

Eugenics for example, appeared scientific in the early part of the 20th Century. It was a prominent movement from 1880 until 1945 and had a large number of advocates, who worked to further the ideas, seemingly based upon a scientific rereading of Darwin, later refined by his cousin Galton. Harry Laughlin, a USA proponent of the Social Darwinist view encouraged the Virginia assembly to pass two laws, SB 219, entitled "The Racial Integrity Act[1]" and SB 281, "An Act to provide for the sexual sterilization of inmates of State institutions in certain cases." This became "The Sterilization Act" in 1924 (Kuhl S. 1992). Thirty other states enacted similar laws in the USA.

These ideas arose from his research into which races were eugenically fit. Laughlin based his viewpoint on a fixed idea of the world, stemming from his personal autobiography, derived primarily from his white upbringing (Nietzsche 1968). This provided him with a basis to categorise other races in a hierarchy. This example defines a number of issues that resonate in this book. The Racial Integrity Act stated there were two classifications of people: white and colored, defined by the "one drop rule." Therefore anyone with any African or Indian ancestry was deemed colored. These were deemed the "other" (Sartre 1943). Interracial marriage was then banned and criminalized until 1967. This was finally overturned by the US Supreme Court, with the case *Loving v Virginia*. Each law was based upon Laughlin's combination of natural and social science research to initially limit immigration, and then to change the internal composition of the American population. Laughlin's sterilisation laws provided the model for the National Socialist Race Laws passed enacted after 1932 in Germany. Laughlin was given an award by the University of Heidelberg in 1936 for his "services on behalf of racial hygiene" (Kuhl S 1992). This is an example of a scientific belief, being socially constructed to create reality, rather than reality being discovered by science.

The first identified problem Nietzsche (1968) notes, is how to overcome this type of autobiographical projection in creating social knowledge. He asks whether knowledge relates to the Praxis of transformation, or whether it promotes despair, drawing from an individual projection. In the above example it could be perceived that Laughlin is defining the white races with a purpose, whilst entrapping the non white races in despair. This is an example of a power discourse. This is built on subjectivity, and rests upon an ability to define reality (Foucault 1995). A power discourse imposes a belief, such as, is addiction genetic, or is there a hierarchy of race? It is the ability to begin a discussion and then set the parameters of the debate.

It is also an example of nihilism, as it erases emotional connections in establishing its thought parameters. It does not seek to understand its effect on the populations it makes pronouncements upon. It erases the idea their emotions exist, thereby promoting mechanistic despair. Although this type of science is now seemingly discredited, it took a World War to bring its ideology to a halt. Its ideas however on race and those who are unfit, are still carried within various scientific discourses; it is an undercurrent of sociobiology. I will be pointing out it has limited the understanding to conceptualise marginalised psychologies and connect to them. It has also stopped any reflection on any remedies. It has become a crucial theoretical problem. Nihilism has also arisen from the Social Sciences shunting the emotional world to one side, and then falsely basing itself on an elevation of rational Science. This entails observing objects, then denying their subjectivity, ensuring they remain distant, and less than, the researcher. This lead to the scientific errors of eugenics, as it seeks to objectify and categorise, rather than create a dialogue to understand. The scientific authors undergo no self analysis or introspection; they merely proclaim their impartiality, when they discover "facts" using scientific methods. As Nietzsche highlights, it is no more than a belief system, a will to power (Nietzsche 1968). Those who are objectified are denied a voice, entailing they either succumb to the dominant view, or create a resistance. When they create a resistance, this again is researched to find the mechanistic causes, as emotional resistance and revenge are erased from academia. This is why those who are seemingly tasked to resolve a problem, have in effect, created it. They only administer discipline, based on their false presumptions, founded on their own emotional erasure. This creates a counter reaction from the objectified. This leads to more strictures being put in place by those who have access to power. This becomes a dialectic of constraint, as new laws and perceptions are based on this counter reaction. It perpetuates the cycles of violence, as the mechanistic discipline fails to curb the emotional behaviour.

Scientific adherents cloak themselves as empirical rationalists, standing back from afar. They discuss their objects as it they exist behind glass screens. In reality, as Nietzsche (1968) highlights, they are projecting their own autobiographies. The case histories in this book show that people who exist on the margins of society can regenerate, when infused with belief. Therefore, I propose only those scientific autobiographies that harness themselves to creating and sustaining regeneration should be highlighted, as "belief requires belief." This is the catalyst, but not the end point of transformation. The fundamental difference between objectified science, and its proponents projecting their biographies and mine, is I ignite social regeneration.

The problems inherent within the social sciences are encapsulated in "The Elephant Man." Think of John Merrick, the "Elephant Man" in the David Lynch film (1980) standing on the stage, as the doctors gather round to discuss him. No one talks to him, they only talk about him. Eventually when they talk to him, they realise he is human. Apply this model to the discussions on homelessness, substance use and mental health. When discussions arise with the "miscreants" they are conducted with a clipboard and a microphone. Would you divulge your emotional pain to someone who appears with these tools? An expectation the most traumatised and brutalised members of society will express emotional honesty to those who survey the world as fixed objects, is a mere figment of the rationalist hallucination. Even if you do speak about emotions, the academics cannot hear it, because it not part of their conceptual world.

"From a doctoral examination—"What is the task of all higher education?" To turn men into machines. "What are the means?" Man must learn to be bored. "How is that accomplished?" By means of the concept of duty. "Who serves as the model?" The philologist: he teaches grinding. "Who is the perfect man?" The civil servant. "Which philosophy offers the highest formula for the civil servant?" Kant's: the civil servant as a thing-in-itself, raised up to be judge over the civil servant as phenomenon."

Nietzsche F. (1895) N29 "Twilight of the Idols,"

The crux of Academic knowledge is its desire for elevation to enhance its legitimacy. This highlights its will to power (Nietzsche 1968). The emotional discourses are a hindrance because everyone has them. Instead rationalist theories hover above humanity, where facts are plucked like apples from a tree, baked into a social cake, and then served as a glazed product. Only the Rational Scientist understands the secret recipes. The academic contemplates (Arendt 1958) and gazes down upon the throng. They forget they are immersed within its body. Looking down through the barrel of a microscope they see objects. This is the pedagogy of the policy makers, transmitted to the bureaucracies. Instead of basing the world on this misconception, an immersion within the throng is needed. However even this, when I explore George Orwell's (1933) experiences in "Down and Out in Paris and London," and the critique of Connell's (1995) Masculinities in "Beaten into Violence" (2007), immersion still becomes problematic. Both authors project onto marginalised groups of men their individual autobiographies, even when they became immersed in their cultures. They did no prior introspective work, and seek to observe rather than connect. Commentators who have undergone no self reflection, see their projections in the world around them, and do not hear or see beyond this mirage. It is a narcissistic reflection. It could be argued the eugenicists see malformed people who need to be disposed of, because they need to elevate themselves above the emotional pain they survey. Eugenics is merely a will to power, (Nietzsche 1968) a desire to create a hierarchy based on a belief system, entailing those who design the system sit upon its apex. It is therefore autobiographical, based on an emotional erasure, and furthermore, it could also be seen as an act of sublimation (Fenichel 1972). It has been used by adherents who seek to disguise their own emotional pain by projecting themselves above a perceived inferior group.

People who are bereaved, recently divorced, families where children have left home, men/women recently made redundant all undergo a change of perception that may lead to emotional crises, when suddenly the meanings and purposes that previously existed are ripped apart. People are taught to suppress these effects, and carry on calmly (Fenichel 1972, Lister 1982, Free 2002). This creates a social silence, not a social science. These emotions are deemed personal, unless relational connections are made (Gilligan C. 1989, 1990a, 1990b). This arena is not part of the everyday social discourse, and talking about these issues creates social embarrassment. It is only through making emotional connection, people share these private moments and fears with one another, because they are taught to be uncomfortable about these resonant feelings. Often they cannot share them with friends for fear of vulnerability. Therefore when a Social Science researcher appears asking questions, these feelings are suppressed and a social 'front' (Goffman 1959) is presented, because the relational bonds (Gilligan 1989, 1990a, 1990b, Whittington 2007) between researchers and researched are deemed to be irrelevant. Emotional erasure within social science research creates a dichotomy, because these hidden emotions have a real impact on the world. They become sublimated (Fenichel 1972) into behavioural forms that emerge as challenging, as they crystallise into depression, or a striving to compensate for a loss (Adler1956). Is it possible to place a measure on loss?

Now consider the emotions stemming from childhood, arising from being raped, tortured, beaten, scalded, witnessing mothers being smashed against walls, guns pulled against children and fired, fathers trying to run over their children in cars, sisters raped, being beaten at school, tied up, robbed and humiliated. These dramatically shift the perception of the world into a negative direction. These same dynamics arose in "Disempowerment and Disconnection-Trauma and Homelessness Report" published by Glasgow Homelessness Network (Collins M. and Phillips J 2003). Can the effects of trauma be measured by science? All of these issues and more have arisen in the therapy I have undertaken, resonating with this Scottish Study. These issues arise again in the Joseph Rowntree publication (McDonagh, T. 2011). Why were these dynamics missed previously? They are not new to the 21st century. They emerged en masse in the 1980's but remained hidden by the Social and Medical Sciences.

The ideal norm is to have a store of pleasant memories. These can be retrieved from childhood; trips to museums, going to watch football with Dad, fishing by the pond, family picnics, holidays abroad, the first kiss, or being helped to ride a push bike. These are emotional anchor points. The feeling of being loved and valued at some point provides personal validation. These memories keep the feelings of dread (Kierkegaard 1844) at arm's length, and instead promote a sense of being valued.

Now imagine none of those anchor points ever existing, and instead a reign of fear and terror enshrouded childhood. There were no pleasant memories to retrieve in adulthood, just pain, trauma and torture. How would you cope? These pleasant memories are the emotional anchor

11

points that connect people into a nexus of emotions that help everyone to move forward with confidence and belief. This anchoring allows people to feel safe within the world, free from existential dread (Kierkegaard 1844). Pleasant memories can be retrieved to create a sense of well being.

Imagine your parents never caring for you and placing you in a Children's Home run by people who wanted to beat you for every infraction? Then you can inhabit the existential horror of the clients who appear in these case histories. The behaviour that Moss exhibits, is not genetic, but a reaction to real events. It was emotional revenge. Not everyone raped and beaten becomes an armed robber is the retort. "Some people go on to do other things." This common refrain is parried by Alice Miller (1983, 1987, 1991, 1990, 2006) who points out beaten and silenced children rise to the head of political parties that proclaim freedom in the name of death; National Socialism or State Socialism. They become Serial Killers, depressants or wife abusers. As Fenichel (1972) highlights when trauma is sublimated, it become transmuted into an effect. Yet Harry Stack Sullivan (1953, 1970, 1974, Barton Evans 1996) highlights when emotional bonds are created, people can recover from, if not entirely forget the legacy of, their trauma. Being abused is not a life sentence. It is however made into one by the academics who firstly have ignored its existence, and then secondly like Robert Hare (1999) claim the academic high ground by pathologising the victims, condemning their counter reaction and assigning a pathological label, based on genetic determinism. This induces further violence. This is enacted on those who have already been beaten, creating the inter-generational cycle of violence.

Ordinarily as I will show in the extensive case histories, unacknowledged trauma becomes transmuted into various substitute behavioural forms (Fenichel 1972). The psychological impact of abuse creates hard, tough, violent masculine responses to stop any further attacks. As "Jerry" shows in his case history, underneath the hard man image, is a little boy who has been vandalised. He does not want to be hurt again, as he has constructed character armour (Reich 1933) in response to his trauma. Robert Hare (1999) however, only sees the thug who needs to be tamed with his genetic determinism, backed with applied force.

The first identified problem is therefore philosophical, and the problem flows from a scientific assumption that genes determine behaviour, a desire to create a moral conformity.

"We need unities in order to be able to reckon: that does not mean we must suppose that such unities exist. We have borrowed the concept of unity from our "ego" concept-our oldest article of faith."

Nietzsche F. (1968) N635 "Will to Power"

The social scientific world becomes reformulated into the image of a presumed imaginary order. This is a self imposition, as irrationality is excluded from this self imposed version of a self composed mirage. In clear language, it means hacking off those memories/events/feelings/emotions that do not comply with being cultured/refined and the above. Faith in ourselves, devoid of introspection is then transposed onto the world. This is the narcissistic reflection of power. It creates a make believe world based on a presumed habitus (Bourdieu 1984), a hierarchy of cultured refinement, an alternate land where emotional pain no longer exists. This is then projected to ward off other people's emotional pain and to create a social cocoon.

Flowing from this identified problem are the research areas that arise from the first philosophical error; the belief in this habitus of refinement (Bourdieu 1984). This is a presupposed set of beliefs about culture. This idea rests upon a cultivated hierarchy basing itself upon a distinct taste and refinement. This distinguishes a hierarchy of cultured people. The individual learns to create an identity through adopting a mantle that is cultured, or alternatively they create an oppositional stance. This is deemed vulgar but can also later be incorporated into a habitus. It is through this process, a person can elevate themselves through a hierarchy, where they can measure and denigrate the "other" (Sartre 1943). The only hierarchy is that based on self knowledge and self actualisation. It is an internal measurement.

Social science methodologies; the way data is captured about the real world fails to acknowledge marginalised peoples psychological realities because it is based on this self composed mirage, a denial of self knowledge. Those who weave social reality, merely seek their fantasy self in the world around them. The induction into social science presumes the authors can switch off their emotions and prejudices with the click of an internal switch. This is merely a ruse, a self deceit.

These social scientific worlds cannot encapsulate existential dread (Kierkegaard 1844), or anguish (Sartre 1943) as a result. The terror of life's meanings, bereft of emotional anchor points, is routinely ignored. The violence involved in demolishing these anchor points is shredded and then stamped upon in the social sciences. It is erased. In an article published in Druglink about a Women's Service I developed at Orexis (Painter J., Riley-Buckley D, and Whittington D 2000) the work on trauma and sexual abuse that was in the original article was not deemed relevant to be published. Trauma was censored.

Social Science usually runs away from its own emotional realities first, before it then censures others. Academics perceive themselves as contemplators, hovering above the mass. This is a form of hubris. Academia lacks Praxis. It does not want to get its hands dirty in the everyday world of immersion in people's lives. Like 1930's Hollywood, it composes academic fictions as they composed musicals, to create fantasies. This provides social glue. Alternatively there is a pandering to pathological autobiographies such as Eugenics and National Socialist Science. This ensures academia maintains its social distance. It keeps itself pristine but fails to connect. This belief in contemplation over Praxis, the idea you do not need to work on the coalface and understand this dread (Kierkegaard 1844) infects the whole knowledge base system. This creates an upside down world where those who exist in bureaucratic worlds, those who contemplate, are regarded as being higher in a hierarchy of order, existing above a practitioner, someone who works at the sharp end (Gerth and Wright Mills 1953). This was the fundamental problem of the British industrial malaise where the inventor was perceived as lower than a lord, and a worker just a pair of hands that puts nuts and bolts together. This led to the problems of work alienation, and the demise of British industry. The lessons have never been learnt, and they are even more acute now as the "objects" being assembled are no longer nuts and bolts, but people. These objects have stubbornly refused to get better. The fundamental problem drawing from Alfred Adler (1956) and Viktor Frankl (1952, 1959) is what is the purpose of getting better?

What is the purpose of treatment? This has not been defined nationally or individually.

Rarely do academics penetrate beyond the everyday "front" (Goffman 1959, Whittington 2007) people present to the worlds in their surveys. Because they fail to understand the emotional worlds, and they do not create the investigative tools to reach beyond this presentation of everyday life (Goffman 1959), the public policies that flow from their research are all based on emotional erasure. Imagine a large computer programmed with numerous miscalculations, but this is kept secret, however the end results are termed "truth" and everyone is told it is scientific. This belief in abstractions entails everyone bowing before the new religion of science. Even though your body may be telling you something completely different from what the scientific computer is instructing you, you negate your needs and acquiesce to the collective belief. These are the fictions of the modern world. People are taught to negate the signs of their bodies (Miller 2006) and their desires, instead accepting the wisdom of the machine. This becomes the new faith promoted into the "steel bath" of invigoration (Lerner 2003).

These basic errors are transferred to the modern bureaucratic (Gerth and Wright Mills 1953) world, where those who administer are raised above those who do. This cascade has stripped the practitioner, those that do, of the tools to undertake their job by placing strictures, based on these ersatz scientific creeds, to halt any process of social regeneration. This has created institutional paralysis and led to a huge cascade of resources (Craig 2008) bypassing those who could have been transformed. These figments rest upon negating the needs of the body and reifying the mind. This begins to expose the academic will to power. The only people who benefit from this exercise are those who have raised contemplation higher than immersion and action. Instead, the people who manage systems or those who theorise should have a caseload, be involved in mentoring, and linked to a human at the end, to remind them of the purpose of their work. This lesson was enshrined in the work of Michael Shiner (2011) who incorporated mentoring with academia, to reflect on the impact of attachment. The reflection was on his attachment relationship with the person he was working with, and the person's relationships with others. This is a shift to a mature social science.

The case histories in the second half of this book highlight the final impact of the academic paralysis on the recipients. This provides the evidence that a new philosophy, methodology, and ways of delivering care are needed, based on understanding these emotional realities. The old forms are not resonant with the needs of the client groups. The main problems are the failure to make emotional connections to ignite social regeneration. Anything that fails to ignite social regeneration needs to be discarded as erroneous. Treatment needs a purpose, and social regeneration should be the aim. This for example would help challenge the anecdotal accounts of people "who have been there." These people claim a special status purely based on their "addiction." This was a significant issue in the substance use field in the 1990's where people claimed all types of hegemony based on their immersion in a culture, without any emotional insight or reflection. The act of taking drugs was seen as creating social knowledge, instead of being perceived as a strategy of negation. Then the pendulum swung away from this discourse, to ennoble those who have never been there, objectifying those who have. All regeneration has to be based on a combination of theory and practice, not either, or. In this way, both of these discourses can pursue; thesis, antithesis and synthesis in the dialectical search for knowledge.

Instead of the contemplator, Praxis; the combination of theory and reflection as noted by Hannah Arendt (1958) in the "The Human Condition" is crucial for understanding how policies work on the ground. Her theories of action can be used to bring the psychology of emotions back into the framework, after they have been shunted to one side by the Social Science obsession with appearing scientific. This has entailed a divorce from the everyday world of people, and a retreat into speculation, leading to systemic failure. The appliance of science within the social world has led to numerous conceptual errors, ranging from scientific socialism, scientific management, scientific racial categories, scientific intelligence, scientific genes and the social sciences. Each is based upon a fundamental error, the erasure of the emotional world and the reification, holding science aloft, as if it exists on a cloud. It only exists in the minds of its adherents. These were the lessons of Stirner (1844) and Nietzsche (1882, 1968) drowned under the shrill noise.

Reclaiming the "Other"

The focus of this book is on the homeless and substance use sectors with a cross over into mental health. These are the areas which until recently were vastly under theorised, as the men and women who exist at the bottom of the social hierarchy were perceived as the "other." This is a term taken from John Paul Sartre (Sartre 1943) to denote a class of people written off as less than human. In "The Second Sex" (1949) Simone De Beauvoir made the links between women's oppression and being seen as an object. Women were and still are perceived as the "other," in relation to the fixed view of masculinity. This is the definitive norm. This resonates with Laughlin's creation of two race categories, white and colored, one and the other.

De Beauvoir (1949) perceived that within the everyday world, everything non masculine is perceived as strange, less than, objectified and exoticised. This has lead to an eradication of the human qualities, the emotions of women. These were seen as weak, unformed, lacking direction and prone to hysteria. They subsequently become sexual or maternal objects both in everyday life and within academic research, until women themselves changed this perception. Alfred Adler was the man who helped to kindle this fire. Equality has not brought an emotional freedom however; instead it has entailed women adopting the creeds of rational power. A process began with Simone De Beauvoir's book (1949) "Second Sex," a new conceptual world was created based on women's liberation. It was quickly co-opted.

Previously women apart from a few notable stars such as Lou Salome (Vickers 2008) were eradicated from academia in the 19th Century. Psychology and Psychotherapy were the entry points for women into the modern world. Salome was the confidante of both Nietzsche and Freud, a woman who transcended two of the philosophical building blocks of the 20th Century. This marked the explosion of emotional discussions. Men's emotions emerged unstated in the works of Sartre (2001, 1943), Rank (1932 1936, 1952), Fenichel (1972), Fromm (1955), Marcuse (1972), Frankl (1952, 1959), Reich (1933, 1946), Jung (1964), Nietzsche (1878 1968) and Stirner (1844).

Adler (1927, 1931, 1956, 2004) and Gross (Heuer 2010) were the first men to recognize emotional freedom, calling for liberation of the genders. Adler in the early part of the 20th Century (1956) identified men's needs within his theory of "masculine protest." He began to see how fixed innate qualities sanctified by science were socially and psychologically constructed, in both men and women. This was the philosophy of transformation, freeing people from the genetic constraints, just as Harlow (Blum 2002) controversially freed everyone from the iron cage of behaviorism.

Subsequently psychotherapy has retreated into scientific respectability, and objectification of its client groups. This retreat has had a real effect. It has stilted the lives of its subjects through eradicating their emotional lives. Chris, in the case studies shows what happened to him when he became objectified in Japan as a gaiijin. It led to a long, slow, torturous collapse, as his self esteem melted. This was a catalyst for a withdrawal from the world. Objectifying people is denying their right to emotionally exist. It is an exercise in power, a discourse. It is a form of bullying as Lynch (1980) showed in "The Elephant Man." This perception is based on an error, the divorce between contemplation and inhabitation of the world. These are both linked to action. People think and act within a real world that cannot be negated by pretending it does not exist, and then be observed from afar. This has been the error of the Social Sciences.

Within the homeless and substance use arenas this Social Science assumption has led to the perception, people on the margins have arrived there due to personal innate failure. Robert Hare in "Without Conscience" (1999) a 100,000 seller, posits that a young girl displaying disruptive behavior arose from a genetic condition, the "bad seed" (March 1997) not because she had been raped as a small girl. Instead he states her genetic condition led her to being raped. Hare (1999) casts his theoretical framework upon his victim and drowns her voice. He silences her as effectively as any abuser silences any child, through appearing superior and applying a powerful ideology that negates individual perception of events, within a broader, alien, rational, framework. This is undertaken through objectifying the "other" (Sartre 1943) and then applying a genetically determined label.

No one has ever found a gene to explain challenging or disruptive behavior, and no one ever will. Aberrant and disruptive behavioral forms are socially

18

defined and constructed. Hare's (1999) explanation is a product of his will to power. He highlights how far science has become divorced from the emotional world. Anyone who works with children, who have been sexually abused, bereaved, or violated in other ways, knows they react emotionally, through either becoming withdrawn, disruptive or they freeze.

The proponents of science ignore children's emotional realities, because they have learnt to ignore their own first (Miller 1983, 2005, 1991, 1990, 1985). Children react to being violated and vandalized. This has been documented by Harry Harlow (Blum 2002), John Bowlby (1984, 1969, 1973, 1980) and Renee Spitz (1965) studying monkeys, war orphans and foundling homes. Children's' realities were written out of science by people such as Robert Hare (1999), Martha Stout (2007) and the other socio biology discourses. Drawing on Nietzsche (1968) these appear little more than autobiographical statements projected outwardly, than a picture of children's emotional realities. The main theoretical problems derive from children's realities being drowned by these theories of containment. This is reflected in the numerous research reports around substance use being genetic. This has had a deleterious effect on social policy.

One issue Nietzsche (1968, 1882) grappled with throughout his work, revolved around how scientists projected their will to power to create collective fantasies. The genetic causation of multiple human behavioral forms becomes transformed into scientific fallacies, when the foundations of their belief cannot be held up for inspection. The creation of labels for human behavior, then ascribing it to a gene, is part of a collective hallucination. This is a rework of eugenics. As I highlight within this book, is it feasible to find a gene for homelessness and vaccinate your children against it?

These belief systems reflect the corresponding ideology; those who succeed are also innately gifted. Yet some of these men in these case studies were ex-millionaires who had built themselves from nothing, into self made men and then lost it. Others were the product of Children's Homes who were raped and beaten, others from two parent families who maintained a deception of providing care. Shifting beyond the externally portrayed stereotypes, connecting to the world underneath the "front" (Goffman

1959, Whittington 2007) highlights the fictions and myths society weaves around reality to create belief systems. These finally collapse when people feel safe to reveal their lives. The academic fictions divorced from Praxis, fail to hold up when emotional connections are made. Genetic fictions promulgated by Social Science and Natural Science inhibit social change, and serve no useful purpose, apart from entrapping people in silos. There is a general promise; a new type of faith, that big pharma will discover a gene that stops shyness, laziness, silliness, alcoholism, drug addiction and stupidity. In reality self esteem, work, education, detox and discussion transform all these "genetic" causations. This requires action in the social world, not contemplation or the inertia generated in waiting to be saved by science.

The perception of homeless men as feckless, violent, lazy and needy obscures the reasons for their immersion into various states of depression. When relational bridges (Gilligan 1989, 1990a, 1990b) are made, and they detail their life stories, uncomfortable pictures of social reality emerge. These are usually shunted to one side by academia. The emotional narratives articulated in these case histories disturb the composed fictions about the nature of socially 'included' reality. They reflect a world existing underneath the composed fiction.

Beyond Recovery

Theoretical problems arise from the psychological entrapment of those at the bottom of society. The "Recovery model" has inculcated a belief change is possible, but this is limited by the same staff teams delivering these new changes without any substantial training in motivating clients.

The same working conditions and psychology of objectification of the marginalised exists. There is no inherent change in perception. I will be arguing perceptions need to be transformed, and a new cultural transition adopted with the enactment of enhanced Psychologically Informed Environments (PIE's) (Johnson and Haigh 2010). These ideas are based on Attachment and Attachment Severance derived from the Praxis of John Bowlby (1984, 1969, 1973, 1980,) Renee Spitz (1965) and Harry Harlow (Blum 2002) linked to Edward Khantzian's (1985, 1995, 1999, 2010)

Self Medication Theories. This provides a platform and a philosophy for social regeneration. The tools for change can be found in the collected works of Alfred Adler (1956), Viktor Frankl (1952, 1959), Carl Rogers (1961, 1969), Eric Berne (1961, 1964) and Claude Steiner (1974, 2003). Teams of highly trained emotionally literate workers drawing on the Orexis 1990's model, incorporating the BME and Gender work, but also linked to action based, psychotherapeutic work. This will deliver social regeneration. This needs Praxis, based on action and reflection.

The aim is to create a different working environment. Currently practitioners have been instructed to change their working practices. Changing the work environment will create new interactions to ignite the process of social regeneration amongst the marginalised. The new model is based on the working model of Orexis in the late 1990's, recently rediscovered by Julian Le Grand (2011), with his work on supporting social work teams. These new working practices will be based on cooperation rather than the current adversarial commissioning system. PIE's (Johnson R & Haigh J 2010) empower the client through engaging and working with them to create transformation, rather than instruct and coerce people into change. The case histories I provide, detail the work with the hardest to reach groups, showing anything is possible when freedom from constraint is allowed.

Enacting PIE's (Johnson R & Haigh J 2010) will require a further paradigm shift. They build on the "Recovery model." This has had a general positive effect in the homeless field as "Harm Reduction" initially invigorating, lapsed into stasis. "Recovery" offers a new transition but cannot be simply tacked onto the old working practices. It needs to operate within Psychologically Informed Environments, a call for a transformation of the current treatment system, if it is to succeed. When enacted didactically 'Recovery' creates problems, and this is a fundamental quandary with the retention of the Commissioning model. 'Recovery' stops people from moving forward, because it is enacted as an instruction. Realistically it needs to generate a purpose, working with the client to realise their potential.

Providing a meaning means adapting to the client groups needs, and using this idea as a starting point. An internal meaning cannot be imposed upon clients. Whilst recovery helps to inculcate the belief in finding a purpose, when imposed didactically, it acts against recovery.

Currently those people needing respite care, those drinking themselves to death, have been stopped from accessing in patient detox, because government instruction has stated only those wishing to access rehab and 12 Step Programmes can use these detox services. Recovery enacted didactically by Commissioners is killing people, through restricting 'Respite Care.' People need to become physically capable of recovery. PIE's (2010) and taking the conceptual leap I propose, will shift this didactic adherence to anti social regenerative procedures. Transforming people, through giving the power to practitioners regenerates people, through providing belief.

The case histories in this book demonstrate the commissioning bureaucracies operate with too many restrictive practices in the substance use and homeless fields. They have become iron cage bureaucracies (Weber 1992). These constraints need to be lifted, to stop thwarting innovation and change. The red tape of commissioning needs to be cut, the layers of bureaucracy condensed, with streamlining based solely on recovery to change. The money saved then needs to be reinvested in front line service delivery, based on therapeutic regeneration. Vested interests seeming to promulgate recovery actually inhibit it, as individual departments' battle against each other for resource allocation and control. This is why PIE's are needed to push the recovery agenda forward. To push the PIE's (Johnson and Haigh 2010) forward needs streamlined emotionally literate (Steiner 1974, 2003), highly trained shock troops (Junger 1920) working directly on the coal face, untrammelled by byzantine practices. Not everyone is capable of initiating emotional recovery with clients. This is a highly skilled undertaking. This needs to be recognised.

Homeless and drug treatment services need to create more dynamic psychologically informed working environments, rather than just pushing clients into recovery. Using the same working procedures as the "Harm reduction model," renaming it "Recovery," will not be unblock treatment. It will lead to staff burnout, as workers lack the intervention and psychological tools. This is explored in the case histories. Treatment is thwarted by the Commissioning process and by charities transforming themselves into businesses. This model does not produce regeneration. They have become too top heavy with bureaucracy and both have drifted from the purpose of the work. These two hierarchies drain resources (Craig 2008) from front line service delivery, as they build their internal structures on a hierarchical cascade, thereby erasing emotional realities. The Purchaser/Provider splits are adversarial and hierarchical inculcating the construction of the "other (Sartre 1943). They stymie change and are inflexible, creating the iron cage (Weber 1992). What is at stake is the structure of our social world, and whether we collectively act to contain problems or resolve them. The riots of 2011 highlighted when the people existing on the margins of society react, the foundations wobble.

Alienation arises from the introduction of "targets" and the response to them is called "gaming" (Berne 1961, 1964, 2010). I draw an example from the Arrest Referral Scheme to highlight the collapse of a good idea. There is a huge problem in the substance use field, as the lessons of attachment theory have been erased in the literature. Treatment has then devolved into a charade between worker and client around satisfying mutual needs, based on game playing (Berne 1961, 1964). This needs to be halted and attachment bonds created to facilitate emotional growth, individuation and independence.

Autonomy and Praxis

These observations arise from an immersion, stemming from Praxis, working on the ground and in academia over the last thirty years. Voices of practitioners are usually absent in the substance use field, written out of the discourse perceived as the "other" (De Beauvoir 1949, Sartre 1943). Too near to the problem their insights reduced to anecdotal. The critique of this book provides balance, through highlighting the hubris of academia divorced from practice, and its creation of systemic failure when it divorced itself from Praxis. It calls for a reinstatement of the worker/academic. It is usually people such as Julian Le Grand (2011) and David Halpern (2009) creating abstract health models who are heard above the melee. In this excerpt, he realises the inherent rationale in Hannah Arendt's (1958) critique, and has engaged in Praxis.

"We developed five pilot projects with the Labour government, which involved social workers spinning out into independent practices, and we discovered that they had more flexibility and were able to make better decisions. It has worked well so far.

"Because that work is similar to the mutuals agenda, I was asked to chair this taskforce."

Third Sector (2011)." Interview with Julian Le Grand," www.thirdsector. co.uk/news/Article/1075751/Interview-Julian-Le-Grand/2011_Accessed_16th September_2011

Le Grand (2011) acknowledges policy makers have no concept how policies operate on the ground, so he went into the GP Practices to establish his working model. This already existed in the Substance Use field in 1997, if he had visited Orexis. Unfortunately his previous emphasis on the market with provider choice (Le Grand 2006) destroyed the therapeutic care system, as the iron cage (Weber 1992) crushed new ideas. Commissioners could not encapsulate the need to provide therapy to people with substance use issues, because it had not been theorised by academia. At the forefront of innovation the conceptual ways of working were crushed between the fine grind of bureaucratic cogs (Gerth and Wright Mills 1953).

The public policy discourses had no concept of psychology, and failed to understand attachment theory (Bowlby 1984, 1969, 1973, 1980) the enlightened witness (Miller 2001) and the impact of early trauma on later life (Miller 1983). Instead discourses that were emotionally illiterate based on an erroneous belief in the science of economics would provide a "hidden hand" to resolve these problems (Le Grand 2006).

Within substance use, the grounding on the medical model linked to Harm Reduction failed to initiate change, because it denied any form of emotional conceptualisation. It uses a static mechanistic model of the body as a machine (Taylor 1911). It is based upon a denial of Praxis, as it uses the terms "addict" and substance user, to define people who have trauma and are self medicating. The term "addict" denotes stasis, a form of entrapment and stymies change. Hear the difference between;

"I am an addict"

"I am self medicating"

Self Medication

The first significant change that would irredeemably alter the current trajectory is a change in belief. Substance use and Homeless agencies need to be redefined as places of respite for people 'self medicating' for trauma. This builds on the work of Edward Khantzian (1985, 1995, 1999, 2010) and John Bowlby (1984, 1969, 1973, 1980). Joining the two together creates transformation. This is based on Praxis and can be clearly seen in the case studies in "Beaten into Violence" (2007) and documented again in "Bath of Steel."

"Chronic substance use is caused by Self Medicating for early trauma. This is due to the severance of early and late attachment relationships and the subsequent desire to find meaning through obliteration. The remedy for obliteration is finding a purpose."

The other philosophies need to be cast to one side as too deterministic, in particular the Social Darwinist theories derived from Eugenics, Socio-biology and the Genetic discourses (Pinker 2003, Hare 1999, Stout 2007). Blaming the genes, robs people of personal responsibility for their personal growth. They have no concept of the emotions, in particular the idea of attachment and the emotional resonances that emanate from connection. Childhood development was documented in the works of Winnicott (1964, 1965) and this highlights how parenting shapes a child's perception of the world. The genetic ideologies fail to observe the emotional lives Winnicott (1964, 1965) researched, and dismiss his findings through erasing his ideas from their debates.

Instead people are informed they can never achieve stability or transformation, because of their genetic make-up. This does not foster belief. It inhibits people from undertaking the will to change from within. They have already been robbed of their childhood vitality, then as adults they are robbed of their ability to change by professional stasis. These theories have no dynamic for personal transformation. Boiling down all behavioural causes to genes, does not provide hope neither does it explain previous transformation. This genetic concept creates vast static care industries and is an example of Max Stirner's (Stirner 1844) "wheels in the head."

Belief systems, taking away any individual belief in change, should not be promulgated, as they are not facts, only beliefs. Undertaking this simple act, changing the philosophy, will allow a new regeneration of society to unfold, through action rather than contemplative medication. Change comes from being inspired. Genetic theories offer no solution and trap people in constraints. These deterministic, mechanical theories prohibit emotional growth by limiting people to their family genetic imprint.

Critique of the mechanistic theory-Let us here dismiss the two popular concepts "necessity and "law": the former introduces a false constraint into the world, the latter a false freedom. "Things" do not behave regularly according to a rule: there are no things (-they are fictions invented by us); they behave just as little under the constraint of necessity. There is no obedience here: for that something is as it is, as strong or as weak, is not the consequence of an obedience or a rule or a compulsion-

"Nietzsche F. (1968) N634 "Will to Power"

The only realities are those based on the emotions, sublimated within the world, as people are compressed into being machines, processed within academia and within work. The end product of this discourse is a split between the outward and the inward.

Within social psychological regeneration, any theory that prohibits growth needs to be discarded. This is the emphasis of the new philosophy, following the ideas of Alfred Adler (1931) and "Social Interest." Recovery can only occur when there is a belief and a defined purpose for change. People need to feel invigorated. They are already constrained by the after affects of early trauma, and then silenced by the actions and beliefs of the people around them. These forces impact upon their internal compass. Changes in belief affect the mind and the body, transforming the self as Viktor Frankl (1959) showed in "Man's Search for Meaning." Emotional care provides self belief, if this basic anchoring point does not exist then later emotional instability arises. This is why Bowlby (1984, 1969, 1973, 1980) and Spitz (1965) are crucial underpinnings for understanding PIE's (Johnson and Haigh 2010) and attachment.

Working therapeutically with people who use drugs, entails an emotional bridge becoming opened. This provides the relational evidence (Whittington 2007) that self medication alleviates the effects of trauma. Self evident, when the relational bridges are built to listen to the people on the receiving end of "treatment." This was detailed in "Beaten into Violence" (Whittington 2007) the product of 16 years therapeutic work in Deptford South East London. "Bath of Steel" is derived from a further four years of work in a South London homeless hostel building on those insights. It highlights numerous case histories, detailing the emotional issues homeless men face based on the impact of early traumatic experiences. This has resulted in many cases of attachment severance, and the subsequent self medication strategies developed as a response, being missed by the agencies who have acted upon these men over the years. The concept of emotional intelligence has been perceived as secondary, over the appliance of technique.

A national recognition needs to follow, that drugs, legal and illegal are highly effective in eradicating emotional trauma. Drugs obliterate the past, the present and the future. They create a meaning or purpose when people inhabit alternate worlds of negation. People ordinarily use a number of strategies to self medicate for trauma, and drug use is not the only strategy. Criminalisation of drug use has not stemmed its use. All that has occurred is a particular self medication strategy has become stigmatised (Goffman 1963), whilst the other strategies are allowed. This sends a confused signal. This is not to condone the use of drugs, but to provide an understanding for their use. Trauma is part of the life cycle of being human, and recognising it exists, in particular its effects, including the coping mechanisms, will allow many people to escape from a psychological conceptual prison. Keeping up the performance; trauma and its effects do not exist, traps whole swathes of people in their self composed worlds of obliteration. These are people who need to be liberated from self destruction. The therapist can build a conduit to allow the person to break out and rebuild their lives. However in the present, there are too many vested interests in keeping these conduits closed. Most of these relate to belief systems.

Self medication (Khantzian 1985, 1995, 1999, 2010) is an issue that ranges across a whole spectrum of human behaviour; gambling, sex, alcohol, self harm, drugs, religion, work, dangerous sports, arson, crime, over eating, under eating, violence, withdrawal, depression, bullying and suicide. People also use power to self medicate for their childhood distress. This includes those who inhabit institutions (Goffman 1963), and this is why psychologically informed environments need to be the template for growth. Ideally work should be a place where people are tested, but also enthused about the test, when stretched in their capabilities. Presently this is not the case, especially in the care sector where the emotional bonds between people are thwarted. Work is perceived as a means to a monetary end. It is through developing the relational bonds (Whittington 2007) of care, people find the purpose to live and transcend the past. This also provides a purpose to the work. There needs to be a reflection on the internal dynamics of organisations tasked to deliver care, as significant issues arise from the various institutional pressures that suffocate ingenuity. These forms of organisation could be termed psychologically uninformed environments (PUE's).

When viewing behaviour that appears aberrant as 'self medication,' the various strategies of obliteration suddenly appear 'rational.' Some are deemed legitimate, and others castigated. They all exist as strategies to overcome the effects of trauma, to bridge an existential crisis, a sense of meaninglessness through fending off despair. These self medicating behavioural forms are regulatory for the individuals who pursue them, and they have an internal rationale. The reasons why they appear invisible are because the wider society has relegated the emotional world to an inferior status, and then reified abstract reason. It is then termed science. Emotions emerge in the arts and are then perceived as feminine, but they are sublimated in all other discourses. There needs to be recognition that self destruction has a 'rational' emotional purpose, and it is not genetic. It is a cry of distress, but the signals need to be deciphered by those who are emotionally literate. It is through building trust with the use of empathy (Rogers 1961, 1969) the relational bridges (Gilligan C. 1989, 1990a 1990b) are built to discover the internal meaning. Working to release the trapped emotional anguish, through helping the person find a voice, creates a meaning to live. This should be the rationale for treatment, not discipline and punishment (Foucault 1977). The Recovery model sign posts a way forward, but the psychologically informed environment will embed it.

Self Medication (Khantzian 1985, 1995, 1999, 2010) allows people to forget about the past but not its effects. It is not genetic, but centred on the emotions. Acknowledging this strategy puts the individual in the driving seat of recovery. Trauma can only be healed through making emotional connections that have been broken. This is the role of the therapist, to act as the catalyst for change, to redefine the life purpose through creating attachment and working through the individuation process. The therapist builds the bonds to eventually let go. The therapist is both the enlightened witness (Miller 2001) and the person who builds the ladder out of the morass, to create meaning, helping the person to realise a future exists. This is a highly skilled job fraught with potential challenges in its processes. This cannot be achieved in six sessions. It also requires a greater onus and responsibility for creating change, than Solution Focused (Berg I. in Washton A. 1995), Motivational Interviewing (Rollnick S. and Morgan M. in Washton A. 1995) or Cognitive Behavioural Therapy (Beck A. and Freeman A. 1990). These are at best partial solutions, and cannot transform people who have had the most horrendous early lives, into people with a purpose. Instead of being the sole focus, these are tools in the armoury.

The people who attend drug and homeless centres are immersed in trauma. To coax them out of their self medication strategies entails building trust and then a ladder of hope. Depending on the skill of the worker and the scale of the trauma, this takes time. The first step is to create the belief that change can occur. Clients pick up from the workers cues, and this affects their internal sense on whether to build trust with them. This is founded on how they view the world. Therapy assists in connecting to these internal working models to make an emotional connection, so the internal becomes externalised. Untrained workers may be communicating their sense of hopelessness to the client, defusing their will to transform, as seen in some of the case studies.

Once these arenas are redefined, the changes in the social realm will necessarily follow. This book details the changes that need to be made once self medication is established as the dominant discourse. Personal liberation will necessarily follow, as it instils belief.

Therapy and therapeutically based interventions need to be at the forefront of a new definition of change, transcending the recovery model into a psychologically informed environment. The focus of regeneration needs to begin with the therapeutic practitioner. Working alongside emotionally trained specialist GP's, nurses, social workers and other specialists, an emotional infrastructure can be built. The therapist should be at the core of social regeneration. Therapy combined with practical support is the only intervention that works, delivered alongside the stabilisation of substitute prescribing. Methadone or Subutex should be provided to help people stabilise, not to keep them sedated. The aim is to work with people to make changes, not to entrap them.

The therapy should encompass a wide variety of models and not just be grounded on Cognitive Behavioural Therapy (Beck 1990), just because it can be measured scientifically by academia. CBT does not dwell on the past; it tries to find solutions to change current thoughts and behaviors to assist functioning in the future. The negation of the past is an error within the philosophy of this model. Early attachment, familial violence and institutional violence all have fundamental impacts on adult perception and create resonating emotional traumas (Miller 2005). These are carried from childhood into adulthood as seen in these case histories. These traumas cannot be simply wished away and transcended by belief; they need to be validated before the client can move forward. CBT (Beck 1990) works well with people who do not have entrenched trauma. The eradication of the past within the model however, ties in with the general malaise within the social sciences of eradicating trauma from the general discourse (Miller 2001).

Solution Focused (Berg I. in Washton A. 1995), Motivational Interviewing (Rollnick S. and Morgan M. in Washton A. 1995) and Cognitive Behavioural Therapy (Beck A. and Freeman A. 1990) are techniques, but not treatments in themselves. They are components in the therapists' tool bag, but not the only one. Who would trust a surgeon who only used a scalpel in his surgical procedures? Science is unable to measure the emotions and has always struggled to provide a measurement. Science needs to recognise the insights Nietzsche (1889, 1895, 1881, 1882, 1886, 1888 1968) made in his collective works about the emotional world, and the construction of social meaning.

Relational methodology (Whittington 2007) is the only feasible way of gaining insight into the process of change, based on Carol Gilligan (1990a, 1990b) and the therapeutic work undertaken in "Beaten into Violence" (2007). This listens to what is being said rather than trying to code it into a predefined academic template. It is the only methodology that highlights the emotional discourse. Science does not offer a cure for trauma; it does help to alleviate the effects. Only human beings can cure the latent effect and this needs specialist insight. Academia needs to be resonant with the emotional worlds, and adjust to the needs of people, rather than make claims that appear scientific but prohibit change, divorced from Praxis.

CHAPTER 2
THE IMMORAL MAZE

The recovery model potentially offers a new pathway. Previously no philosophy apart from a stilted version of Harm Reduction (O Hare, Drucker, Newcombe, Mathews, Buning 1992) existed as a dominant discourse, although addiction also vied for a position in the Homeless and Substance Use fields. In the hostel I worked within, the Recovery Model was initiated, but many clients were not stable enough to attend AA Meetings. With Harm Reduction as O'Hare et al (1992) show, halting blood born viruses was deemed the main focus of the treatment intervention, with the provision of Methadone and Clean Needles. There was no sense of people 'self medicating,' and the emotional discourses were largely absent. Tacked onto this stance in the 1990's were the various criminal justice interventions based on different facets of harm reduction. The term, harm reduction became laden with different expectations and remits. Eventually it collapsed under the weight. This policy provided no guidance or ethos in advocating a psycho-social regeneration of people. Harm Reduction halted HIV, but failed with Hepatitis C and kept a swathe of people on long term Methadone programmes. Harm Reduction, innovation after years of stigmatising drug use, eventually became synonymous with an entrapment on benefits.

The leadership vision was absent. The various interventions lacked internal belief, emanating from the top downwards. It vacillated, as it bracketed emotional research evidence. A lack of direction has been the norm in mental health, homelessness and substance use since World War Two when the Welfare State was introduced. This has become exposed in the 21st century as there is a growing body of research evidence clearly showing the current policy interventions have not created a healthy society.

These interventions continue because there has been so much financial investment, with vested interests wanting them to persist, even though they have not produced change.

An immense opportunity was missed with "Command and Control" (Seddon 2003) instilling "Discipline and Punish" (Foucault 1977). The inability to push emotional literacy as a main intervention stifled initiative, when numerous resources were provided to the substance use and homelessness fields.

The problems became enshrined in the eradication of trauma from research, and the shying away from trauma in the substance use field. Research in the UK has failed to look at the emotions (Miller 1991). Interestingly in Social Work and the Psychological services it was being rediscovered, as Attachment Theory has been used to conceptualise domestic violence trauma. It is interesting this explanation arose in the Statutory Fields, but was ignored in the 3rd Sector, as a cause of ill health and malaise.

This became a huge problem within the homeless and substance misuse fields. I will provide an outline how this inability to conceptualise trauma created a form of paralysis (Miller 1991). Instead, a style of working evolved that had no basis in the emotional reality of the people who were being provided with care. Academia demarcated practice and relevance, and then the government departments followed their line. This affected what could be discussed and what could be delivered as a treatment interaction. This became the nature of a public discourse. A public discourse in this context is a set of beliefs and assumptions made about external reality, communicated as if it was real, and backed with an institutional power to enforce it regardless of is veracity. Lacking Praxis it became a mirage based on the management of appearances. A belief becomes true, when it has power to create adherence. Any evidence to the contrary is bracketed then discarded as this contradicts the main assumption. As an example, any attempt to articulate the emotional lives and the levels of trauma occurring in marginalised men and women, when I was running a substance use agency, was met by a dank blank stare from central and local planners (Miller 1991). It was also absent in the various journals discussing substance use. Discussion of trauma was uncoupled from substance use. The felt and known emotional world was erased. Instead abstractions were repositioned as truth. Trauma was not comprehended because it was deemed invisible in a scientific discourse (Miller 1991). It was not given any credence in treatment planning and therefore deemed irrelevant to the latent causes of drug misuse, homelessness or mental health. Instead a variety of other beliefs were introduced, based on expedience and emotional denial such as genetic, because it had a scientific sheen.

When the parameters, the limits, for thinking have been established, people tasked to deliver the policies, struggle to think outside of the remits imposed upon them. Anything outside of the discourse is considered off-base, thinking outside the contract is deemed irrelevant. This arises in the case histories. A thought-control coup d'état took place. Into this abyss, tumbled academics, bureaucrats and the forces of law and order, in a psychological and physical war, all waged against the marginalised. This erasure effectively shunted them into the sidelines, and they remained kettled, so the main societal vision remained pristine.

"That which has been feared the most, the cause of the most powerful suffering (lust to rule, sex etc) has been treated by men with the greatest amount of hostility and eliminated from the "true" world."

Nietzsche F. (1968) N576 "Will to Power,"

Those who attended psychotherapy when I created the first therapeutic street services in South London during the 1990's until 2005, had lives existing poles apart from central planners and the later local implementators. The only person who became aware, and took any notice of the dynamics was one of the researchers who came onto the management committee from Goldsmiths College.

The templates written by central government were largely irrelevant to running a treatment service in an inner city deprived area. Institutional amnesia entailed bureaucratic inertia, linked to the inability to comprehend the 'other' (Sartre 1943). This became an overwhelming methodological and practical problem. This was based on a psychological split between abstract learning and emotional understanding, a fundamental problem in the Social Sciences. It is another great unstated problem theorised by

Nietzsche and then discussed in the psychotherapeutic work of Otto Gross (Ed; Heuer 2011).

People primarily join care organisations because they have a Social Interest, (Adler 1931) and secondly want to repair emotional damage, by making positive changes for the future. That is until the job becomes purely based on reward, the pay packet at the end of the month (Fromm 1955). Idealism becomes thwarted, firstly by attending academia and learning abstract theory (Stirner 1844). This is where students are taught there is no room for their personal history; secondly they are thwarted by the internal work organisation. A gradual erasure of belief is created, as people are moulded into preconceived ideologies where they are taught to deny their senses. These ideologies are based on the power of the group where the individual surrenders their autonomy to "fit in." Those who had vigour eventually become enmeshed in re-enacting the emotional violence they wished to change, as they become forced into alienated roles. Bureaucratic roles (Gerth and Wright Mills 1953) become performed to keep the emotional truths entrapped in a silence. This reflects the parental commands to a child, to keep quiet and not tell anyone when Daddy is abusing his daughter or Mother her son; the forms of institutional silence Bettelheim articulated in "The Informed Heart" (1960). Institutions collude with emotional violence even if they do not enact the violence themselves, through erasing it as a topic of discussion or investigation. They work in various ways to shroud the knowledge about trauma (Miller 1985). The rationale for ignoring trauma needs to be discussed. The hidden lives of the homeless were never expressly articulated by the leadership in the substance use or homeless fields. It was documented by Goodman L, Saxe L, Harvey M. (1991) in the USA and again by Collins M. And Phillips J, (2003), who worked in Scotland. They detailed the links between trauma and homelessness. Latterly the Joseph Rowntree Trust (McDonagh, T. 2011) drawing on several university studies, has taken up the cause. Previously they were hidden, existing apart from the general social discourse. The past has been deliberately written out of personal histories, echoing the choice of CBT (Beck and Freeman, 1990) as a main therapeutic intervention. Emotional histories could not be articulated. I recollected a Home Office Meeting I attended in 2003 where academic researchers wanted to understand the links between refugees in the 21st Century and their substance use. As someone who had created the first substance use therapeutic services for Somali and Vietnamese I had special insight.

The researchers wanted to implement markers for vulnerability such as truancy, single parenting, Social Services contact, Police, low school achievement and exclusion. The aim was to map these children throughout their schooling. I raised attachment as an issue and the need for therapeutic support/mentoring. This discourse on emotions was greeted with a one minute silence of shock, before the meeting proceeded as if nothing had happened.

People adhere to dominant discourses, because it provides structure and meaning when delivering work targets. These are undertaken without psychological reflection. Currently practitioners are shuttered from the long term consequences of their actions. They can rationalise their impotency by pointing to the levels of control enacted by senior policy makers. Unable to reflect on the long term consequences, they enact the policy regardless whether it achieves its stated aim, just so long as targets are met. Meeting these targets provides levitation through a career structure, so those who "deliver," ascend the hierarchy and eventually take command. This rewards those who bracket out non dominant discourses. The system potentially becomes self fulfilling (Seddon 2008). It will take someone with insight who has ascended through this structure to make the changes to ensure there is a new direction.

The case of Semmelweiss (Celine 2008) the man who introduced hand washing before delivering babies to the world is poignant. His insight entailed him being ostracised by the medical community in Vienna as they were affronted by the idea that gentlemen could be the cause of contamination. Semmelweiss fought the prevailing orthodoxy and was driven into frustration. He eventually committed suicide. All creativity and adaptation to meeting people's emotional needs is initially institutionally thwarted before it becomes orthodoxy.

Presently however, there is a glowering resentment from those who are administered to, as they are reduced to the "other," (Sartre 1943), a type of non-life, an object. Those who deliver 'care' envelop themselves in models or discourses where they can split off from the effects of their actions, by reconciling it to their orders. They adhere to the rational medical model which upholds the divorce between emotions and care in service delivery (Sartre 2001). It negates the healing touch in preference to enacting a procedure, through adhering to an institutional paradigm without any reflection on how it is sustained. This keeps its paradigm intact. Whilst making significant strides in surgical procedure as a technique, the medical model has failed to understand the causes of disease and psychological ill ease, particularly the links between stress emotions and their effects on the body (Harrison 1986).

This medical model is a discourse performed through various decision making processes that have become take for granted. Adherents are indoctrinated within the various training programmes with idealised typologies emphasising the body as a machine. People are tasked to deliver their mental health, substance misuse and homeless treatments in response to these templates. These are handed down from the top to achieve national targets. Targets establish the base lines for funding. If you want funding, you adhere to a narrow template and show within the tender document, how you are going to meet these central aims. Central aims are devised without consultation with recipients in any meaningful way. Academics divorced from praxis create them (Halpern 2009, Le Grand 2006, 2007). Templates stemming from a wider government agenda are engendered to create legitimacy for its economic and political aims. Academics are provided with research grants to investigate the success of the model. Research is undertaken to justify expenditure and enhance its original premise. This is a Durkheimian mechanistic machine, an organic state that exists only to replicate itself, ignoring the world upon which it is based. Addiction built itself into the mainframe as a genetic belief system.

Addiction as a Constraint

This is an excerpt from an American Website the "National Institute on Drug Abuse" where it seeks to; "lead the Nation in bringing the power of science to bear on drug abuse and addiction." It bases itself on producing science around "drug abuse." This details its understanding of "addiction."

"Addiction is a chronic, often relapsing brain disease that causes compulsive drug seeking and use, despite harmful consequences to the addicted individual and to those around him or her. Although the initial decision to take drugs is voluntary for most people, the brain changes that occur over time challenge a person's self control and ability to resist intense impulses urging them to take drugs.

Fortunately, treatments are available to help people counter addiction's powerful disruptive effects. Research shows that combining addiction treatment medications with behavioural therapy is the best way to ensure success for most patients. Treatment approaches that are tailored to each patient's drug abuse patterns and any co-occurring medical, psychiatric, and social problems can lead to sustained recovery and a life without drug abuse.

Similar to other chronic, relapsing diseases, such as diabetes, asthma, or heart disease, drug addiction can be managed successfully. And as with other chronic diseases, it is not uncommon for a person to relapse and begin abusing drugs again. Relapse, however, does not signal treatment failure—rather, it indicates that treatment should be reinstated, adjusted, or that an alternative treatment is needed to help the individual regain control and recover.

NIDA (2011) "Understanding Drugs Abuse and the Facts" http://www. drugabuse.gov/infofacts/understand.html Accessed September 11th 2011

This is a benign view of addiction, where it manifests itself as a disease similar to diabetes, and can therefore be controlled. It does however describe it as a "brain disease." This is incorrect. There is no evidence of any brain disease in people who take Valium, Prozac, Heroin or Crack Cocaine. Only chronic alcohol use can lead to a form of brain impairment. The case histories I draw upon with the most entrenched people who use substances details another reality.

Other more hard line views of the genetic discourse view it as embedded, and passed on as a disease to an "addicts" children. A series of twin studies seemingly highlight its genetic propensity. Twin studies are deemed to be true, because they are perceived as being treated the same by families, and are therefore untainted by the family dynamics known as the "Birth Order," as noted by Alfred Adler (1956). The effect of being born the eldest, middle or youngest has an impact on perception. Twin studies were used by Robert Hare (1999) to explain behavioral differences between two people born on the same day.

"It is perhaps just dawning on five or six minds that physics too is only an interpretation and arrangement of the world (according to our own requirements, if I may say so) and not an explanation of the world; but in so far as it is founded on belief in the senses it passes for more than that and must continue to do so for a long time to come."

Nietzsche F. (1886) N14 "Beyond Good and Evil,"

This approach to collecting data is deemed not to cloud the results, as it follows a rational empirical procedure. This discourse has become embedded within the discipline, as it struggles to provide meaningful data, drawing from biology to reflect on receptors and genetic predisposition. Psychology posits whether it is the result of specific personality characteristics, or the result of an immersion in subcultures. Drug use is perceived within sociology as a learnt response to taking the drug and finding role models. Howard Becker's (1963) exploration of the "Outsiders" is a seminal piece of work as he evokes the drug use rituals and the groups that coalesce. William Burroughs (1977) described the sickness and the day to day drive to find meaning through drug use. None related the need to self medicate for trauma. Emotional discourses arise in Nelson Algren (1949) and Hubert Selby (1976). The links between desolate early family lives and later self medication have been explored by Edward Khantzian (1985, 1995, 1999, 2010) but his findings have generally been ignored.

There are huge vested interests in ensuring the emotional discourse is relegated, as the big pharmaceutical companies pay significant amounts of money into researching the genetic rationale of drug use, based upon a presumption those who take the drug, are deviant and need a cure. This formation of a deviant group resulted after a series of laws (Whittington 2007b) were enacted, to create the distinction between legitimate sources of self medication; alcohol, tobacco, coffee and licit licensed drugs and illegitimate sources; those bought from an unlicensed dealer heroin, cocaine and amphetamines. This distinction becomes less clear cut when licit supplies of heroin, cocaine and amphetamines can be obtained from private GP's, or if the patient defines an illness needing remedy from a bad drug, now deemed good; heroin for chronic pain relief, cocaine for blocked nasal tissue, cannabis for arthritis.

This report was commissioned by the "Office of Science and Technology," based on envisaging the future trends in drug use. It highlights the links between the large pharmaceutical companies and the government apparatus, throwing up a number of non public discourses. Some of these are based on the notion of freedom of choice, whilst also thinking of substance use as an addiction. The underlying ideology is that drug use helps to stimulate productivity.

"High Performance is a competitive world where people work and play hard. Cognition enhancers have become highly popular and, following a period of unregulated use, are now used openly to enhance most types of work, under strictly controlled conditions that minimise harm. After some initial concerns, UK society is now ready to accept the use of some recreational drugs, but only under equally strict and regulated conditions. People are able to identify their personal vulnerability profile and take responsibility for choosing substances likely to cause least harm. Addiction is seen solely as an illness to be treated, not behaviour to be punished, and the number of problem drug users in society is falling. There is still, however, a level of hardcore supply and street use that needs to be tackled, both nationally and internationally."

Office of Science and Technology (2003) "Understanding Drug Futures 2025"

www.bis.gov.uk/files/file15418.pdf Accessed September 11ᵗʰ 2011

This think tank is tasked to imagine the future, based on a series of "drivers." Reading the report, the emotional discourse has been completely written out. Instead a pseudo scientific collation of opinions are garnered together to produce potential outcomes. Within the report, it states drugs are useful for people involved in stressful work, as it allows them to function. These people can self regulate evidently, as they have a social stake and drug use helps productivity. Presumably they are talking about stimulants and their various off shoots, such as MDMA, amphetamines and cocaine. Meanwhile for the rest of the population, it is business as usual. They need to be stopped from harming themselves, because they are feckless and "street use that needs to be tackled." The presumptions within this writing are numerous, and based on a series of fallacies around work stress and medication, as well as street drug use and criminalisation. Yet these forms of discourses are commissioned and written, to think the unthinkable, legitimating illicit business practices, the pressurisation of staff. There is no research into why staff members are taking "cognition enhancers." Is it because they are not intelligent enough? There is no research pointing to what the "strictly controlled conditions are.""Cognition enhancers" range from amphetamines to nootropics (herbs, serotonin boosters, MDMA, Cannabis derivatives).

This viewpoint pervades the subconscious and conscious decision making processes, as drug use is differentiated between the socially included and excluded, groups based upon economic fault lines. One group is promoted, and the other put in prison. Self Medication for stress appears tangentially in the quote; "people work and play hard." It is not viewed as a rationale for the poor. Stress is not deemed a worthy rationale, for those trapped in poverty. This reflects a view that is rarely challenged on its own terms. No one can put up a counter argument within the formal bureaucracy, as thinking beyond the template is deemed off limits.

In academia, theorising takes place through collating statistics, from surveys and from relating back to other academic studies. Occasionally academics will join an out-group to try and understand the world from their perspective. They will then carefully document their appearances and take these acts as forms of social reality. This follows the work of the Cloward and Ohlin's (1966) study of gangs and their revision of the anomie theory. This resulted in significant resources being employed to steer young people away from gang culture, but without sustained success. The theories they employed did not address the psychological need to join a gang, ignoring the emotional precedents, as explored in "Beaten into Violence" (2007) and again in this book, in the case history of Jay. These researchers were dynamic in their perception, but acted upon a problem, rather than seeking the emotional resonances from within.

Genes and genetic causes becomes part of a determinant, poverty is located in causes outside of the social arrangements. If the big pharmaceutical companies could locate poverty as a biological issue, then it could be taken out of the political arena and relocated in the medicinal world. A pill could be invented to eradicate poverty. In this excerpt from a government think tank, sponsored by the Office for Science and Technology this group have envisaged this type of future.

"In Treated Positively, advances in our understanding of the molecular mechanisms of disease have transformed the nature of treatment and of the pharmaceutical industry. New, smaller, manufacturers use open-source technology to quickly create customised precision treatments that match individual disease profiles and the large pharmaceutical companies' dominance of the market is threatened. Greater understanding of genetic susceptibility to addiction means that individuals are able to select which psychoactive substances to avoid and even manipulate their own vulnerability profile. Cannabis is used therapeutically by the terminally and chronically ill and psychedelic drugs are being considered as therapeutic agents. Illicit drug manufacture—which has also benefited from advances in science—is cheap and sophisticated."

Office of Science and Technology (2003) "Understanding Drug Futures 2025"

www.bis.gov.uk/files/file15418.pdf Accessed September 11ᵗʰ 2011

Consumers will be enhanced by the new technologies. Drugs can be used to manipulate their genetic profile, so they are no longer susceptible to drug use. The paradoxical nature of this statement is left unchallenged in this discourse, as there are good drugs, those sanctioned by the state; anti depressants, sleeping tablets, anti psychotics and bad drugs; illicit substances used for hedonism or self medication.

This type of discourse flows (Foucault 1972) from a particular inculcated scientific paradigm, where emotional discourses are eradicated completely, it is all about the genes. The aim is to model the human on robotic life where every choice is based on a lifestyle whim. Alienation becomes complete, where everything becomes based around work. This dominates the mindset of those involved in the scientific field. Productivity is reified. It also denotes emotional forms that would be termed autistic within the psychological field. Within science these are reified as ideal types. This provides an insight into the psychology of science, its denial of emotions is again a reification of the autistic as an ideal type.

The idea of inoculating your children against homelessness could be something occurring at a board room soon. Successive governments have failed to provide any form of leadership around the issue of homelessness, except in the general idealised notion of building homes. Creating sustainable communities was left to the market to rebuild after the 1980's devastation, and its "invisible hand" (Le Grand 2006). This failed, as increased isolation and alienation have been the drivers within the modern world. People have retreated behind locked doors and gated communities. Self medication has filled the existential vacuum, as people have found meaning in internal withdrawal and external shutdown. Trauma has been sealed in the same way (Miller 1985).

"There are no facts, only interpretations."

Nietzsche F. (1954) "The Portable Reader;"

The philosophical principles of "addiction" are fatally flawed and never challenged by academics. Hannah Arendt (1958) highlighted how the

". . . behavioural sciences" aim to reduce man as a whole, in all his activities, to the level of a conditioned and behaving animal."

Arendt H. (1970) P.45 "The Human Condition,"

This robs the person of their individuality. They are perceived as a cipher in a greater whole, their personalities and emotional beings crushed. This type of thinking leads to the creation of social myths, based not on science but on social constructions.

Is addiction to prescription anti depressants part of the same "addiction illness?" If the premise is true, then large pharmaceutical companies are engaged in enticing people with this disease to become "addicts." Why single out heroin? Is it because it is illegal? Alcohol is also physically addictive as are Benzodiazepines. "Addiction" is used to describe heroin users and by default cocaine and amphetamine users, although neither of these stimulants are a physically addictive drug. However these drugs are illegal. The notion of the "addict" soon breaks down in any meaningful medical sense. It does become a sociological category to define the "other" (Sartre 1943). If you mention the term "addict" a picture will form. The picture will not detail a middle age woman picking up her Valium script. However she fits the medical definition of an addict, far easier than a black, rap, cocaine user. Addiction and genetic factors for drug addiction are not scientific terms but power discourses (Foucault 1972). The "addict" is a social construction, part of the "other" (Sartre 1943). This allows the power of the state to be used against these marginal men and women, without considering how they became the bogeymen and women.

Emotional amnesia enveloped the drug strategy, launched by New Labour, as it cascaded downwards through the bureaucratic tiers created in its wake. Various university departments up and down the country, studiously ignored research evidence generated by relational studies (Whittington 2007), highlighting the links between trauma and self medication. Academia is challenged by therapeutic and relational methodology (Gilligan 1989, 1990a, 1990b). They do not understand its conceptual language, which is why it has been negated. As they fail to understand it, they relegate its insights. The term "addiction" is used to denote a pre set condition, brimming with genetically programmed scripts, ensnaring drug users who never change. This allows academics to use "science" to study the disease, divorced from its "carrier." At best these "addicts" can be managed. This appears rational and scientific, until you begin to reflect on what a "cure" entails; gene therapy or selective breeding. Being informed you have a genetic pre-condition does not inspire liberation, but creates a sense of doom.

Furthermore no one has ever discovered an addiction gene. The dissection of a corpse fails to find an alcohol disease gene or a heroin related disease gene. This is a socially constructed disease. Schaler (1999) notes that since it cannot be located in the deceased, addiction it is pathology. Rudolf Virchow (1821-1902) however stated for pathology to exist it must create a change in the body tissues. This socially constructed disease creates an industry in its wake. Addiction is a behavioural form, transferred into science as a given quality, without reflection. The terms addiction gene, is now given a new title "addiction susceptibility genes" because the key cannot be located. This is another act of faith.

"Developing improved treatments for addiction is now becoming easier thanks to the discovery of addiction susceptibility genes. Each new addiction gene identified becomes a potential "drug target." That is, researchers can focus on one gene product and develop a drug that modifies its activity. In so doing, signals or pathways in the brain may be reversed or stabilized to restore proper brain function."

University of Utah (2011) "Genetics is an important factor in Addiction." http://learn.genetics.utah.edu/content/addiction/genetics/ Accessed September 12th 2011

In the genetic experiments, the mice are unable to communicate their thoughts and feelings about child abuse, bereavement, lack of a future, a sense of isolation. These parameters are bracketed, as the concentration is focused upon the internal body chemistry. The social conditions of the mice are also ignored, as the body is reduced to being a machine. It is from these studies of entrapped mice, psychological theories are spun about humans, devoid of emotional content. These theories speak more about the psychological state of the scientist, than they do about the nature of external emotional realities.

This is another projection this book dispels; those who exist in one of the most emotionally chaotic, homeless hostels in London can shift remarkably, when the management team are allowed to display initiative, and invest in emotional support. These were not mice but men. Men who are chaotic move forward when a psychological escape ladder is constructed. The only constraints are the professional "carers," who feel threatened by their will to change. It challenges the carer's belief system, the world is hopeless and the clients are doomed, at best they can be managed. This highlights how the workers entrap the clients in their psychological projections. When the workers believe the clients can change, transformation can be initiated which is why it needs direction from the top.

"Faith" as an imperative is a veto against science—in praxi, it means lies at any price.

"The Antichrist" (1895) *N140: collected in "Twilight of the Idols, with The Antichrist.*

"Addiction Studies" is another projection of what Stirner (1844) would call "wheels in the head;" there is no addiction gene, but there is a belief it exists, it is based on faith. This needs dispelling as another ghost, a modern fiction. The real bonds lie between people and their actions; these can either be destructive, as detailed in these men's histories, or affirmative, as detailed in their description of psychological recovery. Interpersonal actions that denigrate and humiliate create trauma, and a subsequent need for self medication. Affirmation, validation and finding a purpose create recovery.

Scientists do not look for a get well gene? Pre programming for addiction is a smokescreen. It is a mechanistic discourse that offers no cure. Anyone who has tried to fix a computer after a virus should be aware of the various complicated changes that ensue, the process of unintended consequences. A computer is an uncomplicated static object; imagine the problems when this type of analogy is used on human beings who have a will?

The 2010 FDAP (Federation of Drug and Alcohol Professionals) conference reaction to the disclosure of trauma within the client group, created a clamp down from people involved in the management of the problem (Miller 1985). Research departments have spread across the UK, but few works have arisen to challenge the main discourse of "addiction." I will highlight the acquiescence of "scientific research" to the accepted cultural paradigm, promulgated to extend research projects that provide no sense of transformation or invigoration. The NTA (National Treatment Agency) highlighted research departments also failed to ignite change, echoing the critique levelled at academia by Francois Lyotard (1992) on how knowledge is produced and consumed in academia.

What is needed instead is to dismantle the technician, and to bring back the practitioner and involve him/her in various forms of Praxis, the combination of theory and practice. At present all forms of research into "addiction" can be critiqued through the prism of inculcating despair. Science only reflects the various psychological projections of the researcher onto the researched, using unreflected personal assumptions to discover the correctness of their original formulation. This ignores any contrary emotionally literate evidence, because it is not deemed scientific within their habitus (Bourdieu 1984). Emotions have no place in science and are therefore eradicated. Science becomes the discourse of the alienated man/woman. There is nowhere to process any contrary evidence within the current paradigm; therefore it is discarded, creating institutional erasure, science devoid of empathy.

The collusion between academic and bureaucratic hierarchies ensures those on the receiving end of policy, become even more alienated from mainstream society (Gerth and Wright Mills 1953). These are the drivers of extremism. This occurs when people are no longer listening. The next step in social evolution is being less concerned with material wealth (Fromm 1955), as hoarding becomes a signifier of inner psychological unease, and a greater concentration on the quality of relationships. This is the antidote to the drift into alienated imprisoned world.

Social Science Delivery from Paralysis

In the social sciences a vast array of competing philosophies all jostle, push and preen in an attempt to attract funding to their various causes. These create public discourses (Foucault 1972) to disguise nihilism. All hover over the subject to be dissected in unreflected discourses of explanatory power. Each is derived from a habitus (Bourdieu 1984), a culture of manners based on unreflected power discourses. This pathologises the subject as a starting projection. They offer solutions based on various facets of discipline and punish (Foucault 1977), a reflection of individual autobiographies, a form of academic revenge. Violence is one attempt to provide meaning to a body, whether enacted physically or emotionally. It is known people respond to violence with fear, and this is utilised to control their behaviour. It is called Behaviourism. The other reactions to violence are ignored within this discourse, especially resistance; an outward compliance but an inward opposition.

There is a constant belief in fecklessness as a precursor to homelessness. George Orwell (1933), prescient in many ways, failed to see the emotional underpinnings of homelessness when he wrote "Down and Out in Paris and London." There is no reflection between the conditions of poverty, violence and bullying abounding in the society at the time, and the men who tramped from spike to spike. If George Orwell (1933) could not see it, after inhabiting this world, then what could be expected from less empathic writers? The discourse of homelessness, wrapped up in Sartre's (1943) notion of the "Other" always reflects someone who is not quite the same as us. They are less than human, another category of an object. Therefore if they are not quite human, there must be specific causes, lapsing into Social Darwinism. This hits a populist nerve with the work of Hare (1999), Pinker (2003) and Stout (2007). This chimes with an everyday discourse, as people sublimate their emotional resonances and build hierarchies based on this eradication.

A vacuum occurs once again, as Nietzsche (1968) highlights this provides a meaning rather than explanation. The issue of homelessness no longer equates to housing need or any subjective reasons for losing a tenancy. It is recouched as a genetic understanding that resonates with a particular political discourse. Mental health, alcoholism and substance use have all come under the genetic discourse. These are socially constructed behavioural forms. These are mined to ascertain which genes create the behaviour, reducing the human to a mechanism. This mechanistic approach to emotions was used in psychiatry in the early part of the century.

*"Against determinism and teleology—From the fact that something ensues regularly and ensues calculably, it does not follow that it ensues **necessarily**"*

Nietzsche F. (1968) N552 "Will to Power,"

Willpower was deemed to reside in the body like brake fluid at the beginning of the 20th Century (Lerner 2003). Instead it is an infusion of energy that exists all over the body, but is seemingly formulated in the mind. Corpses were dissected to find this elixir. It is this invisible energy infusing the body that Adler (1956) sees as striving for positivity, the difference between a living entity and a deceased body. Discourses cloak themselves in the mantle of science, but are really various forms of will to power. People in power create external public discourses to hide their inward fears. The habitus (Bourdieu 1984) rest upon this fear of sinking downward.

Academic discourses receive funding to prove their thesis. In "Disabling Professions" Ivan Illich (1977) looks at the bureaucratic growth of various professions who have utilised science to colonise aspects of everyday life. This resonates with Foucault's ideas when he looked at sexuality and the desire to order sexual perversions (1998). Academics have colluded with this process of colonisation to provide a platform for their "research." These back up taken for granted assumptions about the world and knowledge becomes self fulfilling. The only problems are the subjects themselves, who do not become better, no matter how many interventions are undertaken. Therefore more theories are introduced to explain their fecklessness and inability to become better people. Moreover there is considerable resistance to these interventions, as the subjects object to being labelled (Becker 1963) and categorised. These sites of resistance then become reformulated as criminal. This creates and sustains more pathological labels, triggering a tranche of research grants to discover these new causes. It is a never ending roundabout that no one wishes to stop, because it sustains a whole industry that tames and herds the feckless. A discourse of power (Foucault 1972) allows various services to project their feelings onto the "other" (Sartre 1943) with some rationale of self serving justification. It provides academics and bureaucrats with a meaning, projecting their beliefs as social reality in various power plays (Gerth and Wright Mills 1953). Meaning for a mass industry is constructed through building it upon this abject (Sartre 1943) "other." Whereas the only true reality is based on the emotional world and this can unpick the contours of the labyrinth.

The Psychological Shadow

All psychologically informed decisions begin at the top, as does its shadow; psychological chaos (Jung 1964). Those underneath the top players, the Tsars become totems representing the policy to the outside world. They deliver it to the news media, whilst the politicians sign it off in the House of Commons. Civil servants are tasked to cascade the policy and ensure it is delivered according to their template. As it tumbles down the hierarchical rungs the various Commissioning bodies makes sense and rationalise the central policy to local needs. They seek tenders from the voluntary sector to carry out these aims. Various voluntary sector organisations put in bids, and the Commissioners work on certain criteria to award the bids. This is perceived as obtaining the best value for money and adheres to the idealisations projected about a market economy (Le Grand 2007, 2007 Halpern 2009); Competition provides invigoration through enforcing rivalry. These ideas promulgated by Julian Le Grand (2006, 2007) and David Halpern (2009) have proved disastrous, as ironically there is no opposition to this policy.

The essential problems are the lack of Praxis, which has led to the failure to capture the emotional life histories of men on the margins. The academic and social backgrounds of these power elites lack internal understanding and the ability to connect with the wider world, as noted by Gerth and Mills in "Character and Social Structure," written in 1953.

*"The superiority of the professional insider every bureaucracy seeks further to increase through the means of **keeping secret** its knowledge and intentions. Bureaucratic administration always tends to exclude the public, to hide its knowledge and action from criticism as well as it can."*

Weber M. (1992) P992 "Economy and Society,"

The lessons from one of the founding fathers of the Social Sciences were ignored by the aides to New Labour. This entailed sacrificing care to the management of appearances. I will be arguing from the outset this process needs to be halted, reformulated or dismantled, so effective work can be delivered. The lessons Max Weber (1992) highlighted need to be incorporated into modern service design. Just as the police were shackled by bureaucracies and targets, so were social care agencies.

Within the substance use and homeless sectors, the two spheres, purchaser and provider, operate with two different psychologies, the practitioner deals with people and the bureaucrat with processes (Gerth and Wright Mills 1953). The practitioner ideally works with people to initiate change, the bureaucratic structure seeks to look after its remit and move upward within a power hierarchy. The manipulation of objects entails people's life histories are codified as statistics, and this needs co-operation with academia. The problems with bureaucracies arise from a clouded vision, as they have not been invested with a clear social stake. They are devoid of belief and purpose, as they have no room to enact a philosophy. If social regeneration was enacted it would act as a catalyst. If they were tasked to think, rather than enact procedures, then the forms of exclusion that currently exist will be eradicated. These are the social visionaries who can regenerate communities. There are inherent difficulties within the commissioning model, as there are no checks and balances to its processes. It operates within a power hierarchy and needs an infusion of purpose within it vision.

Councillors do not understand the intricacies of service delivery, as they revolve around different remits. They are lay people who rely on the Commissioners for information (Weber 1992).

"The power position of a fully developed bureaucracy is always great, under normal conditions over towering. The political "master" always finds himself, vis a vis the trained official, in the position of a dilettante facing an expert."

Weber M. (1992) P.991 "Economy and Society,"

They are also presented with their respective party templates on how processes should be managed. This tells them what to expect and they are then provided statistics by Commissioners. If they ever visit projects they cannot comprehend their rationale. Councillors come and go, but the real power lies with the bureaucracy.

As Weber (1992) highlights, the bureaucratic hierarchies operate within a nexus. This entails secrecy is the first priority. The problem with the present commissioning system is its eradication of initiative and this needs to be liberated. Minimal knowledge of psychologically informed environments exists in many of the tiers. There is no energy invested in delivery, only in a safety first approach of targets that creates paralysis.

Within these tiers it is replete with people who aspire to look up within their hierarchies for guidance. There is no interconnection between different departmental briefs as there is no vision of social regeneration. This was all subsumed under regenerating buildings and making business work, but this has missed regenerating people. As Stirner (1844) highlights the "hidden hand of the market" is just another ghost. The links in the bureaucratic chains need to be broken, made shorter with more effective conductors and catalysts in charge of teams of "shock workers." These are Elites (Junger1920), those who make the substantial changes, those who operate to socially regenerate previously inert communities.

Tiers of Miscommunication

Whilst trying to comprehend why the policy was not succeeding in the 1990's, the policy makers could not grasp the significant problems occurring in the communication between the various tiers of bureaucracy they constructed. Each fought to keep its remit. This was exacerbated by the distance between policy makers, the Civil Service hierarchies, commissioners, managers and finally the practitioners and the power discourses (Foucault 1972) operating to separate those who delivered from those who commissioned. Each was partitioned into a separate mechanic and distinct sphere. The remedy involved local authorities hiring an academic to approach the practitioner for his/her experiences. These could be tabulated into research reports, so Commissioners and policy makers understood how their policies were being delivered. This was called research evidence. These reports were sent back to the Civil Service to verify progress, unleashing further public funds to support the work. The academics were paid by the local Boroughs to comment on service delivery without any knowledge of the emotional realities of the client base.

This conflict of interest within these separate spheres, resulted in all forms of policy and knowledge distortion. Although the purchasers and providers met in various meetings over the year, it needed an outside academic source with no concept of psycho-social regeneration to verify what was being communicated. This outlined whether a new tender was needed, as change was based on "research evidence." This entailed consultants blossoming but they lacked therapeutic expertise to understand the work. This created further policy erasure as the consultants were unaware of psychology, because it had been written out of sociology.

This translated into formulated practice. Clients stated they were on the road to recovery when they eventually met with practitioners. Methadone levels were then increased from a maximum ceiling of 50mls per day according to NHS guidelines in the 1990's, to 120mls of Methadone per day in the 21st century. This could be justified, by basing it on the pioneering work of Dole and Nyswander (Ward, Mattick and Hall 1992) which highlighted the efficacy of Methadone in stopping the need to buy street heroin in the mid 1960's. In the 1990's this was formulated into the higher the dose, the less crime was committed. Clients were then satiated with high levels of Methadone, duly sold to subsidise their Giros. Later reformulated into the higher the dose, the less crime committed. Clients were satiated with high levels of Methadone, sold to subsidise their Giros. Those placed on supervised consumption were humiliated in taking the drug in a special booth in a chemist.

This lack of emotional understanding infused other initiatives, such as sex education, teenage pregnancy, obesity, computer games, self harm, and ADHD, Autism and gun crime. The same psycho-emotional causes were ignored. The solutions offered, only glazed the surface presentation, as; condoms, banning computer games, providing Ritalin and talking about sex were perceived as appropriate interventions. These were the practical remedies for the defined "problem", the pill for the ill. Emotional Violence, cruelty, neglect and incest were all erased as possible causes, as any platform for a discussion about emotional violence was shrouded in an invisible silent curtain.

When Substance use workers were informed Methadone was working, this was left unchallenged. Workers were asked to retain people in treatment, as this was deemed to be the purpose. Methadone was perceived as curing anti social behaviour. Clients satiated with high levels of Methadone would no longer need to take heroin and commit crimes because their synapses were full of opioids. This was the narcotic blockade of Dole and Nyswander (Ward J, Mattik R and Hall W 1992). Medical reductionism dominated the field, as the body became reduced to a regulated machine. As the clients became flooded with Methadone, and more people accessed the defined "treatment module," substance use workers were asked to take on larger case loads, entailing there was less time for any personal support or care. They were placed under pressure to increase treatment slots, by doing less intervention with each client. This resulted in a quick chat called brief solution therapy with a letter provided to a GP. This became the standard procedure in a voluntary service. In the Statutory Services the prescription was already filled, waiting to be picked up. Retention was seen as treatment success. Workers needed to know how to type a letter to the Doctor, fill in a prescription pad and then provide needles to those who were not committing crimes. Treatment aims were based on retention, not recovery. "Recovery" was actively thwarted, to retain people in treatment to secure funding.

Commissioning Roles

The current system of substance use and homelessness needs to be radically changed. Commissioning Services from local authorities has not produced efficiency or success. There is no internal market, only an artificially constructed one. Julian Le Grand (2006) originally had high expectations this was going to drive up standards.

"If patients and parents have choice between competing providers, they have power. For providers then have a powerful incentive to meet the needs and wants of their users; those that do so will succeed, and those that do not will fail.

"However, certain conditions have to be fulfilled for choice and competition to work. First, the money must follow the choice. There must be negative consequences for not being chosen. So funding systems are needed that encourage providers to be attractive to would-be users and to use their resources efficiently. One example is payment by results in the NHS—where hospitals get paid according to treatments they actually provide. Formula funding for schools is another, as it is based on the number of pupils they attract. If providers can reduce costs without reducing quality, they will make a surplus to spend on service improvements and enhancing staff pay and conditions.

Another condition for choice to work is that there must be alternative providers. The illusion of choice is worse than none at all. For proper contestability, providers must have real independence, and be entrepreneurial and innovative. Hence the policy drive towards developing new forms of provider, including foundation trusts, independent sector treatment and diagnostic centres, academies and trust schools."

Public Finance (2006) "A Better Class of Choice." http://www.publicfinance. co.uk/ features/2006/a-better-class-of-choice-by-julian-le-grand/ Accessed September 12ᵗʰ 2011

This ideology is based upon faith when Julian Le Grand's (2006) ideas are transmitted to the substance use/mental health/homeless fields.

"One is deceived every time one expects "progress" from an ideal; every time so far the victory of the ideal has meant a retrograde movement."

Nietzsche, F. (1968) N80 "Will to Power,"

Provider's reducing costs without affecting quality, then using the surplus to spend on service improvements, enhancing pay and conditions for practitioners was never viable and is based on historical amnesia. Marxist economics (Baran and Sweezy, 1989) from the 20ᵗʰ Century showed that markets entailed those who owned the means of production; in this case Charity Chief Executives and Senior Managers benefit from the injection of resources (Craig 2008) whilst those who deliver, are regarded as lower down a scale of hierarchy. In times of recession they are being cut, along with their expertise. The money far from being invested in the work has been used to bolster bid writing and PR departments. These are needed to win more contracts to keep Charities operational.

Charities are caught on a melting iceberg and need to jettison anything they can cut. Those that fail to follow this strategy were previously merged within the bigger charities in the tendering wars. Monopoly Charities saw no purpose in enacting therapy, as it was not needed in the contract and was deemed expensive. In the homeless field, this entailed those who deliver the service being relegated to opening the door to clients. The infrastructure blossomed however. It was predicted by Harry Braverman (1974) who drew from Baran and Sweezy (1989) to visualize the future as standards would be driven down, in the need to sustain an internal bureaucracy. This entailed the management was elevated in overseeing this thriving middle sector. The tiers became self replicating, ensuring the Senior Managers were divorced from the people who actually delivered.

Charities that deliver services grew exponentially under this system, and have become entrapped within a web of contractual relationships. They cannot provide any critique of the current malaise, because they became addicted to its formulaic processes. Between 1997 and 2008 they lost their vitality. The hierarchies satiated with money failed to look ahead and became Commissioner compliant. They were relegated to providers, and given the same status as functionaries. They were asked to operate an alienated treatment system that failed its client base. Only those few noble exceptions, who tunnelled outside the parameters to deliver therapy from their own resources, were able to kindle a torch to see the way forwards.

Commissioners adopt the terms laid down by central government who are influenced by a variety of jostling concerns to manage appearances. The commissioning and tendering for substance use and homeless services has not raised standards. As Braverman (1974) highlighted back in the 1970's, he predicted the deskilling of workers. Commissioning is problematic, as those who commission have limited understanding of the client groups and the work. Commissioning uses a considerable pool of resources. This could be utilised in front line work where emotional recovery is created. This market style militates against creating psychologically informed environments. It is a political ideal that has not ignited change. The current system needs a fundamental rethink. In particular the role of commissioning needs to be redefined. The current system is adversarial, and it needs to be either dismantled, or changed to an enabling system, based on mutual rapport. If it was dismantled the resources used in commissioning could be reassigned to bolstering the training and prestige of the practitioner. Community development skills and facilitation is one option, or perhaps dismantling the apparatus and using the resources on the front line to create more highly skilled practitioners is another.

The people who could be the catalyst for change are GP's, practitioners working on the front line. Working in Deptford South East London in 1997 the GP's were the first to specially commission a drug agency, as we worked in genuine partnership with them. Working in partnership was the most fruitful years of development, later thwarted later by the introduction of Council based Commissioners with no understanding of therapeutic treatment. Travelling around the UK as a consultant the same patterns have been repeated with the commissioning process entailing a swathe of young people are trapped in twilight worlds. The academic failure to understand the critique made by Hannah Arendt (1958) has led to institutional malaise, affecting the health infrastructure.

The major investment needs to be in training new emotionally trained workers. The problem with turning charities into businesses is encapsulated in the Guardian (2006) article by John Plummer. It has driven up pay and prospects for accountants, HR and IT.

In small teams the basis of the Orexis model these posts are not needed. An Admin worker oversees the petty cash; an IT person can be bought in when a computer crashes and HR can be dialled up when needed. In large bureaucratic charities the reverse has happened.

"And now that the government is commissioning charities to run huge swathes of public services in areas as diverse as childcare and prisons, job opportunities have diversified and multiplied almost beyond recognition.

Such rapid expansion has also driven up pay and prospects and the new contract culture has brought greater scrutiny and accountability. Throw in the allure of helping to make the world a better place and it looks like the sector is now able to offer ethical and altruistic career opportunities that aren't compromised by second-rate jobs.

A growth in professionalism means charities need different skills from their staff. The sector is increasingly seeking people with private-sector experience to bring transferable skills, such as finance, human resources and IT.

"Businesses and charities are remarkably similar these days," says Helen Tridgell, now director of external affairs at the Disabilities Trust but who previously spent 20 years in advertising and marketing in the corporate world. "The days of charities being soft and fluffy have long gone. They are just as focused and tough as companies."

She describes her organization as "a business that also happens to be a charity" which is well aware of the benefits of staff with private sector experience."

Plummer J. (2006) "Businesses and Charities are very Similar," http:// www.guardian.co.uk/society/2006/nov/08/charities.voluntarysector Accessed September 12th 2011

This shift to 'business professionalism' is applauded in this Guardian article (2006), just before the financial crash, as Finance Workers, IT and Human Resources (Craig 2008) all shift across from the private to the Voluntary Sector. Far from making them more professional and business like, they have ensured organisations have become embroiled in mission drift. Cumbersome unwieldy organisations, satiated with tenders have created an addiction to the contract bidding. They have reduced front line quality to bolster this idea of professionalism. Charities have become top heavy and increasingly devoid of content, as they project a brand image. The work is inspected by those unaware of what an ideal work situation is. This has created the bedrock for all types of projection.

Charities forced to compete for contracts when dangled before them, were then told to work together by the Commissioners for the common good of the clients. It is a flawed business model when applied to social care. There is no working together, as the process is adversarial. It ensures agencies work against each other. Each is a rival. The commissioners hold the power relationship and control from the centre. The charities seemingly move to their rhythm.

This is the funding rationale for drug agencies and homeless projects. Interestingly it is not used for schools, police forces, CAMHT's, GP surgeries or any social services departments. The reason why, it does not work and these organisations know tendering out services causes care disturbance. Tendering for services used by local authorities is costly; it creates massive disruption, insecurity and leads to constant demoralisation in the workforce. People tasked to deliver care to the most vulnerable are reduced in status. Transfer of Undertakings Protected Employment (TUPE) ensures whoever takes on the contract has to take on the same staff with their pay and conditions as enshrined in European Union (EU) law. There is however a push to circumvent this, through bullying and paying people to leave.

When a new staff team is employed, the providers drive down costs and employ less qualified staff. This devalues the work. It is called deskilling (Braverman 1974). The tendering exercise has not raised standards, but reduced them. Generally commissioners know little about the nature of the work they commission, and view mental health and substance use services the same way as they would invite bids to provide fleet car hire or office decoration.

Commissioners come from a variety of backgrounds but increasingly they need a business degree and no knowledge of the sector they commission. They never assimilated the Hawthorne effect (Landsberger, H. A. 1961); the more support and care people are provided the better the output. Instead the operational mode is Taylorism (1911) based on Scientific Management; engendering fear through breaking down the job role and making each part interchangeable. It is deemed through this process, people are invigorated to achieve more. Praise is therefore withdrawn, and only the hard glare creates the desire for harder work to meet the needs of the omnipresent stern look of the father. All systems are psychologically informed, the workers either adapts to the glare of the bully or is offered the hand in support. Adversarial relationships destroy trust and care, instead creating subservience based on embedded institutional bullying. This is the feature of the current Charities, where non skilled people, are now working with the most challenging of client groups.

The voluntary agencies or charities employ people to carry out the work according to the tender specifications. The tender includes a management cost, used to sustain the voluntary agency infrastructure to make more bids. The person who delivers the policy is a long way away from the government minister and their Civil Service hierarchy. They are often a long way from the Charity hierarchy. As the funding cascades, each chain of the bureaucratic link takes its share of the proceeds.

The division between practitioner and provider created class hierarchies. Those at the bottom delivering front line services are perceived as being on the lowest rung. The bureaucrats who "commissioned" services are endowed with a superior status (Gerth and Wright Mills 1953). This creates a power discourse based on a habitus (Bourdieu 1984) of manners. The career trajectory in the field entails experienced front line staff moving away from working on treatment, desiring to move into the comfort and safety of an office desk. This further undermines the delivery of "care" from inception. Delivering care is deemed to have no value or status. The added strictures placed upon service delivery and the type of work the practitioner is asked to undertake are not congruent with the client's emotional or practical needs. The aims handed down to those who deliver were composed far away from the front line. Formulated around tables in Whitehall, they were enacted to minimise the impact of the escalating fear of crime. This fear helped to fuel an adversarial polarity, developed between commissioners and commissioned. The latter became compliant and less interested in the clients. They became more interested in adhering to the terms and conditions of the contractual arrangement. Practitioners were trapped within a Langian (1960, 1961, 1964) "double bind." If they refused to enact these templates the contracts were pulled, if they enacted them, clients were alienated from the service, prohibiting recovery. Within this power equation the clients suffered.

Command and Control

This is an excerpt from the Drugs Prevention report undertaken by Mike Hough in 1996. This report highlights the role of self medication.

"The 'coping' model (or self-medication model), arguably the most common-sense attempt to explain why problem drug misuse tends to coexist with social deprivation, sees drug use as providing a 'palliative' to poor quality of life.

• The 'structure' model, grounded in opportunity theory (Cloward and Ohlin, 1960), emphasises that those who are denied legitimate opportunities to achieve societal goals substitute illegitimate ones. The model develops—or transforms the idea of drug use as a palliative into that of drug use as a form of work which provides meaning and purpose

(cf Preble and Casey, 1969; Gilman and Pearson, 1991).

• *The 'status 'model develops opportunity theory a stage further, identifying drug use as a solution to problems of status and identity associated with social and economic exclusion. It identifies the positive social pay-offs from drug use in subcultures which respect anti-authoritarian macho, risk-taking and entrepreneurialism (cf Burr, 1987;*

Gilman and Pearson, 1991).

These different psychological and sociological models are neither mutually exclusive nor incompatible with others: different sorts of explanation may be more appropriate at different stages of an individual's drug-using career."

Hough M. (1996) "Drug Misuse and the Criminal Justice System" http:// www.drugslibrary.stir.ac.uk/documents/houghdrugscrime.pdf Accessed 11th September 2011

Self medication was discarded quickly but it is interesting it was seen as the main rationale for substance use just before New Labour came to power; instead Discipline and Punishments rationales never specifically articulated in terms of how they were going to produce change were introduced. They rested upon certain components of Behaviourism. These are the components of a Drug Rehabilitation Requirement that offers a gentle intervention, compared to the list of instruction in Statutory Provision.

"A weekly timetable will be given to you that will include all your appointments you must attend. The requirement will include drug testing twice weekly, group work and weekly key working sessions to discuss things like housing, benefits, drug use, offending behaviours, staying safe, harm minimisation and onward referrals to other agencies which may include an Aftercare Programme or Counselling.

You may also need substitute prescribing, onward referral to residential rehab, alternate therapies or access to the structured Day Programme."

Society of St. James's (2011) "Drug Services and Drug Rehabilitation," http:// www.ssj.org.uk/addiction-services/drr.html Accessed 12th September 2011

This clip from the "Lewisham Safer Partnership" ("2011/2012 Draft) highlights these coercive ventures do not transform the recalcitrant's into making recovery changes. These programmes have again erased self medication, and instead tried to gently coerce. This report details the lack of progress made in the Lewisham Safer Partnership (2011/2012 Draft).

"This Green Paper was published by the Ministry of Justice on 7 December 2010. It details the broad approach to the 'Rehabilitation Revolution' promised by the Coalition Government.

The paper's initial premise mirrors Lewisham's Total Place findings—that despite record investment in prison and offender management structures almost half of all adult offenders released from custody reoffend within a year, and 75% of offenders sentenced to youth custody reoffend within a year."

Lewisham Strategic Partnership (2011) "Integrated Offender Management," 2011/2012www.lewishamstrategicpartnership.org.uk/docs/ SLP%20Marc . . . Accessed 12th September 2011

When the report states "reoffend," this means half the adults released are caught within a year, along with 75% of youth offenders. It would be interesting to know what went right with the other percentage of the population. The problem of coercion and behaviourism is it negates the emotional resistance to being subjugated. Behaviourism did not modify behaviour in the long term.

Discipline and Punish

The underpinnings of the New Labour strategy based on Discipline and Punishment (Foucault 1977) rested on an unswerving belief in behaviourism stemming from a public school pedagogical system of coercion. This only works if there is an escape ladder to force people to take the blows so they can be recompensed with money or power in the future. There is no such idyll promised to people with substance use problems. They are provided with a Methadone carrot, no promise of any redemption. Huge numbers of people are caught in this swathe, trapped within a sense of meaninglessness.

When discipline and punishment is applied to people already suffering from extensive childhood trauma, it fails to make any headway. The various resistances to authority structures (Marcuse 1972) are already embedded prior to becoming involved with institutions and these become hardened by the appliance of discipline and punishment (Foucault 1977). Violence begets violence. This is why there is such a high prison recidivist rate. These men have already created hardened "fronts" that can take on all on comers. Prison means nothing to them. Already taking on the biggest test, violence enacted within the family, beating up a bullying father, (Whittington 2007) those who are meant to provide care; they are pre armed in taking on the state. A common scenario arises constantly with these clients, after years of being beaten they attack the perpetrator between the ages of 14-16, thereby stopping the familial violence. This dynamic arises in Ron's case history. There is nothing the state can throw at a boy, who has endured this violence that has not already been thrown. The hard "front" of the boy needs to be dissolved, not hardened further. Young Offenders Institutes and anti gang initiatives are not going to stop any of the violence, unless these precedents are dealt with. The emotional and social cost to society in keeping up this system is to continue the cycle of violence. This is not going to be remedied by six courses of Cognitive Behavioural Therapy (Beck A. and Freeman A. 1990), Solution Focused Therapy (Berg I. in Washton A. 1995) and Motivational Interviewing (Rollnick and Morgan in Washton A, 1995). Focusing on needles, benefits and Methadone will not resolve these traumas. People need extensive rebuilding.

The current TOPS (Treatment Outcome Profile 2007) undertaken by the National Treatment Agency, measures the client's self reported involvement in crime, thereby measuring treatment improvement. This ostensibly provides a snapshot of their health status, but instead focuses on crime. This clearly is not going to be filled in with any honesty, and yet its function persists. It merely militates against creating any form of rapport, if the first question the worker is asking is if the people seeking help commit crimes. This intervention could only have been invented by academia, ignoring any concept of building a relationship to initiate change.

"Record days of shoplifting, drug selling and other categories committed in past four weeks

Week 4 Week 3 Week 2 Week 1 Total a Shoplifting 0-7 0-7 0-7 0-7 0-28 b Drug selling 0-7 0-7 0-7 0-7 0-28 c Theft from or of a vehicle Yes No d Other property theft or burglary Yes No e Fraud, forgery and handling stolen goods Yes No f Committing assault or violence Yes No

Farrell M. And Marsden M (2007) "TOPS Form" Scanned on September 11th 2011

The Models of Care arose to plot a therapeutic journey. The various tiers have been transformed into bureaucracies, each defending their tier. This "TOPS" tool appears "objective," because Dr. John Marsden and Dr. Michael Farrell (2007) have the power to define "objectivity." These questions are asked nowhere else in the NHS. This is the clearest piece of evidence, linking the various bureaucratic tiers to sabotaging the work of the practitioner. It is aimed at justifying the existence of a bureaucracy who collates the responses into performance statistics, trying to obtain an 80% compliance rate. Used by front line workers to deliver "objectivity," it is a non objective piece of social research, as its whole premise is based on various assumptions. Firstly, it is premised on an honesty that is already presumed not to exist. Furthermore the relational work (Gilligan 1989, 1990a, 1990b) is undermined by the type of questions being asked. It states; I want you to give me your name and address, then tell me the number of crimes you commit each day, so I can send it off to a government agency, that works alongside the police. We guarantee we will store this information confidentially because I say so. Then I can ascertain how effective my treatment intervention is.

There is nothing objective about this "research." There is a will to power in creating a clear discourse; an apparent reality composed using Social Science methodology to sabotage recovery.

"The Treatment Outcomes Profile (TOP) is a new drug treatment outcome monitoring tool that has been developed by the NTA in partnership with drug treatment providers in over 70 sites across England. It is applicable for use in all of the structured treatment modalities as defined by Models of Care for

Treatment of Adult Drug Misusers: Update 2006. For the first time, service users, clinicians, service managers and commissioners will be able to obtain objective and comparable data about real improvements in service users' lives that will be able to inform and improve practice on both an individual and strategic level.

The TOP is a simple set of questions that will improve clinical practice by enhancing assessment and care plan reviews for clients. The data it provides will improve performance monitoring. Data will be reported into the National Drug Treatment Monitoring System (NDTMS) from October 2007 and results fed back to providers and commissioners from March 2008."

Farrell M. And Marsden M (2007) "TOPS Form" Scanned on September 11th 2011

The front of the form records the name and date of birth. This type of interaction has arisen from a lack of understanding the psychological dynamics of psychological change. In particular the role of attachment severance and its subsequent effects is routinely ignored. This creates a research spiral, based on an academic emotional shutdown, cascading throughout the different treatment interventions. Relational (Gilligan 1989, 1990a, 1990b) and phenomenological research have both been abandoned, practitioner accounts perceived as anecdotal, and the universities colluding in this form of "objective" science (Whittington 2011).

These research questions are not asked in any other NHS treatment service. Their remit has been extensively questioned by both the BMA (British Medical Association) and the GMC (General Medical Council). From the outset, this replicates the same set of game playing undertaken with probation, police, young offender's institutes and all the other law and order facilities. It automatically assumes the person is part of the "other" (Sartre 1943). It relies on poorly trained front line staff, with no knowledge of research methods, to ask a set of questions that undermine their primary treatment objective; to develop a therapeutic relationship. The rationale of the practitioner should be in creating change and transformation, this criminal justice remit needs to be left to Probation. It thrusts the practitioner into being a compliant member of "them," a member of the regime who discipline and punish (Foucault 1977) the "other" (Sartre 1943). This strategy as detailed in the Lewisham Safer Partnership Report (2011) has not been successful, yet its precepts are constantly replicated. It sustains a bureaucracy that is built upon the foundations of trauma and upon which bureaucratic citadels and empires aspire forever upward, ensuring those on the bottom are forever trapped.

Substance use workers were synthesised into surrogate probation officers. This is only a requirement of state sponsored substance use programmes, and could not be implemented in private therapy. The worker is being asked to inform on their client's behaviour from the outset, creating the dynamic no one can be trusted. This duplicates the problems inherent in familial attachment severance relationships. This torpedoes any formation of a therapeutic alliance. Workers are aware their clients commit crimes, because they attend the needle exchange in the next room to collect needles, so they can inject heroin. A client can tell a worker they are not committing any crimes in one instant, and then go to the next room, speak to the same workers and ask for a pack of fresh needles. This "objective" research is a subjective hindrance to any effective emotional work. It the state wants its substance use services to become surrogate police people; this should be clarified to those attending treatment. Clients clearly are not going to be detailing their crimes, unless they have mental health issues to their drug key worker.

The over prescription of these intervention techniques is based on an essential divorce between self knowledge and rationally obtainable scientific knowledge, a significant philosophical conundrum within social science and medical research, it barely registers in research methods. There is minimal self understanding from a therapeutic viewpoint, and considerable rational observable scientific amnesia, where self motivation for conducting the research is absent from any self reflection. This absence is projected within the research paradigms, creating a cataclysmic social science research black hole. Research produces a set of social fictions of "bad faith" (Sartre 1943). These are coded into perceived valid claims about social reality, based on a mechanical understanding of human beings. Within the substance use world treatment facilities, this reality rests on a tacit collusion between practitioner and client in a game playing ritual. Clients need the methadone and the practitioner needs the statistic to get paid. Each interaction is reduced to an alienated function, as both have an investment in keeping the game (Berne 1961, 1964) in play. The researcher obtains a result and the NTA meet a target. Claims are made this is a valid treatment intervention, but there is no overall philosophical rationale that proves it. This demonstrates how alienated working practices hamstring the practitioner, making them a functionary, with no personal creativity, epitomising Neo Tayloresque (1911) regimes, enacted to measure the monotony of work. No one has dared to critique this model from a social sciences perspective, and this raises once again questions about how the subject lacks any understanding of the emotional discourse in its methodology.

Social Science methodology becomes conceptually flawed when it ignores these relational bridges, and therefore vast areas of enquiry become replete with the error of assumptions. If someone was asked about their favourite chewing gum or brand of beer within a questionnaire, they could provide a definitive answer. Questioning how many illegal drugs have been consumed in a week is much more problematic. Ask them whether they have been abused as children, and just through making the assumption, anger may emerge followed by a strong denial. This does not mean it is not true, it just means the researcher has not made a relational bridge to gain access to an emotional truth. The style of questioning may even make the issue worse. Unless it is part of an ongoing dialogue, it may entrench the problem, as it triggers the feelings of stigma (Goffman 1963).

Nurses and other frontline workers are not social researchers, but people paid to deliver treatment and "care." Within the scientific discourse the notion of touch, speech, warmth and nurture have been written out of the understanding of cell regeneration within the body (Harrison 1986). Illness is not understood as having a psychological function. It is perceived as a random act. Harrison (1986) changes that perception by looking at the psychological function of illness as an outcome of attachment severance. People learn a life script building on the insights of Transactional Analysis. The case histories seemingly confirm this view that people write their life scripts as a result of trauma and love.

Emotional discourses have become relegated to the arts; literature, poetry, music, theatre despite the work of Spitz (1965), Bowlby (1984, 1969,

1973, 1980) and Harlow (Blum 2002). These concepts are critical for initiating emotional literacy, the idea of 'strokes,' giving praise, as noted by Claude Steiner (1974, 2003) is crucial for a process of psychological regeneration, ideas derived from Spitz's (1965) pioneering work, along with Otto Rank ideas highlighted in "The Trauma of Birth" (1952). It was Rank who challenged psychotherapy for being dead and emotionless bringing back feeling within the work later surfacing in Carl Rogers "Person Centred Therapy (1961). Freud was an originator, who retreated after his Seduction Theory (De Zulueta 1993). He was crushed by Krafft-Ebing into seeing the abuse he witnessed in his sessions as mere conjecture. He relabelled it as the Oedipus Complex; these people really wanted to sleep with and murder their parents. This was the great betrayal. Turning it upside down and drawing on scientific pretension, he reduced thought and action, to a complicated meccano set of preconceptions. Emotional Literacy (Steiner 1974, 2003) needs to be liberated from its walled up confines.

Emotional literacy is ignored in the various government initiatives when working with people with substance use issues. This is a fundamental flaw, and has fatally undermined the whole project from inception. As soon as the first targets were introduced in 1997 with "Tackling Drugs Together" and onwards, a stream of resources (Craig 2008) has cascaded off the edge of a cliff into a vast void based on psychological erasure.

Collapse of a Good Idea; Arrest Referral

As an example of a good idea being saddled with too many ideologies is the Arrest Referral Scheme. It was devised in the mid to late 90's, piloted in Lewisham, Lambeth and Southwark. I was involved in its Lewisham launch in 1997-1999 where the social enterprise I developed, based on delivering therapy, worked alongside the South London Home Office Drugs Prevention Team and the Police/Probation. The rationale for involvement evolved from many service users being immersed in crime to sustain their drug use. At the time, links had not been made between drug use and criminal behaviour. The idea was to forge links with the police, so they could refer people for therapeutic support. I was aware of the connections between drugs and crime because I had the trust of the clients. I was made aware of their various schemes. I also noted that these schemes were linked to a psychological need as well as an economic.

It seemed evident the continuous treadmill of prison and crime wasted public resources. Aiming to break the cycle and allow people to rebuild their lives marked the initial impulse. Drug agencies were the potential agents of social psychological regeneration. Orexis was at the forefront.

The workers employed on the Arrest Referral Scheme had a background in therapy and knowledge of substance use. During the two years we managed to entice 73 people into voluntary treatment who would normally have desisted. This entailed working with them to access counselling and a Methadone script if required. We had developed a strong rapport with local GP's. The highest Methadone level we advised the GP's to prescribe was 50mls and we had 500 clients attending therapy, alongside their scripts. This was why Lewisham in the early part of the 21st century was one of the safest boroughs in inner London, not because of its CCTV systems or summer play schemes. It was because many of its prolific offenders were involved in therapeutic stabilisation. Meanwhile its Labour MP, Bridget Prentice mistakenly announced in the House of Commons that surveillance schemes were having a major impact, unaware the prolific offenders who were receiving therapy were not needing to self medicate. This was because there were no conduits between her role and the role of the agency. We were tiers apart and it was kept that way because there was a lack of theoretical understanding of drug agencies and their impacts.

"People may be surprised to know that Lewisham is the safest borough in London. Crime has fallen by 6 per cent. Over the past year, and one reason is the relationship between the local police, the borough council and the community at large. That partnership has worked extremely well in ensuring that the borough remains a safe place in which to live, work and learn."

House_of_Commons_(2002)_ "Hansard_Debates_for_8_Mar_2002_(pt_6)" www.publications.parliament.uk/pa/cm200102/cmhansrd/vo020308/ debtext/20308-06.htm_Accessed_September_12th_2011

The local Arrest Referral Scheme demonstrated its success, breaking the local drug-crime axis. This was premised on the therapeutic work undertaken at the agency. The Arrest Referral Scheme was eventually launched nationally due to its success in Lewisham. Orexis the drug agency worked in Lewisham on the new contract. There was an understanding everything would continue in the same vein to build trust to create conduits to allow people to access treatment, successfully building upon the previous work. The figures of 200 per annum were high, as we saw over 500 in total each year. This was a far higher case load than most London Boroughs at the time. The effect of the police taking over the contractual arrangements in 2000 entailed less focus on getting people into treatment, which I believed had been the original aim. Instead it focused on assessments for treatment, with the eventual signposting to various bodies that offered tangential support. The figure of 200 assessments entailed seeing 4 people per week, just to take their details. People were visited in the cells, their details taken, and they were finally given a card to attend an AA/NA/CA meeting.

Whereas the previous therapeutic workers had built up rapport and accompanied the clients to our treatment facility, ensuring they received rapid access. The new arrangement entailed the person receiving a card with a number to call upon release a peer support group that did not exist in the locality. Getting people into treatment was not a requirement, making the work easier, but less rewarding.

This numbers for assessment was later increased to 8 people per week. The numbers who accessed treatment at our agency dropped to zero. Accessing treatment was no longer deemed a desirable outcome. It was the assessment that counted. Orexis became the lead organisation in reaching these Met Police targets in 2003. The whole operation descended into "gaming" (Berne 1961, 1964) as it lost its purpose.

" . . . *heavy performance management from the top is not trouble-free. A ceaseless bombardment of instructions demotivates and demoralises providers, especially professionals used to a high degree of autonomy and trust. And targets have their own problems. They discourage continuous innovation and improvement, and can distort priorities: what is not targeted is ignored. As is often said, one can hit the target but miss the point.*

They can also lead to 'gaming': ranging from straightforward fiddling of the figures to inappropriate changes in behaviour (such as unnecessarily admitting patients into wards from accident and emergency departments to meet a four-hour target). Penalties for missing targets can seem arbitrary and unfair."

Public Finance (2006) "A Better Class of Choice," http://www.publicfinance. co.uk/features/2006/a-better-class-of-choice-by-julian-le-grand/ Accessed 12th September 2011

Julian Le Grand (2011) highlights the inherent problems unfolding in being given targets in this quote. This details the forms of alienation that infected Social Care and Health in all the sectors, as highly competent practitioners were shackled and stifled by academic "targets." Orexis was the first substance use organisation to hand the Met Police contract back and not seek renewal in 2003. The whole process became meaningless, collapsing into a statistical exercise. The Police were centrally controlled by the Home Office, and the same exertion was inserted onto drug agencies, destroying the bonds between clients and practitioners. This was the New Labour legacy, and drawing on Harry Stack Sullivan (Barton Evans 1996) this destroyed a vital attachment relationship, that could have created social regeneration.

"Police performance and Targets

The Home Office is taking measures to reduce the police inspection and targets regime. They are working to reduce centralised performance management and the data requests placed on forces in order to free up the police to focus on local priorities.

Policing Pledge, Public Confidence measures have been removed and the Assessment of Policing and Community Safety (APACS) is to be abolished. This allows new arrangements to be developed that best meet the aims of strengthening local accountability, removing undue direction from the centre and supporting professional discretion. Government will also annually review requests made of the police by the 'centre' to ensure they keep meeting needs as the new inspection and accountability arrangements develop.

Lewisham Strategic Partnership (2011) "Integrated Offender Management," 2011/2012www.lewishamstrategicpartnership.org.uk/docs/ SLP%20Marc . . . Accessed 12th September 2011

New Labour's central grip stifled initiative, as Julian Le Grand (2011) highlights. Slowly its fingers are being prised from the windpipe, but with resources being cut to the marrow. Cuts can be inflicted because the treatment system did not achieve any great outcome. There was no regeneration of communities because complex trauma was ignored and treatment agencies were forced into "gaming." Various statutory criminal justice bodies, based on discipline and punishment were launched and these consumed millions of pounds without creating any dent in crime. This could have been used in regenerating marignalised communities. Their abject failure is a searing indictment of the academic and political classes. All foundered on one basic philosophical misunderstanding; you cannot cajole and force people to change their "addictive" behaviour. Addiction is self medication and is premised upon a resistance to emotional violence.

Hidden Lives and the Probation Service

The enforcement of Drug Rehabilitation Orders and Drug Rehabilitation Requirements were introduced by the Probation Service, an agency in the throes of a crisis of meaning in the 1990's. Unaware of the extent of their client's substance use, clients hid their lives from the inspection by authority. I recollect working with one South London Woman in 1995 who pleaded with me not to let her Probation Officer know she was on drugs, even though she had 80 offences for shoplifting. The Probation Officer contacted me when she went missing and queried what my remit was, as the client had let her know she spoke to me about a sensitive issue. Stuck between confidentiality and answering a question about my remit and involvement, I provided details of the agency. She then began to query me on my involvement with the client. I replied I could not answer. She became heated about her right to know. I pointed out to her she needed to make the bonds with the client to understand her background. I gently placed the phone down. This anecdotal account is backed by this report by Mike Hough written in 1996 for the Home Office.

"This review has found no British research directly assessing probation officers' skills in identifying and assessing offenders with drug problems when preparing PSRs, though in Nee and Sibbitt's (1993) survey several probation areas identified this as a problem. Several questions need answers:

• Are probation officers good at identifying problem drug users?

• Are they better placed to do so than, for example, drug workers involved in arrest referral?

• Do they have adequate links with treatment agencies?"

Hough M. (1996) "Drug Misuse and the Criminal Justice System," http:// www.drugslibrary.stir.ac.uk/documents/houghdrugscrime.pdf Accessed 10th September 2010

It was only through the Arrest Referral Scheme, the Probation Service and the Police became aware of the underlying drug problem being directly connected to the 1980's and 1990's crime wave. The Probation service was perceived as part of the "other" (Sartre 1943) by the clients, the agencies of coercion, and they had created resistances to their dictates. This notion of resistance was not accounted for in any research, as it views them as miscreants needing to be tamed. This became translated into practice.

Nursing and Emotional Denial

Emotional interventions are deemed as not being needed within a rational scientific treatment process. The type of training offered within the NHS particularly to nurses both SEN's and CPN's are based on a presumed medical model, the emphasis on substance use as an addiction, which needs to be controlled. The medical model is based on scientific masculine concepts of rationality as opposed to the feminine world of emotions. (Seidler V. 2005) Knowledge discourses are gendered, masculine is deemed strong and feminine ideas are perceived as weak. These were two comments from nurses working in the field. The first was from a Senior Nurse who works in a detox ward and the second comment came from a nurse who delivered an NHS drug service. This highlights the issues inherent in De Beauvoir's (1949) liberation; women have become equal in adopting the rationalist discourse.

Nurse 1

"You mention child abuse as an issue with people with drug and alcohol problems but that's not true is it? I mean I know lots of people who have been abused as kids, they've had terrible times but they haven't turned into drug addicts. They've just gotten on with it. I think people are just looking for excuses for their behaviour. I don't why people keep going on about child abuse; you're either born an addict or not, end of."

Whittington D. (2006) Field Notes,

Nurse 2

"No one I know ever talks about child abuse when they come and see me. I think that's over emphasised in this field, the latest trend. I've been a nurse working in the field for over ten years and not one addict I've seen has ever mentioned they've been abused a kid. That's just rubbish."

Whittington D. (2010) Field Notes

The discourse of child sexual abuse is documented in the Waterhouse Report "Lost in Care" (2000). Sir Ronald Waterhouse and fellow tribunal members heard evidence from 650 people who had been in care in north Wales since 1974. The focus was on seven specific homes concentrating on physical, emotional and sexual abuse. The results were published in this watershed report. The stirrings of child sexual abuse, as a significant issue, arose from the work of Esther Rantzen in the 1980's. Prior to this it was a great unsaid, written out of public life with no discussion, arising from a collective denial of reality. Bruno Bettelheim in "The Informed Heart" (1960) reflected on the public reaction to the "discovery" of the concentration camps. He described it as a form of emotional shutdown, as if people could not encompass the existential horror of what had occurred, instead they sought meaning by imposing forms of denial upon it. These resulted in various explanations at odds with the mounds of corpses; denial, they must have done something wrong, why are they punishing us? I never knew about this, those evil people did that. The numbers, extent and forms of torture reported were too much for people to envisage, so they bracketed it and then closed it off. To accept the deaths would necessitate a shift from an inner composed, compartmentalised picture of social reality, created and held as a fantasy. It would then have to acknowledge extensive forms of violence. This imposition on reality is based on the shutdown of personal experience deemed too painful and the construction of fantasy as recompense.

Sexual abuse scandals followed this pattern, the horrors of the differing forms of torture were revealed, and a societal reaction followed as detailed in "Beaten into Violence" (Whittington 2007). Society switched off because it could not deal with the horror happening within their parishes. It became consigned to the "other" (Sartre 1943). The vulnerable children previously sent to the colonies becoming sexual slaves in Australia, New Zealand, Rhodesia, Canada and South Africa were also bracketed. Sent to keep up the number of white inhabitants they were used as child labourers for farmers. The expose of what transpired, led to a public apology by Gordon Brown for the mass mistreatment after being uncovered by Margaret Humphreys (Melville J. and Bean P. 1989). This only became apparent after her investigations, uncovered a conspiracy of lies that hid the truth. She had faced a number of hurdles based on game playing and duplicity beforehand.

Denial by nurses working within the substance use field stems from a general societal reaction to block out trauma (Miller 1985). It is bracketed as being an antecedent to drug use. The sex abuse scandals and the details of the violence enacted by the "Christian Brothers" carers in Australia were all carefully concealed, through a form of active forgetting, institutional denial and complicity. These forms all emerged in therapeutic work at the hostel. Institutional violence within "care" homes arose consistently as a precursor to later self medication.

This denial of young people's realities is an especially damaging ideology when promulgated by those administering treatment, and who also exercise power. At the very least, it requires openness to acceptance. It does not require the belief every person has been sexually abused, but exploring the antecedents of substance use throws up a variety of causes. As the case histories show, the scale of trauma prior to men becoming homeless is a common experience. This ranges from a variety of causes.

There are concerns that people who supervise staff running groups for people recovering from detoxification may silence people when they reveal traumatic lives (Miller 1990). The success rate at the treatment facility is not particularly high, and this could be a considerable factor in the low performance rate. The Senior Nurse's attitude, beliefs and views are then passed onto staff members through unreflected supervision. They become taught to suppress these emotional realities. The lead person sets the psychological template, and people model themselves accordingly. If there was more emphasis on trauma as a precursor to self medication, then attitudes such as those displayed by these two nurses will need to change to meet the needs of the clients. Their views however remain unchecked, because they reflect the general unreflected assumptions within the sector. The second example highlights the issues stemming from denying attachment and building relational bridges to people seeking support in the substance use field. The nurse could not make the relational bridges with her clients to move beyond the "front" because she was immersed in a medical model that denies connection.

"All credibility, all good conscience, all evidence of truth comes only from the senses."

Nietzsche F. (1886) N 134 "Beyond Good and Evil,"

Whilst the senses can be heightened by the use of science, the emotional world inherent within the senses provides the key to feeling a personal truth. Good science builds upon the emotions, it does not negate them. The split between belief and reality is apparent within the medical discourse, where emotions are sublimated. They are never articulated and those who imbibe its discourse erase emotional realities.

The nurse viewed treatment as a technical exercise in titrating people. This allowed her to ascertain their methadone level by asking them to not take drugs for 24 hours beforehand. She could then administer stepped doses of Methadone to stop the withdrawals. Treatment was reduced to a procedure. It became based on ascertaining the levels of Methadone needed to stop the body going into withdrawal. The body is essentially viewed as a passive organ, rather than belonging to a living being. This reinforces the sense of alienation many substance users feel about their bodies, they are merely receptacles for self medication. It also highlights to problems in taking a piecemeal approach to the problem of substance use. Reducing everything to a technical exercise ensures the mind is split from the body. This replicates a wider discourse within the medical field (Chomsky 1996).

Administering Methadone is perceived as alleviating heroin withdrawal, not as a component in an overall self medication strategy for trauma. Talk around the client's problems was curtailed, as the nurse set about her task. This discourse became self fulfilling, as the second nurse never enquired about a clients background, so they never volunteered any information about their early life. This self fulfilling prophecy can be written as a research discourse, stemming from an inability to draw upon empathy and emotional intelligence to create relational bridges (Gilligan 1989, 1990a, 1990b) based on trust. If these are absent, you have empty unemotional frozen exchanges, all based on a presumed rationality of needing Methadone to stop bodily withdrawal. This highlights the problems which accrue when emotional intelligence is missing.

Issues of attachment, building trust and relationships are absent within mainstream social science methodology. The attempts by the subject discipline to take on a scientific mantle to ensure its respectability. This has entailed eradicating emotional discourses and copying the natural sciences of observing with unemotional detachment.

Legalisation; Psychological Erasure

Social Science research previously undertaken into the causes of male homelessness, drug use, violence and self neglect, has traditionally used ill defined research paradigms, especially those commissioned by the State and Universities. Notable exceptions exist in the Voluntary Sector and in the Multiple Exclusion Homelessness Research Programme (2011) highlighting the links between homelessness and trauma. Traditionally university research paradigms entail intrusive questions being asked vulnerable people by people who have no concept of the emotional effects of their research, alienating the patient/resident/client from treatment. These do not promote a strategy of engagement; instead they appear directly meddling, reinforcing the sense of "otherness," the stigma (Goffman 1963) the intervention is meant to avoid. Questions are routinely asked without context especially of people with substance use issues because they are deemed vulnerable and the "other" (Sartre 1943). When emotional discourses are raised they are then routinely erased.

The inability to conceptualise self medication affects the arguments over which drugs should be legalised. The effective pensioning off of thousands of young people into a twilight existence was not the basis for the rift between Gordon Brown, Alan Johnson, the New Labour architects on one side, with Professor Nutt, Dr John Marsden, Dr Ian Ragan, Dr Simon Campbell, Dr. Polly Taylor, Marion Walker and Dr Les King ranged on the other side. The latter did not resign because of this Methadone satiation. The Advisory Council for the Misuse of Drugs fought a battle of power over who had control over policy. It did not look at the details of the policy itself.

The only positive outcome was the attempt to bring policy and policing substances from out of the criminal justice remit. Criminalising drugs has not provided any satisfactory outcomes as the police have been tasked to solve a crime that is difficult to detect. A fundamental change will be wrought when the war on drugs is suspended, and it is taken out of any involvement with criminal justice. Then the issues of long term self medication will finally become apparent. Legalising illegal drugs will create a major challenge to big pharma. For example, drug users in the hostel would rather take illicit drugs, than those provided by big pharma, because they were more effective in alleviating their need for self medication (Khantzian 1985, 1995, 1999, 2010). These symptoms will not disappear when drugs are legalised. The hard work to create change will entail more social psychological work needed to create positive change.

This second component is neglected in the legalisation debate. Decriminalising drugs is not going to stop their use, it will increase. The reasons for the increase need to be understood. Heroin, Crack Cocaine, Special Brew, Diamond White and Skunk are not consumed because they are part of testing one's skills as an adolescent. These substances are used to obliterate reality. Criminalising these strategies is not going to prohibit people from using them; it only makes them criminals and substance users. The emotional dynamic, the will to obliterate is obscured in the social science and medical research. Deference is given to science, because it appears rational, until closely observed. Then it appears as a belief system. David Halpern (2009) calls for legalisation and then talks about taking out the drug dealers and pushing the users into treatment, but he fails to understand the rationale for obliteration and self medication. This is going to create huge social problems. Legalisation may help regeneration if people are provided a purpose at the end of their treatment, but they need to come willingly, not enforced. If they see a purpose, as my four years in a homeless hostel shows, they come of their own volition.

The social sciences need to encapsulate the differences between the "front," what is presented to researchers, the social role and what has been emotionally "masked" drawing from Goffman (1959) later rearticulated in Beaten into Violence (Whittington 2007). The face value comments of the social actor, when he/she speaks are deemed the truth. This needs to be explored further, through creating and sustaining an emotional dialogue using Socratic questioning (Adler 1956). The emotional actor communicates through creating trust and making emotional connections. Underneath the "front" are the masked emotions sublimated into an act of active forgetting. Self medication helps with this outward composure, a necessary projection to the outside world, as it douses the unease of the inner reality.

CHAPTER 3
THE ABANDONMENT
OF HOPE

"The charisma of office—the belief in the specific state of grace of a social institution—is by no means limited to the churches and even less to primitive conditions."

Weber M. (1992) P1140 "Economy and Society,"

New Labour arrived in power in 1997 and proclaimed a Homeless Tsar in 2000. She was going to create change, someone who could cut through the red tape to solve fundamental problems by being above the various squabbling factions. She was tasked to exude the charisma of the office. The Tsar based on an American model of an all omnipotent slasher through the jungles of bureaucracy, became embroiled in stasis. The main political leadership looked to the news media for their reflection. This was transmitted to those underneath as an effective strategy of engagement. Everyone became involved in various strategies of "gaming" (Berne 1961, 1964, 1964). Any sense of vulnerability was magnified by the media who held the public in a type of thrall. The whole enterprise was based upon public relations, rather than research evidence and long term strategy.

The Tsar failed to acknowledge the causes of homelessness. Whilst Goodman L, Saxe L, Harvey M. (1991) and later Collins M and Phillips J (2003) noted the links between trauma and homelessness, the Tsar made a pronouncement asking for the end of hand-outs to the poor. This was deemed to encourage a culture of transience. People gained more luxurious sleeping bags in the Strand in London, than normal working people could purchase. The discourse transmitted by New Labour ignored research evidence and made anecdotal pronouncements; homelessness was another ruse of the feckless to gain benefits the ordinary worker works hard to obtain. The subtext of this pronouncement is that being homeless is a better lifestyle than working. This stigmatised the most vulnerable. This ignored the other various research reports detailing systemic care failure in children's homes. The Waterhouse enquiry ongoing since 1996 which eventually detailed endemic physical and sexual abuse in its "Lost in Care Report" was published in 2000. Many of these boys who were sexually abused went into a psychological decline including becoming homeless. The effect of PTSD on war veterans as a precursor to homelessness was documented in a series of research reports undertaken in the USA and later again in a Guardian article by Louise Carpenter in 2009 detailing PTSD amongst soldiers. These previous reports have been continuously ignored. The reports detailing the links between trauma and homelessness were eradicated from the public discourse by the Homeless Tsar in 2000 and have continued to be shelved.

Instead of trying to articulate seemingly complex emotionally literate arguments, there was an attempt to play to common sense sentiments. The Tsar reiterated homelessness is a lifestyle choice, another option such as skiing, being a writer or doing a gap year. Those who chose the option of homelessness are stigmatised, because they negate the worlds of those who work. Connecting to the belief there are deserving and undeserving poor, this splits the marginalised into those who need help and those who need to help themselves This fuelled stigmatisation, fuelling popular myths that has real effects on the ground. Countering stigma (Goffman 1963) entailed groups coming together to create subcultures based upon revenge for trauma, isolated from the mainstream world. Simmel (1964) noted the growth of groups formed through violence, and this fed into groups basing themselves on crime. As these case histories show, there are a number of ex armed robbers amongst the homeless population. Moss and Johnny were both sexually abused in children's homes before they went into armed robbery. Institutional violence seemingly creates a desire for revenge (Whittington 2007).

Public discourses highlight the psychology of power elites who fail to understand the "other" (Sartre 1943) except as an object for their opprobrium. This ideology flows from the psychological processes following an emotional split; an escape from childhood bullying into seemingly unassailable power positions. The adult directs events. This is the obverse of being the childhood victim. This is another self medication strategy, deemed socially useful unlike the miscreants who take heroin.

Meanwhile the "other" (Sartre 1943) acts as a baseline for those deemed socially included, it demarcates their habitus, their lifestyle and manners (Bourdieu 1984). Anyone can measure themselves by these "others" (Sartre 1943) failures. A culture of manners evolves to define oneself in relation to the abject. This provides cultural power. The relegation of the "other" (Sartre 1943) devolves them to a free handout as supplicants. In reality those with their hands outstretched are deemed as milking the system with a fake display. Curtailing these people becomes an aim, as they prey on sympathy and the pity of those who have jobs, two qualities creating emotional vulnerability. A feckless portrayal allows the power of the state to be utilised against them, separating the included and excluded. They can be cajoled into a different lifestyle through stigmatisation, and this justifies the commands of a care industry to taint them. This is the transmutation of individual empathy into institutional violence.

The psychology and the voices of the homelessness are missing in the public discourse. It deliberately portrays them as feckless, but provides no dynamic on how they became lazy or workshy. There is an underlying subtext, if most people had the opportunity they would find the lifestyle desirable; the notion of doing nothing is luxurious, with the subsequent projection, most people need to be cajoled into work.

Any interest in seeking the causes of homelessness is currently split between different groups, such as ex soldiers who are seen as deserving because they have undertaken sacrifice; adults from children's homes create a form of bewilderment because it induces the question. "Were they sent there because they were naughty, or were they made into the "other" (Sartre 1943) by their experience?" Thirdly those who were beaten and tortured within their families have few advocates, because these men are silent, and few have ventured into researching their lives (Whittington 2007).

Alternate Realities

The pronouncements from the "Tsar" built on the mockery of people spiralling downwards, adding to their stigmatisation (Goffman 1963). The stigmatised created a resistance to the outside world's critical commands and edicts. Substance use is linked to crime as a self medication strategy, through fending off reality. It enacts revenge in striking back against authority figures (Marcuse 1972). Whilst stigmatisation inhibits any romantic idealisation of this freedom from constraint, those who descend into depression and live on the street ward off the impact of being stigmatised. They enact revenge in everyday 'tit for tat' actions.

The lack of leadership arises from a deficit in emotional intelligence (Steiner 1974, 2003). This has a reverberation, as it closes down any discussion on the topic. As Le Grand (2011) highlights, senior practitioners are shackled. Emotional Intelligence is not a quality needed in the bureaucratic ascent and so people hide it (Gerth and Wright Mills 1953). This is a huge conundrum for initiating change. The transformation in the development of emotional literacy in my work arose from sidestepping bureaucracies. Social pioneers have arisen from experimentation outside of their remits. The money I used in Orexis to deliver therapy was drawn from the Tudor Trust, Church Urban Fund, Comic Relief, Barings Trust and Henry Smiths Fund and latterly the money for the innovation at the homeless hostel came from a major financial institution. Money from the state bureaucracy is always problematic. It is administered to nullify creativity, as it is encased in strictures. The other PIE intervention was originally caught within university forms and processes and hamstrung into inertia. However if the work is to become mainstream, it needs to be harnessed by the senior people in their respective organisations.

A significant paradox emerges; how does innovation become mainstream? It still needs to retain a sense of invigoration. The innovation I propose will challenge mainstream care, but the foundations already exist. As Le Grand (2011) highlights there is a desire for change in working practices. Piecemeal forms of legislation and interventions undertaken to alleviate the effects of street living made great strides to usher people into hostels through employing Outreach workers under New Labour. These were people who went out onto the streets, to entice the homeless men and women to enter a hostel. The challenges occurred when the streets were cleared.

Effective work was undertaken within the hostels when this was left to individual initiative. Emotionally enlightened members of staff worked in contrast to the various layers of bureaucracy introduced into the Charity Sector. This bureaucracy replicated the bureaucratic procedures existing within the commissioning process. These various layers placed within the hostels stifled communication and team work, as the organisations lacked an ethos from central government. This does not require instruction, only an announcement of a philosophy.

In the 3rd Sector this lack of direction induced stasis in the 1990's. It translated into an orchestra lacking a conductor, where substance use workers, mental health workers, housing workers and the activities workers all had their own tiers of managers. Instead of being subsumed under the hostel management, each was managed by a different hierarchy. The result was chaos, replicating the lives of the clients, as group cohesion was shattered. Each had their own "targets," supervision, holiday planning and philosophies of engagement. This also mirrored the lack of direction from the top, as it flowed downwards onto ground level. It encouraged the growth of bureaucratic empires, rather than the provision of front line work (Gerth and Wright Mills 1953). The lack of cohesion between the different empires meant information was lost, and attempts at reforming work practices were met with hostility. Managers were promoted to solidify the power base, rather than engage with the work.

However there were oases as there were a number of managers who were emotionally literate. There was a freedom stemming from having hold of "unrestricted funds" to innovate. The basis of this project was undertaken by the Hostel manager, his deputies and the Area Manager who launched a Kuhnian (1996) paradigm change. It was from this impetus a whole new concept of working occurred within the hostel and this work could take place at all. Without this foresight, these men would hot have been liberated. The impetus for change comes from those who are emotionally enlightened. Those who are not emotionally literate, just emit the dank blank stare.

Case History; Work and Alcohol as Self Medication

Many of the people described in this book have had homes and lost them. There are only two young men who were placed in the hostel awaiting resettlement. They had to wait six months or more for a council flat. This was a test, a punishment to ascertain their need before they were awarded their prize. The psychological process of why people lose a home has never been fully understood. Again it is reduced to fecklessness. As these case studies show, it entails the loss of the following; support structures job, relationship breakdown, social network dissolving, death of someone close, overwhelming debt, inability to face reality and loss of contact with parents. Bill provides a snapshot of someone who lost his home and became homeless through a combination of events, some physical and others psychological. These intertwine. The provision of a home is not enough to stop homelessness. It is about sustaining a tenancy, as he provides an insight into how past trauma shapes the present. Social isolation is a big issue affecting people in a large city. Aspiration does not always lead to success, unless it is built on a sustainable emotional platform.

Bill was the manager of a successful wine bar located in an upmarket part of London. He had worked his way to the top from starting as a barman. One of the problems with the drink trade is the culture of staying up late; drinking after the bar has closed. This was how he had risen to become the bar manager, working hard and playing hard, getting to know people in the business. Therefore he had to stay after the bar had closed, talking and drinking. This had created his social network and it also led to his downfall.

Bill had a previous traumatic family background, which he kept to himself. His parents had split in his youth and due to the problems he had with his mum's boyfriend, he was placed in care. Bill did not want to detail the specific problems initially. However he revealed he did not want to listen to his step dad as he tried to take over the father's role by instilling discipline. When I probed what this meant, it transpired there was an overflow of discipline but not a great amount of care. Bill saw him as an imposter. His mum had backed his stepdad. Bill rebelled against them both, by staying away from the house, drinking alcohol, getting into trouble with the police and absconding from school. His rebellion marked a form of self medication from trauma. This was punished by the state institutions operating without understanding the emotional discourses. They operated sanctions as an enactment of discipline and punishment (Foucault 1977).

This entailed his removal from the family by mutual agreement. Social Services had intervened in the family as everyone felt Bill had become uncontrollable. It was deemed a children's home would be able to provide the necessary support that he needed. This was undertaken in an era that ignored the research evidence of Winnicott D. (1964, 1965), Spitz R. (1965) and Bowlby J, (1969, 1973, 1980, 1984) as there were few people in positions of power, who could encapsulate separation from a child's perspective.

Whereas most who underwent the 'care' experience who became homeless, endured various forms of abuse, he was relatively unscathed by the care system, compared to them. He was however affected by the divorce and his feelings towards his mother in abandoning him in a home. His mother chose a "stranger" over her own son. He also resented his father for not saving him from the home and asking Bill to live with him. As we worked together, this idealisation dissolved, as he revealed his father had gradually destroyed his confidence through operating a critical parental stance when he was younger. Constantly criticised by his father, Bill felt he could never be good enough for him, and his self esteem as a child was poor.

His father worked away as a sales rep and this placed a strain on the marriage as he was constantly absent. He was a stranger in the family in many ways, before the eventual split, and when he returned he was emotionally absent, apart from bursts of anger and violence. Bill had built up an idealised version of how he had wanted his father to be, rather than who he was. This was another reason he did not bring him out of 'care,' as he was never at home to provide any support. His father had divorced his family, long before it had divorced him.

When Bill emerged from 'care' he was rehoused at 16, supported and determined to make a success of his life as recompense. He occasionally met up with his mum who suffered from chronic depression. She had split from the step dad, and had a nervous breakdown. She was under psychiatric care, in and out of institutions. This had a twofold effect on Bill; he was vindicated about his stepfathers actions and he felt a tug of connection to his mother, but also a sense of 'told you so.' He felt vindicated in standing up to him as a kid, but resented the subsequent punishment, thinking his mum should have listened to him. He was also affected by her emotional collapse. This again marked his desire to escape his circumstances.

Bill established himself as a bar manager travelling around London. His last accommodation was tied to the job, so when the new owners took over, there was some trepidation when they asked to see him. He was dismissed that day, and had to clear out of his flat. He had nowhere to go, and he had a chronic alcohol problem, stemming from the late night drinking sessions. His confidence nose dived, as he felt he could not get another job in his condition. Everything he had been trying to avoid, came rearing towards him, He spent seven months on the street, sinking lower with his self esteem. He had lost his job and his social contacts because of his alcoholism. He did not have a relationship because he was scared of being hurt, and this had prohibited him from trying. Bill's fragility was exposed with the dismissal and it took him years to recover. It was in therapy he began to work through the layers of trauma, to gain a self understanding of the various humiliations he had endured. It was then he realised he had blocked out the childhood trauma and his alcoholism was linked to self medication.

The initial discussion we had was based on art and who was a better painter, Rothko or Warhol. Bill was a self taught artist and had visited some of the free art galleries and built up his knowledge. It was through this shared discussion, based on a neutral subject I was able to bring it back to therapy, especially when we began to talk about Pollock and I mentioned his alcoholism. It was through using this strategy, Bill began to trust me. I did not concentrate on what had gone wrong, his homelessness and his alcoholism. This was obvious, and would only reinforce his negativity, so the conversation started on a topic that lifted him up, arising from his interest in art. Then it was a matter of finding which period he was interested in and having enough knowledge to talk about the era. If I was lacking in knowledge, then I would have asked him to explain and teach me. There are always things to learn, and through this type of strategy, the person is empowered to teach. It was through using this technique in the early 1990's that I learnt how to work with people demonised as drug users. It was through building up these intersection points that Bill's resistance was lowered, and he began the therapeutic process. This resulted in Bill beginning to join the art group in the hostel and visualising himself as an artist. We were still in the embryonic stages and one problem that we worked upon was his temper. This arose in a confrontation with the most violent man in the hostel, and for his own safety Bill was moved to another type of accommodation. Otherwise this situation could have escalated into a serious problem for him. I later saw him when I was coming back from a social occasion with my children. He was overjoyed to make small talk with me outside the hostel, a type of validation of him being "normal". He was still doing his art and had cut down on his drinking and looking forward to getting his own place. Whilst he had not stopped drinking, he had found a purpose and was recreating his identity from being an alcoholic to artist. He had made an effort to rebuild an identity based upon becoming an artist, rather than perceiving himself as homeless. A change of identity brought him out of a malaise and this was created through validating the trauma and positing a belief.

Bill related losing his flat as being the catalyst for a descent. He eventually came to the conclusion he had self medicated for his past using his job as camouflage. Alcohol stopped him from being shy and awkward, it helped him to socialise. It also helped him to sleep and forget about his problems. He had sublimated the past. His work as a bar manager promoted alcoholism, as he was expected to socialise with the staff, to build up and know his team. When he left the job, the various negative dynamics multiplied. He could not ask his parents for support because of the gulf between them, and how they had treated him. He had no money to get a flat. Then the psychological dynamics of the past hit him, as his structure dissipated. He began to perceive himself negatively, shaped within the internal parental critical commands. This created his self perception. He experienced a deficiency in finding a meaning in his life, a lack of being anchored in the past and the current negativity pressed down upon him. He suffered its force as an effect. The power of the words from the past wreaked their havoc years later; the critical effects of the parental command were stored within as negative anchors. Bill chose to retreat from the present and exist inwardly, where he was tortured by these critical commands constantly beating himself up as "no good," the internal voice of the critical parent (Berne E. 1961, 1964). To ward off the sense of crisis, he erected a barrier, based upon his desire to self medicate where the world is shut off. This closing off from the outside world entails the person eventually being evicted and forced onto the street. His social network could not cope with his spiral into decline, based on this inward retreat. As Bill had severed links to the outside world, he had shut down any support offered to him by friends as he went into his depression. This became self reinforcing.

The suggestion that hand outs create homelessness is not sustained in this example. Utilising a relational methodology (Whittington 2007), in ordinary discourse, talking to Bill without being judgemental, he articulated his world and his actions had a rationale. His homelessness was a mixture of the present crisis, a loss of confidence combined with a sense of the past compressing his ability to ascend from his descent. Self-medicating to fend off the overwhelming feelings of his hopelessness pushed him further into the abyss of despair. Just getting another job, flat and carrying on may have staved off the date of the crisis, but not its growing build up. Bill's problems lay in the past and these remained unresolved. They could not be wished away, although his drinking was an effective strategy in drowning them in the short term. He could not articulate his problems to outsiders because it demarcated his vulnerability. This vulnerability to denigration led him to have a collapse in self esteem. He was trapped within various double binds (Laing 1960, 1961, 1964). Bill's predicament highlights the crux of what it means to be homeless, the inability to articulate his internal humiliation for fear of being ridiculed. This was not paranoia, but based on a truthful observation. There was no one to talk with independently, and make sense of his emotional world. These people did not exist.

Case History; Emotional Literacy and Illiteracy

Levels of emotional illiteracy also became apparent within the wider commissioned services. The local NHS Substance use service in 2007 set out to put blockages in place against working to initiate recovery. The use of the step approach IAPT to accessing treatment was being used to gate keep and stop clients from accessing detox based on cost. I provided clients with the desire to change, offering them the possibility of a lifeline to detox and then access rehab. The men at the hostel had been caught within the Methadone trap and written off, satiated with high levels; they continued to inject Heroin, smoke Crack and drink alcohol on top of their prescriptions. The levels of use were dangerous. There were frequent ambulance call outs due to overdosing. The main intervention undertaken by the NHS service was ensuring the alcohol level of the clients was under a set level, so they would not be held responsible if a client overdosed on a mixture of methadone and alcohol. This entailed clients blowing into breathalysers.

During the Xmas period of 2006/2007 when the NHS services were closed, I gathered a number of residents together to initiate change. When the NHS Service reopened after New Year, the team leader and some NHS staff nurses complained about these men from the hostel accessing detoxification. They claimed it disrupted their "care plans." This was despite the numerous ambulance call outs at the hostel dealing with overdoses. Whilst one section of the nursing staff wanted to block the recovery, another section were aghast at what their manager and colleagues were doing. The NHS complaints were taken to the head of the charity where I worked along with the local Commissioners, Doctors and outside agencies. This is an example of the systemic inertia linked to trauma erasure. Future referrals were blocked. The NHS service worked to ensure it kept itself funded rather than aiming to socially regenerate people. Instead, it operated instead to meet the needs of the individual service template. There was no wider reflection of "Social Interest" (Adler 1931). Clients had their Methadone increased to 120mls of Methadone per day to create a narcotic blockade. This "treatment" had failed to halt the use of street heroin as the needle bins in the hostel overflowed. This back log of people attending long term "treatment" inhibited new people from accessing their service, as they were placed on waiting lists. This treatment process was overseen by the Borough Commissioners and the local DAAT who did not intervene to unblock the treatment. The long waiting lists for accessing the NHS treatment furthermore created significant crime in the Borough, as there were more barriers than there were conduits. This halted recovery on every level of measurement; access, crime, health and outcome. The substance use services could have been the hub of a social regeneration. Instead they contributed to the general malaise of the area through operating a stepped care approach combined with a peculiar version of "Harm Reduction" prohibiting individual growth.

One person who managed to get through the treatment blockade was Jake, before the door was firmly closed. All this took place in my first three weeks in the hostel.

Jake was born and bred a few miles away from the hostel, in a traditionally white working class area. When I first met him in 2007, he had deteriorated to such an extent, my empathic connections were thwarted. He was trapped in chaos. Jake had turned himself into a human water fountain, cascading cheap, white, cider through the pores of his skin and breathe, whilst carrying two cans in his top pocket. Being constantly inebriated, it poured down his clothes, as he swayed from side to side. Add to this tableau the problem of double incontinence, and Jake was a constant stream of running faeces, mixed with urine and cider. The cleaners and staff were forever mopping up after him, and he had a deleterious impact on morale in the hostel. This affected the other residents and the staff, as they knew he was drinking himself to death. His room was regularly cleared of empty cans, 24 per day of cheap white cider were consumed every day, and there was nothing that could be done to halt it. Jake hardly communicated with staff, as he was embroiled in his self-imposed stupor, rolling into the hostel and then out again. It was difficult to picture the man behind the mess.

Approaching Jake was difficult, because of the smell, as he rarely changed his clothes. The situation was becoming tense, as the staff team were paralysed with fright at his deterioration. I worked on a plan to get him transferred to a drinker's hostel in North London, whilst simultaneously working to get him into detox, with the proviso we could work on the aftercare plan, once he was stabilised. I then worked with the hostel management to ensure he could not be readmitted back to the hostel after he left. This plan would require firm boundaries to contain the chaos. It was also unrealistic, as he was highly vulnerable. However it had to appear to be an option to kick-start a recovery.

Once these plans were hazily concocted, I had something to intervene with. I approached Jake and spoke to him about detoxing, or going to another hostel. He grumbled that he did not want to do either, and that he wanted to stay where he was. Over a period of days, I would make small talk with him, ask him how he was, and we began a rapport. I pointed out to him the impact he was having on everyone else, and he replied he was not bothered, he just wanted to die. The one piece of positive news he conveyed, was that he had a daughter.

As the days passed I asked him about his daughter, how old she was and when he last saw her. This began to ground him in the present. He revealed he had been found by the Outreach Team, sleeping in a graveyard. He had been sleeping on top of his Grandma's grave, talking to her each night. She was the only person who had loved him and he had loved her. This was another piece of information to work on, as I used Socratic Questioning drawing from Adler (1956) to ask him how he would have felt if she had copied his strategy. He paused to think, and he said he would not like it. I then asked him to reflect of the impact of his behaviour on his daughter; his descent into destruction and its impact upon her. The sessions we had were short and brief, as he could not assimilate large amounts of information, being so inebriated. He replied if he was in her shoes he would not like what was happening to him. There, we had the breakthrough, the recognition his behaviour was hurting others, and he saw the value of attachment connection.

The next step was part of a ruse to speed up the process, due to the wider problems Jake was causing to the residents and the staff. Adlerian "Social Interest" (1931) and the rights of the individual existed in a state of tension in working with Jake. I worked with the hostel management to put a proposal to him, offering him two alternatives with the proviso he had to choose one, otherwise he would be out onto the streets. This was not a realistic option because of his vulnerability, but it had to appear realistic to force him into making a choice. This was the only time Zero option was applied at the hostel; a form of narrowing down the options to ensure someone made the choice to detox. This was not Person Centred Counselling (Rogers 1961) and highlights how models become adapted to the situation, rather than the person adapting to the model.

He could in theory be sent to the other hostel for people with embedded alcohol problems, but this was for those who were in their latter years, not their mid 30's. The hostel in North London was for entrenched drinkers in their 50's and 60's; a type of care home. Jake stated he was going nowhere and staying where he was. It was pointed out this was no longer an option, and he had to choose. When he heard the other hostel was in North London, Jake became agitated, saying he did not want to go there, he did not know anyone and it was not fair. This left the detox, and a date was provided for him to access it. In the meantime he continued to drink into oblivion.

Jake was due to go in Xmas 2007. The taxi turned up and luckily one of the workers had enticed him to change his jeans, so although drunk, he did not exude his former odour. The Cleaner had hosed him down in the shower and then scrubbed him with a special broom. This was crucial to getting him into the taxi, as he was already late for his admittance.

Jake was at the door of the car, about to enter the taxi, when he hesitated, saying he needed a can or else. Luckily, when the staff had cleared his room out previously they had taken a few of his full cans to try and limit his drinking. It had gone beyond alcoholism into full blown self harm. A fireman's chain brought him the can. He began to open it, and step inside the taxi, but the taxi driver stopped him, saying he did not want the alcohol in his car. Jake then drank the can in three or four gulps, and climbed into the cab. I went with him.

The roads were clear and we made it to the detox unit very quickly. I accompanied him as moral support. As we began to cross the threshold into the unit, he began to get the jitters, saying he could not do it.

"Take a deep breath and then cross."

"No," he replied. "I need another drink."

With a keen eye for hunting out an off licence, he found one round the corner. He had just enough money to buy one can. I noted it was a different brand to his usual white cider, and compared to his normal pattern, this was a significant change, as it was a 5% German beer. He drank the can between the off licence and the detox unit, a matter of 100 yards.

As we entered the detox unit, I said to him I never wanted to see him drunk again. He nodded. We then sat down, and awaited his turn to be called. Even though he was late, they still admitted him. This was a psychologically informed decision. The nurse came up and asked him if he would like something to drink. I blanched inside, thinking this was another trigger, and he was going to run off and jeopardise the detox. She called out lemon, orange, raspberry,

93

blackcurrant or water. Jake asked for lemonade, the first time something non alcoholic had passed his lips in months, if not years. I knew then, he had made a decision to begin the process of change, and had found some will to live. I left him at that point, returning each day at the agency's behest, to see how he was coping and to undertake some therapeutic work around long term aims. Jake eventually made a full recovery, going onto rehab, rehoused, reunited with his daughter and working in the homeless field. The transformation entailed a great deal of hard work and reflecting on his emotional pain, but he found a meaning to live. Unfortunately the local Borough after a number of other people were due to follow in his wake, stopped them, after the petitioning from the local NHS service. The Borough then employed a gatekeeper at significant financial cost to stop anyone else going forward without NHS approval. Retention in treatment was seen as a more appropriate goal than working to abstinence and rebuilding lives.

Jake maintained his sobriety for four years until a major bereavement hit him. He later rang me to let me know he had overcome his relapse; it was blip as he had dealt with a personal loss and was now at the bedside of his new born son, looking forward to beginning another chapter in his life. In the meantime he achieved the seemingly impossible, pulling himself from the brink of the abyss of self destruction. Having creativity to act fast, brought about the transformation; a window appeared, because the NHS Service was closed over the holidays. The NHS and the local authority subsequently put their barriers in place to stop anyone on a Methadone script from making this same recovery. It was deemed too expensive and the clients within the hostel were not worth the expenditure, highlighting the embedded lack of emotional literacy. They had relegated these homeless men to the "other" (Sartre 1943). The wider impact on the family and community of bereavement is emotionally erased. When he relapsed four years later he was offered a home detox. This again was wholly inappropriate. Services evolved to meet the needs of the NHS Managers. The local DAAT's became trapped in targets. A wider cost benefit or cost effective analysis would show keeping people on long term Methadone prescriptions and (Disability Living Allowance) DLA are not only expensive, but the lifestyle engendered, slowly kills them as they use the extra money to self medicate. If they did not have the money they would be shoplifting or begging. The effect of "Harm Reduction" is sedation. Keeping people on alcohol also kills them. Cutting through the bureaucratic malaise not only saves lives, but as in Jakes case, allowed him to transform. This is the power of making psychologically informed environments, as it slices through bureaucratic layers.

Case History; Informed Practice

Control orders were used to curtail drinking alcohol in public spaces. Special constables were used to enforce them. They could pour alcohol away as they were given the power of confiscation, a harkening back to the ethos of the 1960's school pedagogy, confiscating bubblegum. This intervention only shifts the problem into other geographic areas and neglects to tackle the issue of chronic alcoholism. If the control order entailed pouring the alcohol away and offering a card to access detox, at least it would try to provide a ladder out of the disorder. Instead the state allows alcohol to be sold under the guise of the free market, and then employs someone to pour it away, because drinking in a public space is deemed anti social. These are two mixed messages.

The mixed messages of the State created resentment amongst those subjected to its pressure. This next example, illustrates the micro actions of resistance and revenge that build up in reaction to its enforcement. The situation is finally defused by a police officer, making a psychologically informed decision to dissolve the tension. This scenario illuminates the power dynamics authorities muster in their relationship with the homeless. It highlights the power of resistance, erased in the various academic discourses in the treatment of the dispossessed, the resistance to being infantilised. The objectified have a habit of fighting back.

"Living round here it's such a laugh, "Sammy told me. "I was having a can of Tenants Super in John Smith St. when this copper came up to me and said "Pour that out on the pavement, then put it in the bin. This is a controlled drinking area can't you see the signs?"

"So I looked up, took one look at him, then took one look at the can and tipped it up, not on the floor but down me neck. It went in a few gulps; I then walked up to the bin and put the can in it." Of course this copper was steaming with anger at my effrontery over what I'd done. So I turned round to walk back and

he was right behind me, and then he had a handcuff on me and the other on him. So I said to him "Is that what your boyfriend does to you?"

Next minute he's on the radio asking for back up and I've been arrested for a public order offence. He bundles me into the van, and off he goes back on his rounds. I get talking to the rozzer in the van about what just happened, and the fact I didn't do anything. The rozzer goes "Yeh, he's a well known bully at the station and no one likes him." They drive me round the corner and let me out near the hostel. "Instead of being arrested I got a taxi home. Surreal or what?"

The idea a man's personal space can be invaded and his alcohol use can be controlled through command is naive. The former PM stated he wanted to march yobs up to cash machines, and make sure they paid on the spot fines. The resistance initiated by Sammy to the order, the need to keep up a "front" against perceived authority figures, thereby sustaining his masculine identity was paramount (Whittington 2007). This is also a crucial component in prison, where not giving in, especially in public displays of strength is crucial to upholding masculine status and self esteem. The police officer would have been aware of this when he approached Sammy. He could have achieved his aim by using a less antagonistic command, such as requesting Sammy to abide by the drinking zone rules, leaving him room to manoeuvre and save face. This could have instilled the message around the control zone, without the use of confrontation and humiliation. This request is not the usual discourse of power, as it aims to operate through a series of commands, as acts of humiliation.

Sammy is known as a local hard man; he looks and acts aggressively in formal displays. He has an extensive record for adolescent and young adult forms of violence directed at soldiers and police, anyone in a uniform. It transpires in the therapy sessions; Sammy's dad was in the army. The tit for tat exchange with the first policeman, the exchange of insults escalates. The situation could have escalated when Sammy was arrested, and placed in the van but the second officer enacts a decision to drop Sammy out near the hostel. This is an example of a Psychologically Informed Decision; the long term impact of arresting Sammy would be meaningless. Sammy needs support to undertake a detox and rehab, not more prison. This has not had the effect of changing his behaviour over 30 years. Instead Sammy has become more belligerent and hardened as a result of standing up to authority figures, defining his masculinity through engaging with violence against the state. This became apparent within the counselling sessions as we explored his childhood. Then it emerged, his mother tried to injure him on a number of occasions. He recollected one incident where she dropped him off on the Lancashire Moors in winter when he was 5 years old dressed in jacket and shorts. He survived by finding a bin, turning it upside down and trapping the air, warming himself with his hot breath caught in the container, until he was finally discovered at a roadside. The attachment bonds between mother and son were nonexistent, as she despised him because he represented her first husband. She transferred her negative feelings about her first husband onto her son, denying him her love throughout her life. Sammy expressed unremitting negativity for her in return. The issue of female perpetrator physical and emotional violence (Motz 2008) differs from the traumatic lives revealed in "Beaten into Violence" (2007) either demarcating my skill as a therapist, or highlights the more entrenched types of familial violence in homeless street populations

This was a secret he carried throughout his childhood and adult life, as an emotional deficit. He had projected this hatred onto the outside world, firstly through fighting, then through youth culture, as he became an outsider, and finally settling into a role of father. Since his divorce, his alcohol use escalated as he tried to cope with the effects. Sammy understood why he self medicated, but there was no ladder to escape his predicament. Hard masculinities, how they are constructed and how people progress, is routinely ignored in the substance use field.

Sammy is trapped in his masculine image, a carefully constructed identity; it serves him well up to a point. It garners respect and he knows who he is, even if it is an act of self destruction, the alternative is changing into an unknown version of himself. His drinking is killing him; affecting his liver and kidneys and he has lost co-ordination on a number of occasions falling over and smashing his face on the floor. This has led to four ambulance call outs in the last two months and overnight hospital stays. Sammy has follow up outpatient referrals but fails to keep them. He feels there is no real future. Whereas with Jake we could get him into detox to halt the decline; with Sammy the gatekeepers have stated he needs to attend a

Day Programme to demonstrate his desire for change. The application of the recovery model as a directive command is killing Sammy. If the practitioner, the person who makes the attachment bonds with him was placed in charge of decision making, then a programme could be devised based on these bonds of "trust." Instead he is forced to attend a Social Services Community Care Meeting with strangers and then advocate for his treatment, detailing his life story and stating why he should be allocated funding. This is a barrier to progress, another unnecessary bureaucratic tier and needs to be dismantled. Treatment budgets need to be handed to therapeutic practitioners to make team decisions based on engagement, prognosis and current health needs. These other tiers of bureaucracy prohibit recovery. Sammy needs respite care, as he is drinking so heavily it is affecting his internal organs. His death will shower an emotional legacy onto his children, dad died in a homeless hostel from alcoholism; the bad seed (March 1997, Hare 1999) becomes a generational weight. This is a hidden emotional cost.

Sammy will not attend any meeting with outside bodies because he feels it is another component of the authoritarian regime. As an example of his masculine resistance, Sammy was sentenced to community service. Initially he was placed with the men in the woodworking section.

"I hate woodwork he told me. I'm not going back." Sammy refused to attend. He was taken back to court and resentenced, with his probation made longer. A relative pleaded with him not to go to prison and Sammy relented. He went back to probation and did a community sentence but on his own terms. As a punishment he was placed in the needlework class with the women, before being given the privilege of joining the men in the more masculine fields. After a few weeks he was informed he could now join the men's group, but Sammy refused stating he enjoyed the needle work. He finished his community service embroidering a quilt.

"They thought they were punishing me, but I didn't mind it, sitting there with the girls," said Sammy. "I learnt a lot from sitting with them, much better being indoors than out. I don't think they liked me sitting indoors but fuck 'em."

Sammy completed his order but on his own terms and when he made the decision to finish his quilt, everyone was aghast. Here was the hard man dropping his frontal attack to undertake another form of undermining of the system. If he was going to be punished, he was going to take control of the situation.

He has a number of children, but refuses to let them know where he lives, because of the shame and stigma of being homeless. He is effectively socially isolated, without a job, depressed, with significant attachment severance issues. Various authorities have tried to cajole Sammy, but to no avail. He endured violence within his family and later state forms of violence in young offender institutes. All had minimal impact apart from making him tougher and more violent. His emotional needs refer back to his childhood trauma and the emotional violence inflicted upon him by his mother. These had been kept quiet for years until he explored them with me. Outwardly Sammy is the archetypal hard man, inwardly he is still a five year old boy trapped in the bin, needing to self medicate the memories away. His one connection to shifting the past is the therapy.

Discipline and Punish (Foucault 1977) was the New Labour strategy, the notion people can be behaviourally conditioned. The discipline only impacted upon the "front" presented to the world, and so the strategy failed to stem alcoholism and anti social behaviour. The underlying causes are never addressed. It aims to control public perception of street drinking, after it has sold these men their cans. This strategy was concerned with the management of appearances rather than causes. People can drink themselves into a stupor in their own homes, so long as it is not visible. The reasons why they drink, remains their problem. In the Borough where the hostel is situated there is one alcohol project for a population of 250,000 people. This has some of the highest indices for ill health in Western Europe. People such as Sammy are considerably down the list of priorities for effective treatment, and if he was not connected to the therapy, he would be locked within his alcoholism with no redemption eventually being placed in a social housing estate.

Case History; The Informed Decision

When authority structures make psychologically informed decisions this stays with the men as an anchor point, a retrieval of a positive memory defusing tension. These act as connections of positivity, catalysts for change despite the swathe of negative dynamics that swamp these men in their everyday actions. This is an example of a decision made by a group of police officers, having a great impact on Luigi, a middle aged Italian.

Luigi was in his 50's and was in a hostel. He had spent most of his adult life living on the streets of London. He had a wealth of social knowledge about London that he would relate in bursts of communication. This type of reminiscence was used to encourage him to talk and reflect on his life as he had a habit of hiding away. He would reminisce about the 1950's and the racism he experienced growing up in West London, the fights he had, as he was spat upon, and called spic, wop and dago. He recollected families being firebombed in the 50's by local vigilantes, who despised the newcomers from Europe. At home, Luigi also faced difficulties. His father had come over to the UK before the war and stayed. Luigi described him as a dyed in the wool fascist in every department. He lorded it over his wife and children, expecting total obedience. He was generally out after work socialising, but would return with a venom, then start beating his wife and children, when he was drunk, which was often.

Luigi did not want to speak in the safe counselling space, no matter how I tried. He would gladly relate his life history at the front desk, but not in an enclosed space. He did not like walls, he told me. He had spent seven months in the hostel, and in his years of homelessness, he had never stayed so long in one place. The reason why he had decided to stay in the current hostel was because his heart was palpitating, and he needed treatment. In fact he needed several operations, as the doctors were puzzled by his erratic beat. Taking a more Reichian view (1933) of the body as a store of trauma encased within the musculature, I could see how he had become ill. When he spoke of his childhood he was in a constant state of flight, freeze or fight when his father came home, and started thrashing everyone. This would have had an impact on his body (Harrison 1986), affecting his psychological development. Secondly the impact of sublimating his desire for revenge would have led to high blood pressure, as the anger was forced within. He also had a number of older brothers who were also beaten and so there was constant stress in the family.

His father's love of Scotch whisky ensured he drank at home after work. He instigated a special class for his sons, indoctrinating them into alcohol use. This entailed putting a bottle of whisky on the table and forcing each one to consume a shot in one. Luigi related how he hated the taste and the effect, but he was forced to gulp it down, initially spluttering and then being hit as a result. This continued from age 9 until 14, where he realised he was getting a tolerance. He was also subject to slaps, kicks and thrashings from the belt, from his father for any infraction. This, he related, created a burning resentment. His father believed in discipline, a strong masculinity. He was someone who ordered his family around as a tyrant in his home. This echoed the portrayal of the father as a fascist in Wilhelm Reich's "Mass Psychology of Fascism" (1946). The impact of the violence was traumatic, held in both his mind and the body from childhood to adulthood.

Luigi related he and his brothers, in an act of solidarity, decided to end the violence when their father came home drunk one night. This occurred when Luigi was 14. Each had bought a flick knife. They waited for their father's drinking game to commence. He sat them around the table and then asked one of his sons to get up and get the whisky from the side. As he came back with the bottle, seeing his father's hand laying on the table, the first son plunged his knife through the back of his palm, so his hand was pinned to the table. The other boys each got up quickly and plunged their knives into the trapped hand, as an act of solidarity with themselves and their mother. It was the end of the bullying regime. The paranoid bully had dominated his sons and they had sought revenge upon him by collectively stabbing him.

I asked him what happened next. Luigi smiled and said we all left home that night, and never went back. He hid for years from his family as he was only 14. He was terrified of being caught and sent back home. Luigi then had an itinerant life for 40 years. He had a varied career as a gigolo and other off the record jobs. One involved working on a big building site the 80's, working as a site operator where he recollected living in a hotel he earned so much money. He would spend the money on lavish meals and sex workers.

When the job finished he was back on the street. He never kept in touch with his brothers; everyone went their own way after the stabbing incident. Their father recovered, but always had to wear gloves. Luigi said he never spoke to him again, but attended the funeral, just to make sure.

The act of kindness from the police that he recollected, took place when he was sleeping rough in Central London one Xmas. He remembered it was bitterly cold. He was approached by two policemen on Xmas day. They shook him awake and gave him £200 they had collected at the station. I asked him what he did with it, expecting him to say he drank it, injected it, or perhaps even threw it away. Instead, he said he booked himself into a Bed and Breakfast for two weeks, where he knew it was cheap.

"This gift had saved my life because it was one of the coldest Xmas's on record. It's not all bad being homeless," he recounted, "You meet the best in people as well as the worst."

Whilst it would be impractical for every police station to have a whip round for every homeless person, this decision to assist Luigi had a pronounced effect on him, as it said to him he was no longer alone and he was worth it. It was an act of random kindness, a piece of emotional literacy (Steiner 1974, 2003). Luigi could related a long list of events where he had been moved along, sworn at, kicked and punched by the police over the years, but this one act touched him. Years later, he would recollect the event as an act of kindness that validated him as a human being, and more practically it stopped him from freezing to death. Psychologically Informed Decisions can exist in the most challenging of environments and have real effects. It changed his view of the police, as he stood up for them in the hostel.

As the case studies highlight, psychological factors precede homelessness. This will be explored in greater detail. Attachment is the key issue, creating an emotional inoculation that cannot be replicated by gene manipulation. The most obvious causes of homelessness, attachment and trauma, are researched the least. Homelessness is perceived as a materialist issue, the notion of not having a home. It can also be perceived as an extension of a psychological trauma, the descent into chaos. The everyday world of a homeless man is constructed to fend off meaningless.

Sammy embraced nihilism as the bonds creating meaning were broken; his drinking recreates a purpose. Attachment, (Bowlby 1984, 1969, 1973, 1980) the first bond between mother and son, is the first and crucial relationship that stops the dread of nothing from seeping into the child and enveloping a young mind. It represents an emotional anchoring between mother and son (Bowlby J. 1969, 1973, 1980, 1984) and this stops the vast chasm of emptiness (Kierkegaard 1844) from opening up and engulfing the child in dread. The absence of this bond entails an existential dread floods into the child, the feelings of being alone, isolated and without hope. Those who suffer attachment severance, lack the vibrancy and vitality of the life force that enters through being physically and emotionally affirmed (Spitz 1965). They sense the whole nothingness of the universe instead, an existential crisis enacted at an early age. This deep sense of dread opens, then envelops them, providing children with a glimpse of an eternal living death. This leads to the conditions of hospitalism, Spitz (1965) noted, rocking to and fro clapping the hands. This is a retreat within, and the attempt to find an external boundary by hitting the limbs together to provide an affirmation. Children are brought out of this condition through being anchored in touch, speech and sight by a significant other. These are the lessons derived from Spitz (1965) and Bowlby (1984, 1969, 1973, 1980). If these are not forthcoming, the problems that were discovered in the Rumanian Orphanages occur.

As they develop, children who are beaten, try to make sense of the violence. They use their innate sensory skills to formulate a meaning. Usually it reveals to them the world is a hostile place, and they need to create defences. At least when the violence is enacted, children are validated, even if it is denigration. It is preferable to hospitalism (Spitz 1965). Violence becomes the genesis for various forms of masculinities, as men armour themselves in response to experiencing violence inflicted upon them as children. Hardened masculinities stem from the fragile anchoring children receive. They react to recreate themselves within role models because they have not been anchored. These role models provide a rationale and a meaning, plus they halt further humiliation. They allow the boy to create revenge when older. Those who are nurtured by parents become emotionally stable, unless violated by institutions. Those who have a "secure base" (Bowlby 1984, 1969, 1973, 1980) have a reality woven around them from being validated as a child. This provides self esteem, as the child knows the contours of its body through being touched, and has a sense of its worth through dialogue.

Forms of trauma are invisible; they transcend work, housing, education, substance misuse services, prison, social services and the mental health field. Ignoring trauma (Miller 1990) entails it continues to remain invisible. Few academics have sat down to ascertain why people do not get better. The underpinnings of a descent into the abyss is locked within a cupboard and safely sealed. Instead an overall performance emerges; everything is now safely composed, woven to hide the traumatic underpinnings. There are huge swathes of institutional amnesia; active forgetting that pervades institutions (Goffman 1963) and silences individuals who exist within them. Institutional denial represents various forms of collective trauma, safely sealed off (Gerth and Mills, 1953). New theoretical paradigms, enacted to make sense of the universe are constructed; creating amnesia writ so large no one dares challenge it. No one highlights these hidden realms because each has a vested interest in keeping it intact. Anyone upsetting the carefully cultivated image exposes a huge shimmering charade; an imposition of a cultivated discourse imposed on nihilism. This is a particularly acute problem in the substance use field. Sammy's representation of a hard masculine exterior lies on a polarity to his traumatised softer interior. This is indicative of a wider cultural and institutional malaise involved in disciplining his "front" for 30 years to minimal effect. In Sammy's case he dispensed with the pretence of manners and decorum, sinking into nihilistic belief. A trajectory of self destruction emerged as the emotional bonds grounding him were severed. He could find nothing to live for.

Case History; Invisible Black Masculinities

Talking to former gang members using therapeutic techniques, allows the social "front" to dissolve and the emotional connections to be made.

Jay joined a gang when he was twelve. His father had left home when he was three, leaving his mother, his elder sister and his younger brother in the house. They lived on a large social housing estate in South London. Jay's mother had become ill with stress. Firstly she had the breakup of the marriage then the death of her mother. At the time no one knew what was happening, because there was no diagnosis for bereavement. It was a case of getting on with it.

Jay's mum retreated inside the house, suffering from agoraphobia. For fifteen years she remained housebound eventually making a trip to the local church. Jay's older sister effectively took over the running of the family when she was nine. She became a carer for her mother, and her two brothers, making sure they went to school, shopped for the family, cooked their meals, did the washing and attended parent's evenings when they were older. Jay's mother just stayed in the house watched TV and smoked heavily. She had a form of undiagnosed clinical depression. No one came to see her and the family remained intact through the sister's sacrifice. Social Services were not involved, as the family worked together to halt any outside involvement.

Jay went to the local Primary School, then to another local Secondary School. It was here he circulated with other boys from his area and they developed alliances, creating out groups and in groups, based on locality. Jay had a series of terrible accidents in his childhood that kept him off school for long periods. When he revealed them, I gained a picture of someone glad to be at home who could be with his mother. Together we explored the benefits of staying at home. It allowed Jay to keep an eye on his mother who had deteriorated rapidly. Due to the effects of his mothers decline and his accident, he went through school unable to read and write. I asked him how that was possible. He replied the teachers concentrated on those who were more willing and able. Those who were slipping behind went to the back of the class and were forgotten.

"That is how it was at school." he said.

Jay was also suffering from a form of trauma that remained undiagnosed throughout his school day period. The constant worry about his mother preyed upon him. As he grew older he took more responsibility from his sister. Jay would do the shopping and support his brother.

The Primary School seemed completely unaware of the impact of his home life on his schooling. They were not emotionally literate. The family had learned to outwardly disguise the internal problems, fearing the social services would intervene and take them away from each other. The boys had learnt not to discuss their family life, because they were fearful of the forms of intervention. I explored with Jay how he learnt to cope with keeping secrets at an early age.

I asked him if any other families sought help and he highlighted that no one trusted the authorities, it was "just how it was."

"They are not interested in the likes of us; everyone knows that, you don't need to get involved to understand that."

The Social Service Departments remit was understood as negative and the family created a response to this perception by hiding their problems. The local community had transmitted their decision about contacting the authorities and this was transmitted as a collective decision. Yet Jay spoke easily within the therapy session. It was not a struggle to get him to attend. After an initial hesitancy, he began to talk freely. This highlights how the institutions if they develop the relational techniques can create rapport through building relational bridges. Building relational bridges, rather than applying other models of interaction is crucial.

Trauma is invisible, only its effects are apparent. Jay had automatically assumed that life undertook a particular course. As we began to unpeel the layers in looking back through his existence, he gradually managed to gain an overview. What he saw as normal was socially constructed and this allowed him to visualise other pathways. He had lived within some severely closed parameters. Practically I worked with him to access the literacy support services. This would help him interact with the outside world when he left the hostel. We explored both his past and how he was going to build his future.

As he spoke, it became apparent the gang coalesced into an escape vehicle from his poverty of existence. There appeared a type of depression hanging over everyone. The schools, apart from one teacher, were mainly based on discipline and punishment. This teacher coached him out his protective shell to engage with the school. She helped him for a year before she left. This gave him a lifeline, as she had encouraged him to begin to read and do his work. This highlights the role of attachment, building relations and illuminates the importance of the work of Harry Stack Sullivan (Barton Evans 1996) that people can heal from the most traumatic of circumstances if their emotional pain is validated, they can build relationships. This was the first and last time someone had taken an interest in him, as he connected to an authority figure. This showed how a psychological intervention stayed with Jay who had struggled throughout his life with being recognised. It resonates with Luigi's experience of the police. It appeared from the work I undertook with him around his literacy; Jay could read, but lacked confidence. Within a therapeutic environment I could see he would flourish.

One other female teacher enacted a form of discipline, by hitting the boys in their kidneys for any rule transgression. He felt some enmity to her, highlighting he could cope with the violence, but it was the lack of warmth that made him angry. Jay said he enjoyed school, but it was tough, it provided a level of camaraderie missing in his family life. He met other boys and it was through the gang he began to envisage having people around him and not feeling alone. School systems were for those people who wanted to belong to them. The other boys similar to him, on reflection were also struggling trying to find their own paths through a myriad of unstated traumas.

He did not see the gang as a revenge mechanism against authority; it was a way of finding meaning in a tough environment. As he highlighted there were no other vehicles of success. It was through the gang he exerted himself. He described being stopped by the police when he was 13, and pushed up against the wall. This marked him off from childhood. The gang provided comfort and refuge from the wider world, as it had loyalty and expectations. They were all being harassed by the State, and this provided an internal sense of belonging. They could discuss how many times they had been stopped, what they had said and how many hours they had spent in the cells. The State violence was the making of them. This cemented group solidarity and toughened them up.

I asked him if he attended any youth clubs. He said yes he attended the local club, but had to be careful around some of the people there, as it was violent. I asked him if he spoke to the youth workers, he said no, they work for the police, everyone knows that, so no he would not speak to them. This highlights one of the problems with state institutions, their paranoia and over reliance on discipline and punishment. It halts any attachment connections being made. Whether the youth workers work for the police or not, there is a perception they cannot be trusted. This creates the distinction between us and them. Jay only had the gang as a vehicle for emotional support, apart from his sister. In the area he lived he needed to exert a masculine presence otherwise he would be seen as weak. The conundrum for adolescent boys such as Jay, are the pulls between the social pressures and the family desires. He was caught between the two forces, and had to balance the need to be a "good son, brother" and existing in a hostile environment.

One big loss was his father, who never visited after returning to Jamaica with his new life. The gang as it formed later provided recompense for the loss. It also led him into crime as he distributed Cannabis. It was through this vehicle he gained a living. The problem with this form of immersion is that it led down a path of growing violence.

Violence marked Jay's life as we explored the effects of standing behind someone in a certain part of London and then someone drove past and opened up with a semi automatic. He was showered in pieces of skull, brain tissue and blood.

"How did you cope?"

He shrugged, just got on with it I guess. This demarcated Jay's shut down, he had never even thought of asking the question as he looked puzzled as why someone would ask. This marked his sense of alienation, as he could not even summon up the idea, this was traumatic. This either showed that he had sublimated the trauma, or his life was constant trauma and it did not figure as significant. We worked upon his interpretations and it became obvious, he had actively forgotten its effects.

We later worked on his high Cannabis levels. Jay had effectively sealed himself off from reality through smoking himself into oblivion. Another loss he recollected, in spurts, was saying good bye to a friend who had saved up and bought his first car, after working numerous shifts in McDonalds. Sitting in the driver's seat his friend was beaming with joy, as he had bought a Ford Kia, another car pulled up by the side and blasted him in act of jealousy. Jay went running back after hearing the shots to see the boy's mother cradling him in her arms as he died.

"How did you cope?"

"Just got on with it I guess."

The levels of emotional pain were gradually revealed as trust was built.

"No one wants to know about us Dean, they just write us off, we know that and we have to adjust to survive. They go on about gangs, but no one does anything about it, why don't they have counselling like this, when we need it at school or away from school, somewhere we can go. No one cares."

He had attended various initiatives in his area, and I asked him if he ever spoke to anyone about what is happening inside him.

"No, you know how it is, what the score is, they all report it to the police. There's no one there who can help us. We don't trust anyone, school teachers, youth workers anyone outside ourselves."

Drawing on Harry Stack Sullivan (Barton Evans 1996) and the notion of the "chum" someone in adolescence who acts as a confidante I asked him if he ever had any support. He had mentioned the schoolteacher, but there appeared no one else.

"In the gangs we don't talk about things like that, it makes us vulnerable, people see it as weakness, in a gang you have to be tough, you can't let anything show that goes against that, people need to be able to trust each other. If that ain't there then you are a weak link. No we don't talk about things like that and I think you know that Dean."

Yet for all that had happened to him Jay had empathy. Although he expressed his dismay at being in the hostel, at first, with all these dirty people when I first met him, he had a growing awareness. This grew over the period he lived there. Later, he told me, he realised something, all people are working out their problems, and no one is different to anyone else on the inside. The people in the hostel are just people.

Jay was glad of being in the hostel because it gave him respite from the pressures of living in his area. He no longer felt a gun was going to blast him at any given moment. He told me a story about a boy who wanted to get out the gangs and found God, the gangs had not forgiven him and they waited for a day he was vulnerable and blasted him. If you want to get out of the gangs, you have to get out of the area, because you are forever trapped in your identity. The hostel represented Jay's escape, ironic as the pressure of living with 52 men with deep emotional problems is usually seen as high pressure. Compared to living in his part of South London the hostel was a spa, a place of respite. Jay was one of several new clients who escaped the ravages of the estates.

His one proviso was never to live where he originally grew up; he had a vision of marrying his girl and having children, then working as a youth mentor. We worked to actualise it, as he went through a series of interviews to reach his objective.

"So they don't go down the wrong path like I did Dean."

The conduits had finally been opened.

Black masculinities and the emotional worlds lying behind them are rarely articulated (Fanon 1952, 1965). Instead they are routinely demonised. The presentation of the "front" is everything, the walking gait, the slang, the hand movements are all carefully constructed for the performance. In the counselling session the hard man dissolves, when the pressure to keep the act up is relaxed. Jay found the hostel as respite. He found the therapy session as another retreat from having to sustain his performance, a place where he could discover himself. The gang provided comfort in a harsh economic arena where killing, maiming and stabbing are constant threats hovering over each day. Death is hushed up in news blackouts, as another black on black killing hardly makes a few column inches in the South London Press. With each other, the talk is about "blud, man and beef" whereas in the therapy session, the slang is ditched and the talk is undertaken in Standard English diction. Identity is in constant flux amongst the young black males attending the hostel. The "front" has to be upheld as a buffer against the world, the main defence these men have. If it dissolves they are left raw vulnerable to attack (Fanon 1952, 1965). At least with the "front," it repels all but must the foolhardy, and although plenty of aggressive men exist, it stops the institutions from intruding, as they hit the brick wall of the sneer.

The formal academic theorist would never travel beyond first base. All they would perceive are the eyes looking down the nostril, the performance of the gait, as Jamaican English is performed to keep a distance and uphold certain off the peg perceptions. The little boy hiding behind the adult is eradicated in this discourse, so is the fear that hangs over each day. Family dynamics are also hidden, because each intervention by outsiders is never seemingly enacted as support, but only as interference. They are correct in this perception and this is why they are trapped within various images, locked in a prison of racism. Jay appears relatively unscathed, but this is only because he has sealed off various traumas and operates on a narrow emotional bandwidth. He has sublimated and obliterated various traumatic events, sealed them off within his heavy Cannabis use, never specifically articulated. He then becomes trapped within various outside projections. The perceptions of wider society are enacted on him, as he is subject to various power pedagogies. These are applied onto the black male "for their own good." He has learnt to resist these applications, and the application of further pressure creates a greater resistance. This creates a dialectic of tit for tat.

This dynamic of resistance provides the backdrop for the state to apply various power pedagogies. This ensures the overall habitus (Bourdieu 1984) of manners is maintained. The appliance of violence is routine and operates in physical violence being enacted by the police, emotional distancing in school and psychological profiling in institutions. This creates resentment in being labelled the "other" (Sartre 1943). This resentment is used to justify further sanctions, as it erupts into violence and feeds into more resentment. It is an ongoing spiral with no redemption.

The masculinities that finally emerge are emotionally locked tight. This creates further problems in communicating within their families, leading to further alienation within the home. Families are caught between enacting the habitus, the wider culture and manners (Bourdieu 1984) to try and fit in and be seen as sell outs or resist and remain poor. If they do try to fit in, they are seen as breaking the camaraderie and then perceived as weak. The social system is schizophrenic in its paranoia, as it tries to "tame" these men with force. This ironically reinforces their decision to stay and remain "hard men."

There are few emotional systems created to support the young black male. His problem being that if he dissolves the "front," he will still be subject to being perceived as the "other" (Sartre 1943) and this leads to further

111

wounding. The "hard front" entails he can survive the power applied onto him. Through taking on the system he can gain status and respect. The inability to articulate emotional trauma, because there is no one there to listen, is recast into a hardened masculinity. Jay could slip in and out of this performance, depending on who he was talking to. In an incident that occurred later in the hostel, where another male tried to bully him, he clearly demonstrated his inner resources in eradicating the source of the problem.

The demonising of the black male entails there is little social room to manoeuvre. All around, in the wider society, are images on how black men should behave and who they should be. These are stylised images of opposition. Similar to Paul Willis's (1978) white boys in "Learning to Labour," these oppositional images help to propel them into working class jobs or the gangs. Originally imported into the UK after the war to drive buses and work on the underground, as the UK faced a manpower shortage, the different generations have branched out into the trades and other white working class jobs. They rarely ascend a hierarchy and the rationale for this inability to ascend is not down to Eysenck and the "bell curve" but in an emotional reality encapsulated in the above dynamics, and enshrined in the work of Paul Willis (1978).

Many young people are trapped in social exclusion and the gang becomes the vehicle for propulsion out of the stigma (Goffman 1963) of being labelled (Becker 1963) as a failure. Myths abound around the need for discipline, law and order and harsher prison. No tough men are going stand up and speak about sexual abuse, rape, beatings, emotional loneliness, need and desire. Secondly if a man does stand up no one will listen. This signifies a wider pain.

Instead of emotional vulnerability the imagery of a tough virility, violence, isolation, women as sexual objects and hatred of homosexuals are projected. These images are the reverse of reality and should be easy clues for an emotionally literate population to pick up on. These are emotional signifiers drawn from Personal Construct Theories found in Adler (1956). All hard men were humiliated as children as Alice Miller (1983, 1990, 1991, 2005, 2001) highlights. Stalin and Hitler were the products of child abuse (Miller A. 1990, 1983). Peter Kurten the child killer and Christiana

F were all products of violent homes. Emotional and physical violence are not issues for black families, it is a problem for the wider community as an emotional expression of violence is an act of emotional camouflage (Gilligan J. 1999).

This becomes apparent when the topic turns to homosexuality. Many people, who have been raped as children, cannot differentiate between homosexuals, men who love other men from paedophiles men who rape boys. For them the two are equated leading to a rampant homophobia in certain black, white and other masculinities, a defence mechanism against the past projected as revenge within the present. Gaining the space to discuss these issues with hard men entails building considerable trust, and transcending the race dynamics to operate on another human level. This cannot be quantified by the social theorist, because they cannot create the relational dynamics to encapsulate or sustain trust.

The black masculinities discourse is established in the local newspapers and the media; malevolent killers, not enough discipline at home, feckless fathers with an inability to study at school. The social theorist armed with such conceptions can easily find research evidence to back up the predefined concept. Perceived as the "other," (Sartre 1943) this perception keeps the black male population trapped in being objectified. There are few places of safety. Soul music previously allowed certain emotional discourses to be expressed such as vulnerability, but these have been increasingly squeezed into forms of lust enticement, or bad boy rapper. The musical emotional vocabulary has been compressed into upholding the modern stereotype of power, the individual empowerment of the outlaw. Wherever he looks the young black urban male sees himself reflected as an idealisation. He is effectively trapped within a sophisticated racism, where he now plays the role of the existential bogeyman. He believes the role brings kudos. He acts out the part, but he is effectively suppressed by the law enforcement system whilst being beaten into various forms of violence. The hard image is killing the black male urban population, as they become forced into representations and idealisations that limit their emotional ranges to anger, rage and revenge stoked by more state violence.

DJ was another black British of Caribbean resident who lived in the hostel. He had a variety of roles that he played, varying from gangsta to school boy depending on his mood. These criss—crossed across the day, so there was some uncertainty about his mood switch. He was receiving psychiatric support for chronic depression. He also did gardening being keen to water the plants and this led to some initial confrontation with staff who felt he was taking advantage of a situation because he was paid. I thought his display of empathy with nature was a positive step, given the dynamics of his early family life, its complete attachment severance and isolation.

"Out there it's tough Dean, people don't understand. Now where I come from we don't speak to other boys outside of our area and here they are, and we have to get on with each other but out there it would be different"

I began to ask him if he would hurt someone from another area if they were cousins.

"It does happen, it does happen, but then again you would let someone know from the family, that so and so should drop out for the evening, cos they need to spend time with their girl. That's how it is Dean, it's a dangerous place and people get hurt."

This was not DJ playing the gangsta but communicating the various balancing roles he performs as gang and family member. He was terrified of going to one part of London and pleaded with us, saying he could not make the housing appointment, because if he was seen in the area they would shoot him.

"That's why I come here, don't anyone know that. It's out of the way, no one knows me here, I feel safe."

DJ, again, felt safer in a homeless hostel with 51 men with a variety of psychological traumas, than he did living in the area he grew up in, surrounded by his friends. This spoke volumes about his feeling of personal safety. It was an issue that exacerbated his depression, as this sense of oppression hung over him as a daily dark cloud. This was not just the feeling of being attacked, but potentially being killed. Taking a wider therapeutic brief and incorporating the ideas of Adler (1956) helps to being a broader vista to the therapeutic moment. DJ was imprisoned in his locality and wanted to escape and this issue played on his mind daily as he beseeched the staff.

"You don't know what's going out there. It's different for me than for you. I don't wanna go to these places, it's dangerous. Don't you realise this?"

Just to emphasise DJ's paranoia, I walked home on my last night at the hostel, and was stopped by the police at a South London tube station. Had I any recollection of events two years ago of an incident in Brown St. A young black male was shot dead at 5.30 in the afternoon. His death lay unsolved for two years, despite being shot in daylight. He was 22.

I had advocated for DJ saying the housing appointments need to be undertaken at the hostel, or at the very least he needs to be accompanied and a care plan should be initiated to address his long term educational and training needs. DJ would come to me, and ask me what help he could get, as he felt stuck. As the hostel was being closed down under the government cuts in 2011 ostensibly for refurbishment, but with no alternate provision provided, it was difficult to provide any answers. He was going into a form of suspension where he would be lucky to get more than a two year tenancy on a revolving door of resettlement. Meanwhile the conditions he was seeking respite from, would grow like a cancer with the communities, he and the others grew up within. There was no addressing the causes, as everything that provided structure was being dismantled under the guise of cuts to save the economy.

The help DJ was seeking was already dwindling. The psychiatric team provided more medication to block out the effects. This was the only option, unless the psychological ladders for escape were built.

Even when men such as DJ are willing to work to shift their belief systems and reveal how it impacts upon them, they are still caught within the pincers of disbelief. An issue not easily articulated, because they are self taught to keep secrets, as no one believes them. The defence posture they have inhabited, informs their musculature, the way they carry themselves and the types of speech articulated, to carry out the pretence. If they drop the "front" what do they become?

This "front" becomes ever more refined within each generation trying to express an individual identity, whilst trapped in the same dynamics. It becomes heavily stylised. These identities are based upon the suppression of various waves of emotional pain. DJ spoke no further about his home life, other than it was depressing. Jay revealed his loneliness and frustration when his mother retreated from the world, having no dad to talk to and help him. The gang provided male company and it was through joining other boys in a similar position that communal values were transmitted. The first value he realised from attending school was stay strong, and shut the world out. It was through projecting strength, these men conveyed toughness and this provided status and respect. Another value that becomes transmitted through school is the idea education and learning is not a vehicle for success and there are other routes (Willis 1978). This becomes particularly acute for those young men who are being bullied at home, and have had their attachment bonds severed by emotional neglect or violence.

The various interventions tasked to act upon these communities, enacting their procedures have pushed them into these roles, through the enactment of discipline and punishment regimes. The various communities have become distrustful and defensive thereby strengthening their resolve to keep the "front" intact as an act of defiance. This has led to a tit for tat performance between members of these communities and law enforcement agencies, as outlined in Sammy's case history. It is a battle consuming vast amounts of resources for no definable output, a battle where no one wins and chaos ensues within its wake. Care and anchoring are negated within any discourse that reifies the term "role models" within black communities, the emphasis being on how to act and pretend not create something from within. Looking within is perceived as being off limits, because inside is something dark. This critical command inhibits personal growth and needs to be discarded. This provides the basis of learning for young men, the need to work at assembling an identity through imbibing a role model. The notion they need to emotionally anchor themselves to find out who they are, is never offered to them. Ultimately they are tasked to learn and imbibe a culture of manners, rather than create forms of care themselves. This form of critique arises from the ideas Sartre introduced; "Bad Faith" (Sartre 1943) and "a being for itself." "Bad faith" is a retreat into a performed role, an expectation, the notion of "a being for itself" however is someone embarking on a voyage of discovery. Ironic given that if a genealogy of emotions is undertaken, the early blues artists of the 1920's articulated the depths of depression with a mastery, whilst containing a sense of ribaldry previously written out of the habitus (Bourdieu 1984) of middle class manners within the wider white communities. Later unleashed post war it created a Cultural Revolution. Even travelling back to the 1970's, the Caribbean experiences articulated in reggae were more emotionally diverse, ranging from the love poems of Lovers Rock to the politics of Linton Kwezi Johnson. All these cultural forms have increasingly been written out of the emotional cannon, as the emphasis on acquisition, as a form of empowerment has arisen.

In summary, crucial moral and methodological problems accrue from social science research paradigms that are unreflective and derive from an academic hubris, a belief the inquiries undertaken by the discipline are scientific and are therefore legitimate. The concepts of resistance to Social Science intrusion are wholly ignored. Its foundations are illegitimate and it operates only on the basis of the power it assumes. It says very little about social reality, apart from the one it weaves together and forces people to believe, despite the contrary evidence of their senses.

The Social Sciences needs to adapt to the challenges posed by relational methodology, if it is to become a relevant discipline. It needs a Kuhnian (1996) paradigm shift, if it is to offer any relevance to the 21st century. The Social Sciences need to reflect on the numerous theoretical developments that took place in psychotherapy at the beginning of 20th Century where Otto Rank (1932, 1936, 1952), Otto Gross (Heuer 2010), Fenichel (1972), Freud's work on dreams, Adler (1927, 1931, 1956, 2004), Reich (1933, 1946), Jung (1964) have all shaped the perception of inner realities. It is from these insights Person Centred Therapy (Rogers 1961), a type of phenomenological investigation developed based on the ideas of Otto Rank. Adler's ideas of incorporating the social world into the private world illuminate the relationship between the individual and society. Drawing on Goffman (1959, 1963, 1961) and Sartre (1943) provides an insight into roles, and how these are socially performed. Their social impact is analysed by Bourdieu (1984) and Foucault (1972, 1998). Self medication and the need to find internal meaning was perceived by Khantzian (1985, 1995, 1999, 2010) and this links into the creation of discourses of power. This is an interdisciplinary combination.

A reinvigoration is required because the social sciences have become complicit in upholding an alienated reality. The discipline offers no critique of a mirage. It only works to comply with its preconceptions delivering a modern version of the "Bath of Steel" (Lerner 2003)." Social Science departments based in criminology, health and social care, sociology, psychology and the other social sciences need to reflect on the types of social reality emerging in relational methodology. This decision to ignore this new methodology has created the adversarial scenarios. It sustains a sense of elitism allowing the appearance of objectivity through hovering above the subject in quiet contemplation as Hannah Arendt notes (1958). This is a false dichotomy as it replicates the class position of the objectified and the rational observer, replicating the power relationship of social class.

CHAPTER 4
INTO THE FUTURE

Informed practice is based upon practitioners who are emotionally literate, to contribute and eventually deliver, teaching and research, to enable this paradigm shift. Research needs to be based upon therapeutic practice and delivery. Knowledge needs to be embedded and lived, derived from Praxis. Links between practice and theory are crucial to embed both. Practice becomes anecdotal without being linked to theory and theory exists in the abstract ether, if not based on practice. Creating these links would overcome scientific rationalism, formulated as an empirical mirage.

Universities and colleges need to equip front line workers to engage in a psycho-social regeneration. At present this does not happen. Instead the whole system is based on the same hierarchical arrangements that echo class based systems, encased in the scientific realm of "us and them." Academia has offered no new insight since its mass expansion, due to the alienated forms of learning imposed upon students. Students imbibe at these pools of knowledge to gain the necessary qualifications. These provide an entry into a pre determined job market. Knowledge consumption is based upon imbibing and regurgitating, entailing a stifling of lateral, emotional and critical forms. Taken together this created a paralysed institutional freeze which no one dare critique. As with the wider economy this produces a dammed effect, creating institutional lethargy, seeping in waves at a concrete barrier. Belief in this knowledge becomes eroded, when it confronts various emotional realities, but it refuses to accept them, instead it imposes itself upon the emotions. Learning is reified as a passport to a job.

Innovation and Social Entrepreneurship

Working as a social entrepreneur in 1989, establishing the first therapeutic street agency in Deptford South East London, brought significant insights. Firstly insights into clients' lives were noted in the previous research (Beaten into Violence 2007). Insights also arose from observing power and institutional amnesia, derived from poor social science conception. During the period from 1989 until 1997 I noted a vast array of Task Forces launched in loud fanfares to regenerate the inner city. All disappeared, hardly leaving a trace, after a year or so, the lessons from the previous initiative were never learned. Meanwhile the numbers of people attending our drugs project in Deptford grew.

Regeneration was based on creating new buildings to inject economic capital into the neighbourhood infrastructure. Iconic buildings have a psychologically positive effect, but they do not transform areas. This was because they failed to regenerate the people. The various Quangos were composed of local people with a stake in the community. They obtained funding through creating various layers of social capital, but they failed to tackle the underlying issues relating to the psycho-social problems. Formal public consultations were undertaken with community representatives to ascertain local needs. No one pointed to the emotional problems existing within communities. Social stigma (Goffman 1963) would be enacted if domestic violence, alcoholism, substance use and child beating were raised. These were necessarily hidden, because endemic fears existed on breaking the silence and the repercussions. Instead more visible issues were highlighted such as graffiti, dog faeces, youths' congregating on corners, dampness and fear of crime. The result was the mass installation of surveillance cameras, caretakers, community police, diversionary programmes and house renovation. These visible structural problems were remedied, but they still failed to tackle the underlying causes. These were invisible and related to the relationships existing between people (Wilmot and Young 1969). To understand these causes needs emotional literacy. The well springs within communities ensuring neighbour helps neighbour, people talk to each other and they support their children are invisible. The issues that needed remedying have no conceptual vocabulary, other than stigmatised problems. There were no community champions to articulate these needs. Another crucial arena that needed support included the types

120

of family interactions, and how institutions related to families. There was no sense of an open discourse, only people being harried and chastised for their outward behaviour. The idea of building self esteem and confidence was missing.

Linked to community cohesion, education and support to start a business is needed for those wanting to be autonomous. Ideally social housing should have sustained community activities, binding people together. These existed in Wilmot and Young's (1969) kinship studies in the East End, later erased through the change in city dynamics. Old communities offered support to insiders and resistance to outsiders. They provided solace for families during hardship, but were constraining on innovation and individualism. They also promoted hard masculinities as a norm.

The Quangos had one advantage, due to their limited shelf life, their aims could be customised to meet client needs, rather than funders tick boxes. They became highly effective in their delivery by default. By the time the funders became aware the work was being used for social psychological work, their remit would relapse and the next organisation would begin the process. The problems accrued when various Social Sciences academics turned up to assess the work. They lacked basic psycho-social concepts and could not understand therapy. They researched the therapeutic work using outmoded research paradigms, as they lacked the methodological understanding of how therapy worked. The same concepts for understanding the installation of double glazing, were applied to understanding and tabulating the therapeutic work. This led to distinct methodological problems and clashes. Clients did not want to talk to academics because they were not on the "wavelength" and represented the authorities. This was because they intuitively understood the difference between the contemplative lives of the intellectual, based on perceived class differences. The nature of the psycho-social problems remained hidden, as academia rests upon amnesia. This spurred me to write "Beaten into Violence" (2007) as the conceptual apparatus did not exist; therefore it had to be invented. This was based on Otto Rank's (1932) idea of the artist as innovator.

Whilst funding bodies did not understand the work, it was noted the Orexis agency was seeing considerable numbers of people. The Home

Office became interested in the project based on these numbers, and the agency subsequently delivered all the prototypes within substance misuse. The work in Deptford involved pioneering; young people's services, arrest referral, ethnic minority services, men's services, women's services, the first Crack Services, the first joint Probation /Substance Use, the first agency wholly funded by GP's, the first to work alongside the Home Office.

The funders never understood the therapeutic work and this caused problems. We were constantly asked to curtail it. This would have made the work easier, but less rewarding. The therapeutic work was the bed rock upon which everything else was built. If the therapeutic work was cut the only support available was a letter to the GP, asking them to provide Methadone. The Lewisham Commissioners, although we saw more people than other London Borough's, thought we could see even more, because they refused to tackle the problems within their NHS flagship. The Deptford clients were fearful of attending there, and eventually it was decommissioned in the 21st century.

Commissioners did not seek to improve the NHS performance, because it was backed by a large institution. Ironically its facility was located outside the council chambers, so the local councillors walked through the problems caused by their council officer's inability to deliver. The council's reaction was to place an alcohol exclusion zone outside the chambers. This highlighted the inherent problem of the commissioning model. It aimed to usher its mistakes away from view.

In 1997 the agency I ran was funded by local GP's for two years and this was the golden era, as we worked alongside those who funded us in a joint partnership working on clients needs. The problems occurred when this was halted and funding streams were then administered through the London Boroughs. Commissioners did not understand the therapeutic processes, and this lack of theorisation created difficulties. Whilst money was poured into substance use, it did not cascade into front line staff, but was placed within a bureaucratic apparatus that administered finances, paperwork and targets. The issuing edicts enacted neo Tayloresque (1911) time and motion studies that inhibited growth, as they wished to control the providers, not inspire them. Staff sickness not an issue beforehand, became one, and is still a major problem in the substance use field. People resented the targets, because they lack direction and purpose, thereby deskilling those who take up the job. As someone with a therapeutic background who had weathered the previous storms, I stayed until 2005, when I handed the contracts back to the Borough and went free lance. The work had lost focus.

Emotional Literacy and Emotional Shock Troops

Instead of bureaucracy, building on the "Recovery Model" should be the focus, with emotionally trained therapists, an elite cadre of emotionally literate men and women employed to liberate the potential of those who live in the twilight worlds. They should be working to regenerate people. This should be based on the academic tenets of Community Education, Psychotherapy, History, Geography, Sociology and Psychology. This would incorporate those elements relevant from media studies and criminology to build relational bridges. The teaching would entail high levels of knowledge being generated and dispensed in Praxis; an engagement with communities. These forms of knowledge would necessarily create a vanguard of people who can initiate a new cultural renaissance by liberating the potential of those people who have languished. This will obviously disturb the carefully cultivated habitus (Bourdieu 1984) existing in universities.

Academics, who wish to embrace the new change, can easily join the new renaissance by reflecting on the various assumptions their knowledge base previously rested upon, and this would provide them with a conduit to go out into communities to create and distribute new forms of learning. The old distinctions between those who engage in the university habitus (Bourdieu 1984) and those who are excluded would gradually be eroded. People will gain confidence through a linkage between the new literacy tutors and embracing knowledge culturally relevant. This would also be culturally challenging to make sense of the world. This is not to deny academic knowledge, but to make it more accessible, relevant and create transformation.

As an example of the latter I recollect showing Passolini's "Oedipus Rex" (1967) to a group of black female team members of the Deptford Staff

Team. This created a subsequent stir of "Why is this relevant?" afterwards. Months later I was thanked, as people were confronted with Freud on the various training courses they embarked upon. They were able to contextualise what he was saying back to the film of the myth. At the time it appeared just another dull foreign subtitled film.

Lectures undertaken by practitioners could create new university courses based on Praxis. The Attachment Journal is the template for this new writing as it embraces academia and wider formats of poetry and stories. Students can reflect on the various aspects of discipline and command shaping their lives, then understand how they have reacted to them. This provides the self knowledge to understand the "other" (Sartre 1943). It is through the process of self investigation and wider reflection that Praxis can be enacted.

The fulcrum of delivery needs to be shifted to teams of emotional "shock troops" (Junger 1920). These will be emotional elites, trained to a high level in therapeutic interventions to transform stagnating communities and marginalised people, working in small teams. The Child Adult Mental Health Teams potentially offer a template where they have embraced holistic individual psychological therapy. This encompasses many aspects of CBT and Family Systemic models.

"One should not understand this compulsion to construct concepts, species, forms, purposes, laws ('a world of identical cases') as if they enabled us to fix the real world; but as a compulsion to arrange a world for ourselves in which our existence is made possible:—we thereby create a world which is calculable, simplified, comprehensible, etc., for us."

Nietzsche F. (1968) N 521 "The Will to Power,"

Praxis is needed to create a cultural transformation. There needs to be less emphasis on academic models and more interaction with clients to see what works. In returning to the origins of psychotherapy, there was a belief nothing was off limits and although there were huge disagreements between Adler, Jung, Freud, Gross, Fenichel and the others, this stemmed from defining the discipline. This energy needs to be rekindled to bring therapy to the marginalised. The new elites need to be eclectic, and become integrative through Praxis. Therapists need to be willing to experiment to see what transforms people, rather than become rigid, operating predefined scripts. For example some clients did not like enclosed spaces, so we went for a walk, to a cafe, to a museum or a park. These were areas they had not visited previously and this was part of the process of normalisation, connecting back to the everyday world. This was not part of a therapeutic model, but it had the same effect. One Afghani client spent an hour on UTube showing me the devastation of his country and discussing his fears for his family. I would never have encapsulated his world unless he had led me to it. Another client showed me his favourite music, someone who had remained shuttered for years. These clients had retreated from the real world and needed to remake connection. These are just some examples from experimenting, rather than relying on techniques.

What works will evolve from Praxis in an engagement with universities, practitioners and clients. There will be no more top down prescriptions, only catalysts for change and the evidence will be discussed in learning units, where it will be refined through immersion.

Small teams will work on the coal face, where people are marginalised. There only previous emotional outlet was a potential appearance on the Jeremy Kyle Show. The focus of regeneration should be on working with the homeless and then the wider communities, to allow people to take part in the social world. This will bring those people who have been left on the margins, back into mainstream society when they realise they have a social stake and a life purpose.

Confidentiality should be the cornerstone of people regeneration. A separation between social regeneration and the needs of the surveillance state urgently needs to be initiated. Otherwise this will break the trust between therapist and client, then render the whole operation another initiative burdened by too many expectations. The job of the police needs to be redefined to give impetus to social regeneration. This will release their potential and take away a great deal of the adversarial pressure they face, when confronted by the effects of childhood trauma in their day to day work. The arrest referral schemes need to change to meet the needs of social regeneration. Police training also needs to encompass these changes.

Psychologically informed environments are not soft options; confronting the self is the hardest task anyone can set them self.

Communities need to take over management of these emotional shock troops (Junger 1920) with a mixture of professionals and local people sitting on local management committees to help sustain the work, and to act as intermediaries between those other professionals who feel threatened by these new arrangements.

Batons of Trust

The emotional turmoil revealed in the therapy resonated with the work already undertaken at the drugs agency I established in Deptford. Accounts of familial and institutional violence abounded. Whereas in the 1990's I was a blind man searching for answers, in the 21st century I was a hard bitten veteran. Working in Deptford had been my "Bath of Steel" (Lerner 2003) and delving into the worlds of the homeless, was a return to the front line. Except this time, I no longer had to manage people, just concentrate on a therapeutic intervention. The men at the hostel were similar to the people I worked with previously, and on three occasions the very same people, who had slipped further down the ladder. I was relieved that each person was glad to see me, and greeted me as a long lost friend. This baton of trust helped me to make initial inroads into the hostel because each was a "hard man" in his own right. When they spoke people listened. I built a platform to ease the sense of resistance I encountered in Deptford. This eased into co-operation. I was now a trusted worker, and no longer "one of them." The fact I had given up the agency in Deptford and not complied with the New Labour initiative of discipline and punish, a career suicide manoeuvre, entailed that when I moved back to the front line, I was lauded. It helped me to create this intervention.

This baton of trust passed on by these men, helped me to make even more significant in-roads into these hard men's emotional lives, as they opened up. They passed this information about me to the others in the hostel, and this is how the counselling work became embedded so quickly, I was a known "face," one that helped rather than hindered. This belies all of the government initiatives, as they have no conception of building trust and perceiving it as a form of social and cultural capital to be called upon.

Clients make judgements whether to engage or not, and this is embodied. Clients can feel whether a person has a bridge to them or not. This is not just a 'rational' decision based on gratification. There are no immediate benefits in talking, no Marks and Spencer vouchers, no Methadone. The whole process promises emotional pain. Yet they arrived.

"Essential: to start from the body and employ it as a guide. It is the much richer phenomenon, which allows of clearer observation. Belief in the body is better established than belief in the spirit."

Nietzsche F. (1968) N532 "The Will to Power,"

There is never a sudden engagement but a period of circumspection and appraisal. Clients feel the worker out. Just as in the real world people weigh up safety, confidentiality and whether it is worth the time and trouble. At first there was a regular client group because the numbers of people in the hostel was stable, with people living there for 3 years or more. Due to making these initial connections, the newer arrivals began to attend. This is how I became successful.

The benefits and the negatives of self disclosure are undertaken before the men begin therapy. At the hostel, a fast move on rate occurred, due to the success of the team. After a year of therapy, there was a constant flux of new clients. Relationships then had to be constantly built and maintained. This was due to the success of the intervention and it became a challenge to the positive work undertaken. The therapeutic work helped to speed up resettlement but then made the interventions shorter (Whittington 2011).

The changes in the dynamics at the hostel entailed the need to be continuously involved in outreach work to keep up the numbers of people in treatment. A notable increase in informal referrals from key workers and specialists to the therapeutic service gradually arose with hard to reach men, when they saw the benefits. This also increased from personal

127

contacts, but I noted those workers more attuned to therapy made the most referrals.

Self medication is the main barrier to accessing therapy, as the use of substances entails people emotionally shutting off. It is the most effective self medication strategy. It negates having to talk about problems, as it creates a safe cocooned world of warmth. Problems occur in keeping the mirage intact; it needs a constant supply of drugs. Khantzian's (1985, 1995, 1999, 2010,) model of self medication, highlights how alcohol and drugs are utilised to create a sense of euphoria in the present, to block out memories of the past.

It is from small talk that bigger talk emerges (Whittington 2011) Small talk involves discussing current events such as news, football scores, talking about music or films. These are the cross cultural intersections that help to make connection. It is through sharing these snippets of information the men make the decision to make a connection or not.

Therapeutic Models

Adlerian ideas flow from one current of Nietzsche. Adler (1956) is crucial in recovery. Adler (1956) envisaged people moving towards a positive impulse when the layers that bind them are released. The work with the homeless justifies many of his original premises, as the case histories demonstrate, his original premise is correct. When people undergo a process of retrieval of their self esteem or custom build it from scratch, they can shift remarkably.

Adler (1956) is a crucial theorist because he has been neglected, as the march of scientific discourses has replicated the social divisions. The operation of the discourse has created us, the socially included and them, the socially excluded the "other" (Sartre 1943).

Education becomes an indoctrination where energy and zeal is zapped and the machine takes over. Nietzsche highlighted the pedagogical process of turning a person into a machine through ensuring the process of learning becomes as abstract and irrelevant as possible. Inner subjectivity is replaced with a need to learn external concepts that replace internal focal points. Learning should build upon and expand upon the emotions, not squash and eradicate them. Unfortunately the concepts learnt in therapy are often applied as webs the client needs to fit within, rather than used to gauge where the client is and then build a custom structure to meet their needs. Moving beyond the various therapeutic models; cognitive behavioural, family systemic, brief interventions, solution focused, person centred, existential is needed, as humans are far wider than models. Drawing on Khantzian (1985, 1995, 1999, 2010), Adler (1927, 1931, 1956, 2004) Nietzsche (1878, 1895, 1881, 1882, 1886, 1888) Deleuze and Guattari (1972, 1980), Fromm (1955), Yalom (1991), Sartre (1943, 2001), Illich (1977), Arendt (1958) philosophical insights can be gleaned to understand what works. The conceptual ideas of Buddhism, drawing on everything, are a starting point rather than the dogmatic idealism of one faith that fits all.

Therapy needs to be built on building self esteem, and then the pieces can be assembled from the different models, it becomes customised to a need, rather than an off the peg model the client adjusts to. Yalom (1991) speaks of his jazz method, as he details his interactions and this encompasses the reality of working with clients. Models are based upon a concept that offers a template, rather than a one size fits all. Components should be taught and then reformulated within universities through Praxis, to ascertain what works with whom, when and how. I only posit the above ideas to broaden the current paradigm from being foreclosed from conception. The starting pistol for regeneration needs a wide open vista and does not need to be colonised by any 'model,' only by Praxis, social regeneration, self medication, attachment, trauma, recovery and purpose. The practicalities can be formulated and theories and models tested to seek what works. In the case histories that follow, the models are derived from Behaviourism to Adlerian. There is a room for all the models as they are "tools" rather than tramlines. The starting point is defining the issue, and then using a specialist tool to construct the psychological escape. I visualise the therapist as a 14th Century craftsman who in the 21st century also transmits and reciprocates from the insights of women.

Dissolving Self Medication

Working with a self medicating client group presents particular challenges. A significant issue within the therapeutic field was the appliance of stigma (Goffman 1963) onto marginalised groups, and the old notion you cannot work with people who are inebriated. Previously it was deemed people would have to cease their drug use to be firstly assessed, and then to begin the therapy. This is the reason why therapy was not seen as relevant in the substance use field, as this false notion was based on a presumed assumption. There is no need to stop self medicating prior to accessing therapy. The task of therapy is to work together with the client to look at the purpose of their strategies, what it contains, then work to alleviate its effects. Very few people would access treatment if they had to be well beforehand. This idea people have to stop using substances to make use of therapy is derived from a division into us and the "other" (Sartre 1943. These perspectives cascade through the social sciences as part of the Habitus of manners (Bourdieu 1984). Psychotherapy adopted the discourse of us and them, divorcing itself from Praxis, and then deciding not to engage with the hard to reach client groups. It became a contemplative discipline, instead of being active.

Vast numbers of people take prescription drugs and are alcohol dependent. Refusing to work therapeutically with people who are taking substances, asking them to stop, marginalises and stigmatises significant numbers of people. Few men would expose their emotional selves to engage with an unknown talking therapy that brings all the submerged memories to the fore, when they already have a strategy in place. Self medication works instantaneously, and erases discomfort. Substance use is a coping mechanism. Working with people who are using substances empowers clients to make changes by ignoring the stigma of their drug use and working on their emotions. It humanises them.

After working to overcome this therapeutic projection, the next major challenge entailed creating a relationship to reduce the reliance on these embedded strategies. This took nerves, patience and an ability to walk into the abyss of various human catastrophes over a four year period. This helped the men make sense of their desolate worlds. Whilst an immersion in pain is seen as transformative within the 1st world war, the "Stahlbad,"

(Lerner 2003) the homeless lifestyle, compounded these men's problems. The person who is changed by the process of becoming immersed into these worlds, is, ironically the therapist. The "Bath of Steel" (Lerner 2003) only applies to the therapeutic/bureaucratic and academic immersion into the worlds of pain. The clients already inhabit the steel bath (Lerner 2003). It has not cured or invigorated them, because no one has developed the ladder to help them escape from it.

Clients need to see the therapy as working and that it has a practical application for them, so they can trust the process. The first expectation is for something to happen, and working on sleep deprivation brings the first results. Explore the dreams, but do not slip into the Freudian net of interpretation. The client needs guidance not instruction. The role of the therapist is to find meaning that resonates with them. There is no science of dreams, only interpretations.

If the client suffers from chronic anger, then trying to defuse this with CBT (Beck 1990), or any other "let's pretend this is not happening," will only sublimate a legitimate emotional release. The task of the therapist is to enter the 'steel bath' (Lerner 2003) and immerse themselves within it. This means walking through the painful and nightmarish worlds of those who have been emotionally decimated. In practical terms, this means sitting there and facing its full frontal effect. When a client becomes angry, Person Centred Therapy (Rogers 1961) allows them to explore it within safe parameters. Let it blow and contain it within the room. The therapist cannot respond to the anger, as I note in the case histories, it ferments the energy. This is what it means to be an enlightened witness (Miller 2001), to be there in the here and now, feeling the full emotional effect. Expressing anger is not a personal attack on the therapist, but allows the waves of rage that lie suppressed to be finally given a voice, a safe space for the furnace to blast. The task of the therapist is to shape the rage and then to heal it. This is a crucial skill, and it takes finely tuned, judgements. It involves neither condemnation ("I am uncomfortable with your anger"), nor collusion ("let's go and kill those abusers"). The defusing and rebuilding of those who have been humiliated needs a safe space for the emotions to be unleashed, and then for them to be harnessed to a life enhancing purpose. This may take one session, or twenty sessions of immersion in the "steel bath" (Lerner 2003). Time is a healer. You will feel it in the gut when it is time to shift, listen to your body not the psychology manual, and then when the fury has been expired, it is time to build the ladder of escape.

Taking an interest the client's previous positive achievements with less focus on negative life choices, creates the alliance derived from the tenets of Motivational Interviewing (Rollnick S. and Morgan M. in Washton A. 1995). These are the rungs of the ladder. This provides the client with the clear message, this not another authoritarian lecture. The main initial intervention tools are derived from the Person Centred Method (Rogers 1961) listening, empathising and an immersion. This is the bedrock upon which the other counselling modules are built upon, as listening creates the bond. The pace of the sessions varies, depending on trust, client insight and the extent of their depression. Sometimes the client reveals a fundamental issue in the first session, other entrenched clients; particularly those with dual diagnosis issues may take up to 12 months. There was only one person in four years who I worked with, who I never reached, and that was seeing five people a day over two days, ten people a week over this period roughly 1800 hourly sessions. The most complex diagnosed dual diagnosis residents were able to shift forward and make changes.

Once the therapeutic relationship has solidified, the client can be gently probed using Socratic Questioning derived from Adler (1956), to explore beliefs, attitudes and behaviours. This helps the client to focus on different options and explore divergent opinions they may hold around the hostel, substance use, the future and the present. It is effective in shifting negative perceptions, by pointing out positive achievements in the past and present. The clues occur within the listening.

Severance of attachment issues entails negative critical feedback and the internal voices knocking self esteem. These need to be replaced with positivity. The internal voice, the thinking voice, described by Eric Berne (1961, 1964) and Claude Steiner (1974) needs to be encouraged to grow and develop, then stop condemning. This is the voice that commands action. It is this voice, based on the stored memories of the past which needs to be reached beyond the everyday presentation. This draws upon Transactional Analysis looking at the critical voice, the one that screams

"Idiot," "you are never going to be good enough," "you will never make anything of yourself," "Destined for failure" or any other critical put down that inhibits growth. These can be contrasted with successes, times when the person has overcome adversity, been in love, had happiness and joy. The idea is to build the positive profile and create the foundations for growth. If the client does not have the store of positive memories to anchor them, work with them in the here and now to build them. Harry Stack Sullivan (1953, 1970, 1974, Barton Evans 1996) and Alice Miller (2005) speak of the adolescent chum, the ideas/beliefs that carried the client through adolescence. In the case study, Rickie had Jimmy Cagney and Rod Stewart. Alice Miller (2005) writes about the therapist being the enlightened witness (Miller 2001) to validate trauma. Whilst the client goes through the trauma build them up by highlighting their survival skills and provide the emotional literacy in "strokes" (Steiner 2003) that were denied at the time. If they have nothing from the past, then these "strokes" have to be built in the present. People are survivors of trauma, not the victims although the process needs to be carefully paved from one feeling to another. This is the process of individuation, separating the client from their substance, the new rebirth.

Finally, when the process has been worked through, when the bond between client and worker has solidified, it is then time to think of the future. This can be tentatively explored at any time in the process, but there comes a moment and this is akin to electric in the air and a feeling in the gut when the major shift begins to turn into an avalanche. Finding a purpose can be drawn upon to reflect the future. Using this technique with homeless men provided startling outcomes, just asking the question when we had the therapeutic alliance created a shift entailing the future could be faced.

"Do you have a purpose? If not what do you think it should it be?" Did you have one when you were younger, dreams, visions an excitement?

When the future is defined then the self medication strategy can be tackled, not before. Coming off drugs and alcohol needs to be carefully constructed. Coming off Methadone needs to emerge from an internal rationale, not an external command. The structure that holds a person is based upon their social network, their hobbies, education/training/work, partner/children/family, housing. To come off drugs entails far more than "you can do it." It entails a rebuild to find a meaning to exist, to fend off meaningless through having hope. This comes from an immersion within the world. A Social network based on people in recovery, or people not involved in the previous subculture, reinforces the dynamic of change; hobbies provide an outlet for creativity and social networks. They allow a person to recreate their identity, no longer a drug user or homeless person but a writer, sculptor, artist, singer or musician. Shifting self perception entails shifting social role. Education and training provide the means to obtain work to live independently, free from the State and to have a disposable income. This creates the ability to choose a lifestyle, no longer based on self medicating. It allows a person 'to be' in the world, instead of walling off. Reconnection with the positive components of family creates emotional attachment, the sense of being anchored, loved, valued and the sharing of memories. This provides validation. Housing provides the end point of the homeless journey, and the beginning of another life chapter.

All of these components need to be addressed within the therapy, drawing on the internal and outside resources to build this psychological ladder. This is beyond therapeutic models, but builds upon Adler's idea of Social Interest (1931). This is an engagement with the world. This arises in Paolo's case history. A man who lost social interest after the bereavement of his partner gradually retrieved it, despite facing up to life threatening illnesses and furthermore transcending them through belief.

When the bonds have been created the self medication issues can be explored. Drawing on Khantzian's (1985, 1995, 1999, 2010) self medication hypothesis, the following questions could also be asked, as part of an ongoing dialogue, not as a quantitative tick box exercise

"What role do the drugs play in your life?

"When did you notice you were relying on drugs as an everyday experience and what else was going on in your life?

For Adler (1956), the impact of the social realm is just as important as the familial realm. The social world is not just locked within a family and parents but lies within the birth order, the way institutions and the wider world impacts upon the family.

Adler (1956) drew on these insights to influence the training of parents, teachers, and social workers in changing the ways they interacted with children. Changes in Child rearing practices empower children patients/ clients to seek emotional growth.

Ideal for Living

Drawing on positive adolescent coping strategies also allows the clients to retrieve emotional strength, the coping mechanisms of childhood and early adolescence. These are the foundations for building self esteem. This involves exploring the importance of significant others, who may have provided support during early adolescence, crucial if family structures were primarily negative. Jay for example recollected a teacher. This creates the foundations for future growth.

Crisis Interventions often occurs at particular junctures. These are an opportunity to work through and solidify the therapeutic relationship, then work towards a self defined future vision, undertaken using primarily Cognitive Behavioural Therapy techniques (Beck 1990). Drawing on previous positive coping strategies, allows the client to shift from a negative present preoccupation to retrieve and utilise earlier positive strategies. The aim is to work with clients to re discover skills and use them in the present.

The main form of intervention is providing a space for men to articulate their emotions. This ranges from expressing anger, sadness, depression and frustration to exploring their hobbies and interests. The length of engagement with the service should be open. The level of engagement depends on the scale of the problems the client's identifies and their ability to create a meaningful vision in a care plan structure. This structure arises from the chaos and cannot be imposed.

Working therapeutically with homeless men entails thinking differently about therapy, and then critically reflecting on the various therapeutic models. Adaptation and flexibility is the key. Waiting times, punctuality, appointments and referrals all need to be undertaken flexibly initially, as people cannot be forced into counselling, they can be enticed (Whittington 2011). General therapy is based upon a specific model and mindset, evolving from working with people who have a stake in the social world, and therefore wish to engage on that basis. Once the bond is created, appointment times become part of a structure.

Formerly homeless men have foregone this social interest (Adler 1931). The therapist ideally uses their skills to meet the needs of the client group, not force the client group into a pre ordained therapeutic model. Homeless men are forever missing crucial appointments for Doctors, mental health services, probation, police signing on and medical reviews where their benefits may be stopped. Maslow's (1968) hierarchy of needs is no longer a concern for the homeless population as warmth; shelter and food are not the overriding priorities they are for those who have a social stake. Self medication for trauma becomes their overriding objective. Men, who have been in and out of prison, see appointments as another authoritarian device to contain them. If viewed from their perspective and seeing life within a prison as essentially structured chaos, the imposition of structure resonates with this sense of being constrained by powerful authority figures. The projection entails a belief people are going to be asked to explain their behaviour. This creates problems for the therapist as there are numerous subconscious projections they need to overcome to meet the clients' needs. Dissolving projections is undertaken at the beginning of the therapeutic relationship, to create the foundation to begin. The therapist needs to be conscious of these strategies to defuse resistance.

Trust is the crucial ingredient; this is built and sustained to engage bemused populations. This requires reflection on which strategy to adopt. This provides the space to allow people to make informed choices around engagement. These men cannot be forced into therapy as this only reinforces their defences. Therapeutic engagement necessitates a new form of interaction, not based on the strategies of discipline and command.

Homeless men have largely ignored structure. Homelessness is its complete negation. The therapist has to create an intervention using lateral knowledge, rather than rely on the preconceived structures of conventional therapy. The aim is to gently build a structure, working together, rather than presuppose it exists and expect the men to respond. Many therapeutic projects have floundered within the homeless sector, because they expect the socially included model to be applied at inception. This is an aim to work towards. Appointments are a social construction that can used to measure the therapeutic journey, something that people aim for and eventually meet. Structures are not innate, but are imposed systems to create meaning for those who adhere to them. It is part of having a social investment.

Carl Rogers in "Freedom to Learn" (1969) helped me to reflect on the foundations for rethinking the whole therapeutic process. In adopting an initial client centred approach, I built a structure where the client is, rather than where they should be, or using any other form of imposition. The clients meaning, and how they view the world is the therapeutic starting point, and the client centred model allows this to be expressed from the onset. Empowerment is part of the therapeutic process. Within my work the paperwork became less and less, until it became a minimum. Paper work gets in the way of effective therapy. It is a requirement of bureaucratic procedure, but if it does not assist with the therapeutic process, it needs to be dispensed with. In my private practice the paperwork is necessarily kept to a minimum of case notes and invoices. Assessment, care plan, risk assessments should all be used therapeutically to draw the clients past out of them, to jump start the therapy, and not used as a bureaucratic hammer to bludgeon the client. They can be filled in over a period of weeks, depending on the mood of the client.

Presupposing people will attend agreed appointments for therapy en masse is an unreflected projection of the standard therapeutic model. Appointments and time keeping are part of a socially included discourse of manners. For people who are socially included, time is a precious commodity measured by money and it is necessary time is used efficiently cut up into segments. Homelessness entails time being used in different forms; it loses its importance. It is no longer a commodity to be measured. Time is measured by its effect on the body and ensuring the self medication strategy is maintained. The body becomes the repository for measuring time. The effect is felt when alcohol leaves the system, the handshakes or the heroin withdraws, then the stomach cramps and runny nose begins.

This is the standard time measurement for someone engaged in a self medication strategy. Other forms of measurement occur, whether it is day or night, wet or dry, hot or warm. These mark out the days.

Beginning the therapeutic process where the clients are starting from is not the same as condoning their chaos and adopting cultural relativism. The chaos that engulfs homeless people is a real event, it has a meaning and purpose, as I explore, but it is also debilitating. It is another self medication strategy to fend off the world and when given the choice, behaviour they wish to escape from. No one I have ever worked with had a childhood aspiration to be an alcoholic or heroin user. At one time, these men had childhood dreams and hopes, but they were vandalised by powerful adults.

Trapped within this chaos, they can fend off the world through using this chaos as a defence. It is built to negate emotional trauma. It is not just another lifestyle choice. The behaviour has a meaning, difficult for those who are socially included to decipher, unless they know the signals. These are not difficult to decode when people become emotionally literate.

The homeless men's behaviour provides some significant challenges to preconceptions of being socially included. These men at one time were children and part of families. Their journey into homelessness resonates with many other populations who have had less traumatic experiences (Miller 1987). The emotional rationale to self medicate becomes apparent when the trust is built. Then it becomes perceived as a rational choice given the circumstances. Homelessness and substance use are differing forms of self medication to fend off emotional realities by replacing it with oblivion, nihilism and the negation of meaning. The world of comfort has been negated, and instead they have embraced the rigours of the street in various states of depression. This has compounded the original depression, as they have internalised the stigma of their role, leading to a dialectical descent.

Therapy should not reflect the client's chaos and condone this lack of structure. It should however begin where the client is psychologically, and then aim to build meaningful structures to create a purpose. This can be undertaken through engaging with the world, inspiring someone to transform their internal world into an external positive reality. Entering into the personal maelstrom of these men assists in creating routes out of their predicament. The men need to find an internal meaning, and this is individual. The aim is to support the men to work towards finding a purpose to live and then succeed in the world. This is built from practical interventions ensuring they want to attend breakfast, Doctor Appointments for illnesses, wait in casualty or go to their Jobcentre meetings. They gradually ease into the everyday world through being supported, and seeing its relevance, as something they want to join in with. Time becomes acknowledged as part of a care discourse. They begin to act within the world and eventually shape it, rather than ignore it and fend it off.

Therapy is often feared by the men because it involved a presupposed invasion into the personal realm, the one that lies beyond the "front" they project. The internal world must be kept silent at all costs. They have learnt to keep themselves silent and separate as a survival strategy. Otherwise the surrender of the "front" involves a loss of face and respect. This makes them vulnerable to the bully. Any type of alliance with a perceived authority figure is deemed to be avoided, because the internal command tells them authority figures let you down just like parents. This is the first internal command. This is a projection needing careful dismantling, as the therapist approaches the client.

Therapeutic engagement involves being grounded by the basic tenets of therapy, whilst adjusting to meet the needs of the client group. It requires a new cultural perspective on the meaning of therapeutic service delivery. Previous therapeutic structures for these homeless men, prior to my work, were offered off site, used only by those who were extremely motivated, referred there, because the worker understood the relevance of therapy to recovery. These were people who could keep appointments. This left the mass of people trapped in their chaotic lives.

Trust allows the clients to explore their psychological histories. This relieves the physical and psychological stresses on the body. Early physical abuse issues appear to be carried within the body as well as the mind expressing themselves as latent anger and bodily illness as adults (Miller 1983, Harrison 1986). Stored anger as memories impinges on the body creating high blood pressure when recollected. This retention generates poor sleeping patterns and induces nightmares. Inability to de-stress ensures clients remain awake for long periods, drinking alcohol, taking sedatives or heroin to induce sedation. Sleep is shallow, inducing lethargy, affecting concentration levels. Dousing memories in substances is a process of active forgetting. Sleep often perceived as a condition of rest, is re-experienced as another site of stress. When awake at they feel in control, asleep, they are at the mercy of their dream worlds. Therapeutic work on dreams and in particular nightmares allows the clients to interpret the meanings to dissipate the effects. Talking and relating dreams, particularly the incessant chase, articulated by Simon, or falling off buildings and hitting the bottom mentioned by Rickie occur repeatedly.

Releasing memories through recollection creates validation and then dissipation. Not being understood and dismissed is a huge denigration of existence. Memories recollected in a safe arena, explored for their meaning and consequences allows a future to appear based on freeing the client from negative historical effects. The safe release of memories relieves the constant "fight, freeze or flight" syndrome, keeping the body in a state of heightened suspension. Poor sleeping patterns become enmeshed within the general hostel conditions as there is considerable night time noise. These intertwine with the latent affects of childhood abuse as the body lies ever alert. Much of the sexual and physical abuse of their childhood took place at night time. Trauma is externalized in the form of nightmares, sleeplessness and making noise, which then distresses the other hostel residents, and a culture of noise then envelopes the hostel.

Each client life history differs, but over the years commonalities relating to shame, anger, self blame and sexual confusion have emerged. A significant issue in the homeless client population differing from the work I undertook previously (Whittington 2007) are the levels of disclosed female perpetrator abuse. This may either be due to my improved ability to work around these issues, or a significant differentiation between homeless men and men who are already housed. In Deptford the men primarily lived with their mothers. In the homeless hostel this is obviously no longer the case.

The recollection of memories and their dissipation are crucial for undertaking an emotional release. The childhood abuse is accompanied with years of adult silence. (Pezzot, J and Pezzot Pearce, T. 2006) Many men tried to articulate their abuse with emotional caretakers but were not believed. This harks back to Freud's attempted articulation of his "Seduction Theory" (De Zulueta 1993). This has added to the emotional hurt that has accrued. I have to tread carefully to generate and maintain therapeutic alliances. The previous articulation of abuse was often accompanied with strictures stating the person was fantasising about their abuse experience. This compounded their humiliation. This also echoes Freud's experience of the "Seduction Theory," as he later reinterpreted it into the Oedipus complex; the child fantasising about their desires. Not being believed undermines their experienced reality, this self doubt creates a basis for later "mental health" problems as the men have retreated inside. Accepting and believing the clients accounts, is a major breakthrough for these men, and provides a tentative release from a psychological prison.

The therapist has to be aware that client strategies for emotional coping are their main focus. Intertwined is criminality. This is more than just an economic necessity. The calls for the legalisation of heroin to resolve the crime issue ignore the emotional dynamic that drives the self medication. One crucial dynamic in the relationship between heroin use and crime is a desire to gain psychological revenge for past humiliations and hurts (Whittington 2007). It is an attempt to wound those who failed in rescuing the child. The basis of this revenge arises from childhood, where children are still systematically bullied by adults and peers. The child either withdraws into dream worlds, or acts upon the world, to grasp and then shape it, as an emotional recompense. This is undertaken to ensure the child is not beaten again and the bullying ceases. This reflects Adler's ideas on organ inferiority (1956). The articulation of this issue is thwarted by the lack of trust between the homeless men and the institutions aiming to manage them (Goffman 1963). This is why it is rarely articulated, and only emerges in a relational methodology (Gilligan 1989, 1990a 1990b).

New Visions; Social Regeneration

The first psychologically informed decision is to make self medication for trauma the starting point for social regeneration. Then a training programme based on Community Education, psychotherapy and sociology linked to history and geography needs to be initiated. This needs to be delivered by academics with formal links to front line delivery. These are the people, initially, who will pave the way. Either they work directly through mentoring young people on the margins, or sit on management committee members of small charities. These people need to be part of an inclusive society. Creating an apprentice scheme within the universities to reach out to the organic intellectuals in marginalised communities will assist them to gain skills, subsidised with local bursaries, with the proviso they return to rebuild the psychological and social infrastructure. Academia and rebuilding communities is a two way process, not academics directing operations or local anecdotes swaying professions. The relational methodological (Gilligan 1989, 1990a 1990b) template creates a new format. Quantitative methods provides a statistical breakdown of structural inequality, the qualitative provides the effectiveness for emotional change.

Secondly, practitioners need to be rewarded in line with those who regenerate areas. The expectation is they deliver in line with their enhanced training, morale and effectiveness. Rewards need to be redirected to those who are practitioners, redirected from those who "monitor." This monitoring has stifled change. This type of remit needs to be swept aside with no more micro managing. Instead new highly trained emotionally literate front line staff needs to bring about rapid transformation. They rejuvenate the areas that have slipped into abjection and depression. These people need to be recognised within their communities as those who not only act as old fashioned role models, but also within this new paradigm, they are the emotional anchor points for change. Their remits should be to stimulate fresh thinking and innovation.

Links need to be forged between the knowledge these shock troops accrue and local university departments and local colleges. University and Colleges need to be repositories of knowledge for psycho-social regeneration. This is where these shock troops will embark on educational programmes to bring about a new elite cadre of organic intellectuals to return and continue the rebuilding process. This will aim to rebuild all communities even those deemed affluent, to share meaning, camaraderie and vision. The emphasis initially will be on those who are marginalised and then work to create a national regeneration.

At first, to avoid confusion two departments need to be created, one in north of England and one in the South before they spread to all areas. The notion of Praxis needs to infuse university departments where too long the same class divisions between academic researcher and researched in the social sciences (psychology, sociology, health and social care, community studies, and counselling / psycho therapy) all needs to be transformed. These disciplines need to be made relevant to the populace. Departments need to make connections with local communities to create the conduits for innovation. This is not about lowering standards but raising them higher.

The work at a homeless hostel provided a template for a new rebirth. This shows Alfred Adler (1956) was correct in his original premise. Human beings do move towards positive change if given the chance. They may move slowly or quickly. The dynamics of change occur according to the bonds of trust established. These are the dynamic catalyst for change. This account of life within a homeless hostel provides an insight into the challenges that arise. It is based upon numerous case histories arising over a four year period. These highlight the psychological challenges when working with people on the margins. It provides a platform for my critique of past government policy and its architects within the homeless sector. Major policy flaws have had significant repercussions, creating alienated working practices based on targets. It is time to unleash human potential.

CHAPTER 5
THE PSYCHOLOGY OF
THE BUILDINGS

The main hostel housed 47 former men who were either former rough sleepers, who made up most of the population, people released directly from prison, or those referred from social services or Borough housing departments. The hostel rooms were spread over 3 floors, with long corridors and the small rooms feeding off each. The initial reaction to the hostel is "this looks like prison." Few people are enthused about living there, because the rooms are small and it has the ambience of an institution. Yet remarkably, the staff undertook notable inroads with a chaotic client group.

There is an annexe built in 2003 which houses 5 men in 3 rooms and 2 self contained studio flats. This is used to ascertain if people are ready to move on, as these residents cook, clean and budget for themselves. This is a halfway house between the hostel and eventual resettlement for those that can sustain independent living. The challenge for the men in this annexe is to spend more money on food than on self medication. Those that cannot manage, return back to the main hostel.

The residents refer to their small rooms as prison cells, and it is no exaggeration, as they are small, enough for a bed and a cupboard, they are basic. There is a projection onto the environment because so many of the homeless are former prison inmates, nearly all previously incarcerated in police cells or psychiatric wards. The front counter is referred to as the "jump," a reference to prison and the corridors are called "landings." The considerable noise in the hostel becomes another flash point along with the non payment of debts for violence.

There were various projections placed onto staff, all primarily negative as they were seen as "other" (Sartre 1943), authority figures (Marcuse 1972) that tried to dominate or overwhelm the residents with rules and power. These men had years of being involved in institutions (Goffman 1961). One of the issues explored in Reflective Practice, group work activity undertaken with staff for an hour per week, was a reflection on the different modes of authority, (Marcuse 1972) how these were formed and the effects on the worker/resident interaction.

Staff brought a number of ideas to work, some positive and others negative, gleaned from personal experience, religious institutions, college courses and the wider media. These projections were worked upon in the Reflective Practice, as they led to assumptions made about the residents and potentially created conflict through transference. One acute problem when I first began at the project in 2007 was the appliance of psychiatric diagnoses without any confirming evidence. These became written up as truths. These were all assumptions derived from the DSM manual.

"That person X he appears to be a borderline personality."

This ensured everyone would nod in agreement, but in reality no one knew what it meant. There were all types of labelling (Becker H. 1963) taking place which objectified the residents without seeking their views. This initially hamstrung the therapeutic work, as these appeared based upon empirical science but these practices needed rigorous challenging, as it led to another form of determinism and paralysis. This practice was abandoned after the workers who had used this discourse moved to other areas.

Within reflective practice I introduced some theoretical knowledge, to ground the practice on something other than anecdotal evidence, and this also helped to shift perception. If a psychologically informed environment is to be enacted, then it needs to be nurtured within a safe environment, rather than people engaging in an encounter group. I raised the issue of staff being psychologically aware and for this to be incorporated into the recruitment process. This should be the crux of the interview, as all other aspects of the job can be built upon its foundations.

Project Workers are caught between policing the rules and developing relationships with the clients. Ideally, rules could be reformulated as boundaries to keep the hostel safe. This was one of the aims undertaken within the reflective practice. Staff needed to act consistently in their decision making and support each other in making collective decisions. The staff were involved in key working and they put in a considerable effort to ensure the practical needs of the residents were met. This created the basis for therapeutic engagement, and it was through this process project workers referred people to me for support. Although a vast array of projections were cast upon staff, they dealt with the residents fairly. It was when a perceived sense of justice flared up, that tempers frayed.

The architectural setting of the building impacts on perception, but if the team is connected, they can overcome design. Aesthetics are important for psychological perception, but it is the human contact that brings about change. The building I worked within was nearly wholly negative in design and setting, yet big gains were made.

The building stated from the onset, people here were the "other" (Sartre 1943), housed in an old Victorian building, echoing with the history of the workhouse. Even in modern buildings, specifically created for the client group, the layout inhibits a psychologically informed environment and problems have accrued. The old hostel was more effective in providing the space for therapy, than a brand new state of the art building especially commissioned for the homeless. One particular hostel I worked in, previously redeveloped, had the acoustics of a swimming pool, so all the noise collected and rebounded around the open space. Open planning created considerable therapeutic difficulties, as there was no safe space to conduct therapy. The layout resembled the ideas of Bentham (Foucault 1977) as an update of the Panopticon, where all space can be surveyed by those who manage it. This was not conducive to undertaking confidential therapeutic work. The building was designed before the notion of therapy was envisaged with this client group, and the structural conditions militated against it ever occurring. As it could not be undertaken, it was written off as something people did not want to engage with. The whole argument became circular. The end result was the population was managed rather than assisted in moving forwards. Building design is crucial to create a Psychologically Informed Environment, as it needs to be built into the fabric. This also entails architects being made conceptually aware, rather than aesthetically aware. Ensuring buildings are psychologically designed, rather than just aesthetically created, is a novel concept that needs urgent attention.

Recasting the rules as boundaries provides clients with a meaning and dissolves the adversarial nature of the relationship. This helps to lower the projections made by residents onto staff. They have already spent considerable time in prison, psychiatric wards, police cells and children's homes. They are used to authoritarian systems and finding ways to circumvent rules. This resistance needs to be negated, not reinforced.

Move on, to the outside world should be the end result of a psychological ladder, stretching from induction, after creating a tentative a care plan. Future plans should be part of the induction, even when the client is entrapped in chaos. Building a framework to allow people to become equipped to move forward should be the priority. Whilst therapy should not be compulsory, it should be embedded as a core component. The residents have the option of attending the in-house, or external support services; Day Programmes, Substance Use Services, Mental Health Services as alternatives. The residents should work through a programme of change, within the hostel before they eventually move into outside accommodation. Some residents need considerable support, others need less, but they all need to develop a future plan, detailing their aims. The rehousing of residents with entrenched drug and alcohol problems has entailed other people taking advantage of their vulnerability when they move out.

The therapeutic work needs to be the central component of any psycho-social regeneration. This places greater emphasis on the therapist and they need to have the abilities to meet the challenge. This entails being trained in Praxis to a high degree, beyond the current levels of DANOS competence or IAPT, therapists are expected to achieve. Hostels could be reformulated into stage 1 rehabilitation centres undertaking the ground work before people access other long term rehabs, outside the Borough or become rehoused within.

Flash points in the hostel revolve around drinking alcohol in the pool room, smoking in the building and using the main telephone for personal business. The staff team monitor the residents' rooms for tidiness, which for those who are untidy, results in a letter being sent to them to tidy up. I was always hesitant about this process, recognising the need for boundaries but also reflective on how they were enforced. Whilst hygiene is an issue, many residents struggle with the concept, and need support to understand its importance as part of their emotional growth. This should be part of a therapeutic engagement, so they find a meaning in the wider world. Policing the rules in the hostel within a psychotherapeutic milieu requires reflection. Therefore taking cues from the long term rehabs as therapeutic models could help ground the adherence to boundaries within these wet hostels. However the main differences are the punishment regimes for infraction. The wet hostel has to operate in a far wider mode of flexibility. The Hostel Manager and his team had those skills.

There is a pool table downstairs where people can also watch TV and access a computer. There is also a TV room on the first floor where the canteen is situated. Two meals are provided each day, breakfast and dinner; the residents also receive free food from Prêt a Manger and Japanese Sushi Bar. This provides their main nutrition, and the diets need to reflect the various nutritional needs of the clients derived from the health problems people have experienced on the street. Those with hepatitis, cancer and HIV all need special diets, based less on red meat, than on white meat and vegetables. The canteen was another flash point with people perceiving the food as "prison grub." The portions were deemed too small, the food not of sufficient quality and lacking in variety. These were constant complaints.

The whole notion of making a service Psychologically Informed is far wider than just employing a counsellor to deliver therapy; it entails a complete rethink of the whole purpose of having homeless services and redefining their purpose and rationale. Building design is crucial, because some safe therapeutic spaces need to be created to provide an appropriate healing environment. In my therapeutic work I note the nature of social class informing the forms of environment created for clients. Within my Harley St. Practice there are sumptuous rooms with air conditioning and relaxing chairs. Where I attend supervision it is less aesthetically desirable than Harley St. but the rooms are quiet, the chairs are comfortable and the space welcoming, a form of middle class environment. At the hostel the work takes place in a surgery where the chairs are basic, sound leaks in from people shouting outside. However at least it is a room we can shut off for an hour or more. It is an environment reflecting the homeless world.

The building used at Orexis, the social enterprise I established in Lewisham was purposely refurbished to ensure there were numerous therapeutic spaces and the degree of comfort aimed to ease the therapeutic relationship. Whilst not as ostentatious as Harley St. in design and sumptuousness this would have militated against the client group we were working with, it was a welcoming environment. The building and room design has to be commensurate with this notion of easing the therapeutic relationship. Having a client on the management committee helped this process as he provided input.

Familial violence and the severance of early attachment relationships marks the lives of homeless men, in particular the relationship between sons and fathers, and an issue which became more apparent, violence between mothers and sons. Emotional trauma as a precursor to homelessness is the crucial issue. The increasing tendency to ally trauma and socio-biology is eschewed, as these men showed they had empathy even though it was not initially apparent when they first arrived at the hostel. They needed an "enlightened witness" (Miller 2001) to bring it out. They did not suffer from damaged brains, but defensive psychologies, as the institutions acting upon them could not envisage a process of change (Goffman 1963). These institutions kept them locked in their roles, through applying discipline and power. It is my contention most people exist in a state of emotional flux over their lifespan. Emotional difficulties ebb and flow according to what happens within everyday living, there is no fixation. Bereavement will affect everyone at some stage of their life and those who have empathic connections between those who have deceased and those who survive them will bring significant changes in their brain chemistry. Relationship breakdown will impact, as people cope with the racket feelings from their childhood events. The deterministic use of the attachment model seeks to reify institutional practices that build on discipline and command structures, as it is applied to poor people, without seeing it as a model that applies to all of us.

Public Schools which send a majority of pupils to Oxford and Cambridge are seemingly the social pinnacle, but there is another shadow to this perception when the therapist works through the layers. They inculcate a particular pedagogy based upon emotional suppression. When corporal punishment was rife, this was used extensively to discipline and punish young people. The discourses presuppose the pedagogy of public school is beneficial because of the eventual positive economic outcome. What it fails to review is the type of regimes that were initiated in these schools. These forced young people to escape into dream worlds to negate the effects of the real one. This became their vehicle for adult success but at an emotional cost.

Socio biological explanations are deterministic and lock the subject into a particular discourse, where they are trapped within a biological philosophical prison. This presupposes that people cannot change and live different patterns. This is patently untrue and the discourse of emotional brain damage being touted as an explanation for the entrapment of the poor is another power discourse (Foucault 1972), a habitus (Bourdieu 1984) created to define the included from the "other" (Sartre 1943). It is a form of delusion, because as these case histories highlight, not all of these men are from the poor backgrounds. The notion of the feckless degenerate poor, dominates the conceptual thinking of the included. These case histories highlight a set number of performances initiated for the onlooker, in a charade of middle class manners that hides various forms of child abuse. Because people, sit on various committees and play roles of decency, this does not mean they are decent. It just means they can act the role. The significant problem within the homeless field are the various types of expectations cast onto the "other" (Sartre 1943), and the forms of labelling that take place. These have real effects. It alienates the men from being supported.

"Thus the complex professional remedial tools have come to justify the professional power to define the need—to decide not only the appropriate remedy but the definitions of the problem itself."

Illich I. (2005) P84 "Disabling Professions,"

It could be argued the different professions have moved into homelessness to carve out niches of explanatory power when it received an increase in funding. They have used the opportunity to colonise the arena, claiming a special remit based on non robust research evidence justifying their particular form of intervention. Talking to the homeless people about their past is not deemed as relevant, as they are already provided with various scientific labels.

Therapy could be construed as another intervention, except it has another key difference to the others. It engages with the homeless person to ascertain how they have constructed their meaning. It does not pronounce onto them, as it focuses on building trust to create a joint venture. This provides the entrance into a shrouded world where the effects of the past have been closed off.

This is the key issue that informs the psychological interventions and defines their role. The notion of trauma being an issue within the homeless population is a relatively new discourse. Previous discourses focusing on why people become homeless have related to issues of mental health, genetic, feckless and criminal. At other times it has been seen as a romantic aspiration, a chosen lifestyle. Whilst these elements combined within the role of being homeless the fundamental issues have remained silent. Silence has helped men to cope with the effects of institutions. Many have been victims of child abuse when they were younger, and this was undertaken systematically within institutional settings. Feelings resonant from childhood are projected onto all institutions and barriers have been created. These barriers are necessary for survival, as they are the dictums formed to ward off further emotional pain. Institutions (Goffman 1963) working with these men have noted their responses to help is sometimes grudging, without thanks and in some cases hostile. This has fed back into the perception homeless people are different to the mainstream population, through their behavioural displays of aggression. On other occasions the thanks can be effusive, and it marks a real breakthrough, as they appreciate the lengths to which people have put themselves through to support them.

Therapeutic Environments

The work was undertaken over two days, as the first part of the morning entailed liaising with project workers, then undertaking outreach with the clients in the corridors and across the front counter. This creates the appointment slots for each day.

The therapy was undertaken in two confidential rooms, the surgery and a larger meeting room. Neither was ideal for therapy, as both represented a makeshift quality; however both were secure and quiet. Generally I aimed to time the sessions between 50 mins and an hour. Sometimes due to the complexity, a session lasted up to two hours, and on other occasions, judging the fragility of the client it lasted 10—30 minutes. The sessions underwent a particular process, as I worked to ground the client in the latter stages of the session, so they could return to the hostel environment without being traumatised. I would also need to take breathers between each session, as I felt drained by the levels of concentration and the energy taken out of me. I would often be physically drained at the end of the day, and learnt to rejuvenate myself by joining a swimming club, to act as a refresher before going home. The work is enjoyable because of the progress made, but it is also emotionally and bodily demanding, particularly the attention levels needed to follow the client. With the clients who lacked structure around time, this was gradually introduced into the relationship to build on any inherent fragility. The room did militate to some extent against the counselling, and Rickie remarked on in the incongruity of talking intimately about his personal life, whilst facing a picture of someone demonstrating safer injecting practices, standing naked in front of him.

The therapy needed to be flexible, because it was competing against the chaos of unstructured lives, and more importantly the demands imposed by upholding a self medication strategy. It was also competing against the history of past interventions by authority figures and institutions. The self-medication strategy is more important than everything else in these men's lives. Families, children, food, warmth, light, heat and therapy are all secondary. In my ability to engage, where all the other connections had been severed, I tested my abilities.

Along with the self medication strategy, there arose a number of other competing pressures; the long list of appointments homeless people have to attend to deal with their health and benefits including court, probation, resettlement, substance use and their friendships. I would see on average 8-11 men over two days, for four years. As the process began to be embedded, more people knocked on the door, and the maximum I saw in one day was seven, and there was one day in four years when I saw no one.

It is from the small talk that bigger talk emerges. Small talk involves discussing current events such as news, football scores, talking about music or films. These are the cross cultural intersections that help to make connection. It is through sharing these forms of information the men make the decision of making a connection. This highlights the reality of therapy, as opposed to the machine rhythms envisaged by the bureaucracy.

Evidence Based Relational Methodology in Action

"The difference between psychosocial interventions for problem substance misuse and formal psychological therapies targeting a client's co-morbid mental health problems is that the latter interventions are specialist psychological treatments (such as cognitive-behaviour therapy for depression or anxiety, cognitive-analytic therapy, dialectical behaviour therapy, or schema-focused therapy for personality disorders) aimed primarily at the non-drug psychological problem. Such interventions should only be delivered by specialist practitioners such as clinical and counselling psychologists, suitably trained psychiatric staff or other specialist therapists with relevant training, qualifications and supervision in the therapy model being offered. This would be delivered as part of the care plan but would not constitute a "structured psychosocial intervention" for problem drug use itself.

NTA (2006) "Models of Care for Treatment of Adult Drug Users," www.nta. nhs.uk/uploads/nta_modelsofcare_update_2006_moc3.pdf

"The 'apparent' world is the only one: the real world has been lyingly added . . . .

Nietzsche F (1895) P46 "Twilight of the Idols"

The NHS is fixated on CBT and its offshoots, these are replete with paperwork. This is another straightjacket devised by academia, imposing its machine world to compose order from emotional chaos. It has been "lyingly added." The past as these case histories show cannot be wished away with meditation or creating positive messages. The "steel bath" (Lerner 2003) has to be entered by those who are emotionally strong enough, to face the abyss of meaningless that shrouds these men's lives. Substance use is intertwined with trauma and cannot be neatly separated into scientific components. This is a fallacy of therapy as a mechanistic discourse. The human emotional range has been reduced to a set of machine cogs.

The real work however is undertaken through improvisation and adaptation to individual needs. This is why Individual Psychotherapy is crucial. These case histories outline the emotional realties from sitting down and talking to the homeless men about their lives. Validation of these accounts in terms of a synopsis, of who was seen and the main themes were provided to the hostel manager at the end of each day and discussed in supervision with a clinical psychotherapeutic supervisor, twice per month. Reports were also written on the work once a year and these were circulated within the hostel with the men's details being changed. These following case histories are disclosed anonymously, with names, dates, ages, numbers of children and places all changed. Some of them appeared in a briefer form in the attachment journal (Whittington 2011). I have represented other facets of the relationship that highlights a wider spectrum. They are based upon building relationships to shift beyond the 'front' to connect to what has been 'masked' (Whittington 2007). This moves beyond normative Sociological method, which insists on codifying social interaction in a form of mechanics, to understand the emotional resonances contained within language, the thought and feelings that create the song rather than a depiction of the notes.

Case History 1; I only wanted to be loved

Ron was a 63 year old man who had been in prison for fifteen years consisting of numerous short sentences and two long ones. Emerging each time to return to the streets, he had spent ten years sleeping rough, the rest of the time was spent in institutions. He had been caught in this spiral since the breakup of his marriage when he was 28. He had been entrapped for 35 years.

He related the catalyst for his self destruction was finding his wife in bed with another man when returning home from work. In the first session, he felt justified in his anger in attacking the man, asking me what I would have done.

He beat the man to near death in front of his two young daughters, who watched the violence. He recollected they were terrified as they entered the room, as they heard the screams. He was angry, each week he would return to this incident and repeat it. This was his choice, an incident that haunted him, and he could not shake it out of his head. He was trapped within Post Traumatic Stress. As he explored his life, it appeared this relationship was the only piece of stability he had ever known. His life prior to the marriage was chaos, and his life after the split was turmoil. At first he expressed bitterness over the man in the bed who had destroyed his life. He also felt aggrieved over the betrayal of his wife, blaming her for the split, pushing him to act in front of his children. He asked me "Why had this man had done this to him?" "What was she doing?" "She was nothing more than a slut?"

Ron initially portrayed himself as a victim. At first I listened sensing the inherent fragility of his position. I did not say anything to push him to look at the dynamic, as it was extremely raw. Ron was creating a narrative for his life where he had been victimised at some point and still perceived himself as forever under attack. It was clear in this account that he repeated over eight weeks, that he was the protagonist but had recreated himself into the wronged man; he was the one who had been cheated upon. There was no other way of working with Ron. He was stuck in this scenario, and this was the first time he had spoken to anyone about it. The idea of doing six structured sessions would not allow time to engage with his incoherent rage.

It was after we had created a bond, I asked him how his daughters reacted. Then we began to shift from the continuous repetition. He looked startled, and then began to cry for 40 minutes. He let out huge, heaving sobs. I spent the rest of the time sitting with him, as the racket feelings of the past rose in waves. I handed him numerous tissues to help him mop up the sobs. The hard man had dissolved of his own volition. At last we were getting beyond the "front." I felt trepidation for him, because he was caught in a double bind (Laing 1960, 1961, 1964). His lifestyle was killing him, but returning to the past was traumatic. He could not shake it out of his head. It was clear he was self medicating for the past, and that he was trapped in trauma.

After 50 minutes he became calmer as I gently switched the topic, to try and rebuild him. At the end of our session, he had to return to the hostel. Therefore, I had to ground him in the present, to bring him back out of the past. It was clear he had no sense of purpose and failed to embrace the present, except to satiate his immediate alcohol needs.

The next session he told me;

"I never spoke to her again. The only time we communicated, was when I received the divorce papers in prison."

Ron couched himself as the victim again, the open door had closed, but he had opened it briefly, for the first time. Glimpsing his role as a perpetrator created an immense reaction. He began to shatter under the impact. He only viewed his actions as someone responding to an attack, not someone initiating violence. I was unsure who he was crying over, his children or himself as a child. Drawing from experience I had more than an intuition where the feelings of victimisation stemmed from. Trying to steer him away from the incident which haunted him, I asked him about his earlier life and what had happened.

Recounting his early life, his anger began to rise again and then subside. Ron stated he was from a travelling family. They worked on the fairground. As far as he could remember his recollection of his father was violence. The man was extremely aggressive, and he described him as "knocking his mother around." When it was happening he felt one day, he was going to put a stop to it, but he was physically incapable of taking him on. As they travelled, he never had a stable schooling. He was being reared to take his place within his family, as a copy of his father. The violence was continuous as he grew up. His father was always beating his mother. He described his fright, his incontinence, and his feelings of being under a cloud of fear. The violence was a lead weight that oppressed him as he felt helpless. He described his father's rages as he was lashed with a leather belt. As the eldest boy, he received the violence first, and then it cascaded onto the others. When his father finished, the family was a mixture of tears, bruises and screaming. No one dared challenge him and everyone lived in a state of perpetual fear.

He was 17, he had grown and he did not feel as vulnerable. He described feeling different, being on the verge of early manhood. He no longer felt like a child, someone who was vulnerable. Instead, he felt as though he should stop his father the next time the violence erupted. He had vowed to end it as a child, but was too frightened to act. He recollected his father returned home drunk from the pub and went to hit his mother. She ran away from him, Ron and his father left in the room. He remembered his father sneering at him. Ron waited until he turned around and then smashed him on the back of the head with a full beer bottle, knocking him over. He then kicked him repeatedly in the head until he became unconscious.

"I thought I'd killed him. I wouldn't have been bothered if I had"

Ironically that was when the violence stopped. His mother returned and pulled Ron off from beating his father, otherwise he said, he would have continued to beat him until he killed him. His brothers and sisters never entered the room. His mother found a pulse and found he was still breathing. She told Ron to get out, and then she sat crying, as she attended to her husband's injuries.

"What happened?"

"I cleaned up and went to the pub."

The violence in the house ceased, when Ron had overcome his father. This marked the latter's descent, and his ascent. Ron was already seeing a young woman he had met. She was his sweet heart, everything opposite from his family. The atmosphere in the house was uneasy, as Ron still stayed there after the incident.

"What was it like?"

"Strange looking back, very strange, he kept out of the way. We never really saw him. I went to work and did some bricklaying but I wanted to move out. There were too many of us trapped in a small space. My other brothers all became alcoholics, there are six of them who drank, three of them are dead, all my sisters are divorced, and we are a mess."

The dynamics of the violence follows a pattern, constantly re-emerging within the numerous accounts over the years. The violent, paranoiac, father vandalises his family, cowering everyone into submission through anger and beatings. The woman stays with the man through fear. In the 1950's she had nowhere to go. Her family could not look after her, because they had no money or resources to support their daughter. At the time, there were no refuges. The masculine culture allowed a man to dominate a woman. If the children had been taken and put into a "home," the outcome could hardly be considered an improvement. There are numerous other men in the hostel who experienced extensive violence in the children's homes. These families were trapped in the double bind (Laing 1960, 1961, 1964) of gender roles and economic straits, and then finally wrapped in cultural expectations. It was a mind prison.

The attack destroyed the psychological hold by undermining the physical prowess of his father. Ron had described his ability to wield and enact violence at school, the fairground and the pub prior to the attack. Ron had a previous reputation as a street fighter. He had no fear in the outside world, but was terrified at home. The violence within the home was externalised into the wider society, enmeshing with a wider culture of masculine violence. Other boys who had been beaten within their families were also externalising their violence. This created the masculine culture they inhabited, where a slight would be avenged by violence. Ron needed to expend his energy to defuse the racket feelings of familial humiliation. This was kept as a secret. Those who existed outside the family could only view the man from the front, not from within.

Although Ron beat and attacked his father, the hatred still brimmed over. Years later, Ron was tortured alive by the various incidents. He was still trapped within them, as he recounted his early life. Clearly, he was still suffering, and he needed his memories to be validated and externalised. He recounted an incident after his father died. He went to his grave and poured a beer over it, then urinated onto the gravestone to wash it all down. The act of defilement marked the bitterness and anger that seethed within. It was this anger that he had held onto throughout his life, as he pushed everyone away. This created further attachment severance and led to further self medication.

"He liked a drink, so I gave him a drink, and then gave him something to wash it down with. He was a horrible bastard."

Ron had endured endemic violence. He was emotionally shattered by his childhood and adolescence. As an adult, he tried to overcome it, and then later adopted a self medication strategy to cope with its effects. It haunted him, and once the story emerged, he could not keep his masculine silence. He would stand at the front counter in the hostel, crying in front of everyone, telling the hostel staff about what had happened to him when he was a child. The emotional gates had been opened, and Ron's dammed past rose like a torrent. It drowned the present in waves of regret.

The attachment bonds within his family were shattered by the rages and violence. His mother, although he idolised her, had little time to spare. She was in a constant state of childbirth or nursing when he was growing up. There were 11 children who survived; all, as we worked through the genealogy, had issues with alcohol or mental health. She could offer support at a distance, as she was constantly under stress from the violence. This negated the support she could provide. It appeared his father wanted to isolate his children from any form of emotional support and to exist only within his shadow. His sense of fragility entailed him annihilating his children's self esteem, turning them into copies of him.

Ron had one attachment bond that acted as a lifeline, his relationship with his girlfriend. This allowed him to build a platform of stability away from the family. He met her at 15. He married young and escaped the family dynamics when he was 17, just after the fight. He went into raptures when describing his wedding day. It was the best day of his life; he achieved his dream of marrying his childhood sweetheart, now he could begin again. He viewed it as a new chance to wipe the slate clean. He stopped drinking and there was a period of stability.

Problems gradually surfaced when his wife became pregnant, then the dynamics of the relationship shifted irrevocably. She no longer had the energy to go out, she was tired and he could not understand these changes. He described their sex life as altering; he began to feel left out. Unable to understand what was happening, he would disappear to the pub. When his child was born, these feelings of ostracism became even worse. He described feeling jealous of his child but could not understand why. This highlights an enormous problem for men who had their early attachments severed when young. They can escape the effects through finding an "enlightened witness" (Miller 2001) someone they can build trust with. The problems surface when this becomes ruptured, then the old racket feelings begins to emerge again. Ron felt as though he was being pushed away. He was not emotionally equipped to look after children. He described his sense of unfolding isolation.

"It was as if she no longer needed me apart from handing over the money."

Ron felt alienated from his new family and now felt used. He spent more time in the pub drinking, and then returning home in a rage. Ron was turning into his father. The rows started, Ron did not feel wanted, so he verbally attacked her, thinking she was seeing someone else. Eventually the rages shifted from verbal to becoming physical. She only had sex with him when he forced her. Ron started crying again. As Ron recollected, he revealed the various narratives he had constructed, to fend off the reality of his actions. It was then the dynamics became clear. As he attacked her, he became filled with remorse. He would seek forgiveness and then go off to the pub to drown his regret. Returning home filled with rage, the problems would reoccur. It was a continuous cycle of suppressed emotions and rage.

As he recollected his experiences, he realised he drove her away, as he felt he was no longer "good enough," for her. He needed his wife, but could not connect with her. He could not show his need, because this would undermine his sense of masculine identity. This was built on being aggressive and strong, another double bind (Laing 1960, 1961, 1964) that entrapped him. He was caught in various emotional knots (Laing 1971). His sense of identity was equated with being strong. It was an immense conundrum for Ron, as he became tied in more emotional knots. This entailed him wrestling with love, need, distance, violence and lust. This became enwrapped in his traumatic past. He also became caught in a twin cycle of violence and guilt. He resolved these tensions by self medicating everything away. This had the effect of creating further distance between him and his partner. He sought solace in the pub, firstly drowning then fuelling his anger. This was the dialectic of pain and anger that tore his stability apart. He realised she sought the love that he could no longer give, because he was paranoid that he was unlovable. His actions confirmed this.

We worked together to try and draw the pieces of his life together delving deeper into the problems with this relationship. During the sessions, Ron would turn up intoxicated, sometimes incontinent, and then we had to abandon the session.

After his divorce, Ron had hung onto his status as a hard man. He had an extensive history of confronting authority figures in prison, in hostels and on the street. He had been excluded from numerous hostels for violence. He had killed someone in another statutory building over a disagreement, resulting in a charge that involved manslaughter. This was later deemed as self defence, but he was remanded, spending time in prison whilst the case went to trial.

We worked together for over two years, and at one point, for the first time in his life he was on the verge of making a momentous change. He went into detox and gained community care funding to go to a rehab. The work we had taken had paid off. He was in the detox awaiting his rehab slot when they informed the money had been rescinded. The energy he had galvanised to make the effort dissipated. Ron felt the authorities who he had trusted had let him down again. His self coping reaction returned to deal with the loss; he went off to the off licence and drank himself into oblivion. Turning up at the hostel swaying from side to side he screamed;

"They took the piss out of me."

Ron felt that he had been set up to fail, it was all a big joke played on him, setting him up to think he could change. Then at the last minute it was all swiped away and he was left to fall. It later transpired it was a bureaucratic mistake. They called him back to complete the detox and rehab, but it was too late. A brief window had been opened; Ron decided to take the plunge, and then he believed he had been ridiculed. It brought back all his fears, he was changing at 63, but who would he become, what would he have to face? He

161

had an internalised message that everything would always go wrong. This was his life script, and this miscommunication helped him to replay this message. It was the story of his life, why would it change now? This details how the decisions to change need emotionally literate bureaucracies.

Ron lived off this story, detailing the mistake and how he nearly got there, but slipped back to his old ways at the last minute. We worked together as a team to try and put some boundaries in place, to rebuild the fragments, but he had collapsed internally. The energy he had gathered together had dissolved. He seeped into a big puddle of alcohol and incontinence. This demarcates how the numerous remits involved in care, fail to inter connect. It needs someone to make the decision and then to enact it. The numerous tiers do not communicate. The practitioner should be in charge of the decision making processes as they build the psychological ladders.

Ron pressed the self destruct button. If the process had been managed in-house, this could have been easily navigated. There were too many people involved in his "care" and each person had to be convinced of his desire to change. Ron felt vulnerable having to attend the different meetings and tell everyone his life story. This entailed him having to relate the confidential events he had confided to me then being communicated to others who were not part of the hostel milieu. Narrating his life story to strangers, especially people who represented the authorities was a significant challenge for him. He stated they never helped him when he lived on the streets.

Instead, he gradually returned back to the street. Sitting outside the hostel, drinking cider, he made some indecent remarks whilst intoxicated, to a young girl walking past. The nature of the remarks and their emotional cruelty resulted in a management ultimatum to either attend the rehab or return to the street. Ron out of spite said he would rather return to the street. When he felt he was being pressurised he would put up a masculine resistance. The hostels hands were tied, as Ron had broken the bonds of social interest (Adler 1931) by denigrating a young girl, the act of a bully, the return of his father (Whittington 2011). Ron lost his vision of the future, as he did not feel worthy of it. He later accessed a B&B, but the problems relating to his forensic history, entailed few, if any, organisations would work with him. He now lives alone, having driven everyone away.

Ron had built a resistance to the outside world based on anger and alcohol. This fended everyone off. The therapy helped to dissolve these presentations. It allowed him to view them as "roles" he inhabited. These arose as fronts of self protection. Seeing them was one significant step forward, dismantling them was another. He needed to know how he was going to make the change, and what he was going to change into. This marks the resistance to being coerced to change. Ron would never respond to enforced therapy. Given the options between being forced to doing something for their own benefit; many men will resist. It is the only shred of respect men like Ron can hold onto. Ron had transgressed the rules and they had to be enforced. This was for the greater interest, as the social interest (Adler 1931) involves balancing individual needs with those of the wider community. His remarks could have resulted in a criminal prosecution, instead the rehousing team were contacted, and Ron was eventually found alternative accommodation. He lives by himself isolated.

Ron's life story marks the intricate complexities of how violence weaves into family life and destroys the self esteem of children. It also highlights how someone desperate not to repeat the dynamics in his relationship, is drawn back to repeat the same dynamics. Torn by emotions that are unarticulated; jealous of his children, he remains silent about his emotional world. As the case studies highlight, this becomes a powerful unspoken conundrum in relationships. This drives men and women apart because men cannot communicate and women cannot decipher. Attachment severance as previously highlighted (Whittington 2007) arises from jealousy when the children are born. Women are unable to see beyond the front men have created. These are acts of camouflage stopping anyone penetrating beyond this facade. As he said to me towards the end

"All I ever wanted is to be loved."

Case History 2; Only Making Plans for Jamie

The standard view of the social world is that homeless people are products of the underclass, people from the social housing estates. Within the hostel the homeless populations were derived from a mixture of social backgrounds, some men were from poor families and others were from affluent families. Jamey came from an affluent family. What he had in common with the residents who grew up in impoverished families are the levels of violence inflicted upon him. Violence is often perceived as an issue occurring within poorer families, but as these case histories show, this is a problem that cascades throughout all of the social classes. The autobiographies of Leaf Fielding (2011) and Andrew Motion (2007) provide an insight into the violence inflicted by public school institutions and the coldness of middle class families. They are constrained by emotional strictures that are passed through the generations as currents of emotional coldness.

Jamey came into the hostel, and began to interact with the therapy from the second week he moved in. He was open from the beginning, in talking about his family background. He came from a county family, and had run away from them, along with his older brother, when he was 14. Up until this point he had been living with his father who was the epitome, outwardly at least, of decorum within the local community. His father sat on the all the local committees in his village and was seen as someone who was a pillar of the infrastructure, outwardly upright. He also ran a local business that was a sizeable employer. This provided him with a significant amount of social capital (Halpern 2004) as well as economic capital.

Both sons had fled in their teenage years leaving their father alone. They had run off to join the circus, as it provided an escape from the seeming tedium of life in their town. This appeared to be the case from observing the situation outside the family, as Jamey recounted. He said people saw us as two odd boys, because our father seemed such a decent person. His mother had left the family first, when he was around three years old. She ran away to live in a poor part of town. Jamey recounted how he had hated her for leaving him and his brother alone with their father. They were subsequently deemed odd, because their actions as wilful rebels, seemed to be undermine their father's outwardly cultivated image.

His father to the outside world, exuded a badge of respectability, at home Jamey described a violent bully, who beat both his boys with fists and canes. He later enacted customised punishment regimes until they both screamed and bled with internal pain. This took place from the time his mother left, until they finally ran away together to join the circus. Attachment was severed through neglect and violence. The situation for the boys become more problematic because of the awe his father was held within, in the local community. No one could understand the discrepancy between this seemingly cultivated man, and these two ungrateful, wild, and untamed, boys.

As they grew older, Jamey recounted how the beatings increased in ferocity and frequency. The physical violence took place until they went to Secondary School, then it changed. To keep the silence, they were both threatened with further violence if they told anyone about the beatings. They were also told it was for their own long-term benefit. Jamey revealed he lived within constant state of fear throughout his life, unable to sleep properly as many of the attacks were undertaken whilst he and his brother were asleep. He was also incontinent, until his teenage years, ensuring he was disciplined for this lapse in decorum. He was trapped in a constant double bind of fear and retribution (Laing 1960, 1961, 1964). It was also a constant cycle of violence and humiliation, as he recounted the family dynamics. Violent outbursts happened two to three times a week. This still had a physical effect on him as an adult, as he described his sleeping pattern as shallow. Years later, he still describes himself as forever alert. Another trigger point for violence was when they were caught watching TV.

"When we were younger we would be watching TV and he would come in, then start shouting and screaming about us wasting time."

"He would go into his cupboard and bring out his cane and start whacking us across the legs and face, if he had the chance. He would drive us up to our rooms, chasing us up the stairs. This was when he was in a rage. Other times he would line us both up, and then we would take it in turns to be beaten. When you're that age and someone is screaming at you, that you're useless and stupid, you don't think they are wrong. OK, I felt humiliated with the beatings, but it was the lying, that's what got me. He lied in order to beat us. That is why I hated him. There was no reason."

The local Primary School was in the same village and the marks on the legs and arms were visible. Jamey recollected these were explained away as young boys playing rough and tumble. No one seemingly suspected the local dignitary, the man who single-handedly decided to look after his two young boys after his wife had "cruelly deserted him," of abusing his children. It appears any thoughts local people had that the children were in danger, were completely shut down. Instead, they were left to their fate.

Jamey described how he came to accept the violence as being normal, part of growing up, a great unsaid until he went to Secondary School. He felt an internal rage at the injustice which had to be sublimated because it was being undertaken for his long term benefit. The other issue he faced were the dynamics of a closed community, where everyone knew each other. No one challenged his father due to the power he had accrued, sitting on all of the local committees. No one suspected, as he explained all the bruising away, as two boys on various escapades. He adopted a different stance to the village people, than he did at home.

Secondary School brought other problems, as an emotional reality dawned upon him; Jamey recounted sitting in PE, then looking around. He noticed the other boys were not covered in bruises. It was then he realised, his home life was not the norm. Jamey related he became curious how other fathers behaved. He recounted raising the subject with his friends, to try and find out if their dads were as violent as his father. It was through this form of feedback, he began to realise the peculiar circumstances of his family life. He realised his father was abnormal in his care patterns, even by the standards of the 1970's. He came to perceive that not all fathers attacked their sons. It was through gaining this perception he recognised his strategy of stubborn resistance was a response to being bullied. He described the whacks on the outer skin as feeling like stings. He recalled these beatings bolstered his inner resolve to obtain revenge at some point. His brother reacted differently, and Jamey noted these changes, becoming anxious for him.

Jamey became more aggressive, whilst his brother retreated inwardly. He became subservient. His brother was being broken by the violence, mentally and physically. This marked their responses to the dynamics at home. The main attachment bond was between each other. Adler (1956) for example, noted that attachment bonds can form between siblings, as much as between parents. It was this bond that seemingly saved them both from complete mental health collapse.

As they grew into puberty, the physical violence was replaced by a different form. His father must have sensed it was having an opposite effect on Jamey to what he intended, by making him more rebellious. Therefore he used a more invasive technique to break him. He changed his dynamic and mode of operation by putting the boys into "stress positions," forcing them to carry books for hours, standing still, kneeling and other silent postures. He realised his dad had learnt about modern interrogation techniques and was applying them to his children.

This form of torture went beyond the surface of the skin and was aimed to destabilise the mind. Jamey said now he fully understood he was trying to break his children, so they would become compliant, like drones. Pleading and crying had no effect, withdrawal did not invoke pity. Meanwhile, his father expected his sons to work within the family business and take a role in the operations. I asked Jamey, why he was never sent to public school? He replied;

"He did not want to spend any money on us; he wanted to break us himself."

It was through undertaking therapy, he began to realise why his mother had left and not wanted anything in return. He recounted how his father had imposed himself upon the family, wanting total control because of his position. He stated he felt hatred for her for years, because she had abandoned them to their fate. He felt she should have returned and saved them. Looking back, he realised she was in a hopeless situation. His father had married beneath his social class, a very beautiful woman. It appeared she could take no more put-downs from him. She left him to return to penury.

"That," Jamey said, "spoke volumes of the type of relationship they had. She had been swept off her feet by his attention and wealth, but it was only three or so years, after having two children, she decided she would rather abandon them than stay with him. He had probably forced her to abandon us"

In exploring if he had any "enlightened witness" (Miller 2001) validate him, Jamey recalled how he had told a school friend about what was occurring at home. He felt he needed to tell someone, because it provided an outlet, a release from the tension building inside him. He swore his friend to secrecy. He recollected he felt trapped at the time, and was self harming. Sent to a psychiatrist by the school, he kept quiet about home life, fearful the man would breach confidentiality. Jamey was suffering from acute anger and it emerged in his behaviour. When this emerged, this was subject to further punishment. Jamey was labelled as troubled, but no one was taking the time to explore how this had emerged. There were no tools at the time to gauge his behaviour. At the time, Schools had minimal emotional literacy. They worked on a particular hormonal model of young people, equating their recalcitrant behaviour with their puberty.

Another outlet for expelling his sense of injustice emerged in petty crime. As a teenager, he disclosed he stole from shops and smashed up telephone boxes, but no one ever asked why. He was forced to pay fines and his father would punish him. Jamey said it was his way of undermining his father's prestige in the local community, as he could not articulate what was occurring at home. No one would believe him if he expressed it verbally. This highlights a key emerging issue within this work, the levels of emotional literacy in the 1970's. No one was able to decode the behaviour and instead applied labels as an ungrateful, errant, son. People began to sympathise with his father about his plight, struggling to look after his boys. Instead of seeing a bully, the onlooker only saw a man who needed to instil more discipline onto his two aberrant boys. Jamey recollects people goading him to enact more structure to keep them both in order.

They found solace with his father's mother, who provided some form of protection from her son, but she was not strong enough to stop him from attacking his children. Eventually they created an escape plan to run away to the circus and leave their father. This lifeline out of their environment became their saviour. Jamey had found a meaning and purpose in an itinerant lifestyle, an escape from their middle class upbringing. Finally they both chose a day to leave and Jamey revealed the exhilaration in finding freedom from constraint. The exhilaration he would never have to return to his family home filled him, as he ventured out into the wider world with his brother by his side.

This was 3 decades ago. Jamey had a golden period for a number of years with relationships and travel. It was when his brother died 10 years previously from cancer; the past began to whirl towards him. Jamey nursed him during his illness. The cumulative effects of the past began to arise, as he watched his brother wither away. This had a devastating effect. The closest attachment he had to the world dissolved. After his brother's death, Jamey described his trauma, a descent into meaninglessness that was rescued only by his heroin use. This helped to seal off the past and the terrible feelings that nothing was worth it. He drifted, lost his desire to live, existing only to self medicate. Eventually he dropped out of the itinerant lifestyle and became street homeless. He had become the reverse image of his father's dream, the product of being beaten into violence. His self esteem and belief were shattered.

My role within the therapeutic relationship was to validate Jamey's experiences and provide a release, through allowing him to articulate the trauma. I was an enlightened witness (Miller 2001). Validation is crucial for people in gaining the ability to move forward. The punishments he endured were accompanied by threats, curses and vitriol about the worthlessness of both him and his brother. These lay as silent commands from the critical parent. The two boys had been objectified. His father sounded as if his status achievements were his main form of validation. He could not build attachment and instead, needed to construct objects that existed only within his shadow. Listening to Jamey, it appeared he was still trapped in an ongoing psychological crisis. His father seemingly re-enacted his own upbringing on his own children, driving them away from him. Remarkably he still kept up the pretence of appearances to the outside world. I asked Jamey whether he searched for his sons. Jamey said that they buried themselves so deep away from him, so scared of being returned to him, they ensured he would never find them. It appeared the father had shifted the discourse onto his errant sons who were deemed; never any good. This scenario had been ongoing for 3 decades with no word on whether they were dead or alive.

Jamey stated he did not want anything to do with his father when I suggested writing to him to open up a dialogue about the effects of the past, as a healing process. He stated firmly, that his father would never change his behaviour. He was such a sadist at home but with a remarkable ability to perform a role of charm to the outside world. It was this ability to carry through this discrepancy, this double life that rankled. Jamey was puzzled how he managed to keep up the pretence. It took such energy and why did he need to annihilate his sons?

Jamey rebuilt himself within the hostel but still carried the scars. He self medicated through using heroin and crack to block out the effects. He blamed his father for his brother's death, feeling the stress he had carried, had eventually led to his body breaking down, years later. As he said, he could see it coming all those years before. His brother caved in under his father's regime, the cancer had begun then. These dynamics were extremely painful for him. They had been haunting him since childhood and he had maintained his silence since, as he felt no one would believe him and he could not build the trust.

The homeless population is varied, with people from all over the UK, the Americas, Asia, Europe and Africa. Jamey came from an upper middle class family, a recipient of violence. Violence is not just a pedagogy of the poor. The effects of his childhood were carried into his adulthood as heroin was used to self medicate. Jamey was still trapped by his childhood dynamics never escaping them, and they were still affecting him as an adult. Every day he was drawn back to the past. He obliterated it away. Jamey differed minimally from the other men in the hostel regarding his desire to self medicate. The level of affluence in his family did not save him from being bullied.

There was no one who could rescue him during his childhood as his father was so dominating, no one could step in to contradict him. This amnesia created a blanket around the family dynamics. The PE teacher, when he attended school, never noticed the bruises on his legs and back, his mother remained distant, his grand-parents remained acquiescent and the institutions turned a blind eye. The current substance use services could not make the connections. This reflects the nature of institutional amnesia existing in the 1970's, spreading into the 21st century as children's psychologies were invisible. This has spread to an institutional amnesia about the role of self medication in people's lives.

Case History 3; Beating the Brat

Simon was the product of a middle class family who lived in a small close rural village. He described his family as living in a detached house with a garage. He lived with his mother, father and brother. Simon was now ostracised from all members of his family. He did not want to make contact with them. His younger brother, he disclosed, went on to have a successful professional career when I asked him about his family.

"They were just horrible, really horrible. I don't really want to talk about it, what's the use. What good will it do me?"

He went on to describe having been extensively disciplined by his father from an early age. Initially his mother let it happen; she stood by, but later joined in with the violence. As he grew up he described the violence they enacted as frenzied. He related one incident where they both held him down, whilst his father then ripped off the plastic flexing that held the curtains up and whipped him, whilst his mother pinned him to the floor.

He described how they would come home after going out, and then beat him together. His father then fashioned a special tool out of metal and rubber naming it the "Brat beater". He would drag Simon out to the garage and beat him on the legs and backside. Hitting him on his body ensured the marks were not so visible. Any type of excuse was needed, late home, not doing his homework, being punished at school, watching TV. As they lived in a detached home the dynamics could not be overseen by the neighbours, but as Simon related the levels of violence, they must have heard his screams. No one did anything to intervene. Simon was left to himself. He described himself as undertaking an inward retreat, to protect himself. The levels of violence enacted by both his mother and father alienated him from all forms of support and created an attachment severance. He would often return home late to avoid them and then be beaten all the same.

"They beat me on the outside but they never got me on the inside." He explained.

I asked him what strategies he used to help him cope with the violence, what carried him through when it was happening drawing on Harry Stack Sullivan (Barton Evans 1996). He told me listening to punk rock helped him, as he realised there were other people who felt as angry as him. This belief carried him through the violence. It was through the music scene he made the connections to run away from his family. Simon described the peculiar dynamics of the family as his younger brother was feted. He was not beaten and later went onto university. Meanwhile Simon ran away from home to live in a series of squats from the age of 14.

It was here, he was taken in by a group of people who were creating their own community. They provided him with space and time, so he could try to heal himself. Simon began to talk to them about his home experiences and this also helped him to validate himself. He was able to perceive his family life as abnormal in its provision of care. He was however turned onto drugs in these squats. He smoked Cannabis initially to block out the past and create *euphoria. The people in the squats supported him financially, as he could not sign on. It was here he learnt to beg for money, as he stated he felt guilty about taking things from them, so he began to help out by bringing in some money.*

Since he ran away, he had never spoken to his parents for over twenty years. He had kept quiet about his early family life, since the squatting, until speaking to me in the therapy sessions. Simon was still traumatised. This could be seen in his body posture, as he was stooped and he held a distant gaze. At the hostel he was hooked on alcohol and heroin when I met him. We met each week, but the general options for detox were foreclosed by the employment of a Borough gatekeeper. She refused to process the referrals for treatment. Instead the Borough policy entailed all parties working with a client needing to agree on a joint care plan. This effectively sabotaged any progress, as all agencies involved in someone's care needed to agree on their progress and provide resources. This was a logistical quagmire.

Dutifully we arranged a case conference to try and build a platform for his recovery. Simon had expressed his desire to detox, before he was rehoused. We had been meeting for weeks and he was making significant progress. The case conference required tact and persuasion to get all agencies to agree on a way forward. People had different professional remits and were varied in their psychological awareness. Simon had been in and out of hostels for the past three years with his chronic heroin and alcohol problem. He had kept quiet about his family dynamics with all the other agencies, as he did not trust them. This created a hurdle, as I was privy to more information than everyone else. Therefore it was up to me to convince them, yet I could not divulge his confidential information. These agencies had no awareness of the traumatic background of the clients. This was not taught on their course colleges and neither in their CPD training.

Simon had a relationship and this was violent. This was his only current attachment relationship, and it was a tumultuous mutually violent affair, although he held the ultimate power. Simon related how he was scared, she would leave him alone. I pointed out to him, hitting her would drive her away. No woman wants to be denigrated. He looked shocked, as he reflected on his actions. He was turning into his father.

Simon wanted to go into detox, then rehab with his with his partner, as he did not want to lose her. No local detox would facilitate this, as it created problems in the group work. At the case conference the various assembled agencies commented upon his problematic behaviour, and how it was creating difficulties for his move on. This problematic behaviour related to his alcohol and heroin use. I encouraged Simon to provide a context to his self medication strategy, and how it had affected him psychologically. Given the opportunity, the floodgates suddenly opened, and Simon volleyed his childhood dynamics onto the table. Everyone sat there stunned by what he recounted. No one moved, everyone looked perplexed, the room went silent and within a few minutes the conference ended. Simon was asked to wait outside.

Afterwards people from the agencies sat around trying to reflect on what Simon had recounted. They were shocked, as he spoke for fifteen minutes, in depth about the variety of tortures his parents had inflicted upon him. This was to be a recurrent theme in the various case conferences, as the professionals from Social Services, Housing, Probation, the Drug Services all blanched before the issues of familial violence and trauma. In 2007 there were no cohesive strategies or training days around childhood trauma and substance use in the Borough where I worked. In 2011 having checked it still remains emotionally erased.

The case conference could have built a platform for Simon's recovery. Detox, rehab and being rehoused, linked to training and emotional support, these were the obvious psychological rungs of an escape ladder. Simon needed to break out from his situation. This escape route was not in anyone's brief. There was no inter-departmental collaboration. Each had set targets that needed to be adhered to, and that was all they were focused upon. The conference highlighted the inherent problems of inter-departmental working, as each was trapped within their own modes of working. There was no holistic strategy and no long term vision or sense of purpose coming from the Strategic Services with their interventions.

Each had a particular intervention that needed to be addressed, but there was no one who could conduct the orchestra. Each asked Simon to meet their aims, and thereby ensure he could proceed further with his goal. He identified his aim as wanting to live with his girlfriend in a flat. He wanted to be stable, drug free and requested their help. Their aims did not coincide with his aim.

Simon's partner came from a wealthy family. She had dropped out of a city job to live with him and then descended into substance use. The narrative that people had constructed is that he had a Svengali type hold over her that was entirely negative. She had succumbed to his will and he was a bad influence. I was not sure this was entirely true reflection, as I tentatively broached the subject with him in a therapy session. I had established the first women's service previously and had a different understanding of co-dependent relationships. The dynamics of attachment were paramount in understanding how these relationships were sustained. The women gravitated to men who reminded them of previous issues. They had minimal self esteem and looked to self medicate. I worked with Simon to help him build the relational bridges with her to understand how she was formed. When a dialogue was established it appeared there were significant intersections in their childhood lives.

The agency representatives at the conference saw it as a simple equation, he was bad and she was good. During the case conference, however, she expressed her undying love for Simon and this torpedoed one of the underlying aims, to prise them apart. Instead everyone was left wandering what the next steps were. No one had thought of any contingency plan because the idea that trauma bound them together, creating the desire to jointly self medicate, was not a dynamic any professional could conceptualise. They tried to dangle a flat before Simon if he stopped his co-dependency relationship. This failed to motivate either him or his girlfriend. They still wanted to be together and requested attending a joint detox. This was eventually deemed not feasible.

After the case conference finished, no structure had been agreed and the two continued to operate in emotional chaos. This reflected the institutional chaos, now replicated in the client's lives. A few months later, Simon gained a flat and his partner moved in with him, regardless of what the professionals envisaged. There was no care plan, prior to him moving in. He continued with his alcohol and heroin use in a co-dependent relationship. Last time I spoke to him, he and his partner were begging on the street. He looked sheepish when he saw me. Whilst he had engaged with me to a certain point, we had reached a limit, thwarted by the institutions. I was under a funding threat and the first contract I had at the hostel ran out. In the meantime I worked with him to access an art course. I also gained funding for him, but after I left, there was no one to support him. He was very fragile despite appearances. He dropped out after three weeks. When I returned back to the hostel, he had moved on.

Emotional trauma from an upper middle, and a middle class background both had latent effects on Jamey and Simon (Miller1987). Both were self medicating and both were homeless. In my previous work, Deptford mothers provided the family backbone. In the work with the homeless, the mother in Jamey's family severed her attachment with her two sons. She left them to the caprices of their father. In the second vignette, the mother joined in with the violence. She was an active participant. This role of female violence within the family is a significant difference between the men who lived with their mothers in Deptford. Although female violence did arise, mothers generally provided support and nurture. They tried to protect their families, operating under threat from their husbands. The significant difference between the men who accessed the treatment services in Deptford, as noted in "Beaten into Violence," (Whittington 2007) and the homeless men in this hostel, were the reported levels of violence enacted by their mothers.

Further problems occur when then these issues are articulated in case conferences. As no one has the training or knowledge to understand what is being expressed, the professionals back off. This leaves a vacuum, as no one appears to have a remit. The therapist needs to be given the kudos to work with the problem and the other agencies to act as adjuncts. Confidentiality needs to be carefully constructed with the client and the outside agencies. There is a huge learning deficit as the outside agencies are unaware of the psychological dynamics of these men's lives. This can only be undertaken through a massive re-training programme.

The case conference needed leadership and direction. It lost focus because the participants were unable to conceptualise the links between trauma and substance use, in particular the impact of attachment severance. The levels of violence Simon disclosed created an emotional shutdown amongst the participants. This reflects the overall leadership shutdown. This highlights how the institutional guidance affects the psychology of the people who deliver services on the ground. This guidance has a surge effect, the currents of institutional power cascades downwards through the tiers onto the ground. Understanding violence as an enactment of those tasked with care, is a major omission by care services. The inadequacies of the leadership, in this case not just homelessness/ housing but also mental health, substance use and probation are translated into real impacts when working with complex emotional dynamics. The conceptual language is absent and this leads to different facets of emotional paralysis, as people retreat into their performed roles. This creates a barrier for change, as agencies cite budget constraints. None of the people round the table knew how to react when Simon disclosed the familial violence he endured as a child. They were clearly uneasy and then they looked to me for guidance. I suggested they needed to work out a collective care plan that would allow everyone to add their input, but each stated they would need to refer to their manager and consult their budgets. No one returned with any plan. Simon later told me, he thought it was a waste of time. They were more concerned in breaking up his relationship than helping him to get better. This perception was correct. Although he did say he felt better in getting his past out of his system, then seeing everyone look aghast. He said he did not realise it would have that effect, and queried why they did not offer him any help.

There was a distinct institutional malaise when a window of opportunity arose. This is because there were too many people involved in Simon's care. In effect, it meant no one took control. It appeared to an outsider everyone had a stake in keeping him in a form of stasis. The main problem was the lack of emotional intelligence and the clear inability to understand what was being articulated. The second issue was the inability to react to his emotional narrative. Everyone backed away in fear. This vignette represents a wider malaise within these institutions and is an archetype rather than a "one-off."

Case History 4; Attack!

The institutional revenge theme became more acute when I worked with Jerry, as the stifling remits of the different professions and their various defensive projections were revealed during another Borough case conference.

Gerry was a white male from Glasgow in his mid 30's. Shaven head, covered in tattoos, he had previously resisted all attempts to engage him in any form of interaction, with any member of staff for months. He never spoke to any staff members, except to bark commands. He had been cited by a number of residents for bullying; attacking them for money, but nothing could be proved. He refused to go onto a Methadone script and seemingly gained his money, through extorting finances from people inside and outside the hostel. This allowed him to self medicate.

I worked with him, through small conversations to build up a rapport. I asked him what religion he was, and where he grew up. He was taken aback at my audacity. I told him I had lived there, so I understood the dynamics. This meant I went up in the world, and he asked me what religion I was, and I went back down again. The ice however had been broken. We began to talk about football, and the areas we both knew. This style of interaction lowered his resistance.

Eventually we decided to meet once a week in the counselling room, just to help him offload and talk about life in Glasgow. Reminiscing about the past, allowed Gerry's "front" to completely dissolve. As he recollected, he began to talk about his home life and broke down into floods of tears, revealing that his father had raped him continuously as a kid. This occurred after three months of meeting once per week.

"That's why I'm such a mean hard bastard." He said. "I don't want no fucker ever touching me again." "No one fucking understands, they just think I'm a thug. But if that happened to you, you'd make sure no one does it again."

Jerry had established a relationship with his father as an adult, but he had never confronted him about his behaviour when he was a child. His father seemingly had amnesia about his actions. Jerry felt caught between the past memories and his present need to build a relationship with him. This 'great unsaid,' was driving him to currently self medicate. As we continued to meet, I worked with Jerry to visualise his best option, this included detox and then to move to rehab. He was in no position to talk to his father or confront him about the past. Despite outward appearances, internally he was very fragile. Although he presented as a hard man, this was a role he had constructed to fend off any further violence. He had been under psychiatric care for a previous attempted suicide. He related he had not disclosed to the psychiatric services about his sexual abuse history. He had become involved with them, after trying to hang himself and was later fished out of the Thames after throwing himself in. He was currently being treated for the symptoms of depression. Jerry wanted to shed the hard man image he had cultivated and move on from taking heroin to sublimate his emotions. This was a golden opportunity to assist him to make changes. Jerry was currently involved in seeing the psychiatric services once a week and was taking Olanzapine to help him cope with his depression and it seemingly helped with his anger.

A case conference was needed, after the local care authorities had blocked the hostel from making any direct referrals for detox. This needed the combined support of the internal mental health worker, the outside mental health service and the statutory substance use worker. In Jerry's case this required contacting the local substance use team and the psychiatric team. To manage someone's care plan, involved a combination of teams, all with different remits. This was also a bureaucratic balancing act of personalities.

The case conference was scheduled for 2pm on a weekday afternoon. Jerry turned up on time and sat facing us. I was apprehensive because I had qualms about the personalities that had turned up and the lack of empathy displayed before the conference had taken place. Flippant remarks about Jerry were made about his alleged psychiatric illness. I was caught within the confines of confidentiality. Only Jerry could relate his dynamics. I was also wary of mentioning abuse, as they had already decided he was a liar, prior to the conference commencing.

The case conference unfolded as a dynamic disaster. It highlighted the inability of the statutory services to conceptualise emotional intelligence. Again there was no agreed Chair, no agenda, no one knew what to do and so the workers took the opportunity to attack Jerry for missing their previous appointments because as he demonstrated, he could keep them when he wanted. The focus of the meeting was meant to be about Jerry's care plan, and whether they would support his application to detox and rehab. It descended into the professionals goading Jerry, bullying him about his lack of adherence to their organisational aims. It appeared they were embarking on a process to stop any more referrals from the hostel to the detox and rehab.

The Statutory Drug Worker asked Jerry why he had not kept her appointments but was able to make this one. The dynamics were based on denigration and failed to provide the "strokes" that assisted psychological change. Jerry should have been congratulated for turning up on time, and thinking about change, after months of skulking and bullying. Instead the professionals set out to challenge and undermine his fragility. The work Jerry and I had undertaken over the months was flattened in an hour. He became an object in a coconut shy as they threw barbed comments at him. The workers all backed each other up. They concentrated on every negative point they could muster to denigrate him. Jerry still sat there and took it, although rattled, he stood his ground. This only spurred the three women to keep up the attack. In an attempt to try and change the dynamic, I attempted to highlight the positive work we had done together.

Jerry related how he had discussed his sexual abuse issues with me. The drug workers and the mental health workers stated this had nothing to do with his drug use and mental health issues. Jerry replied it had everything to do with how he had ended up.

"If you can't trust your father who can you trust?"

The hostility continued from all three women as they mocked him openly. At this point Jerry collapsed emotionally and broke into floods of tears, then stormed out the room screaming. The three women turned round to each other and smiled. Meanwhile Jerry had to walk though a crowded meeting of the hostel workers to get through the door outside the hostel. I had intervened for nothing, and had set him up for a humiliation from professional people who clearly had no empathy. I sat staring at the floor, then one of the workers looked over.

"Oh Dean you don't look too happy. What is it?"

This created a double bind (Laing 1960, 1961, 1964) for me, because the commissioners had stated all referrals to detox and rehab needed joint approval. If this was not forthcoming then there would be no more. This highlighted the power politics that inhibited psychological regeneration at the hostel. Every attempt to shift people forward was hampered by agencies that saw clients moving forward as an organisational threat. It highlighted their inability to do the job they were tasked to do. It undermined their power base. I just shrugged and smiled.

"Do you think those tears of his were real" the Statutory Drugs Worker queried. The In house mental health worker laughed and said he had put on a good show.

"Is sexual abuse something that people make up?" I asked

An advert for "Survivors" was on the wall.

"Perhaps he can go there, we can refer him there." they agreed.

I looked it up on the computer and the website said the therapy had to be paid for.

"I don't think he will go, because you have to pay for it." I pointed out to the drugs and mental health workers.

"If he needs the support bad enough he can find the money." The Statutory drugs worker said.

"He doesn't need to. I can work with him around this issue." I said.

There was a stunned silence and they all shuffled their papers about uncomfortably.

This scenario summed up the hostility from the Statutory Services, to any form of emotional recovery. Instead they enacted a power play, a distinct form of institutional bullying where they abused their authority. In this case Jerry's attempt to move forward was sabotaged. Unfortunately I was trapped within this system. Complaining to the commissioners I learnt previously, only exacerbates the bullying. There are no checks and balances within this system. When a complaint is made, they pile on the pressure to the complainant to halt any discussion The bureaucratic gate-keeping ensured no one was provided any form of ongoing treatment unless it was agreed by every agency. In effect, this stopped any further referrals.

Jerry never spoke to me again after this case conference, and ignored any attempts at small talk. He also withdrew from the hostel. Eventually he was evicted for smashing a window, and then embarked on a campaign of localised terror. This became so pronounced that when I met a local councillor at a private function outside the hostel environment, she asked me what was happening in the area. She had received numerous complaints from people who lived there. It was difficult to convey the dynamics of the meeting to her, but what Jerry had undertaken in retrospect was a campaign based upon emotional revenge. He held all night parties in the street after being evicted from the hostel. The police were called, and he refused to move on, arrested, he returned and made more noise and nuisance. I could not condone what he was doing, but I could understand why. This had all resulted from the meeting to plan his future escape, it had been closed off, and he was letting us know that he was not happy. He later went to prison for violence. This highlights the ripple effect of institutional violence as it cascaded onto the wider community, the residents and eventually a complete stranger who was beaten senseless.

Case History 5; Pin a Label

Labelling (Becker 1983) is another issue that arises within the professions. These are passed on as part of a bureaucratic folk memory transmitted between workers, ensuring the person on the receiving end receives a label. They are then treated according to its dictates. Once a label is applied, it is extremely difficult to shake off. It is passed on from agency to agency. No one checks to ascertain its veracity. As it becomes written in the notes, its truth is taken for granted.

Peter was placed in the hostel by the local Social Services. It was clear from the offset it was an inappropriate placement. Peter had severe special needs issues and was therefore highly vulnerable. Social Services looked after his general support needs. These realistically needed one to one input, to help him control his epileptic symptoms. The arguments about funding, hamstrung his care. It was expensive to keep him at the hostel and this highlights another significant issue amongst the commissioning bodies. They operate within a silo, unaware of a cost benefit analysis. This inability to map services is symptomatic of a leadership vacuum that has flowed from the top, down to the bottom. Keeping Peter within the hostel where he was potentially subject to bullying was costly at around £500 per week. The cost of his care in a specialist home would not be much more expensive. His quality of life would be improved. Especially as there were concerns he had some form of brain tumour.

Peter suffered from a severe form of epilepsy, although when perusing the notes these questioned whether he was acting. A cursory reading of his hospital summaries would have dispelled any doubts. A significant problem arose, as no one had looked further than the presentation. It became apparent he was admitted into casualty, between 4-8 times per month. This was another added cost, which should have been taken into account using an economic index. Whilst in the hostel, because of the stress he was under, there were numerous ambulance callouts, then he was observed in a bed space, then discharge summaries were compiled and after care appointments arranged. This could all have been halted.

Pete attended therapy readily, and related he had attended special schools as a child. He also stated he had been in prison for sexual offences against children, after being set up by his brother. This was backed up in a Social Services report. This also described him as an alcoholic, difficult to engage and highly problematic, displaying challenging behaviour.

As we looked into his case, only one of these diagnoses was correct. The rest were labels and folk information, passed on from agency to agency. Peter was deemed hard to engage, yet Peter engaged to such an extent with hostel services when the bridges were built, you had to usher him out of the door. He was desperate to continue after the therapeutic hour, and he would have spoken all day if he had the chance. Afterward, he propped up the front counter, still wanting to speak. Far from being reticent Peter was extremely lonely and wanted company. He was trapped inside his epilepsy, and because he had deteriorated physically, everyone was apprehensive about approaching him. It was also clear he did not touch alcohol. The room where the therapy takes place, soon fills with the fumes of people who use alcohol extensively. Peter never touched it. His Aunt appeared one day, out of the blue. She said he drank weak lager when he was younger when he looked after his mother. This occurred when she was seriously ill, but this was the only period he drank. Peter said he never drank because he was worried about the effect it would have on his epileptic medication. He was tortured by his illness.

Another more concerning issue placed on his notes, detailed allegations he had sexually abused his children. Peter stated he had been in prison for ten years to add to the confusion. Clearly, when I began to work out a genealogy with him, detailing the ages of his children there were discrepancies. He could not have been in prison for sexual abuse offences for ten years and be the paternal father to four children. The dates did not tally. When the relative appeared again she was asked whether he was ever in prison. She said no. The Social Services department had taken his children into care because of neglect and physical cruelty with one son going abroad. This cruelty was undertaken by both parents, as they could not cope looking after their children. The case notes *appeared to be a psychological projection, assembled from various bodies who had made assumptions, rather than based upon evidence.*

Reflecting on his childhood Peter related how his older brother had enticed him to climb a wall when he was nine. This had collapsed on him and this was also verified by the Aunt. This was the trigger for his epilepsy. His brother was seemingly jealous of the attention he gained as the youngest in the family, from their mother. Adler (1956) speaks of the birth order and how this impacts on the psychological outlook. This enmeshes with the relationship with the parents and shapes perception. In this case Pete was the youngest, and Daniel his middle brother, was extremely jealous. Peter later in life reciprocated this care, when he looked after his mother when she became housebound. Their father had issues with alcohol and anger, attacking both his wife and his children. This was stopped when the brothers banded together in a rare show of solidarity, attacking him when they were adolescents.

Peter was unaware where his older brother lived, as he had not seen him for years. The middle brother was in and out of prison, and had a heroin habit. Peter's condition in the hostel over the two years gradually deteriorated and he needed support. Apart from the one relative, he appeared socially isolated, as no one ever visited. Over two years the number of epileptic fits increased in severity and frequency. This entailed him going into seizures where he banged his head continuously and because of this, he slurred his speech. Few fits took place inside the hostel, and this had led hostel staff after reading the notes to initially doubt the severity of his epilepsy. The hospital discharge notes finally dispelled this. They all seemed to take place in one part of South London, and there were concerns these were related to people taking advantage of Peter. As his condition deteriorated, my role became more based on advocacy. Peter needed ongoing care and I worked with his key worker to get him relocated to somewhere where he could receive support for his epilepsy. This entailed a move far away from the South London he knew. Social Services were deciding on their care budget. Meanwhile the ambulance call outs were mounting up, as were his admittances to A&E, his speech was becoming slurred and he was dribbling from his mouth. The wheels were always grinding slowly for people such as Pete. His life had had been labelled, and he was passed from agency to agency. The fundamental errors, entailed he was ostracised from further support as he was labelled a hard to engage, a sexual abuser, who faked his illness. I saw him every week for two years. During this time he expressed his anger about how his life had unravelled. In particular the entrapment in his illness had stopped him from being able to express himself.

Pete's case notes were gradually challenged, as I worked with his project worker to provide evidence to alter the entries. It was clear from Pete's standing at reception for hours, the difficult to engage remarks could easily be over turned. We worked to get hold of his forensic history to overturn the sexual abuse. We had numerous copies of hospital discharge notes and referrals to head injuries units, to overturn the queries about his epilepsy. This entailed, when the referral was made to the Social Services Commissioners for his care, the old notes made by their department could be challenged. This case clearly highlighted that information passed by different departments is not checked for veracity. It takes time to elicit information from Pete, and patience to understand his speech. His memory is poor and he contradicts himself. It appears convenient to apply a label, as time is not what statutory agencies have.

The labelling issue arises within the police, social services, mental health services and the substance use services. It is a significant issue, as there are a number of presumptions included within these labels around, race, gender, class, sexuality and mental health. The clients are then forced to internalise the label, as they are offered treatment on the basis of accepting the diagnosis. What they are not offered are forms of treatment which look at the precedents of how their externalised trauma occurred. There is a conjecture they belong to the class of the "other." The habitus of genetic origins is constantly trumpeted. This has entailed creating a whole industry to pathologise the homeless, forming classes of exclusion. Ironically there is also a payoff for those on the receiving end as they claim enhanced DLA (Disability Living Allowance Benefits). Previously this produced a collusion between professionals and the clients, who worked together to provide a label, so they can access high rates of benefits. This makes everyone's job easier.

Peter was one of the few people in the hostel who did not self medicate. He was worried about the effects of alcohol on his epilepsy. He was however vulnerable for those who wanted to dispense of their surplus clothes He bought anything that was being sold, having a room stacked from the floor to the ceiling, with Puffa jackets and Bob Marley tracksuits. He also had a number of girlfriends, who helped him to dispose of his DLA and benefit money. He showed me his mobile phone text messages, as he did not have the manual dexterity to reply *to the texts. A woman had contacted him about his two timing behaviour, and it was clear she had been following him around South London to see where he was going, describing his contacts with women. This blew some of my projections about him away.*

Case History 6; Lost in Rooms

Whilst violence is a significant issue in family life, another impact is bereavement. The effects of bereavement are debilitating, the sense of grief, the loss, the feeling of solitude, loneliness and the chasm of meaning. It creates a nihilistic despair. Previously religion provided a rationale to death, but in a post religious age the loss cannot be easily explained as a journey to a better place, the reappearance as an angel.

Paolo eradicated his sense of despair through self medication. It took away the emotional pain and allowed him to live within a narcotised bliss. He was enveloped in an alternate world where the pain of losing his partner was dispelled for the hours he remained opiate and alcohol satiated. When the substances were no longer present, he faced a chasm of despair. Taking more substances created a meaning for him. The problems with this self medication strategy is that he neglected the other areas of his life, going to work, paying council tax, keeping up his car insurance, eating, sleeping and keeping warm as he drifted to living on the streets, living out of bins. Paolo went into a form of nihilistic despair that was leading to self destruction. Eventually he was rescued by an Outreach Team and placed in a hostel. Then he reinstated his strategy of negation, by barricading himself in his room, hardly venturing out. He had lost his purpose.

Paolo kept himself locked in his room 23 hours per day. He only ventured out to collect his meals and go to the toilet. Apart from these events, no one saw him, for days at a time. I stopped him in the corridor one day on a rare occasion he ventured out during the day. I spoke to him, asking him where he was from and what his country was like. He asked me if I had ever been and I said no, but perhaps one day. We struck up a conversation on a regular basis after this. He began to tell me about the good areas to stay in Portugal. I used this strategy to push him to reminisce, to think about the positive things about his country. Spending so much time in his room is an indicator of institutionalisation or depression, or both. Judging by his unkempt appearance and his body odour, I guessed it was depression.

We spent a few weeks making small talk; I listened to him speak about Portugal. He would then come to the front counter and talk about the national football team and how well they were doing well, especially compared to England. The impact of Mourinho and Ronaldo on English football was crucial to the engagement. It was through these small intersections I noticed Paolo would come and pick up the free Metro newspapers lying on the counter. This strategy of engagement connected him to the present day world. He was still locked in his bereavement and his depression. He had closed off the outside world, but he was beginning to engage.

After a while, I suggested he come and talk to me in the surgery about his life. Paolo attended regularly, nearly every week for a 6 month period. He was born in Portugal in the late 50's and had grown up in an affluent family. His father had opposed the fascist regime that existed in Portugal until 1974, and he was imprisoned for a number of years. During this time he was tortured. The family lost their social prestige and they had to move out of their former residence. They relocated to a poorer area. Paolo however was still stuck within the school system run by the Church, the same people his father had opposed. He described the difficult conditions he grew up within. During this era, he related how the police came to his house regularly along with a whole army of snoopers. They searched the premises for a radio; if they found it, the family would be taxed. The whole thrust of the regime was to seemingly keep the people in a state of infantilised entrapment. Paolo had internalised the dynamics of the regime as a form of emotional suffocation, that he wanted to rebel against. His father was later released after a few years and the family continued as before, except they were much poorer. His father, as we reflected, was traumatised by his incarceration, but there was no language to express it. Post Traumatic Stress Disorder (PTSD) was not a concept people were aware of.

In 1974 Portugal changed, and it was during this transition life became freer. Paolo had been drawn to the hippy culture, a negation of the rules, previously imposed by the Catholic Church indoctrination he had endured as an adolescent. He later found meaning in listening to Bob Dylan, Stones, Hendrix, and The Beatles, even though it had all happened years previously in the UK. 1974 was a big opportunity for Portugal to join the nonstop party that had been seemingly happening in the West. Portugal, he felt had been kept in a state of enforced emotional suspension, whilst everyone else was seemingly having a good time. Substance use helped him to become a rebel in Portugal, as many middle class children gravitated towards the counter culture. Drugs became a bond between them, a form of negation of everything they had grown up within. The counter culture allowed them to overturn these old values. This was the hedonism, the reversal of all values based on doing the opposite to the old ones. Everything that was forbidden was now allowed. Paolo recognised he was part of that steady rush to embrace this new freedom.

Paolo became suspended within this culture, noticing people passing away. Within a few years most of his friends had died from overdoses. He tried to get clean and settle down, but he failed at least three times. He revealed he had attended rehabs in Portugal and France, paid for by his parents. As we reflected on why he had not succeeded it became apparent these were run by priests. He realised he was trapped within the drug subculture and relied on his parents for hand outs. He also subsisted by stealing. When his parents died, he was left alone and this was a turning point, as he had recognised he had existed in a suspended adolescence. This was the impact of their bereavement and the exposure of meaninglessness. He also felt lonely, until he met a woman and fell in love. She also used substances but was from a professional upper middle class family from another South European country. They met in Portugal and decided to move away and begin a new life with the other Portuguese in the East of England.

Paolo stated he wanted to rebuild his life by escaping the drug scene. His partner had been ostracised by her family because of her drug use. Their main attachment was to each other. They built a life together working in the chicken factories in East Anglia and East Midlands, working on the production lines. Paolo described working on the production line then rushing in the toilets to inhale heroin. He inhabited an opiate dream world whilst working in the factories. This echoed the stories of early industrialisation where narcotics had been freely available until 1916 (Whittington 2007b). Paolo and his partner built some stability renting a cottage, buying a car and living in bliss, despite their drug habits and the shift work they did to survive. Then one day she came back from work and said she felt ill. She went into hospital and they suggested she stay there for tests. She died within a week. Her family alerted by Paolo, flew over; took the body back to their country, ignoring his state of shock, they took over the funeral preparations and buried her. Paolo was left alone and suffered an existential crisis based on the bereavement. All his foundations had been crushed in a week. She was sanctified in the family plot and a marble mausoleum was built to honour her death. He expressed his bewilderment and hurt, as they had never contacted him after this. He was ostracised from her, when her family took control of the situation. They brought her back to their world and separated him from the process, doing more for her in death than they had in life.

He recalled his feelings after her death in the sessions. He stated it was a numb sensation, a vast emptiness, meanwhile he kept thinking it was just a dream, that when he awoke she would be beside him, just as before. He spent hours waiting by the window thinking she would return. It was the sudden nature of the loss, how she became ill, and then the sudden disappearance from his life. As it began to dawn upon him she might not be coming back, he became sick with grief. Initially he stayed inside the house and did not venture out, still waiting for her, locked in a state of disbelief, thinking she would still return. All he had to do was wait patiently. Meanwhile the world continued without him.

He lost his job, the bills piled up and finally he was evicted from his house. Unaware he could sign on, he drifted onto the street, eating from bins and stealing from shops. Meanwhile his car tax had lapsed and he was accruing fines which would impact on him later. Paolo was trapped in a cycle of despair driving him downwards. He gravitated to London, because it was easier to sustain a habit and be homeless. Eventually after three years he was picked by the Outreach Team and placed in a hostel. It was there, he realised, he could have claimed benefits and that if he had been supported at the beginning of his crisis, he would not have lost three years. During this time his Hepatitis had worsened.

Paolo was ambivalent about life, as he felt it consisted of pain and torture. It was only through returning to the pleasant memories, buried under negativity he began to change his inner mantra. We looked at the good times in Portugal, the music festivals, the fun he had, rather than concentrating on the negativity. The negativity appeared without any prompt. The first step was to work with Paolo to ensure he has a meaning to continue living, so he would invest some of himself in the real world, instead of hiding away from it. He began to engage *with the hostel and I referred him for specialist support to ensure he claimed his benefits. The Benefits worker accompanied him to the Panel Adjudication Meeting.*

Paolo could have gained DLA, if he had lied to the panel. Evidently they were looking for a reason to support him. He made them aware of his health status and spoke about the impact of the bereavement, providing a context for his descent. The worker who accompanied him said they gave him every opportunity to use their discretion, but interestingly his morality stopped him. He was stuck on the bare minimum of JSA, suffering from chronic hepatitis. I worked with him to find an inner meaning to the disease. He had missed several treatment appointments for his Hep C after the bereavement, subsequently his physical condition had worsened. He was now in serious health difficulties. My role now switched to try and help him to find a meaning to his life, drawing from the logo therapeutic work of Viktor Frankl (1952, 1959).

If Paolo could find a purpose to his life then he could find a means, as he had demonstrated he was extremely successful in surviving on the streets. It was through this intangible, abstract idealism, Paolo began to define his inner meaning, in particular through taking up writing. He would attend the local library and write about his experiences.

Problems for Paolo arose when he chose to re-engage back with the world after burying himself away after his bereavement. He was hit with the unpaid car fines. These were deducted from his benefits leaving him even less money to live on. He had to face up to the severity of his illness and was then diagnosed with diabetes. This meant he needed a special diet. He had very little money coming in and the only way he could sustain his health was through winning the Hostel Quiz competition, which is why he avidly read the Metro. He found his meaning in the brief chats at the counter at the beginning of our therapeutic relationship. He then realised he could supplement his income, and improve his diet through reading the free newspaper. This small talk sparked his greater interest.

Therefore the hostel activities are crucial to this client group's psychological and physical welfare. The activities are more than just occupying their time, but are embedded as survival strategies. Paolo went on to take new forms of Hepatitis treatment. This was working at the time of writing. We had worked on guided imagery to help him fight the virus and both fell about laughing as he said I was better than Paul McKenna (Whittington 2011).

The main issues emerging when speaking to Paolo were his descent into depression as he had lost his will to survive after his partner's death. Instead he had become trapped within an abyss. He could see no way out. The idea was to assist him by building a psychological escape ladder but he needed to climb the rungs. This could only be undertaken if he found a rationale to live. I provided a spark and he then built the escape route.

Case History 7; Beaten into Violence

Les was a white working class man in his mid 40's with a shaven head and large physique. He had grown up in South London and had spent twenty years in prison since 16 for various violent offences. His main drug of choice was Cocaine, "Charlie." He was a cocaine sniffer and used it in conjunction with drinking Weak 4% lager. Les epitomised one aspect of a South London white working class masculinity; emotionally and physically hard, prone to violence and outwardly confrontational. I have had years of experience working with men from the local environment and I could see beyond the initial presentation. I worked with Les in a number of sessions to reflect upon the past. Les had grown up with a step-father who was alcoholic and prone to violence. He had beaten Les ferociously from an early age up until he was 14. Les had been attacked once too often, and decided to retaliate. This demarcates a common occurrence. It marks a particular rite of passage as it draws a line between being a recipient of violence as a boy, and an enactor of violence as a man. This illuminates how white working class masculinities are created within this white working class culture. It is the difference between being bullied and someone who can inflict violence. I asked him how he felt, reacting to the violence and fighting back.

"I dunno Dean. You ask me how I felt. That's a good question. You know in all these years I have never thought about it. I s'pose I felt fucking good. I will need to think about it. I dunno."

Les was the least introspectively honest man, I have encountered. He had no initial concept of emotions other than anger and serenity. They were two modes he had operated within for five decades. Talking about how he felt, was novel to him, like wearing a new Mohair suit, he would take it on and off, and look at me quizzically to see if he was doing it right.

"I need to think about all this stuff. You've got me thinking. Why was I violent? Is it linked to my step dad? I don't think so. It's just me."

As we worked around his emotions, it became clear to me, he represented the foreclosed man, wearing his self constructed, character armour. This was the type of man Wilhelm Reich (1933) had written about. Les sat emotionally tense in full character amour, not letting anything penetrate beyond his facade. He was the archetypal hard man, his voice, the way he carried himself, his physique and his facial structure.

Les related after he beat up his step dad, the latter only returned to pick up his belongings. That was the last they saw of him. Afterwards, Les became part of a gang, becoming embroiled in a career inflicting violence in organised and semi organised criminal associations. As an adolescent he was initially sentenced to juvenile detention, due to his violence, when he was 16. He described the institution as being based on applied violence. The first day he had a confrontation with another inmate over a locker. This resulted in him "battering the boy into submission." This scenario appeared to have been set up by the Prison Officers. After this fight, he thought he was going to receive more punishment but was instead feted. It turns out the "screws" as he termed them, had been recently investigated after a serious incident regarding their previous propensity for violence. They had been told to restrict their enactment of punishments. A particular individual had sensed the backing off and had asserted himself within the power vacuum. He then dominated proceedings. This was Les's narrative as he recounted his tear between being an antagonist and siding with the institution. He was set up to attack the other boy, and he beat him. After beating the other boy, he was given special privileges. This was how the punishment regimes worked, through formal and informal arrangements. He described one prison officer making a group of prisoners do bunny-hops as a punishment humiliation.

Les was left out of the routine because he was seen as an enforcer. The regime he inhabited was devoid of any notion of emotional intelligence. It was all based on hardened masculinities, either receiving or giving violence in hierarchies to inflict humiliation. This was a reflection of life outside the prison, a representation of the dysfunctional family he had lived within as a child and adolescent. Far from changing his behaviour, this type of environment reinforced all the signals he had received as a boy. It displayed and enacted violence, and he was tough enough to take it. He had already been subject to abject bullying as a child. He described his step father punching and kicking him, until he could take no more. He had learnt to emotionally retreat within, to protect himself. The prison had nothing to offer a man who had already emotionally shut down. Les thrived in prison as a hard man. It was the making of him.

In the therapy sessions, he began to make the emotional connections between his early life and how he had constructed himself over the months. He would look at himself in awe. I was uncertain whether he was actually making the connections or just showing he was changing, as a form of elucidation. Les had different ideas. He began to take an active interest in the hostel, protecting the more vulnerable residents and working to change. He vocalised how the hostel was helping him discover old hobbies and he began to engage in public speaking. He developed a passion for a schoolboy hobby, cricket.

Dismissing it in his youth as a toff's game, and not for him, he met a friend from his school days who encouraged him to play. Les the archetypal white working class hard man began to relax, his facial musculature changed, as he began to smile, live life, and enjoy himself. His cocaine use diminished as did his drinking.

At last he found a meaning for himself through his hobby rather than being enclosed in a reaction to the humiliations of the past. Les was completely unaware the past had affected and shaped him. When he reflected on his history it became obvious to him where his anger had emerged from. He then began to make the emotional connections. It was through therapy he transformed.

Hobbies are a key component of psychological development. They create an engagement with the wider world, and this allowed him to make a new set of friends away from the pub, clubs and gangs. At our last meeting, Les asked me where he could buy a copy of my book "Beaten into Violence." He stated the title was enough for him, as he realised it represented who he previously was.

"That was me." he said. I returned home and found a copy and gave it to him. When the resonance is so acute, this speaks louder than any academic treatise. It is a pure connection of an empathic flow beyond academia, as the world is finally understood for what it is rather than what it appears to be. The hard man had been transformed, as he began to connect to himself, rather than continue with running away.

Case History 8; Isolation

Delroy was a middle aged Black male, who whizzed around the hostel. He was forever in and out the door. The first time I stopped him, I slowed him down for an instant, asking him if he ever considered doing some therapy. He quickly retorted he got a bad vibe from me. From then on, he refused to speak to me and pointedly spoke to the other workers when he needed anything, completely ignoring my presence.

Then one day, he had no option to speak to me. He was desperate to make a phone call. I was the only person present on the front counter. His benefits had not arrived, and he needed to pay someone back, or he would be in trouble.

"I know you and I don't get on, but I really need to use that phone right now, because I am in trouble."

"Ok" I said, "Go ahead."

This small exchange broke the ice. Whilst dialling, he asked me what exactly therapy was. Did I think he was mad enough to need it? I began to explain that therapy can be about visualising the future and this instantly clicked. We began to meet regularly every week. At first, we steered away from the past and concentrated on the future. Delroy had aspirations of being an artist; he had excellent skills in sketching cartoons, and had contributed pieces to a small magazine. He also wrote about his life at a workshop he attended. As he relaxed, he related he used heroin and crack occasionally and I worked within to look at his self medication strategy. He was part of a fractured West Indian family. He had been looked after by his Grandmother in Jamaica and was then sent for by his parents after they had established themselves in the UK. This was in the 1950's. When he was brought over, the family had internal difficulties resulting in his father leaving and his mother then looking after and raising 7 children.

Delroy was then put into care because she could not cope. He resented his mother for choosing him and keeping the others with her. This was another "sting" he had imbibed, as he was estranged from his family, yet again. When he was an 18 year old adult, he remade contact with his mother and was accepted, but he was bitter about being left in Jamaica and then being sent away. His mother remarried during his early adulthood, but he never established a rapport with his stepfather. He felt there was something unsaid. His mother had a large house in East London, which she had bought years previously. Due to the escalation in house prices this property was worth a considerable amount of money. Delroy stated the stepfather wanted to get hold of the house, because it had a high value.

Delroy felt he had engineered a series of accidents to try and kill his mother. Delroy eventually confronted him. The result was a violent tussle in which Delroy was initially charged with attempted murder. He was later given a verdict of Not Guilty. However, the stepfather had seemingly put a price on his head and Delroy then hid. This marked his ostracism from his family yet again. Delroy then lived on the streets for years, forever fearful he was going to be shot.

The relationship with Delroy had to be carefully nurtured. Initially, I spent considerable time building up a rapport, and then I worked with him to allay his fears about the contract placed upon him. Delroy spoke as if these incidents had happened last week. He had lost sense of time.

As he had a connection with his family at one time, I reviewed with him whether it was feasible to rebuild it. The past was clearly still disturbing him. I perceived my main focus was to be an enlightened witness (Miller 2001) as he revealed the various emotional wrenches he had suffered in his early life; being left with his Grandmother, being torn away from her, being sent away from his family to be placed in care. His life narrative emerged over weeks and not in one straight sitting. It was an issue I had to piece together from fragments. I suggested he recontact his family. He was in palpable fear when he visualised meeting his stepfather again. I worked with Delroy to count through the years to help him realise, the man would be in his 80's. He needed to make some tentative enquiries and ascertain whether it was safe.

Delroy eventually made contact with his family. I worked with him to write an anonymous letter to his mother, to let her know he was still alive. He then became aware through contacts; the family had been searching for him. The step father had died years ago. Delroy had lived as though the twenty years had happened two months ago. It was clear when he spoke, he had no concept of time passing and people changing. I worked to break this perception, and it began to achieve results. He began to reformulate attachment.

Eventually Delroy informed his family where he was living. He made an instant rapport with his younger brother. It was the return of the prodigal son. However, the underlying resentments against his mother were still running deep. Over a series of weeks, we worked on these issues. Delroy became frustrated on how his life had turned out. He was bitter about the rejections and became angry towards his mother, as the past resurfaced. He would stand up and act out the dynamics in the counselling space. He felt she should have sided with him when his stepfather was trying to injure her. He expressed his sense of neglect and abandonment. There were also issues with the other older brothers that had remained unresolved. These were the issues he faced in reconnecting to his family. I worked with him each week to try to allay his anger and build up a connection.

This was ongoing painstaking work that lasted over a year. Delroy would return each week to voice his frustrations about what had happened to him, how the others had benefited from his sacrifice and why his mother had not helped him sooner. His anger welled up and I sought to defuse it, otherwise he would create further barriers between the hands outstretched to greet him and the isolation that beckoned. I could empathise with his sense of rejection, but the anger was driving everyone away from him, and this needed to be worked through.

Meanwhile, his art became his main focus, as he realised he could make a living out of drawing cartoons and writing. This provided him with an identity. He could now interact within the wider world as an artist. Previously Delroy had inhabited the identity of a homeless man. What we looked at, was *how he could switch this identity to being a Bohemian artist, and shift away from being psychologically homeless.*

Hobbies are crucial in assisting people to make social contact outside of their self constructed worlds. One of the significant issues reported by homeless men when they move out of the hostel is the deep sense of isolation that envelops them. It is through having hobbies; men such as Delroy can shift beyond the stigma of being homeless. He can then join a wider community of peers. Delroy's writing and art helped to move him beyond the confines of being labelled. He became a writer of street experiences rather than being a homeless person that writes. Delroy could create another identity based on his hobby. The conceptual apparatus I used was derived from Otto Rank (1932) and a quote I half recollected from Nietzsche. The idea was derived from the concept; if you want to be an artist you have to inhabit the role. It is then people will believe the representation and eventually become the role. This was the spark I gave him. The rest was created through his initiative.

Case History 9; Finding a Purpose

Ricardo was an Italian male who had been deported from the USA for a violation and then sent back to the UK where he had some family connections. He was extremely distraught about what had happened to him. Furthermore because of his brown off-white skin he had been detained under the Anti Terrorist Legislation in the UK. As it transpired, a significant error had been made, as Ricardo had definite ideas around race.

Ricardo related he had been brought up with a Norwegian father and Italian mother. His father was an alcoholic bully who had attacked him and his brothers. Ricardo detailed how he was beaten with metal rods and as a result of the violence, he had run away from home a number of times. He was continuously returned by the school welfare people and the police. No one had questioned why he had run away, and as he became an adolescent, he made a vow to run away for good. This was enacted in response to the ferocity of the violence he was facing at home. Ricardo had originally helped his father in his engineering business, but became increasingly frustrated by his critical put downs. The resentment built up inside him, and is spilled over as he eventually attacked his father with a baseball bat, before finally running away forever. He never saw his father again.

Leaving home at 16, Ricardo initially supported himself with drug dealing. This allowed him to keep himself afloat financially with the money he earnt, ensuring he could survive without going near his family, or the state for support. His younger brother also ran away from home because of the violence. He joined Ricardo. Ricardo looked after his younger brother until he stole a considerable sum of money from him. This created the final break from his family ties.

"What happened?" I asked

"I beat the guy to near death. No one should be doing that to another member of their family. The guy was having a tough time, I put him up and he did that to me. That's not family, that's a betrayal!"

The impact of the events finally caught up with him after this episode. Far from feeling exhilarated, he recounted how he felt alone and desperate, after attacking his brother. Depressed, totally cut off from his family, laden with trauma from the past, he tried to commit suicide by jumping off a building. He was badly injured in the process, but it did not kill him. He did break both legs. In hospital, lying up with his legs broken, he vowed to keep on living.

Over the next few years, Ricardo rebuilt his life and learnt some carpentry skills. Gradually he built up his own carpentry business. He became a successful entrepreneur in his early twenties. He even began to hire people as his business expanded in his mid twenties. Then he met a woman, fell in love and had children. He could not cope when his wife had his first child and felt her pulling away from him. Instead, he sought solace in heroin use, feeling as though he was isolated within his new family. The attachment loss was great, as he felt he was losing a family once again. Then everything began to slide downwards, and he lost his business, his relationship fractured and eventually he was arrested after undertaking a robbery to support his drug use. He was then deported under a technicality; all of his remaining goods were seized as he was put on a plane and sent to Heathrow. Later discharged, he was again picked up for suspected terrorism and held in a special camp. He then spent years living on the street. Ricardo was incensed at his treatment, in particular

197

that he had been mistaken for a person of Arab descent, describing himself as a patriot. Out of all the humiliations he had received, this was the most heavily vocalised. Ricardo was incandescently angry, and my role was to sit and validate his life story. Through allowing him to talk, his anger eventually cooled. It was then I envisaged we could build a structure. The events of the past were too raw, and we needed to build a bond first. Ricardo attended each week for six months. The first sessions were full of rage.

It was easy to ascertain where the roots of his anger lay. It existed as layers and we journeyed through each one, as he undertook a therapeutic journey. The rationale for his anger lay as sediment. The first layer was his sense of frustration at being homeless, and the stigma attached. Then it was the anger at being held as a terrorist. Excavating further, revealed his anger at being deported after putting so much into the country. Then there was the shock of losing his wife and family. Underneath this were his family dynamics. Then we hit the hatred he felt for his father for the bullying inflicted upon him as a child. We waded through the layers over the months.

It appeared Ricardo had endured a treatment lying beyond Kafkaesque, as he had been stripped of everything apart from his life. He was chronically choked with anger, and this surfaced towards ethnic minorities. He despised them, even though he was one himself. This was not a subject I broached until much later, as the anger he displayed was initially too vitriolic to point this out. I could not challenge his world view, until we had a definite bond. My strategy in working with Ricardo was to let him just blow the anger out in the room. I only needed to close the door and sit down, and then he would rage about his sense of injustice. I never probed or stated I was unhappy with his anger; I just let him pour it out, and then waited for him to cool. Once he realised he was understood, I felt I could dig deeper. That was when I asked him about his initial family support, and this provided another catalyst for him to rage again. This concerned his sense of humiliation endured at the hands of his father, who beat and ridiculed him as a child until he ran away. This was undertaken over a period of years, until finally he attacked his father and disappeared for good. There was a distinct hatred still directed at his father for the bullying. This was also aimed at his mother for not protecting him. It transpired she was also relentlessly bullied by her husband. However there was also a lack of connection between her and her children.

Lastly, we tackled his masculine role and how it affected his relationship, the sense of loss he felt when his children were born. The one person he had formed an attachment with, seemingly emotionally abandoned him, when his children became central to her care. He could not communicate this loss to her because he felt he needed to keep up his sense of masculine identity. He was trapped in a double bind (Laing 1960, 1961, 1964),caught between playing a masculine outer role and then hiding his self perceived more feminine emotional needs, to connect to others. He felt admitting he was jealous of the children, would allow his partner to get a hold on him. He found heroin as a solace, a get out clause, from the double bind (1960, 1961, 1964), as he escaped into a blissful state. It allowed him to wall himself off from reality. Once he entered this porthole he never could return again. It provided him with a meaning and a set of friends away from his wife. As he developed his habit, he lost his trade and then his heroin use became a hindrance. They eventually split and this caused more emotional heartache, which he self medicated for. Eventually committing the robbery and then being caught, put him further into the abyss. A discrepancy was found in his immigration papers from years previously and before his lawyer could assemble a case, he was deported to the UK. Working through the anger and the injustice provided a sense of personal validation for Ricardo. This allowed the anger to subsume to managed levels. He had kept up a hobby, despite his anger, heroin and crack use. He could carve wooden tubes and make ornate artistic designs, which he would sell. Ricardo had found a purpose in life and it was from this purpose we began to construct meaning. We could never alter what had happened to him. He would always carry the emotional scars, but at least we had now found a rationale for living, a sense of overcoming the worst that events could throw at you. This was the only vestige of his self esteem he had left. We built up on this one residual quality and constructed a future out of his imagination, an idealisation based on what he wanted, given the conditions he existed within, and what was available. Ricardo sensing he could find a way forward, grabbed hold of the rungs. He attended the necessary pre-detox courses. They helped him to visualise and strengthen his resolve. He gained community care funding and did a detox. Ricardo had finally escaped a life of entrapment, emotionally and physically. Whilst never emotionally free from the past, he had stopped it from haunting him every waking second, overpowering him, to produce chronic surges of anger. These surges had pushed everyone away from him in terror. The role of therapy was to engage the man hiding behind the maelstrom he wove around him, to use the energy for recovery, rather than self medication.

The key to Ricardo's recovery was to use Person Centred Therapy (Rogers 1961) initially, as there was no need to say anything. It was just a case of sitting in the room and letting the gale force inferno blow around the space without flinching on what was in the narrative. I could understand why Ricardo was angry, it was layer after layer of abuse; family, institutions, all combining to enact discipline and punish. His voice was absent from any sense of articulated discourse. He was bereft of hope and could not communicate his feelings. He had erected a hardened exterior and this had led to the collapse of his relationship. This was another deep sense of ostracism. The deportation from the USA and his reception in the UK was bizarre even by the various narratives related around institutions within the therapeutic sessions. The fact he was deported to live on the streets of the UK had no justification. The use of Psychologically Informed Decision making such as the relationship between the police officer in the van and Sammy would have forestalled many of the problems within Ricardo's life. The services in the USA failed to pick up on, why he was running away from home, when he as an adolescent, even though he was covered in extensive bruises. Everyone turned a blind eye to what was occurring, in the hope someone else would pick up the pieces. The issues rebounded across department to department, from agency to agency and remain unresolved. Within the vacuum more carnage followed in its wake. Decision making is Trans Global not just limited to local decision making processes. His release from a terrorist holding prison, based on nothing more than skin colour, outlined the paucity of the decision making processes during the alleged war on terror.

The therapeutic work assisted Ricardo to recollect his memories in a place of safety, whilst he was still self medicating. This is a crucial difference from just sending people into detox unprepared, or attending the skills development workshops undertaken by the Borough. Through the therapeutic process, Ricardo became fully aware of what he was facing emotionally, when he finally stopped using heroin and crack. The pre preparation work is crucial for men such as Ricardo, otherwise they will be overwhelmed by memories and feelings, when they decide to detoxify. So much had happened as he had been the victim of traumatic forms of violence. This had encased him in rage. The heroin helped to soothe him internally from exploding, as it provided him with a meaning and satiated is anger. Taking the drug away would not help him psychologically, in fact, it would have potentially led to a severe episode, either involving harm to others, or self harm. Detox is part of an ongoing process that needs to be managed amongst practitioners. Ricardo needed a number of support structures to achieve his aim of being free of his drug issues, therapy was the catalyst for the change by working with him to define a purpose. This was built upon his definitions of change not a preconceived template.

Case History 10; Gun In Your Hand

Johnny was a middle aged East London man, second generation Irish, in outlook he had become a fully fledged Londoner. He spoke about his life as a series of segments. His early life was based on crime, mainly shoplifting, as his father had a drink problem. There was not enough money coming into the house to feed everyone, as his father drank away the finances. As a child, he had to assume a carers role. This entailed going out to shoplift to supplement the family income. One day he was caught when he was ten years old, and one of the conditions of the sentence was that he was sent away from his parents. They were deemed feckless and unable to control him. Johnny felt aggrieved at the label, but could not tell the truth, that the family was not managing because of his father's alcoholism. This was kept as a family secret, and Johnny sacrificed himself to uphold it.

He related that during the first night in the hostel, a priest came up to his bed and instructed Johnny to masturbate him. Frightened, Johnny said he complied as there was no one to turn to. All the other boys appeared asleep. The visits became frequent. Johnny tried to speak to his mother about what was happening. She would not hear of priests doing anything wrong, as she went to Mass each week to pray for her son.

He was caught in a double bind (Laing 1960, 1961, 1964) between being sexually bullied and then punished for non compliance with various statutes, enacted to contain his subsequent aggressive behavior. It was through being caught in this web that his adolescent anger crystallised into hatred, as he stated he shunned all feelings for others. This was to serve him well in his chosen career of armed robbery, but to devastate him in his relationships. After he left the "home," he went straight into a career of armed robbery. This lasted thirty years. We worked on his ability to empathise, feeling the severance attachment he had endured, had created a psychological shock where he had learnt to emotionally shut down. Using this strategy allowed Johnny to articulate his internal feelings. He spoke about the humiliation of being violated, and then the silence, because no one wanted to believe him. He felt betrayed by his mother, who he had supported as a child. In his hour of his need she had not reciprocated. He felt a form of disgust towards his father for putting the family in such a situation, but had a greater understanding of his alcohol use, as he had been reliant on heroin for thirty years. He had brief periods of employment in-between his various bank jobs, and he felt a certain pride and amazement at his capabilities to obtain money. He never kept any of it, as soon as he made money, he would be in a hotel having a fix, drinking champagne and dialling for sex workers. Johnny described it as an addiction in itself, the thrill of power, of being able to spend money on nothing. It was this feeling that he craved, when undertaking the armed robberies. The anecdotes were spiced with self deprecatory humour, as he related how he would practice his technique in the mirror. He would make appropriate grimaces, altering his voice to imply menace. He went into one Building Society after cleaning his gun, pulling it out to demand money. He had not put it together properly and so it fell to pieces in his hands. Quickly trying to reassemble it, he picked it up and ran out. We also looked at the impact of his behaviour on the cashiers, and Johnny began to make the emotional connections between his early childhood shutdown and his adult ability to wield a gun with impunity. He also began to develop some empathy for the victims when he finally made the connections.

Prison had not changed Johnny's outlook when he had been caught. His entire life purpose had revolved around enacting revenge against the state. This resulted from what had happened to him as a child. Authority figures were his substitute priests. He cared little for his own safety or for others, as he had no specific boundaries. He had been married, but had conducted an affair with a close relative. This was revealed by his lover to his ex partner and this shattered his marriage. She would have forgiven me everything but that. Johnny revealed he had been a fool for throwing everything away. It was only through undergoing this painful process that he finally confronted himself. Usually he ran away from himself. His life had been constructed around revenge and making himself invulnerable. The problem, as he now realised, was that his emotional invulnerability had entailed shutting out everyone else who had a connection with him. Johnny's transition was remarkable. In the therapy he began to reflect upon himself. He began to assemble the pieces of his life, similar to the components of the gun he had dropped on the Bank floor. Picking them up piece by piece he created his life narrative. This allowed him *to care for himself, as he had some severe physical problems that needed ongoing support. He had neglected his health and he was in severe physical danger.*

Johnny needed to find a purpose for living and this process of talking and reflection helped him to find validation. He spoke about the abuse and how it affected him, the terror of childhood. He was unable to sleep and was beaten for incontinence in the home. The denial of his anger emerged as rage. He found revenge through wielding a gun. It was the power of being in charge of the situation and being outside the state boundaries that appealed to him. Johnny worked through his issues and eventually left the hostel to live in his own flat. He maintained his tenancy, but the problem he now faces is social isolation. He has however created a non drug using network for the first time in thirty years.

Johnny's story highlights how boys learn to keep a code of silence. He tried to articulate what was happening to him as a child and adolescent. He was told he was making up stories. Denied his reality, he was forced to keep a silence. This became converted into a burning anger that became unleashed in violence. When he was caught, he still kept to his code of silence due to his previous dealings with institutions. His anger stemmed from having his physical and emotional realities denied. The armed robbery was a sublimated discharge of this violence. The same dynamics appear repeatedly in working with these men. These psychological insights transcend the traditional forensic psychology paradigm.

Johnny was another homeless man, who could have claimed compensation for being sexually abused as a child. He was not interested in claiming; it would entail reliving the whole nightmare once again, in public. As someone with an extensive history of armed robbery and heroin use he was sanguine about his prospects on the witness stand. He had previous experience of facing the prosecution. This sublimation of the terror of the past allowed him to cope. It turned into a strategy of self sufficiency, fending off authority figures. This becomes the golden rule of survival and becomes enshrined in masculine forms of individualism. These hard men of the streets were all soft children at one point in their lives. They learnt to develop the hardened "fronts," to survive in hostile environments. They have no reason to shed their "front" (Whittington 2007) because it has served them well by fending off enquiries. It allowed them to gain status. However it locks them in a role and Johnny felt

203

constricted. The therapy helped him to escape and deconstruct, whereas other impositions such as prison had kept him psychologically locked within. This had only constrained him and had not cured him. The therapy helped him to escape and deconstruct, to find a form of solace.

Case History 11; Will to Live

Jim had been in the hostel for four years prior to making contact. He ignored me for the first year I was employed in the hostel, as his focus was on self medication. When he did speak it was a gruff barked command. He was involved in a co-dependent heroin relationship with Jeff (Whittington 2011) another hostel resident. They both begged on the street to sustain their drug use. Jim had cared little for his personal appearance. This was epitomised by a plastic hospital tube protruding from his stomach. This leaked internal body fluids. No amount of cajoling would entice him to see the nurse or go to hospital. Eventually it was bitten off by a dog. Jim was in agony, but it passed through his system and he eventually healed.

I asked him why he never cut the end off, and he just shrugged. He had no reason to live, no emotional investment. He had no long term relationship or children. His only attachment was with Jeff. Jim did reveal he had been active in various political groups and this had created a previous purpose, but he had drifted away into being homeless. He was adamant he had no further interest in his past life. He did not want therapy, but was happy to talk informally about confidential issues. This was the dichotomy of the work, the clients dictated their own rhythms and could not be coaxed into arrangements they resented. These talks usually rested upon legalising drugs and why the state made it so difficult for drug users.

Towards the end of his stay at the hostel, Jim began to speak about his emotional life with me, understanding the role his heroin use had played in helping him to cope with first his mother's death and then his father's death at 16. In the subsequent will, he was given a considerable sum of money from the estate. Lonely, isolated and full of trauma, although he never acknowledged it at the time, he spent it on self medication, walling himself off from the feelings of bereavement, loneliness and isolation. He had not thought about it until he spoke to me. It had taken 3 years of brooding to make the decision to explore an event that had dominated his life over 30 years ago.

"What do you know when you're 16 and both your parents die? How do you respond? Of course you're gonna go off the rails. No one teaches you how to cope with bereavement. It was even worse then, there was no one like you to talk to"

This self medication had continued for 30 years. Trust had been built up slowly over a series of small interactions talking about Manchester City Football Club. Jim never wanted to attend any confidential space of a counselling room. This was the first hostel he had stayed in, for more than two weeks. The walls reminded him too much of prison and it was claustrophobic. He loved the freedom of being homeless, away from constraint. Instead of the room, he spoke in the garden outside the hostel. I experimented with safe space, essential in everyday practice, by using the garden going to cafes, and going to museums with the clients. Even going for a walk with people changed the dynamics.

Jim In one of our last sessions before he moved out to his own accommodation spent the session talking about his new flat. He had expressed apprehension about moving out of the hostel, unsure if he would cope. This was always a big psychological hurdle for these men. Those who were keen to move out began to baulk when the leaving day loomed. The hostel for all its dynamics represented certainty. The bills were pre paid. Venturing out into the world entailed uncertainty. Jim was unsure how he was going to furnish it. He had ideas for colour schemes and what he was going to buy to make it habitable. He had made strides in informal therapy. He needed to build trust with the outside world, as for too long he had languished in a twilight world. He had closed himself off from the mainstream world and existed inside his head. The death of both his parents before he was 16 had created a huge emotional shock that he had obliterated through heroin use, and active forgetting. As long as he kept up the self medication, he no longer had to think about their deaths because he could exist within his self constructed world. Over the years the pain had dulled, but he had estranged himself from connecting to relationships as a result. Jeff was his lifeline and Jim was his. They were in a co dependent relationship, not so much with heroin, but supporting each other to make forays into the real world. Both had similar bereavement issues. Jim was older and shook himself out of his fugue first. Jeff still remained trapped and eventually teamed up with another man in a similar position as himself, replicating the dynamics. Meanwhile Jim began to pull away. The changes were noted by staff and they responded to him. Jim sensing everyone was treating him with greater dignity began to respond in kind. This marked the dialectics of change.

Jim spoke to me about his fears, his loneliness and isolation, worried he would not cope. During this process he bathed, bought new clothes, shaved and cut his hair embarking on a process of identity change. He also stopped begging. The informal sessions we had helped to ground, the impetus for change came from somewhere within. When he eventually moved out he sustained his tenancy.

Case History 12; Codes of Silence

Nick had accessed two sessions, the first time in 50 years he had revealed his inner fears to anyone in "authority." His early family messages were all based on keeping the authorities away from internal family issues. His father was a hard man who had extreme notoriety in his locality. Nick lived within his shadow. His father was still a powerful presence, even though he had died ten years previously. He still cast a long pall over everyone's life. I used to speak to Nick in small exchanges as he whizzed in and out of the hostel.

"You won't want me in your sessions. I used to disrupt all the counselling in prison. I was famous for it. I bet I will end up analysing you."

Nick saw attending therapy as a challenge. He self medicated extensively using heroin. During one of these small exchanges, he told me, he previously had a well paid job but lost it over a fracas involving an off duty policeman. He had tried to settle down at one point in his life, but his temper had boiled over. The fight had stopped him from gaining any stability. Although the charges were eventually reduced when he went to court, the amount of time he spent on remand, ensured he could never return to his former job. The one avenue of escape had been foreclosed. This meant he could only follow his father's direction. Nick was sucked back into the criminal subculture.

He then went into his father's profession and descended into using heroin to cope with the stress. This meant he lost his family, as a result. It was a series of chain reactions. Each was a Russian Doll.

"You should've seen me when I was younger mate, a right tearaway, you wouldn't have got me in here then."

He told me when he was younger he was involved in armed robbery, torture, extortion and theft. Then, he was the social archetype of a hard white working class masculinity existing in certain areas of East London. His father was a man with a considerable local reputation. He had become involved in certain components of organised criminality after leaving National Service, where he had taken a special interest in fire arms training. Later joining the main army he was sent to various conflicts where his sense of aggression won him many accolades. Demobbed he was caught within various entrapments and unable to adjust to civilian life. A decorated hero with the former Special Forces, he moved into a life beyond the law.

The catalyst for Nick to begin talking to me was his anger at an injustice. Social Services had become involved in his family, and he felt powerless. Nick's daughter, looked after by his Auntie had been taken into care because of her frailty. This triggered a series of incidents as Nick tried to contain his rage. The seemingly placid man of the hostel had turned into the Hulk of his early adulthood.

I was asked to speak to Nick by the management. This was a considerable breakthrough, as his sense of self sufficiency had been a barrier to accessing support for the years he had lived within hostels and inhabited prison (Whittington 2011). Nick related he felt he was heading into a dangerous place, as he had beaten someone to near death over a minor disagreement. He had also become involved in another outside fracas over some petty issue that had escalated. Nick realised he had transferred his feelings about his daughter onto strangers. He was taking his anger out on them as a substitution. This interaction was a crucial breakthrough, as he reflected on his internal anger and its external consequences. Previously he would have gone to prison regardless of any consequences. This is how he had defined himself, as a hard man, just like his father.

Nick was a serial offender and was well known for his capabilities as an armed robber. He also related that few people can make a living at it. Even the people who go to Spain eventually return for a last job. Armed robbery was a type of power addiction, he related. When you are wielding the gun, you feel as though everything that happened to you in the past has been erased. The money becomes secondary to power.

I worked with him around strategies for coping. He had spent 20 out of the past 30 years in prison for a number of convictions. They were all based upon his recklessness, including one event where he was released after seven years, then recaptured within a day. This resulted in another long term jail sentence. It was an expectation that he would live up to his family reputation. He felt ambivalent about the consequences, saying, it was another form of stress as well as excitement. This is why he liked living within the hostel as it relieved him of needing to act within his former role. He made no attempt to move out, because he valued his freedom. He did not want to return to organised crime, and remaining low. It meant there were no expectations placed upon him. Nick revealed the culture he had grown up within. He was expected to become involved in armed combat. He described how his father had taught him from an early age to jab, box, slash, cut and twist utensils and limbs to maim and kill an opponent. Nick both idealised and was terrified of his father. Describing, if he failed to carry out the instructions properly he would be hit across the face. His mother was also drawn into the subculture. It was an expectation that he would join in. It was a belief that Mr. X's son would follow into the family trade. He had fought against it by trying to "go straight." Nick began to let his defences down, and spoke about his heroin use. It helped him cope with his childhood as he recollected the lack of emotional warmth. He revealed he was sent out to thieve for the family dinner on a Sunday. It was through the therapy, he realised he was socialised by his father to be him. He had originally believed he was a chip off the old block, a genetic copy. He began to become jittery at the thought, feeling as though he was letting everyone down by denigrating his father. Nick had waged an internal battle, fought out between his critical parent, the voice of his internalised father, battling with his own emotional needs.

"If he knew I was talking to you now like this, it would not be OK."

He told me one day. This was the psychological power his father still held in his imagination. He had died whilst Nick was in prison, and he could not attend the funeral. This was a significant local event by all accounts. Nick felt aggrieved the authorities refused him a pass to let him attend, creating a sense of injustice. Nick retreated back into the hostel milieu after an initial foray in articulating his internal emotions. Terrified of moving out, he stated he was institutionalised and did not want to leave. The hostel was the only piece of stability he had ever had in his adult life. He hung onto his room and was scared of leaving.

"I like you Dean, but I don't want to move out of the hostel. If I keep speaking to you, they will move me out, but I won't be able to cope. I have spent too long in institutions."

Nick was scared of success and what it entailed. He had built one platform of stability, hanging onto his position within the hostel for three years. He did not want to disturb it because his past was extremely fragmented. He expressed ambivalence about going to prison because it was an expectation. Discovering freedom disturbed this view. Although he was self medicating, he was putting down some roots into the world outside of incarceration. I understood what he was trying to do, but it was difficult to articulate his position. The rational pathway was to move out of the hostel as soon as a flat became available. For Nick however, letting people know he was back, would lead to more pressure and a potential return back to a former way of life. For three years he had endured a reprieve from it. All attempts by the housing worker to make contact with him were rebuffed. He could not envisage a future beyond the hostel in the sessions. He eventually stopped seeing me, although promising each week to return. As he explained, talking meant betrayal, and his status was the only thing he could hang onto. Nick lived in a limbo world. He did however stop his violence.

Case History 13; All I feel is revenge

Loll attended counselling for three sessions after I undertook an initial exploration of his needs. He was clear in the first session that he was in a desperate state of chronic anger, and was on the verge of committing a murder. He had a homicidal ideation plan, and he had been working on it for a number of weeks. He wanted to go and kill some men and their families. These were the men, who, he stated, had raped his girlfriend. He revealed he had been following the men around for weeks, and had noted the times their children were picked up and dropped off. At first I was perplexed why he was telling me the details of the plan, as he knew I would have to report it. These

209

were distinct and clear threats to others, and this entailed confidentiality being breached.

I reported the issue to the Hostel Management, and they took the appropriate action to eventually relocate him. In the meantime, I worked with him about his rage. He was seemingly suffering from Post Traumatic Stress. The revenge ideation was also a normative reaction to a series of traumatic events that he outlined. As he detailed his plan it allowed us to stop any further violence. At first I listened to his account, then when I felt it was safe for both us, to gradually introduce Socratic Questioning, in order to understand whether murdering the men's children would alter the past. It would entail these men suffered, but their children were not responsible for the adult's actions. Perhaps the children were already being bullied within their families by these men? Seemingly men who are capable of such a lack of empathy in the outside world would have issues at home? The violence they enacted were not the actions of people who display attachment and who are supportive to their children. The actions were indicative of men who had no clear boundaries. This approach had a clear impact on Loll as he revealed his "disturbed childhood" in snatches. This began to halt his homicidal ideation plan. He realised that it would not assist him if they were hurt.

With the first session I could have abandoned it at any point and called the police, but this would only transfer the problem and not heal it. I was also torn between providing support and a certain initial scepticism at the description of the events. They needed to be checked out, to ascertain their veracity. There was a considerable amount of detail involved as the details emerged through careful questioning. This highlighted the veracity of what he was saying. What was unusual is that Loll had not built trust beforehand. His plan just tumbled out as soon as we closed the door in the first session. It appeared that he was about to explode, if he did not tell anyone. When I made enquiries around the hostel, no one really knew him. He was not known to any mental health services. It also appeared what he had told me was true, that he has lost everything and was waiting to go to trial.

He related what happened in the session. He had been drinking in a bar in London with his partner. They were standing on one side of the bar, as a group of men assembled on the other side. They made suggestions they wanted to have sex with his partner. Loll had stood up to them by telling them to fuck off. Instead of leaving at this point, he continued drinking in the bar until closing time. Both he and his partner were inebriated when they left, and the men were waiting for them. They beat him to the floor, and then held him down whilst they took it in turns to rape his partner. Loll said they deliberately made him watch the act. This made it even worse, as he felt humiliated and powerless in being emotionally tortured.

She was pregnant at the time, although he was unaware, and later had a miscarriage. She then descended into depression and became suicidal. He felt helpless at what had happened and also partly to blame, by not spotting the danger signs and leaving sooner. This had sparked his feelings of revenge, as a response to the after effects. He was trying to cope with a deep sense of helplessness that pervaded him this had turned into rage. The men had been arrested and were let out on bail. Meanwhile his partner had committed suicide.

I had described the confidentiality procedure, and what I needed to do. This did create a conundrum for me, for a brief period. I empathised with his reaction to the events, but by detailing them, clearly he wanted someone to stop him. He wanted to break out of the double bind, of revenge and violence, but also wanting to live, whilst also needing to act (Laing 1960, 1961, 1964), these dynamics entrapped him. He was not expecting me to collude. Evidently the men who had committed the rape were well known to the police for violence, when the hostel management eventually spoke to them. The judicial system, although flawed, is the appropriate arena to try and create some structure around justice and the use of violence could not be undertaken outside of this structure. The therapy we undertook aimed to provide some closure for the double bereavement and trauma.

I often wondered why Loll told me. I checked out the location of his story and everything was true. There was a bar in the area he mentioned. I knew the schools he had spoken of. This was an example of someone who wanted to have his boundaries enforced. He felt compelled to act, but torn about the consequences. He veered between revenge and trying to put a brake on events by not wanting to enact further violence. In the third session he revealed he had empathy for the children of these men. He spoke about how horrible it must be for them, living in the same family and speculated on what their lives must be like. It appeared I was in the right place at the right time to avert a local catastrophe. It was clear he was building up to undertake a revenge attack. This would have entailed him being locked up for a long period of time, or being killed in the process along with others.

I spoke with Loll about needing to speak to the hostel management about safety. It would also be beneficial for him to be moved away from the London area. This was undertaken finally by the CPS after the third session. This case marked the scale of the intense emotions relayed within the therapy. It also highlights the complexity of the issues that emerge within the present needing extreme diplomacy to try and create some structure and support.

Case History 14; Violence Grows

This is the narrative related by Moss who was brought up in North London and was then sent to an institution outside of the city, seemingly for his own good. Moss presents as the proverbial hard man. When he entered the hostel he was still trapped in prison mode. It takes a while for men to adjust to the new dynamics. Moss was covered in ornate and homemade tattoos; he had a shaven head and expensive designer clothes. It transpired he had recently served a long prison sentence for violence. During this time, he stated, he had spent a year in solitary confinement "down the block," where he had smeared faeces, attacked prison officers and fought the system. Anyone who dared to approach him was attacked, as he generally behaved without limits. It transpired that Moss hated authority, and any attempt by the hostel to impose any structure was met with extreme hostility. The probation service had told us to stay away from him because of the danger he represented. Yet interestingly he responded to therapy within the first week of being in the hostel, and did not seem to be any different to the other men. As it transpired he also shared many intersecting dynamics.

In prison, the authorities had responded to his anti authoritarianism with increased violence, escalating his tit for tat exchanges. Moss would attack prison officers and anyone, including other inmates who were placed in his cell. This would entail the officers entering his cell and taking their revenge. Moss said he would take what they had to give, and then enact his form of revenge. This was a continuous process, enacted between warder and prisoner, a "tit for tat" dynamic.

He described being woken up and beaten and then dragged semi unconscious before finally he was placed in isolation. As he was placed in isolation the psychiatric medication was increased to sedate Moss. He was using four anti psychotic drugs plus Valium, Temazepam and 120mls of Methadone per day when released.

In the sessions, Moss stated this was the first time he had spoken about his life. He never spoke to anyone in prison as that was deemed off limits. He had a reputation to uphold. He had extensive previous offences for armed robbery and violence towards others. He related how he used the money from armed robbery to gain a sense of power for a few weeks after he had received his haul. He would spend it on Escort Girls, Crack, and Champagne until it disappeared, and then he would go out and do it again. I asked him why he never saved the money and put it into a legitimate business. He replied it was dirty money, and he wanted to dispose of it as quickly as possible. This was an intriguing observation he had made. Despite his desire to gain revenge for his childhood violations, he still had a notion of morality. He had a belief the money was not his, and that he should dispose of it as quickly as possible, before someone caught him. This was embedded. The money was psychologically tainted in how he had obtained it, and its only purpose was to provide the backing for a sexual and drug related release. I explored with him whether he enjoyed the experience of power it gave him. He looked at me, to see where I was coming from. Of course he did, otherwise why do it? But I pushed him, what did it represent to him this feeling of power?

He then related his family dynamics; he revealed his adult behaviour was recompense for all of the misery he had been through as a child. He had suffered an attachment wrench. He had grown up in North London with his mother, father and siblings. His father was a violent bully who had dominated the family. As he grew older the violence intensified, and it was coupled with ostracism, being locked in his room, being woken at night, dragged out of his bed and beaten. As a child, he lived in a constant state of terror. Trapped within the bodily state of fight, flight or freeze he recounted going through all three states every day. His mother provided no solace as she also beat him and berated him as he grew older. This was the pattern until they finally incarcerated him in a children's home at around 9 years old. Moss had been subject to extreme, pathological bullying within his home environment, and there was no sense of safety in the "care home." There were however distinct similarities between what happened to him as a child and the dynamics that occurred within prison.

He had been discarded from his family by his violent father who had put him into care at the age of 9. This was the final humiliation as the Social Services took him away. This should have been a decision that saved him. Instead, it locked him within a prison of rage as he related the abuse he experienced at the hands of the state. All the years later, he still expressed an outright visceral hatred of both parents. Placed in a "home", he tried to reconnect with his parents by running away constantly, and then pleading to come back. He related he undertook this at least a dozen times. It was all to no avail. If his parents saw him, they would phone the police straightaway. Then they would come and pick him up and return him to the care home. Moss was trapped in a double bind (Laing 1960, 1961, 1964).

Moss had one attachment figure, his Auntie who took pity on him, but she could not look after him long term. This appeared his only attachment relationship. Moss described the conditions of the home as brutal. The staff team, it appeared, were primarily psychopathic bullies who attacked the children constantly. This created the conditions of fight, flight or freeze as he described being incontinent into his teenage years. The children were needy and full of resentment at the world they had been forced into. Ejected from their families, they were now subject to increased punishment regimes, to make them into docile bodies. There was no hint of a psychologically informed environment within the home, unless pathological psychology is considered a benchmark.

Moss related the emotional impact of being tied down and raped by staff members who used sexual violence as a weapon of humiliation. He was penetrated; it appears, to break his resistance to authority. He asked me if I had heard of "Pin down" and then spoke about the hours he had been sat upon and crushed (Whittington 2011). He was emotionally and physically suffocated by their control methods, as it aimed to break his inner will. In response, he had created an internal command, to revenge his childhood humiliation when older. These linked back to the childhood script (Berne E. 1961, 1964) a rework of Adler's idea of organ inferiority (Adler 1956). Moss had a desire to gain recompense for something that was lacking and that was love. These day-dreams were based on revenge, the opposite of being loved. He wanted to inflict violence instead. These ideas, he revealed, sustained him until he entered adulthood when he later re-enacted them. It was in adolescence they formed. Moss had projected a hard adult masculinity as a defence against being hurt again. This formed and then continued, in response to the extreme humiliation he had endured. This highlights how personal constructs are created and maintained to create a meaning, a recompense. Hard masculinities seemingly exist in a tension to a brutalised childhood. This toughening involves being the recipient of extreme violence. This arises from attachment severance. These are the ingredients that create men who become extremely aggressive and competitive when older. The remarkable aspect is that despite everything, Moss did have empathy, notwithstanding the violence and humiliation he had endured.

His anti authoritarianism ironically created an emotional silence as he revealed, years later, the police had visited him whilst he was in prison. They were undertaking an investigation into the care "home," and they asked him whether he would testify against those who ran it. He said he refused.

I asked him why he decided to refuse. He replied, he had already made an internal command to always be anti-authoritarian. This command, undertaken in adolescence sustained him throughout the time he was subject to violence, echoing Billy in "Beaten into Violence" (Whittington 2007). This energy kept him intact, whilst he endured the brutalisation. He could not surrender his younger self now. He did not want anything to do with the police, as he viewed them as the coercive authoritarian structure. He could see no difference between them and the people who ran the home.

I asked him, "What about other children in care, what about doing something for them?" This made him pause and reflect, he said he would think about it.

I pushed further. "What about the compensation?" I asked, "Is that not an incentive?"

"Nothing could compensate me for what happened," he replied. "You know what happens when you go into the box? They have some smart arsed barrister bludgeoning you with questions. They only have to raise my past, armed robbery, violence towards others, violence within the prison and so on. I would never stand a chance within the legal system, it's all sewn up. I would come out even worse from the experience having to relive it, and then be called a liar from someone who has probably got a thing about kids anyway. I would be

humiliated and what for? For people like us, there is no future except violence and drug use. That is how we are made. You cannot rely on the system because it is corrupt. That's what I learnt as a kid, and nothing has changed that view."

This highlighted his internal command to stay safe and never surrender the result of attachment severance, violence and humiliation. The making of a hard man is based on the brutalisation of a soft child. In his adult life as soon as he was 16, Moss became involved in crime. By his late teenage years, he became involved in armed robbery, kidnapping, torture and involved in a variety of extreme, violent events. We looked at his need to revenge his childhood, and the notion of empathy. Moss stated he had no empathy at the time for anyone. He was completely empty and full of rage. This had become channelled into wielding a gun and feeling the power of exercising it against someone's head. When he was conducting torture, he could see nothing wrong. He revealed when he was inflicting violence he saw himself as a child. Then he was a victim but the roles had reversed and now he was administering violence, rather than being the recipient. This was the cycle of violence being enacted. We did a considerable amount of work around pain, torture and the cycles of violence. I had to tread carefully, but this was a key point as he described the abused child becoming the perpetrator.

His adult life was focused on revenge for his pathological hatred of authority and his institutionalisation. He could sustain this image in early adulthood but the problems for him became acute when he fell in love with his first partner. His lack of emotional preparation for the birth of his first child created a spiral he could not control. Moss could not adapt to his new family and felt a dread when his first and then his second child were born. It was as if everything was collapsing. He had fought to overcome his adolescent rage, met a woman, built a successful legitimate business, then had children and he should have felt better. For him however, the children were a catalyst for an emotional descent, as his relationship dynamics changed, he had the feeling that his partner was seeing someone else. This haunted him, and he began to self medicate on Crack. Within six months, everything he had worked for had gone, and he had nothing to show for it. In the meantime, sensing he was about to hit the floor, he tried to put some controls in place, by handing his money to his partner. As he became increasingly desperate and paranoid he became more embroiled in his self medication strategy. Seeing no way out, he attacked his partner for the money and strangled her. She refused to hand it over, and then the violence escalated. She was then forced to escape and he was left alone. She disappeared and she was eventually rehoused with a new identity. Moss was sentenced for violence against others. He received the maximum sentence and did the full amount of prison due to his anti authoritarian stance.

"They didn't like me, they made that clear, but it was mutual."

Whilst Moss was on a danger list, and should only be approached with caution by the authorities, at the hostel we undertook a number of clear constructive sessions. Moss took to therapy and made full use. Working to disassemble his hard image he revealed the abused boy behind the ferocious "front." Moss had no respect for any staff member particularly anyone who used authority. This created a problem for me, because he was making headway in the therapy, but was very confrontational with other staff members. He felt they were trying to control him. If you spoke to Moss as an equal, he would respond in kind. It you tried to direct him he would dig in and make life difficult. I could not reveal his past but at the same time the staff needed to understand the psychology of the residents. This could only be undertaken in reflective practice as part of an ongoing process. Moss's temper, when it was unleashed was incendiary thereby alienating staff. He appeared as a hard man to them. This is part of the conundrum of working with men encased in trauma. I knew the boy, hiding behind the man, whereas everyone else just saw the malevolent front. I could advocate for Moss, but he expressed extreme disrespect towards the other hostel staff, because of their modes of authority. He did not want to be told about his room being untidy, or how to wash his bowl. He would turn up at the sessions with his eyes bulging about some minor infraction he had been picked up on, saying to me

"Do they know who I am? Do they know how dangerous I am?"

He would be perplexed this was not taken into account, as everyone had access to the numerous psychiatric reports. To some extent the normalisation of Moss helped to contain him for so long. Although I could see his point of view, as a man who had spent a year in solitary for extreme violence against prison officers to suddenly being picked up for having a dirty plate was a potential catalyst for revenge. I worked with him to defuse the violent intent, and Moss tried to accommodate himself to the house rules. The problems accrued from

217

the other workers. No one else believed that change was possible. His probation officer provided minimal support, believing it was only a matter of time before he went back to prison.

Finally, working on his vision, he stated he wanted to live with his girlfriend away from the hostel. He worked towards this outcome. It was through embarking on questioning every decision made by the hostel management structure; he finally propelled himself through the door. It was a war of attrition. In using this strategy, he was eventually moved out of the hostel by his Probation Officer into private accommodation. He had burnt his bridges in the hostel through his challenges to staff backed with his apoplectic anger. He felt the design of the hostel and how the staff operated was no different to prison. Towards the end of his stay he became less concerned about being rehoused and he became more focused on his girlfriend. This was a positive aspect to his life, despite this outflow of anger, he described to me that he had fallen in love, and wanted to make the relationship work.

Moss found empathy, once again, after all the years of brutalisation. No one expected it to last. She became ill, and the hospital placed many barriers between Moss and his partner. They tried to stop them from seeing each other, seeing him as a negative influence. He used the sessions to vent his frustration and work patiently to walk around these barriers. I worked to defuse his anger. I supported him in working with authority structures, instead of constantly fighting them. Previously Moss would have taken a head charge against the wall, to try and force it move out of the way. Now he began to use diplomacy. In ten sessions, he had made a significant shift, but he needed long term support. As the therapeutic bond solidified, I suggested he needed to go to detox and rehab to build on the changes he had made. He expressed ambivalence. Moving out of the hostel after being asked to leave, he found a B&B. This was the basis for him to build his relationship. It could not take place in the hostel because of the rules about overnight guests. The men could only have their partners with them during the day.

I see him on the street every now and again. He informed me after a short stay in prison, she came out of hospital and they began living together. Although still self medicating, he was not involved in his former lifestyle. He wanted to make the relationship work. Whenever I see him in the street, we wave. Moss finally found some form of connection with other people other than hurting them. *Whilst Moss and his partner are not the idealised loving couple, they have created a bond that has transcended their respective traumatic histories.*

Case History 15; Emotional Rescue

I had known Simon from Orexis in the early 90's. Then he was a young man who had just dropped out of a Maths degree. He had been sent to the UK to study by his parents, a prestigious accolade in a country still trapped in poverty. Simon told me there was a drugs problem in his country back then. Living in the locality, he began to sell drugs to fund smoking heroin. He was from Liberia. He stayed with the agency for two years on a Methadone script, and then disappeared one day. Ten/fifteen year later, I walked through the hostel door on the first day of working there; I was greeted by a thin black man with dreads, resting on a crutch.

"Hello Dean".

Looking over I had no recognition at all. Later when I learnt his name, I felt a tinge of recognition, and it was only in the second week, the identification dawned. Simon had been in the hostel for years and had not engaged with the in-house services. Remembering me and calling out my name, turned out to be a crucial event. He not only refused to engage, but barely spoke to staff. He had been on the streets of London for ten years, and had deteriorated over that time. Injecting heroin into his leg due to poor practice, entailed he was in danger of amputation. He injected like a drunken darts player stabbing the needle into his limbs. This was self harm. Moreover, Simon always denied he was injecting to everyone else, and refused to seek treatment for the open wounds. He also refused to see the nurse, to learn how to inject properly. He had erected a barrier of denial that had created a wall to the outside world. He existed internally. Later I found out this defence was erected to stave off all bad memories from the past. Simon lived in a perpetual state of now, where nothing existed apart from the moment. This perception was kept intact by his self medication strategy. When this was no longer available, he fragmented internally.

Simon had deteriorated to such an extent within the hostel; he was eventually sectioned by the mental health team who oversaw his care. He had spent a weekend refusing to eat or drink and had made wolf like noises late at night in his room for hours. After being sectioned, he would return to the hostel to obtain drugs, either Methadone or Heroin. One day, I came across him when he should have been in hospital. I asked him if he had been discharged. He told me, it was none of my business, and started becoming abusive. This was not his usual stance. He then told me, he was going to burn the hostel down, if anyone got in his way. He needed heroin or methadone because he was in withdrawal. He was still in danger of having his leg amputated, so I quickly called the hostel staff to phone the hospital. We tried to usher him down the stairs. Simon made it clear, he felt I had betrayed him. When he was finally escorted from the premises by the police, he pointed at me shouting

"I'm going get you, you, you've betrayed me."

Two months later he returned. Silent, staring and shuffling his limbs, having had a depo, along with an assortment of anti-psychotic medication he was sullen and withdrawn. He had retreated within. Still injecting into his leg, but less frequently there were still severe concerns about his levels of self harm. Simon could no longer communicate, even on a basic level. He just shuffled, looked ahead and then nodded. He had retreated deep inside himself and remained locked in a shutdown, unfocused, trapped in a glazed dystopia.

Over a period of nine months, instead of seeking revenge, Simon would shout out "Dean." This would be my cue to sit with him. He would sit for an hour and remain silent. This went on for months. Simon stared into space and the notion of the Rogerian silence suddenly became a reality rather than a textbook technique (Whittington 2011). Gradually I began to probe, questions about his thoughts, acutely aware of the fragility of the relationship. Simon had returned to the past, trapped inside his head, pulling the shutters down. He began to nod to my questions. Eventually he revealed in short bursts; he had spent nine years on the streets. I worked with him to gain recollection, working on his dreams and nightmares. As with many people in the hostel he suffered from constant nightmares. This disturbed his sleep and so he was constantly fugued. Simon's reoccurring nightmare consisted of walking down the street and suddenly someone was chasing him, then he began to run. As he ran and looked over his shoulder, he noticed more people joining in the chase, so he sped up and stated he was running down Oxford St, then around the back streets. As he kept on going, more people kept joining in, until they caught up *with him, and then he suddenly awoke. The problem with this dream is that it put him into flight, fright or freeze mode. When awake he was stressed and when asleep, he was also under stress. He was never at rest. Simon was terrified during the day and had no respite in the night. It was vital to work with him to gain some respite. His heroin use could then be seen as rational, providing a euphoric solace, whilst the injecting was a form of self punishment. It also appeared Simon was haunted by dreams of persecution. I worked with him, to try and understand what they meant. Reality was too painful to discuss, as when my questions became too persistent he would just shut down and stare. He would grunt, nod or just sit there looking ahead. I asked him if he could confront the people in his dream and ask them what they wanted.*

He nodded, smiled at me, and said he would try. It was a breakthrough.

We continued with the therapy, and I tried my reminiscence technique. A key moment occurred when I recollected how he had helped me fix my push bike in 1993 (Whittington 2011). This opened the floodgates, and he began to reminisce, connecting back to the past; it was a moment of connection that transcended the years. It was then I asked him, what happened to the man of the 90's? This created a jolt, arising from the connection, as he began to think back. He stated he had lost contact with his parents when the Civil War in Liberia was ablaze. He had not contacted them for years, fearful over what they would say. Now he was unsure whether they were alive.

When he was on the street, he did not want to tell them what was happening, because of the stigma and shame about his decline. He said he had the hope one day he would recover, but it always seemed too far away, so he put it off. Then when he came into a hostel, he was too much of a mess to write, thinking he will get better at some point. I probed him about the relationship he had with them, to ascertain whether there were any underlying issues. From his mono syllabic answers, I surmised there existed a foundation to build upon, and then I suggested he write to them.

During the week, he wrote by himself, suddenly spurred, without waiting for me. It took a few days for the letter to be delivered to his parents in Liberia. When it did, they instantly telephoned him at the hostel. This was the crucial moment for his long term recovery, as attachment bonds were restored. He began to retrace the path from his inner shell to relate back to the real outer world. They welcomed him back regardless of what had happened to him. He stopped using heroin and I, along with a project worker devised a strategy where he could save his money.

I suggested now he had made telephone contact, he return to Liberia for a holiday. Simon stared long and hard at this,

"Do you think so?" he replied.

I worked with him to visualise his return using a CBT technique, where we pretended to go to the airport, do the checking in, wait in the lounge, board the flight and arrive at the other end. When he embarked, he was greeted by his family. I asked him to comment how he felt at each stage. Simon began to inhabit the experience. He had been backwards and forwards, but over two decades ago, and had forgotten the sensations. These began to return as we rehearsed the flight each week. Simon gradually unlocked, became less armoured and walled off. He was returning to the present with the various exercises we were undertaking. I stopped him from being bullied by another resident, and the two became friends. I also worked with Simon to attend a plumbing course. This stimulus began to have an effect. Gradually Simon was returning to consciousness and living in the present moment, inhabiting it, rather than fending off the past or the future.

Simon eventually went back to Liberia and was met at the airport by his mother, father and sister. After a long absence, he was feted, the prodigal son. Problems did occur as Simon had to adjust to a new Liberia. It was a changed land, as so much carnage had taken place. Simon came to realise that whilst he was living rough on the streets of London, all his school friends were dead, murdered in one of the early culls that took place. Whilst the time with his family was happy, adjusting to so many traumas was difficult. Whilst living on the London streets, Simon had escaped a worse trauma at home. When he returned, we worked on two levels, the elation of being accepted by his family, and the deep sense of loss created by the deaths in the Civil War. He began to see the dreams he had, as the people coming to him to warn him about what was happening back home. They had a purpose. He began to adjust to his past, as it no longer mattered in a country that had seen so many traumas. The living all inhabited post traumatic shock. Simon was no different to many men in Liberia.

Eventually he left the hostel and went into semi independent accommodation. He gained stability travelling back to Liberia, and then getting a part time post in a cafe in London. Later he returned to see me; he had clearly sustained the gains he had made. He was now a businessman travelling to Liberia at least once or twice a year. He also had a girlfriend there. This was a remarkable transition for someone who was on the extreme edge of trauma, shuffling in his shoes, nodding his head. He had recovered some of his poise from the early 90's, after twenty years of mental health chaos. All it took was a descent into his void and to stay there whilst he unlocked and presented the key.

Case History 16; Madness is a State of Mind

Rickie was a long term, entrenched, hostel occupant, originally from outer London, he had grown up in Children's Homes in the suburbs. He had an emotional breakdown when he was 24, and he was now in his mid 40's. He was still suffering from the after effects of trauma. Previously, when he was in his early adulthood, he had a period of stability from the ages 16-24, holding down relationships and jobs.

Since he had his psychological breakdown, he had many brief spells in prison, psychiatric units and hostels. He was usually locked up by the police for being drunk and disorderly. His various spells in hostels were marked by his increasing anger directed to staff. He was frustrated in being caught in the revolving door of homelessness and hostels. His extensive rages entailed him being sedated. He had been given accommodation previously but had turned them into Crack Dens, according to the notes in his file. He would then be evicted back onto the street. Rickie was therefore extremely vulnerable and subject to having his accommodation being taken over by more aggressive men. Rickie was known as a very difficult resident. He was trapped in limbo.

Rickie was also involved with the local psychiatric services and had a diagnosis for schizophrenia. He had high levels of income derived from having the full amount of DLA, (Disability Living Allowance) and he was bullied by other residents. When intoxicated he gave away everything he had. He attended the therapy twice a week for over 18 months, and embarked upon a therapeutic rollercoaster ride.

He had had various parts of his body broken in numerous fights, all started by his lack of personal boundaries. Rickie always refused to back down when faced with overwhelming circumstances. Rickie was verbally aggressive, but he was no match, when pitted against the hardened men of the homeless subculture. Rickie would approach the most armoured male and challenge him to a fight, knowing he would lose. It was self harm. It entailed him having his arm broken on three occasions, his teeth knocked out and numerous blows to the head.

Rickie would turn up to the sessions in various guises, the gangster, the Irishman, Rod Stewart, Jimmy Cagney or the madman. I worked with him to deconstruct the personalities and find the real Rickie. Drawing on Harry Stack Sullivan (Barton Evans 1996) I began to perceive the strategies he used during his adolescence being carried through his years of loneliness as support structures. Jimmy Cagney and Rod Stewart were people who had helped him when he had been wrenched from his family. He had drawn on their imagery during his late childhood and adolescent years. Jimmy Cagney was his mother's favourite actor. She had an emotional breakdown following the death of her brother. Rod Stewart was the glam man from the 70's, who represented another adolescent daydream world, glamour that opposed the mundanity of his existence. This was a type of mantra Rickie carried, as he lived within a self composed fantasy world. He told me he created these worlds because the real one was too awful. He lived in a world of glamour, divorced from reality, a world that he could inhabit inside his head.

When his mother had her mental health breakdown, back in the 1960's, his father was unable to cope with looking after his children by himself. He had placed the children into care, initially temporarily. When he was placed in the children's home, Rickie broke out in a series of carbuncles. This entailed him being taken from the home around the age of 5 and put into hospital isolation. The hospital was unsure of the diagnosis, so they kept him isolated for months. This, I perceived, was the genesis of his later emotional breakdown, the enforced attachment severance, the bodily reaction and the isolation from the family. This was terrifying for a child as his attachment world collapsed around him, leading to a form of entrapment. All his certainties were ruptured and instead dread loomed over each day. He was trapped in isolation and was barrier nursed. He was left alone, bereft of touch and care. I began to see how his reaction differed to his siblings. It transpired, whilst caught in this situation, he wrote a childhood script (Harrison 1986) that allowed him to escape the horror of existence, and he composed an alternative world inside his head.

Following the work of Wilhelm Reich (1933) I explored with him how this outbreak of boils occurred to see if it was a bodily reaction to the trauma he had endured. His mother's breakdown ensured she was deemed not capable of looking after her three girls and two boys. This attachment severance from his mother and now from his brothers and sisters, drawing on Reich (1933) and Spitz (1965) could be perceived as the foundation of his illness. It transpired he had suffered a condition known as hospitalism (Spitz 1965).

These were the precipitating factors we identified, as he recollected how his mental illness formed. Strangely, during these sessions Rickie became lucid and as coherent as I had ever seen him. Returning back through the door into the main hostel, he would drift back into his performed role, but for moments he emerged as someone else, the man who existed before the emotional collapse. It appeared these were guises he adopted, as we surveyed his early trauma. Everyone else just saw the "madman," a role he performed to perfection when he wanted.

"Yes that would send anyone mad wouldn't it, all of those within a space of six months. Not good is it."

He used an understated irony to express himself. This belied his sense of innate meaningless that existed within his world. These were the seeds of his trauma. He had functioned up to a point. We looked at the point of collapse. This occurred when he took an acid tab when he was 24. This was a trigger event, and Rickie blamed his collapse on the drug, before we looked in depth at his early life. He felt he was still trapped inside the trip. He asked me continuously how long it lasted. I informed him they usually last around 12 hours, not 20 years. The trip triggered something inside him, as he saw himself in what he had repressed. The anchor points that held him, snapped one by one. He was left isolated. He saw the small boy trapped in the bed for months, and this triggered a reaction, as the events of the past he had actively forgotten, arose, and then overwhelmed him. The LSD appeared to be a trigger for reliving the trauma of his childhood as he explained what happened. At 24 he had repressed it, and then it reappeared in floods of angst. It overwhelmed him.

225

Rickie had spent 11 years in two care homes, which he had previously described as idyllic. Gradually the image began to melt and then eventually break down in the sessions. He said the first home was caring until he went to Secondary School, then things became harsher. He recollected the other children were taken back home at some point, but he was still left at the care-home. This demarcated his anger towards them, feeling they had received more care from his parents than him, and this had strengthened them. Meanwhile he was abandoned in the home and no one cared.

At 16 he eventually left care and was given a flat. This provided independence. He was however vulnerable to older people and it was during this time he was attacked by an older man. This occurred because he said he trusted older males. Raped at 16 he managed to have two significant relationships with women. He worked at home and abroad in a high pressure industry before having a psychological collapse. Placed in a secure unit at 24, he was then provided with psychiatric medication. When he was discharged, he became homeless and revolved around the homeless hostels for years, as he could never find stability. He had few emotional anchor points; those memories people can retrieve to make themselves feel loved.

During the time I met with him, I sat and endured his initial volcanic rages, sitting there unflinching. My initial strategy was to draw upon Person Centred Therapy (Rogers 1961) and let the rages blow. This was a common strategy I used to build and then sustain trust. Trying to subdue his anger was a non useful strategy, as Rickie clearly had immense reasons to be livid. Denying his anger would stoke the fears even further. Sitting with him over the year and a half brought some surreal responses. After screaming and shouting how he hated the hostel, its design, the staff, the food and wanting to return to the street, he would get up to shake my hand and say;

"Same time next week?" Laugh and walk out into the hostel."

It was not however a game, it was a conduit for him to safely defuse the anger that infused him. The anger was stored within his body and it needed a release. As the anger abated over the weeks I began to work with him on a vision for the future based on turning these negatives into a positive. Working with colleagues, a structure was devised with Rickie. This entailed him visualising he could shift forward. Encouraging him to attend detox, then rehab, thereby creating a life purpose became the focus. Rickie was a binge drinker who would buy expensive presents on his pay day such as rings, boots, clothes and alcohol then give them all away in two to three days, so he had nothing left. He would remain sober for the next few days until the next batch of money came in, and then he would repeat the cycle.

When he became drunk, Rickie would also become suicidal. He would phone an ambulance for companionship. These were called out at least twice a week. In exploring why he called them, it became apparent this connected back to the isolation ward. Rickie saw being hospitalised as a form of solace. The ambulance service worked with the hostel to ascertain how they should proceed. They were at their wits end with the number of call outs. It was only through the therapy, headway could be made. Rickie located his need to his earlier state to eventually shift out of it. It was then finally the call outs began to cease, until they eventually stopped, as he worked on his vision. It appeared that all his actions had an internal meaning, and were symbolic. What was needed was an ability to decipher the emotional code he had written.

His parents were deceased, but he did have supportive siblings. These were a lifeline for Rickie, as these were the main attachment ties he had to the real world. Although he railed about them, he was also deeply grateful for their support, as they learnt to manage Rickie's behaviour and contain him. He also had a girlfriend and she was from a German family. She also had endured a breakdown and Rickie had met her whilst on a section. They both shared a love of Rod Stewart and this created their attachment bond. Rod had carried them both through their adolescence.

His other connection to the real world was based on a surreal form of mockery. His sense of being without limits pushed him into virtual suicidal situations. He narrated upon the world with the insight of King Lear's fool. Whilst performing the role of the madman, he had an x ray vision. The local police brought him back from one escapade that involved singing to the commuters on a Friday evening "to cheer them up." They related how he had turned up in the middle of a riot, in just his underpants, shouting for the police to stand down and shake hands with the other side. Even they had found it funny, as they later recollected the story of him appearing unexpectedly to try and defuse the situation. Rickie was well known by the local police because when intoxicated, he would begin singing and shouting in the street, causing a disturbance of the peace. Usually they arrested him, kept him in the cells until he sobered up and was then released. The police were careful with Rickie.

Over the 18 months Rickie made considerable progress. He became stable enough for the first time to consider detox and rehab. He attended outside support such as the local alcohol service and went to AA meetings. Rickie eventually completed a detox for the first time, as the consultant at the NHS service had changed and someone more psychologically informed helped to create a change in the system. Rickie spent two weeks in a rehab before absconding, stating he missed the inner city. Rehoused, he managed to hang onto his flat, but shifted from abstinence to binge drinking, although nowhere near as bad as before. He drank once a week, rather than three to four times per week. He had made significant gains. His sense of the absurd however was never curtailed.

He later spent some time in prison for armed robbery, after walking into a village hall with a pretend, plastic, toy—gun during a WI function he told them to put their hands up. He then walked out again. He was sentenced to prison for several months for this escapade. When asked why he had done it? He replied;

"It was the anniversary of my Dad's death and I remember him buying me a plastic gun when I was small. I just wanted to go and show them what my Dad had bought me, but they thought it was a real one. I walked out of the hall but someone had called the police. Next minute I was covered in red dots and surrounded by an armed response unit."

After he was released Rickie turned up at the hostel to thank me. Stretching out his hand, he stated;

"I think you helped me as much as I helped you. Let's call it quits." This was his parting shot as he burst into laughter; shaking my hand again, he disappeared out of the door.

Case History 17; Equal Opportunities

Michael was a 49 year old white working class London man. Although he had physical disabilities, he overcame them through being extremely flamboyant both in dress and personality. Michael accessed therapy twice a week with a long list of complaints that he wanted attending to. He was also outwardly gay and broke hostel boundaries in pointing out the various male staff members he liked as figures of his lust. This was often challenged by staff. Michael took to therapy as an actor to a stage, it allowed him to shine. He was constantly drunk and would perform a thespian's soliloquy on the evils of the world and his position within it.

"My dear boy, we must do coffee. Come, come I'm buying. Or do you want me to take you to the pub?"

Michael had few conceptions of professional boundaries, which as we explored them, seemingly emanated from his childhood. He revealed in these "talks" he had been married and he had two sons. They were estranged. He would remark at the beauty of women and the horror of their personalities. Trying to disentangle Michael's views was not easy, as he shrouded himself in obtuseness. He would reveal himself as whatever sexuality he wanted to show to the world at that particular moment in time. Shocking people was his forte. Similar to Rickie, his desire was to prick the bubble of complacency. He had his own drinking club who assembled within his room. His rate of DLA entailed he could buy drinks for a few days and then expect his kindness to be reciprocated, when everyone else became paid. This kept everyone in his club in a state of perpetual drunkenness, trapped within a culture of expectations.

One evening Michael turned up in the canteen dressed as a woman to test the views of everyone else in the hostel. This caused a considerable stir. Open homosexuality did not exist in the hostel. It may have taken place behind closed doors, but before this event it was a taboo subject. After Michael appeared in the canteen dressed as a woman, the number of gay relationships within the hostel suddenly blossomed from none to two/three. This was a watershed event. The hard men of the hostel were torn between wanting to beat him, laughing at him or acceptance. The final result was acceptance and those who critiqued Michael were told to mind their own business. The main appraisal however was that Michael was an ugly woman, and he needed to put more effort into dressing up, so the other hostel members would find it less offensive.

It became a watershed event as previously there was no differentiation between men who were paedophiles and those who were gay. This was part of the *general consensus. Men who had sex with men were the same people it was deemed, as those who had sex with children. This is why homosexuality was seen as taboo and those who practiced it were subject to violence. With the increased exposure of homosexuality as a lifestyle choice in mainstream society, this view, formed in the furtive secrecy of families/institutions, changed. Families and institutions were where boys were sexually assaulted, and this perception that gays were paedophiles began to break down. The men could see there was a difference between men who had adult male relationships and the men who had attacked them when they were children. This was a major change within the culture of the hostel. Being gay was no longer equated with sex with children.*

This had created great confusion in the lives of these marginalised men, especially those who had been previously sexually assaulted. There was no differentiation between the two groups in mainstream society. Both were perceived as deviant out-groups, reflecting their own position within a hierarchy of being the "other" (Sartre 1943). The hidden nature of both homosexuality and paedophilia and the general lack of discussion, made it difficult to ascertain the differences between men who had sex with men and men who had sex with children. These issues became ever more complicated when it emerged boys had been raped by women.

Michael was also trapped in his disability, however he was the taboo buster. In the therapy we made some headway, but he was more concerned in trying to entice me into his make believe world, where he spun his web. He was a gale force wind, that ripped through the hostel and he left a type of emotional chaos behind him.

One issue he did relate was that he had an accident on the first day of school when the scaffolding collapsed on him. This had led to his injury and long term lay off from school. His mother had looked after him, but his brothers and sisters became jealous. He became extremely tearful in the sessions when we looked at the past. It was then he began to relate issues around the formation of his sexuality and childhood. His vulnerability as a child because of his disability and inability to fight back, entailed he decided to harden himself as a result. This was his adult stance to life, a type of full tilt at it based upon being inebriated to emotional pain. I explored options around detox and rehab but Michael sidestepped any notion of change stating

"Look at me, who is going to employ me, no one. If I stop now, what are the prospects?"

Eventually Michael left the hostel one day to return back to the wider world. Impatient in waiting to be rehoused, he felt he could take his chances in bed and breakfast and see what happened. Before he left the session, he stated his intention that he was going to move away.

"I don't like the hostel. I think I will leave then see what turns up old boy. It's all a game isn't it."

Case History 18; Waiting to be rescued

Phil was difficult to engage in the hostel. He never spoke to anyone for months. He would enter the front door briefly and like a small mammal he would taste the air with his finger. Then he would disappear for the day. I spoke to him in fragments about the weather, as he was extremely dishevelled. It transpired he spent most of his time begging to support his heroin habit. Unusually, he had never been arrested whilst living at the hostel. It transpired he did not have a criminal conviction. The weather was a significant factor with him, because he went begging every day in the sun, rain and snow. He was affected by the climate. He later related to me the effects of different forms of emotional coldness, based on his observations of the weather and his heroin use.

It was clear in the first contact; Phil was suffering from some component of severe trauma. He only just acknowledged where he was staying. He referred to all of the workers as Miss and Sir, as he could never remember anyone's name. The servile deference arose from being institutionalised. It had become easier for him just to recognise and acknowledge gender differences. Gradually through small talk, we developed a tentative rapport. Phil never changed his clothes for years and he was in his mid thirties. He revealed he had bathed around 12 times in his life. Nothing had been undertaken recently. His room was completely bare, apart from the bed and table. He had no spare clothes, only the rags he wore. These were completely filthy. He also carried a dirty blanket which he used to keep warm when he was begging.

Eventually, through the small talk, he attended formal counselling. It became clear Phil needed to be grounded in the present. He was stuck in the past and he lived in a dream world. What emerged when talking to him, he had built a fantasy world that allowed him to escape the dynamics of the past and his previous sense of entrapment. He also revealed he had been estranged from his partner for 12 years, and this haunted his conversation. He could think of nothing else other than his desire to be reunited. He said he was waiting on the streets for her to pick him up and take him home.

"You need to find Ellen for me. Tell her I love her. What is the matter with that girl? Why has she left it twelve years? Why hasn't she come to get me sooner? What is the matter with her?"

This was his continuous mantra. Phil was stuck within this feedback cycle. He told me he went out begging, hoping he would meet her, then everything would be alright and they would get back together. We went around like this for weeks; until I felt we had a strong enough bond for me to begin to challenge him. I sensed that I needed to try and ground him in the present, but it would need to use a directional strategy rather than rely on any non directional engagement. He needed to focus on the present and in particular his health which was deteriorating. Another issue became apparent; Phil was too chaotic to adhere to structure. He rebelled against any thought of it. The idea was to try and work with him to build a structure out of his chaos.

"If you want her to save you then you need to think how it is going to happen. You need to work towards this belief and then to make it happen."

"Yeh, of course I do."

"Well what about taking care of yourself?"

"She can take care of me, that's what I need."

Phil had surrendered himself to an idealised Ellen. This was the name of his former partner. Ellen would save him and make everything OK, she just needed to know where he was.

As we explored the importance of this relationship it became apparent, Ellen had released him from the effects of institutional violence, as he grew up in care. Phil was traumatised by his early life events and this relationship with Ellen was his one attachment. This provided him with stability, helping him escape the rigours of living in "care". After five years his partner who had two young daughters asked him to leave the house. It was meant to be a year's break. Phil had been working at this point in a steady manual job. He spoke about how he had tried to make the family work.

When she suggested the break, he moved out, and firstly he sofa surfed, expecting to be called back at any point. Then he began to use heroin and finally ended up living on the street. He believed Ellen would still look for him, when she realised what he meant to her, and then ask him back. As the months went by, he still held onto this vision. 12 years later he still believed. I worked to prise him away from this. It was an error that was holding him back. Whatever the reasons for the original split, the distance between them was now a gulf. Phil needed extensive ongoing care from a hospital. His poor injecting practice had transformed his legs into a tableau that represented the surface of the moon. He revealed he wanted to have his legs amputated; stating Ellen would surely have to look after him if he had no legs. Phil was deeply estranged from his body and he spoke about it as an object. This marked a split he had created in his head. He told me about a boy in the "Care Home" who was constantly raped in the dorm and he related the attacks. I never put it to him that this boy was near to Phil, but guessed the way he had walled off, there were connections. Phil was extremely fragile and this was not an appropriate time to explore what happened in the home. We needed to embark on shoring up his fragile state in the present.

In trying to gain some form of emotional truth I used Adler's Socratic questioning (1956) to try and shift beyond the seemingly autistic outer shell he had created, to fend off reality. This was utilised, once the foundations had been created using Person Centred (Rogers 1961) and then a form of rational emotive. I put it to him that he would not be able to meet his estranged partner if his legs were taken off. She would not want to push him around in a wheel chair. This made him pause and reflect. He became fixated on finding his partner and asked me if I had found her yet. I knew of a way to do it but was not sure if he was ready. Eventually after three months of him asking me, I showed him the locality where she lived and asked him if he could meet the plan guidelines we had worked out. He never asked about her again after I confronted his illusion. This marked a break. I was flying into a void with Phil, not knowing if what I was doing was helpful, but it was clear from his health, something needed to be done to try and get him to take care of himself. He was in danger of having his legs amputated.

I encouraged the substance use workers to try and key him into services. Phil made all the right noises, but his drug dealer had warned him, Methadone gets into your bones and you can never get off it once addicted. Phil would begin a course of Methadone at the low titration rate of 30mls, with the expectation he would return to have his dose upped, but each time he abandoned treatment. He felt Methadone did not do anything, and therefore why continue. Heroin was instantaneous. He did not need to keep going backwards and forwards to a clinic. Phil tried, and abandoned treatment around five times, stopping within the first week because it didn't do anything.

I eventually worked with him to speak about the past. He revealed to me his mum had put him in care because she did not want him. He reminded her of his father who had absconded when he was born. He had spent eleven years in total in the home. She had rejected him, and there was no sense of attachment between them.

In response, Phil regularly travelled to where she lived when he was short of money. Their "adult" relationship consisted of her shoving ten pound notes through the letter box, telling him to go away. This type of interaction was clearly not healthy from either perspective. Phil used the money to buy heroin when his begging was not bringing in enough money to buy a bag. His bedraggled presence was seemingly too much for his mother to cope with, so he emotionally blackmailed her, feeling entitled because of her previous neglect. The relationship was based on the dialectics of revenge and shame. Mother and son were trapped in a performed role. Phil could not recollect a time when she had supported him, or even travelled to see him at the Children's Home. He suffered from a severe form of attachment severance.

I estimated that Phil was trapped at around five years old. The therapy would entail his growth, but it would also create problems, as he went through the various growth stages. Phil needed to go through adolescence. I visualised him as someone who was locked in a state of infantile dependence. He had never obtained a sense of being an adult. Clearly he was traumatised and trapped in a childlike state. Gradually he emerged from his shell to connect to the world outside. A significant transference issue emerged when he asked me if I wanted to have sex with him for £20. This appeared to be a cultural norm he held, and when I explored how this projection had arisen, he revealed this had happened previously with other workers.

Phil's self medication always took precedence over every other need. He did however begin to become less frozen. One day he came to speak to me to talk about the coldness of the street, the biting cold that gets into your bones, that is even more ferocious than withdrawal coldness and this differs from a mother's coldness. Phil had begun to reflect on the different types of being cold, thinking physically and emotionally. I asked him about his legs and he spoke about the pain he felt, as he had to walk everywhere. It was like walking on broken glass, is how he termed it. He had been taking his anti clotting injections, to stop any blood clotting, but these had not repaired his legs. I asked him if he bathed, and he said now and again. He had been trying to keep clean, and in the six months he had three baths. During lunch I went to the pound shop, and bought him a bowl, Dettol, salt and coconut oil for his feet.

I had the idea he needed to reconnect to his body. For the first time he touched his feet, as he bathed and massaged them. Previously he viewed himself as an object. Phil lived in the citadel of his mind and his body was a dart board for him to put a needle in. When he became bodily aware, I presumed he would not be so keen to destroy it. The hunch I had began to work. He had found it painful to bathe because of his open wounds, but he did begin a process of cleansing by ensuring his feet were bathed. Phil began a healing process and whilst the produce from the pound shop is not going to heal the internal damage, it has halted his desire for amputation. At last Phil has begun a journey to discover himself and undertake self care.

Case History 19; Magic Carpet Ride

Jason had been living in the hostel since 2005. Diagnosed with schizophrenia he was a patient of the local mental health team. Since he had been in the hostel he had gradually deteriorated, undertaking an inward retreat. This entailed him surrendering all concerns about his outward appearance. He had rarely washed himself or his clothes. Isolated within the hostel he lived within his room, he stared at a series of maps he had assembled whilst occasionally smoking Cannabis. He rarely spoke to staff. He wore shorts in winter along with football boots. I noticed something incongruent however when I was talking to another resident in his room. There was a tap on the door. Jason asked to buy some Cannabis then caught himself when he saw me. He mumbled and then went away.

Davie, whose room it was beamed out "All the loonies talk to me, although I've noticed they never speak to the staff." It appeared Jason could make the effort to straighten himself out when he needed.

When I made a bond with him much later, I asked him about the relevance of the maps. Jason said he escaped into dream worlds with them. Although trapped in his room he could transport himself anywhere in the world, and live a fantasy life. It meant he could have a foreign holiday, without any of the problems of travel. This was his inward retreat, away from reality.

I began to get to know Jason over a series of small exchanges. Football was the main focus. Initially he never spoke to me, and it took a year of nods and hellos, before any contact was made. The incident of tapping at the door was as much as he spoke to any member of staff in the years he was there.

In between his health deteriorated, he stopped washing altogether, stopped going to the canteen and began buying and eating dog food. He also made strange high pitched whistling noises, forcing the other residents to attack him when he did this during the night. Eventually he was sectioned and emerged six months later with a clearer focus. When I learnt he was a fan of Crystal Palace I would show him snippets in the London Evening Standard. I began to talk to him about the players and their prospects. This strategy had the impact of grounding him in the present. He would build on these small exchanges to let me know what happened over the week end. It was through small talk he developed trust. Eventually we went into the counselling room and then we began to meet regularly.

He related his childhood experience of being constantly systematically bullied by other children. This entailed he retreated into his bedroom to escape the torment. *He was also affected by his parents' divorce. He escaped their rancour by locking himself in his room.*

Jason made tentative steps to shift out of his shell, and the staff team alerted to these changes, encouraged him. These tentative steps, and the encouragement created by the emotional literacy of the staff team, allowed him to gain more self esteem and confidence. It was an ongoing process. This was a psychological environment in motion. It was akin to building a psychological structure from the foundations. Encouraging him to enter the mainstream world, entailed he gained confidence to recount more of the earlier trauma of his life; having a gun pulled on him, being ostracised by his mother for smoking Cannabis in his bedroom, surviving on the streets for five years, the impact on his fragile self esteem. He then revealed he was raped as a child by a close relative, and this was another reason why he retreated away from the world. He could no longer face what was happening to him. The real world was too awful, smoking Cannabis and playing computer games allowed him to drift away into a dream world. This is where he lost contact with the outer world and his "madness" began. Talking to me about these issues helped him to validate his early life.

I explored with him why he had improved after being sectioned?

He replied "You try living with a bunch of fucking loonies for six months and you would want to get better."

This was not him revealing that he was play acting. His trauma was real. Faced by the shock of recognition, he invested his energy in pulling away from what he saw in the reflection. Jason made great strides in engaging with the world, shifting away from someone with a mental health diagnosis. Interestingly the psychiatric team told everyone it was because they had put him on new medication. It was on this basis they decided he was ready to attend another dry hostel. This was after a year of therapeutic work. Jason became very anxious before the move and I alerted the team he was becoming scared of the change. The crux of the issue was what was deemed best for Jason. He had initially agreed to being moved, and the planned exit was set in motion. Jason had previously been bullied in the hostel, when he was in full retreat, and escaping from it was deemed desirable.

I was in two minds believing he needed to be moved as part of a dynamic, but I also thought even though he had been in the hostel for a long period of time, the current gains were fragile and needed cultivating. Perhaps a new environment would bring that out? Moving him needed more planning than just whisking him from accommodation to another, but the psychiatric services were adamant it was the new medication that had made the gains. Jason had built himself up within the hostel as someone who played pool, taken part in activities and was part of the social scene. Surrendering these gains would not be easy. He had developed a social interest.

The fragility of the gains became apparent. When he left he looked fearful, hardly spoke or said good bye. Within a week he had returned to a catatonic state and was subsequently sectioned, put back onto the psychiatric ward. The crux of the issue was the status of the talking therapies. This intervention was perceived on a lower order than the medical input. This needed to change in the future. This particular incident made it clear the therapist should be in the driving seat and the medical model is an adjunct to the main intervention of building attachment. The workers from the psychiatric service varied in their understanding of the emotions. There was some very good joint work where they would consult whilst other workers would ignore the therapeutic input. This highlighted a training deficiency. Mental health existed within a mechanistic world of drugs and effects. The impact of this type of intervention denied relational realities. This had a real impact on Jason after a very good psychiatric nurse left who used to consult jointly. The new workers had not concept of the emotions and based all their views of a mechanical care plan. This worked to Jason's detriment and the therapeutic gains all unravelled.

Case History 20; A Waiting Game

Mickie was a fifty year old Londoner who consumed large quantities of Cannabis. He also drank heavily. The combined effect of his self medication strategy was impacting on his lungs, kidneys and liver. He drank 8-10 cans of Special K Cider per day. He was tipsy but never drunk.

When he first accessed the hostel he kept himself to himself. Initially closed off, he gradually emerged from clouds of Cannabis to play pool. His social world revolved around drink and Cannabis use. He was involved in a social club that involved other residents, as they lent money, drank alcohol and smoked Cannabis, all sharing amongst each other. Mickie attended counselling when this arrangement collapsed into retribution. He was stabbed in the face, after lending money to someone who refused to pay him back. Mickie had tried to cajole him to return the money and then finally insisted. This provoked an attack, as the man stabbed him to keep up his "front." In the ensuing melee the police were called and Mickie was left to press charges against his assailant, after spending time in the police station under questioning.

Mickie was furious at the "liberty" that had been taken and was swearing vengeance, saying if that had been his younger self, who had been striped, then this man would be dead. He had clear homicidal ideation plans. The other man was in the police cells, so they could not be enacted. It took weeks for Mickie to calm down. He said he was tense, he could not sleep, feeling full of anger, having flash backs and in a constant state of alert at every knock on his door. The attack had stirred up old memories, bringing the past back to haunt him within the present.

I spent weeks with him to calm him down, as he expressed his rage and intent in the sessions. Used to men venting their anger, therapy became a safe space to blow the energy into the room; whilst I balanced the idea of letting them express anger whilst reflecting on how much danger existed to others. The protagonist had been arrested and when released was moved to another hostel, so there was no real threat involved, as Mickie was unaware of what was happening.

After the anger subsided, following several weeks of therapy, Mickie began to talk about his early life growing up in the East End, and his love of Leyton Orient. This helped to cement the relationship, as I knew little about this team, but prompted him to reminisce. As the bond developed, he recalled a recurrent dream that haunted him every night. This stopped him from getting to sleep afterwards for hours, because although not frightening, it held a message for him he could not decipher. Exploring sleep was one of the strategies I used to get people to talk, as the dreams held a key. When we worked on them, the anxiety usually subsided, and the amount of sleep improved. This provided a practical application to the therapy, as getting five hours or more sleep, was a significant achievement for many men in the hostel. Mickie slept between 2-4 hours per night, waking constantly, then nodding off, drifting into a shallow sleep, lying *forever alert. He revealed he wanted to have his legs amputated; stating Ellen would surely have to look after him if he had no legs.*

He stated he drank because alcohol helped him to get to sleep, as did the Cannabis. I explored with him whether the Cannabis speeded up the heart beat, and actually kept him awake. Mickie went away to ponder and experiment with his Cannabis use, and noted its impact on his sleeping pattern. This assisted in him in cutting down and listening to his body before he went to bed.

The dream concerned him being in a room with his painting materials, where he painted one wall, then turned around to get his brushes and paint another, but the brushes were gone. He turned back again, and the wall returned to its former unpainted state. We worked together on the meaning, so Mickie could begin to unpick it. It was important he found the meaning, rather than I interpret it, so he could understand and then grasp what was being said. He used to be a painter and decorator and had to give it up when he became homeless. He recognised the dream was telling him there was a sense of futility in achievement as everything he set out to attain collapsed. Events were always conspiring against him, so he had resigned himself to fatalism. It took us a few weeks to get there, but it did begin to create a spark in Mickie, as he began to visualise his future based on looking at how he had negated his life. He had spent years not making any decisions, thinking everything would sort it out, then everything would be OK. He had drifted into his 50's with no aim or purpose, believing other people would rescue him. He had surrendered any personal responsibility.

In particular he revealed he was waiting for his partner to contact him, even though they had split up eight years previously and had not spoken since. He recounted they had never lived together independently as a couple. Initially they had both led separate lives until eventually he went to live with her family, when his son was born. She lived in her mother's house. There was tension after the baby was born and Mickie then drifted into going to the pub to relieve his feelings of being ostracised.

When I worked with Mickie, his son was now a young adult who had recently established contact with his father. This had brought him out of his self imposed isolation. Mickie had another dream; they would all be reunited if only she made the first move. I asked him how he would react, if he found she had found someone else. He went bright red as the anger flushed his face.

"It's a good job we know each other", he stated. Just the thought of it . . . No she wouldn't do that she is a proper woman not like the others you see around the hostel."

She would be waiting for him. This appeared as an idealisation, and I felt I needed to tread carefully around his vision; I needed to prepare him for a reality that may not match up to his idealisation. The reminiscence work led him to talk about his family. His father was a quiet man who went to work, whilst his mother stayed at home to look after the children. He described himself as a naughty kid, always getting into trouble, never able to sit still. When he was at school he was the class clown. He learnt to read and write, but lost interest in school after a while. School was not for him and he was impatient to leave. He wanted to go to work, to earn money. There was an initial incongruity between his narrative and his position in a homeless hostel. I tried another tack and looked at his periods in prison. He had expressed some anxiety that he would be return to his former life, when he said he was intent on revenge for the initial attack.

This produced a breakthrough, as he related a story about his last spell in prison. The incident arose when he returned to see his mother, after he had left home to live with his partner. He had minimal contact with his mum after his father passed away. He described her as closer to his sister than him. His mum had been drinking, and Mickie said he should have walked away when he noticed the bottle. It was a warning sign from his childhood telling him there was danger in the air. However his sister was present and he thought he was safe, as he was close to her.

He then related that his mother was a continuous binge alcoholic, who would become chronically drunk, be mean and spiteful, then the next day deny everything she had done. This had a huge impact on him because she had a dual personality. When she was drunk she would attack him verbally and physically. The next day she would claim amnesia. She not only beat him, but then denied his reality that he had been beaten. This form of amnesia was enacted as a power play. It created a burning sense of vitriol inside him.

He would try and point out to her the effects of her behaviour, and in return she would just scream at him he was making it all up to try and humiliate her. He would back off, confused and hurt. I probed further what "spite" meant and he said; "very spiteful". As the trust grew, Mickie stated she used to pull the wooden slats out of the airing cupboard, and beat him with them until they broke. She would then punch and kick him, when he was a kid. The next day she would be completely different, cook his dinner and ask how his day went. This continued until he left home to live with his partner. As he recollected he realised how bizarre the behaviour was. Interestingly he still believed all mothers behaved like this, until he asked me what I thought. Feeling safe and having a strong bond with him I said to him that this was not everyday behaviour. His face flushed and he said he thought so. The worst injustice however was about to emerge. When he returned home as an adult his mother began screaming at him.

"It was like I was still a kid again even though I was a 40 year old man. Then she went for me. I was stuck; I went rigid with fear and then felt her hand digging into my face. So I pushed her and she came back with a weapon, so I grabbed it off her, but she came at me again. Then we fell on the floor. I managed to pin her down and called the police on a mobile."

"They eventually came, as I had her pinned down, but they took one look, made up their minds and took me away in cuffs. She then pressed charges against me. I was on remand, thinking they're going to think it's a big mistake and they will let me out. It went to trial, and my solicitor was useless. They didn't even get the call transcript, and they asked me to plea bargain, saying it will all be knocked down to a misdemeanour. I could walk out of the court with no fine as it was going to be a bind over. It was an easy decision, even though I was the wronged party. Like a fool I believed them and instead I was given four years. I did half of that in the end."

Expecting his sister to back him up, he was disillusioned when she backed out of providing any support when he appealed against the sentence. Mickie's sense of injustice was raw, as he recalled the past events. His anger was seismic, bubbling beneath the surface. He had been put in prison by his mother, after she had attacked him and then she had lied to the police. Mickie was caught in another double bind (Laing 1960, 1961, 1964) in revealing his mother had lied as she would be imprisoned for perjury and violence. Alternatively he could keep quiet. He vowed never to speak to her again unless she went to the police and told them the truth. They had no communication for years.

Another problem emerged in the sessions, later, when the trust had been established. His former partner decided to get married and had sworn her son to secrecy. This was a red, hot, wound that seared Mickie across all his levels. The anger frothed, bubbled then erupted when he eventually learnt about the marriage. He became incandescent. This was the last strand before he went on a rampage. I had already prepared the ground earlier, not knowing, but sensing she would have found someone else. We worked through the violent blasts. Hurting his son's mother would not bring her closer to him. Eventually as we worked it through week by week, Mickie realised he would always have part of her memories and this was good enough for him in the end. This marriage, released him from the past and we navigated the crisis. This provided the final spark for change.

We worked together to make the connections between his childhood and what occurred later when he was an adult. Mickie had never made the links. We then began to try and understand why his mother was violent towards him, Mickie began to identify the reasons, forced into marriage at a young age, and she had resented the baby. It had chained her to the life she did not want. His mother did not want to abandon her family and instead had directed her rage onto her eldest son. Mickie represented someone who had denied her the life, she thought, she should have had. He was the symbol of her entrapment. This meaning provided him with a sense of elevation, because he thought it was personal, something in him that she did not like, rather than what he represented.

I knew Mickie was arranging a detox and rehab by himself through Community Care because he told me. One week, I turned up to work and he had gone. He eventually completed detox and went to rehab, the last anyone heard of him he had achieved his aim. He had not paid his debts in the hostel, and this created some consternation amongst his drinking fraternity. If he ever returned he would be in trouble. However he escaped from the spiral of despair that entrapped him. Sometimes all it takes is a spark and for the outside events to fall in place.

Case History 21; Faith

Jimmy was a middle aged man from the North, who lived in London for years and had raised and lost a family in the capital. His eldest son was still in rehab recovery, and his second son was one year clean. He was estranged from his wife, who ran a wine bar and although she had remarried, she still provided emotional support to him. Jimmy was a regular attendee at counselling. He would stay for the full hour, and reflect on his life. Initially I could see a great transformation. He had found a purpose in attending AA, reading the Bible, wanting to be a counsellor and drugs worker. He cleaned himself up, bathed and appeared focused.

Our first point of contact revolved around trying to help him sleep. Jimmy would go to sleep each night and wake up after half an hour. He had the same reoccurring dream, walking up a high building and then walking off the end, then suddenly, with a jolt, waking up just before he hit the bottom. Sometimes he did hit the bottom, then picked himself up, and climbed the stairs again. Each night, Jimmy fell off the building five or six times. He described it as a type of agony, as if he was drowning in dread (Kierkegaard 1844).

It meant his sleep pattern was severely disturbed, and his body never rested, as he was forever on the climb to his death. Fearing going to sleep, he would drink himself into a stupor, to try and curtail the effects of the dream. As he began to relate it, the effects diminished, but it never stopped. Only the length of time between falling became longer, but the dream was continuous. It was a form of self torture, his sub conscious screaming something to him, and we tried to work out the hidden message.

He had started drinking at 14, and had left home at 15, to live with girlfriend's parents. His Dad made money semi legitimately, and was away a considerable time, working as a bookie. He was distant, but supportive when he returned home. Jimmy related he was taken to football matches and had a good relationship with him when he was at home. The main person in the home was his mother. Jimmy was nonchalant about her, telling me she was a wonderful person but at the same time it was delivered as a script, like something he was reading and had learnt to say. This was how Jimmy related his life, as a play, where he was an observer.

"What happened to your mother?" I asked him.

"She died when I was 15. I was living away from home."

"What was the emotional impact on you?" Sensing this may be crucial.

"It had a terrible impact on my father. He was devastated. He lost his home and had to go and live in a shelter with the other kids."

"What about you? How did it affect you?"

"I just got on with it, you know. I had to. It was just a question of soldiering on. When you're 15 and something happens like that, of course it affects you but you can't let it dominate your life."

In retrospect these were clear clues, but I failed to pick up on them. I had been used to men eulogising their mothers in the previous work I had undertaken. I had misread what Jimmy was telling me. I had the view he was trapped in trauma and had self-medicated the impact of the bereavement away. Instead he was telling me her death did not have a great impact on him. I tried going around his blockage, and received this reply to my question.

"Did your drinking go up after she died?"

"Yes of course it did. I was affected. It went up a lot but I still went to work and I had my girl friend to support me during this difficult period, and of course God was looking over me."

This was how the next six months took shape. Jimmy attended the therapy and we explored the past and hit this brick wall. The bereavement was a shock, a loss, and his drinking went up, but it was not the reason for his alcoholism. This was an individual choice, because he had an addictive personality. He needed his AA groups to help him through this period, to become alcohol free. He also needed to get back to the church, as this also provided an anchor point as talking to God helped. I supported Jimmy in both these strategies, as they provided meaning within his life. They helped him to create a structure, but I became despondent. As Jimmy attended each week he began to deteriorate. He had managed to get a detox sorted out, but failed to attend. Instead he roamed around the hostel with a can, sinking further into alcoholism. He became dependent on the AA meetings, attending 2-3 meetings per day but this was also having no impact on his drinking. Jimmy was sliding off the stool and sinking into the floor in front of me. I still kept up the weekly meetings feeling helpless, thinking we had done so well at the beginning, and now everything was descending into chaos, as his drinking soared. All his support mechanisms; me, AA and the Church were not enough to hold him.

I worked with him to keep in touch with one of his children, and they provided one form of support. I became alarmed however, when I learnt he was tapping them for money to keep up his alcohol use. The hostel was initially keen to move him on when he was sober, seeing a great improvement, but when an offer of a flat arrived, he was in the depths of relapse. There was no way he could be rehoused. This was setting him up to fail. Jimmy took this as another insult, and redoubled his drinking, turning up inebriated at the session, as we continued for the hour. He recounted events in his life and I tried to work on a future vision. Jimmy paid lip service to everything that was agreed. Then he went out and bought some alcohol and sabotaged any sense of recovery. Discussing him in supervision, I tried to find out what was happening in the relationship, as Jimmy was unique in attending regularly, but getting worse. Usually if people relapsed, they stayed away from the therapy.

After a year, we began to make some headway over a vision, and Jimmy became excited over a rehab he had found. This was non Christian and therapeutic based. He brought in the brochure to show me, telling me this was what he wanted. I worked with the substance use team to get him into detox and rehab. The rules were relaxed, as there was a new Consultant who had more empathy and due to Jimmy's deterioration he was fast tracked. It was felt he was drinking so heavily, the only other alternative would be for him to leave the hostel on a stretcher, be transferred to intensive care and then to his grave. This was a psychologically informed decision that saved him, due to the perception of the workers.

Jimmy eventually went off to the detox. I recollect shaking his hand and wishing him well, with feelings of bewilderment. Jimmy had attended around 50 sessions but I never had the feeling we had actually achieved any breakthrough. Jimmy told me he had an addictive personality and had passed this onto his children as a genetic condition. He was deeply shameful and wished to God *that he had not done this to them. This was all there was to his condition. It explained everything. Other people may look to child abuse or beatings but he had a normal childhood, and there was no other explanation. I sensed there was something else, but he was so adamant, I shrugged inside, and thought I needed to know the boundaries of my expertise.*

I saw Jimmy briefly in the next one and a half years, as I passed an off licence in South London. Then I glimpsed a bedraggled figure, buying a can of beer, rushing past, I thought what could I have done different? A year later he turned up at the hostel asking to see me. I took one look and realised some form of transformation had taken place. He had returned to thank me for my help. I was a little nonplussed, as I have never felt so helpless when working with someone. I felt we had never got anywhere, yet here he was with new teeth, his skin glowing and a smile spreading across his face, exuding warmth whilst firmly shaking my hand.

We went into the counselling room and I was curious what had created the transformation. Jimmy recounted what had occurred, his battle with alcoholism, two detox's with a relapse in between. That was when I had seen him in the off licence. Then after the second detox he did a 12 month rehab, where he was forced to confront himself and he remembered our talks.

"He remembered me saying that there must be something."

I jumped in, "So it was your mum's bereavement that affected you?"

"No, that wasn't it, he said. "I was shut off when she died; I had had enough that was why I went to live with that young girl when I was 15. My mum was terrible, a terrible temper and a hidden alcoholic, hiding bottles around the house and then erupting into violence. My Dad never saw it, because he was away all the time, but we felt it. I kept it a secret, feeling I could not betray her, but finally I let it out in a group, and it was such a relief. I didn't have to carry that burden anymore"

The obvious was there all the time, but neither of us was prepared to explore it. Jimmy had kept a nonchalant idealised picture of his mum, because she had died so young. I was still trapped in my previous work, where mothers were the backbone of families. Jimmy taught me a valuable lesson. This was why he left home early, not because he was in love and his girlfriend's mother was liberal. It was because he was terrified and could not articulate his fears.

He had however come to thank for standing by him during all those sessions. He acknowledged he was not ready to delve into that space, and needed to be away from the hostel to look into it, because it was too painful.

"There were the unacknowledged feelings around the bereavement," he said. I sat back transformed at his transformation. Whereas we had waded into these currents previously, Jimmy had always led me away from himself into a brick wall.

"No point looking there," he would say, "I know what you counsellors want me to say, but my childhood was OK."

Now his whole demeanour had changed, we were no longer engaged in a hidden quest with him leading me around in circles. I was intrigued at my role during his time at the hostel, as I had felt lost in working with him.

"It was just being there," he replied. "That was enough. No one could really help me where I was heading, but you managed to help me put the brakes on. The rest of it was up to me. I needed to have someone to have faith in me, so I could find the faith in myself."

Jimmy was one of the most challenging people I worked with, because of the various hidden meanings he had created to hide behind his trauma. When the addictive personality dissolved, he was left with an existential meaningless, the idealised mother did not exist and he had to live with this void. In the rehab he learnt other people suffered from having mothers who did not provide nurture. This form of negative validation of his internal pain helped him to shed his idealisation. As he explored the trauma he no longer needed to self medicate to keep up the pretence. This was the stress he needed to sublimate. It was all in the emotions.

Case History 22; Anger Blasts

Davey was another hard, masculine, man from Northern Ireland, a former paratrooper. He was a large 40 year old male with a chronic alcohol problem. Sleeping on the streets since his army discharge, he spoke very little about his past. He described both his parents being supportive, but there was a considerable amount of sibling rivalry. This had become exacerbated after his father's death. This resulted in almost a murderous intent in the after effects. Davey had joined the army to spite his father.

He related, "He had moaned about my lack of direction and that I needed more discipline. I turned up at the house and told him I'd joined the British Army, he wasn't very pleased."

Davey spoke little about army life and what he endured. He revelled in stories of his parachute drops. These brought back those special times. He also recounted a series of tales from the homeless world. At first, when he attended counselling, it was akin to having a gale force wind trapped in the room, as the energy ripped through the air. The sheer level and volume of anger was ear wrenching in volume. Davey had a considerable amount of chronic stored anger, that appeared inexhaustible as the weeks spun by. He was angry with the hostel, sleeping rough, and his life pattern. My strategy was draw upon the Person Centred Model (Rogers 1961), and look for forms of rapport. Keeping silent and nodding whilst following his narrative helped to create an entry point. In creating a safe space for him to discharge his anger it meant he became calmer when confronting the project workers. Previously he discharged his anger at the front line staff. Rather than fuelling his anger I began to work to put some boundaries around it. In this way the free formed anger, which flowed from a combination of his chronic alcohol use, combined with past trauma was channelled. It took several weeks of sitting in the room with Davey to achieve this type of change. His years spent on the street, entailed he was estranged from institutions. He was also extremely wary of creating any rapport with authority figures, as he had been self sufficient for years.

"My people are out there." He told me pointing through the door.

As he had been sleeping out for years, he was well known in the homeless arena and he commanded respect. Along with his alcohol use he occasionally used Crack and Heroin but he was not known as a habitual user. He would however drink two large bottles of cheap cider per day. This was always a recipe for uncertainty with Davey, as his mood swung with the vigour of an over wound pendulum, just before it stops.

The strategy I used with Davey was to let the anger blow whilst trying to see where we could move to. I sat there unflinching as any attempt I made to communicate was akin to throwing a gallon of petrol onto the fire. As he began to cool, he articulated other aspects of his life, a love of archaeology and a desire to move into the field. He was interested in Roman architecture, so I shifted the discussions away from the hostel. The conditions in the hostel reignited his anger. Talking about the positives in his life and in particular discussing Roman Emperors, battles and conquests brought out another side to him. I began to show him courses he could study without needing a degree and then he could go on weekend digs. I also pointed out he would need to do a typing course and learn about computing.

I worked with him to sign up to an adult learning class. Davey had been banned from certain parts of London. We had to be very careful about where he could go for support. The bans had all arisen from his time on the street and subsequent appearances before magistrates who had given him various Asbo's and fines. Davey was not particularly interested in the consequences of breaking any order, as he regularly flaunted them. His personality was based upon the negation of all law and order. He was a big man and not easily controlled by the police or any other authority. The issue was to build a psychological ladder that allowed him to try and shed the adolescence he still adhered to.

He attended a typing course and completed the whole ten weeks. Sitting amongst the middle aged women provided him with a new status, and he revelled in it. It was a significant psychological leap for a former paratrooper who had spent years on the street with an alcohol problem, to engage in a mainstream activity, and complete the course. All of this whilst residing in a homeless hostel. The next step was to work towards a detox which he completed. This was the first time he had completed any type of stabilisation. He did not want to go to rehab but instead opted to be rehoused after returning to the hostel. He relapsed from being abstinent, keeping to a form of controlled drinking. This was a huge step away from his previous chaos. The key to working with Davey was to let his anger blow as there was a deep rationale to its expression. This was seemingly related to his family dynamics, and in retrospect it was the relationship he had with his mother that was most intriguing. He spoke warmly of this father but his mother was invisible. She was deeply submerged. He was not going to share it with anyone and that included me. We never located the source of his chronic anger or his suspended adolescence. He was enticed to change through building a future vision, based on his hobbies.

Before he left he came up to me and asked me;

"One thing that's always puzzled me is why you bother with the likes of me. What motivates you?"

"No bigger challenge than you Davey, you are the Mount Everest of the emotional world."

Smiling, he went through the door and I never saw him again.

Case History 23; Disdain

Not everyone was enthusiastic about attending therapy or talking about themselves. Joao was a 30 year old Portuguese male. He expressed a distinct hostility when I asked him if he needed any help. He looked down at my shoes, ranging his glance across my clothes until he finally met my face and then said "No" as a form of emphatic statement. From that moment on, he perfected the front of nonchalance, as he offered a scowl whenever we met. Joao expressed a general hostility to the hostel and everyone who worked there, but took a particular shine to ensuring he always greeted me with exaggerated indifference. He never asked for anything in the hostel, he only ordered. My role was subsumed within the general hostel, as someone to be ignored, but more pointedly than the other workers.

He also behaved with the same indifference to the local drug services, and treated the staff with scorn. He had created a total shutdown. If he felt he was not getting what he deserved, he was would launch into a screaming and cursing fit, where he dredge up curses in Portuguese or English specifically tailored to wound his victim. Joao had very strong ideas on race, which he would use on occasions, either by dismissing black staff and wanting just to talk to white staff, or alternatively not talking to any project workers and only communicating to the management. He had a sense of perceived hierarchy. Staff felt alienated by his manner and the notion of hierarchies he employed. These were designed to elevate him at the expense of the world around him. It was his protective shell. He was telling everyone, although he was homeless, he was neither black nor a mere worker, but someone who had lapsed into losing a home. He would return one day to his true status, sometime soon. Joao had a high opinion of where he was going. Normally this would be positive to have such a high self regard after hitting the streets, but with Joao this seemed based on a type of denial of reality. It would have been easy to be sucked into his dynamic and I felt drawn, but pulled back. I was always tolerant to his exaggerated insults. The key to working with the client group was never to take anything personally. The men were working out their inner projections. I obviously represented something to him.

He made some effort to join in with the other hostel residents for the social events, and went along to the ten pin bowling, ice skating and music activities. He also spoke to the other Portuguese residents, using the same self high regard. They also complained about his haughty manner, but he was tolerated as he always seemed to have a ready supply of heroin. He used the same mechanism to keep himself elevated. It was a carefully cultivated "front" of haughtiness that had the effect of isolating himself. He no longer had to deal with anyone else, and lapsed into a solipsist world. This was further sealed by his heroin use. It took two years for Joao to talk to me. This happened on two occasions towards the end of his stay. He had been making some calculations during this period on whether to talk to me and how he could drop his defence without appearing weak.

One day he approached me out of the blue and began to speak, not in the counselling room but in the benches outside of the hostel. The first time he had spoken to a member of the hostel team, outside of regaling the management with a list of complaints, or being challenged about his behaviour. He explained to me why he left Portugal, because there was nothing there for him after his mother and father died. Both had died young and this had created a sense of embitterment. His parents had died from heart failure. He too had a very weak heart and extremely high blood pressure. I worked with him to look at the causes working on the after effects of the bereavement and how he had retained the effects inside him. I suspected his high blood pressure resulted from trapped forms of anger that remained unresolved. I had noted the effects between high blood pressure, alcoholism and violent childhoods when I did some case work for an alcohol agency. I pointed this out to him.

Joao could relate to this bodily impact of an emotional effect. The impact of the bereavement had been significant, as he revealed his sense of loss, the descent in depression, the feeling nothing existed. He had used heroin in coping sealing off the effects of the trauma. He had shut himself off from all emotional responses as a result. His anger simmered from his sense of injustice about his loss, and he cursed religion because it provided no solace. He spoke no further about his childhood and the types of parenting he endured. He had said more in an hour than he had in 24 months. I suggested to him that he needed to work on exorcising the trauma that lies within, as it was affecting his body. He said he would go swimming to see if it made a difference. He then asked me if I was a father and I replied I was.

He then said something quite remarkable given his unflinching critique of staff.

"I bet you are a good father."

He then stood up and the meeting was over. Joao never spoke to me again and kept his silence, although he always greeted me in Portuguese and called my name, a significant improvement to the years of invisibility I offered.

In the meantime Joao had another blow up with the black staff, screaming and shouting racist abuse. The management asked to see him, and put it to him that he was a racist. Joao was genuinely shocked that anyone could think that of him, as he had a black girlfriend in the past. It was however a turning point for him, as he apologised for the first time for his racism. Previously he would have denied everything, and point to some form of provocation first. He was skilful in his use of racism, as he said enough to push the boundaries, but not enough to be evicted. Joao had made a major breakthrough and everyone was shocked, as he normally treated all the staff with disdain, now he was acknowledging that they existed for the first time.

He had been put forward for being rehoused, and although he was not stable he was no longer chaotic. He had found a steady girlfriend and was talking about working. The day before he moved out, the ice man came up to me and thanked me for the support I had given him over his stay.

"I like your heart," was his four words and after a handshake disappeared into the wider world

It appeared from his reaction after the death of his parents; he found nothing to believe in and descended into chaos. It was only because of the people in the hostel he was kept buoyant, as he battled his internal trauma. The bereavement had caused a fugue that he could not shake off. Instead he retreated from the world with the shock then slowly had to find a meaning again. Joao never returned to the hostel and although not drug free as reported by the drug agency, he kept up his stability and stopped his violent outbursts.

Case History 24; Dispelling the Fugue

Ian was a fifty year old man who never changed his clothes, never shaved and looked like a middle aged Karl Marx. Always scouring the ground and communal ash trays for dog ends he was an avid smoker of other peoples cast offs. He would collect them, tearing open the butts and rescue the remnants to make a super strength roll up. He was a connoisseur of the scour, preferring to walk to certain areas of affluence, where throwaway cigarettes had high grade tobacco butts. If he was desperate he would raid the bins in the local High St.

Ian had a mental health diagnosis of schizophrenia, he also had chronic hearing problems. When I first met him he spent an hour telling me about radio waves being emitted from spy satellites overhead, and the electronic signals coming from computers. These were all affecting him and he had to block them out, because these would send him mad. This also stopped him from thinking, as the signals mingled with those in his brain. He also told me he thought the CIA were behind some of these electronic signals. He would not turn on his hearing aid because of this. Coughing and spluttering because of his smoking habit, he could not hear the seriousness of the affect on his lungs of his smoking.

Taking him at his word, I explored with him why the CIA would be interested in him, and trying to find the meaning behind the version of reality he had composed. Previously other professions had written him off, when he spoke of conspiracies. I was interested in the meaning of the events and what they signified rather than the events themselves. Ian felt under attack for some reason, and I guessed this would stem from a real event, rather than the mirage he had composed to hide behind. The issue of electronic signals attacking people was a common phenomenon in the homeless sector. Its construction meant something, as it was dangled as a piece of camouflage to fend off reality that was locked inside. Trying to reach Ian used a great deal of my personal energy. It tested my patience in going beyond the facade he had constructed. There were various layers to descend and using an initial Person Centred Approach (Rogers 1961) helped to create trust and meaning. This created a platform to use the Adlerian (1956) notion of Socratic Questioning; exploring how the various contradictions arose to probe his personal constructs. This could only be undertaken if he had trust in the process. This all needed to take place at his pace. Ian was very fragile.

The past was a blur for Ian and he recounted multiple realities. I guessed these were pieces of concealment he hid behind. He was dangling pieces of himself but then ensuring I would need to work hard to decipher the riddles. His family history was a muddle, as he related having numerous mothers and fathers, attending various schools, never being settled and always too big for his age.

Within the present, Ian related how he attended Job Search regularly, as he wanted to return to work. Clearly he was in no condition for any job. He was very keen, but this was part of his delusion. He could pick up dog ends, but was not connected to the wider reality. My job was to find a conduit to bring him out of his isolation.

We met over books. Ian had been an avid reader in the past. As an autodidact he had read; Nietzsche, Marx, Jung, Freud and Crowley. I turned the therapy sessions into discussion groups to bring him into the present. This strategy worked although, my knowledge of Crowley was stretched, and therefore I allowed Ian to instruct me. Empowering him within the sessions boosted his self confidence and it made the sessions more rewarding. They provided him and me with a purpose. Ian then related that when he went to do his job search he was spending time searching on the computer looking up various research interests, such as space, magic and other esoteric forms. When the sites were blocked, he was going to the local library.

This was a construct we explored using Socratic Questioning, as he had expressed a fear of computers, yet he could use one in the Job Centre. The aim was not to catch him out and denigrate him, but always to bolster his self esteem and engagement with the world. This was the premise of using this method to broaden his scope. As we began to develop a rapport he would explain Kabala, Alchemy and John Dee. He had a keen interest in the ideas espoused by Carl Jung, Paracelsus, Hitler, Stalin and Thatcher. He would go in to libraries and read philosophy books along with historical biographies and esoterica.

As we worked together over the months the mention of electric spy satellites diminished and his memories returned, gradually. He recollected smoking when he was age 11, buying a packet of Woodbines and sharing them with his friends when going to the Cinema. This was a narrative he would return to, and was a memory anchor point for exploring his rebellion and his friendships. Cigarette smoking appeared to be a real passion. I began to work with him around reminiscence of the various brands. Having worked in a shop as a child, I remembered the various brand designs; Kensitas, Guard, JPS, Park Drive, Senior Service, Capstan and this made some inroads into bringing the past back for him. He began to narrate life events around the cigarettes he smoked, telling me about smoking "Mores" and Sobraine's the exclusive cigarettes when he was going out with his friends and showing off. Ian was still heavily guarded about his life and any attempt to make sense out of a family history was thwarted by his various recollections. I remember saying to him that he was an enigma and his response;

"Some people think that and others don't."

This was his full stop to that probe all stated with a straight face. We continued to meet once a week and Ian would expand on philosophy. The fugue around his life extended everywhere, as I was unsure whether he was a Marxist or Nationalist as he spun between both positions in his recollections. My aim was not to become bogged down with politics and views, but to get him to engage with the real world. Then the aim was to work with him to connect to the real world of emotions, as he had retreated far into his interior.

I finally began to get some concrete pictures from him when he was discussing his early adult life, living in the West of England in a small village. He also related he had three relationships, as I noted the various tattoos with women's names on his neck. At first when I asked him about them, he stated he could not remember who they were. After six months of being entwined in the layers of his fugue, a narrative began to emerge. In one session he showed me his position within his family, as both his mother and father were involved in attacking him when he was a young boy. Firstly they would attack each other, he said, and then when he appeared, they would attack him. He would therefore spend hours and later days away from the family. Various family members supported him. This helped to formulate a picture of someone who was brought up by various relatives, attending different schools. He had gone to the library as a strategy to study philosophy to get away from his parents. Ian came from a working class East End Family and his choice of escape into books arose from an escape from violence. He initially read magical books to cast spells upon them, and then gradually he moved into philosophy.

Over a year Ian of therapy, he became more grounded. Although he had a mental health diagnosis, he did not want to claim Sickness Benefit. He steadfastly refused to be moved off Jobseekers Allowance. This would prohibit him from using the computer. He had been attending his Job Club for years and clearly he was in no position to hold down any type of job. Ian had refused to be put on any Sickness benefit as he believed; he could get work if he wanted. We worked with him to dispel this delusion. With most men working with them to want to work is a huge task, with Ian this entailed trying to shift him away from thinking he was going to get a job. Clearly he was unemployable.

Ian did not drink or take drugs. He needed the extra money from having his benefits increased. This would be useful in his recovery rather than another spoke in a self medication strategy. He eventually relented and we worked to increase his benefit levels. These were eventually approved. This created a significant change in his outlook. When the money came through, he was ready to change his image. He cut his hair and shaved his beard, and one of the project workers took Ian out to buy new clothes. Previously he had worn the same clothes every day, now he had a choice. Ian regained the art of conversation by listening and then speaking. All talk about the electric currents and the spy satellites had finally gone. Emerging instead were layers of childhood trauma. He now stood up and showed me what happened. Through recollecting with the past he was transforming the present. He related he had been married in his early adult life and when this had broken up, he had been independent for years, but had developed an amphetamine habit. Taking base amphetamines *for twenty years after the break-up of a second marriage finally entailed his descent onto the street after his wife asked him to leave. He slept out for years in sheds and railway ducts, until he was picked up by the Outreach team. He was in severe mental health difficulties suffering from relentless delusions. This resulted in a section and mental health medication. He had remained trapped within this state for years, until he sat down and began therapy. This allowed him to articulate and gradually make sense of the disparate confusion that enshrouded his memories, where everything had been shut off and shut down.*

Ian eventually left the hostel to live in semi independent housing, where he looks after himself. Someone checks in with him to ascertain how he is doing. The change in him was remarkable. He went from the dishevelled man to someone proudly wearing and washing his Northern Soul T Shirts, clean shaven and bathing every day. The personal hygiene delineated his self confidence. It was through the reading discussions he found a rationale to engage with the world. It was a platform we built upon to transform his self perception. As a team we worked with him to engage with the world rather than retreat from it.

Case History 25; The Inward March

Les was a fifty year old man who originally appeared during the harsh winter of 2010. He was offered a space in the hostel due to the significant drop in temperature to 0 degrees. This was part of a government initiative, to shift people off the streets into temporary accommodation when the weather froze all normal life. When he first appeared he was glad of a bed, and delved into the food with a flourish. Les appeared to have no discernible problems, apart from not being housed. He did not drink, smoke or take drugs. He also appeared not to have any mental health problems. He would talk, smile and engage in general themes about the hostel. He appeared personable. After the cold weather spell finished, Les was given a vacancy in the hostel as the management and workers thought he would be an easy move on. After a week in the hostel Les appeared agitated. He felt that he was not in the same position, as the other people in the hostel and they were more deserving of the bed than him.

"If only I hadn't fucked up, I'd be OK now."

This was his steadily repeated mantra. He suffered from an existential anguish that mounted in its ferocity. Les steadily declined, as he related his sanitised life history to anyone who would listen. Gradually be became stuck in this self feedback loop that amplified his internal failures. This haunted him day and night, driving him downward. What Les feared was occurring, as he dropped off the cliff, and no one could save him. He had pressed the self destruct button and he went into a perpetual orbit of decline. He was descending into a deeper pit than anyone else in the hostel. This was causing consternation amongst the other residents, who were becoming wary of him.

He had lived with his parents in Sussex for 32 years before moving out with their support. He had grown up in a family with his brother and sister. His brother had married in his twenties and his sister had moved out of the house. This left Les alone with his parents. He had a spell of rebellion in his teenage years, marked by his tattoos. He stated he had ridden motorbikes and listened to Heavy Metal. He had then tried to commit suicide in his early twenties by slashing his throat.

Asked why? He replied he was bored. We never went beyond this statement. He lived with his parents up until he was 32 when his father gave him the money for a deposit and he bought his flat. Les lived there for eight years, and then decided on a whim, that he wanted to move to Spain, then sold everything he had within a week. He managed to sell his flat and was all ready to go when he was stopped by his work colleagues and his father. They all suspected there was something dubious. Les heeded the advice and stayed in the UK, renting a series of properties which ate into his accumulated capital, after he sold his flat. After another eight years, Les was penniless. He could no longer pay the rent and left the premises unaware of housing benefit. He lived on the streets for three years, wandering around the UK. Les would look back on each section of his life and express bitter regret. He could not exist in the present or envisage a future. He had no relationship with a woman, since he was 16 and felt too shy to talk to one. He also stated he had an alcohol problem, but I could not detect any alcohol use. The counselling room usually fills rapidly with the fumes when someone is using heavily. It later transpired he had exaggerated his use to fit into the hostel milieu. When it was discovered he was not a habitual user, he suggested he should hand himself into the police as a benefit fraudster. This was a continuous refrain and we had to spend considerable time to stop him from wasting police time. Clearly he was severely depressed and had minimal

259

self esteem, the worst within the hostel. This highlighted a quandary around the various self medication strategies and their meaning. The other men appeared to stave off this sense of meaningless through their self medication. Les had a spiralling sense of depression and did not use any substances.

Les would look wistfully at the other people in the hostel who had alcohol and drug problems and would say at least they lived; they had exciting lives going in and out of prison doing their robberies. He had achieved nothing in his life; he had bought a flat, held down a job and existed.

"I haven't even done that. All I've done is go to work and then go home. It feels as though I have just frittered my life away."

This deep sense of the meaningless of his life haunted him. I worked with Les to look at the highlights in his life. He had travelled abroad to Australia and been on a cruise. He said he felt alienated by the middle age people on board the ship. I asked him about motorbikes and heavy metal but he just shrugged. Everything appeared hopeless. Gradually it emerged he had been on holiday to the Far East, Europe and around the UK. There appeared to be some adventurous moments and that it was not all work and going home to watch TV. There were internal hostel events he attended and participated in, pool completions and quizzes. He struck up a friendship with another resident who was coming out of a fugue. The problems for Les were demonstrated in the pool competitions and quizzes, the other residents were more aware. The Portuguese residents beat him in the quiz because they studied the free papers for the clues. The other residents practiced their pool shots. Les was dwarfed by them, even though they were inebriated and he was not. He had lost his sense of purpose in his middle age. He could not regain it. He did attend two workshops and appeared to enjoy them as these built on adolescent interests; cycling and swimming. Each session we had would see Les being caught in the same negative spiral of;

"I've fucked up I had it so good in X place. Why didn't I stay there? I should have listened to my Dad."

His father's voice played a significant role in his life. He was terrified of being told off or censured by him. As he deteriorated within the hostel I suggested he contact his parents to let them know where he was. He became terrified;

he couldn't possibly tell his dad that. His Dad would not like it. This was a very fragile area, so we left it. Although a significant problem for Les was his isolation. As he did not have a self medication issue he could not join the other informal arrangements that existed around drinking, smoking and drug taking. His relationship with the other resident drifted, as Les deteriorated and the other man improved. They bypassed each other on an ascent and descent, from and into, the pit of depression. Les could find no purpose to live, trying to envisage the future was impossible, as it was coated in a shroud. He constantly referred back to the past where he would self flagellate. All the grounding techniques I had learnt had no impact. Taking him away from the hostel improved his mood, but as soon as he returned, he was enveloped by despair. He began to haunt the corridors on the first floor of the hostel. He stood there for hours. The other residents became wary of him, feeling he was about to explode. They asked staff to do something about the man who just stood and stared. His decline marked their fear.

The mental health services initially could find nothing wrong with him, which given the state of his depression was questionable. He was expressing suicidal ideation to me and I spoke with Les, stating I would need to develop a support plan and speak to outside agencies. As he had been found to be coping by the mental health team in a previous session, he was requested to attend A&E if he felt suicidal. They would undertake an assessment. This was inappropriate as the local A&E was one of the busiest in Europe.

After a few months, Les began to stop eating, he would only respond if he was told to go and eat. He needed direction and any Person Centred empowerment would entail him chasing his tail around. Everything with Les became directive. As a team we worked to halt his decline. Using any empowering technique with him would just allow him to unleash a circular pattern of personal failure that would descend into a spiral. Therefore strong boundaries had to be asserted around eating and cleanliness to help him maintain his health and self esteem. He only responded to orders, and seemingly fell into being an adolescent.

It was the last pattern of standing in the corridor, staring and repeating his sense of failure, the voice of the critical parent in constant repetition; this finally triggered the mental health team to meet with him. He was then found to have one of the most substantial degrees of self denigration ever witnessed by them.

Les had managed to remain in the hostel without leaving for nine months. This had put a roof over his head but then he had to confront what had happened to him over his life. Whereas Chris and Ian had positive memories that could be retrieved to anchor them, the same techniques of reminiscence with Les produced a type of shrug of the shoulders, as we went through the motorbikes he rode and the gigs he had attended. It was the fear of his father finding out about his life that ensured his pronouncements finally came true. His son was sectioned.

"You'll never make anything of yourself. This is what he told me and he was right, it was true"

The critical command barked at his son had left a powerful mark upon him, a form of psychological wound that could not be stemmed. Les repeated that his father was right, he had foreseen the truth long before he/Les, anyone else could see it.

"Why didn't I believe him when he told me this?"

This halted the therapy as I tried to find ways around this belief system. Les looked around the hostel and saw the mirror of failure. He heard his father's words echoing inside his head, that he was destined for failure and here he was, he had finally arrived. He was not even good enough to be "an addict."

I felt there was a huge portion of his life walled off, which no one could access. Les was guarding himself and stopping anyone from peering in, because he felt so helpless. Clearly keeping up this strategy through years of isolation, then wandering from place to place and finally enacting a locked groove of self denigration helped him to sustain a semblance of coping. It was not enough to stop him from descent. The trigger was seeing the other men in the hostel involved in a form of swagger. This induced in him a feeling that at least they had lived, whereas he felt he had not. He looked upon their lived experiences of being arrested and kept in prison, their being sectioned and arrested, he viewed this as part of a lived experience.

Finally after standing in the corridor for a week, Les was sectioned for his own benefit, the only time I felt relieved when someone was led away. Everyone had tried to support him but no one could find the key. His despair was too over reaching and his ideation too strong. Les marked the limits of my competence. As it transpired the section did little to help him. After a week after his discharge, after four weeks inside, he readmitted himself as a voluntary patient. Les, it seemed, felt enveloped by an institution.

Case History 26; Melting the Ice Man

Chris arrived at the hostel after a stay in a mental health ward. When he first arrived he was locked into an emotional shutdown. He would look around the hostel like a bird with large soulful eyes. He could see you, but I had the impression he was staring straight through you. Darting in and out of the hostel, scared, timid and meek, there was also another component to him. Seemingly someone who had been without structure for years could adhere to one very quickly when he wished. Hardly speaking, when bolting out of the door for his various appointments, he returned to his room. He was rigid, like clockwork, in attending everything he was asked to do. He would then spend the day locked away, turning up for the meals in the canteen and then disappearing again. I guessed from his accent he had lived in a town similar to where I had lived. I began to speak to him about football, but he had no interest. Then I mentioned music and some of the venues, and from this basis of reminiscence, he slowly began to recollect his home town. It acted as an emotional grounding, allowing him to exist within the present, through talking about the past. Slowly Chris began to thaw, as he recognised who I was, and gradually differentiated me from the other staff members. This groundwork took around 3 months, until he attended therapy rigorously, once a week in the counselling room.

We worked on some of the practical aspects first, as he suffered from isolation. This entailed working with him to access some of the occupational therapies on offer and talk to people on the courses. We then worked a vision on how he could turn his burgeoning hobby into a possible outlet for obtaining work in the future. Chris was very hesitant in thinking long—term, but I pushed him to try and visualise his expectations. If we could build a future then we could work backwards to uncover the source of the trauma. This was a gentle pushing, Chris was extremely fragile, but I sensed we needed to move beyond Person Centred into more task orientated therapy. Chris was looking for structure, whilst not wanting to be constrained by anyone's demands.

Chris was extremely traumatised and very agitated, initially terminating the sessions early because he felt so anxious. He was on high levels of anti psychiatric medication and this helped to calm him down. He became more relaxed however when he changed his medication. Chris was very respectful towards Doctors and spoke of their expertise. There was no sense of resistance to any diagnosis that was made. The medication calmed him, and he became less agitated. This belief in Doctors was one of the boundaries that constrained him. He had a great deal of investment in authority figures and responded to their words, as edicts for living his life. Alternatively he had wandered around Britain and Europe for ten years paying no heed to anyone. This was the enigma of Chris.

I did not let Chris know about my qualifications, until near the end of our time together, feeling it would create a strange dynamic of him taking my pronouncements as edicts. I felt he needed to find out who he was, under the layers. Chris revealed he had been deported from Japan after being sent to see some Japanese doctors after he had lived there for years. They had diagnosed schizophrenia. He later returned to the UK, and was placed in a mental health institution. When he was released he embarked on a ten year wander around Europe and the UK on foot. He survived by eating out of supermarket bins, where he said fresh food was carefully placed. This was a lifeline for these itinerant people, and part of a psychologically informed decision by the supermarkets. Otherwise he would have died from starvation, such was his inward retreat. He detailed one bin that was regularly used by the homeless in Central London. Homeless people organised queue's to create order, to pick out the food placed there, past its sell by date. Chris recollected he returned back to the same spot five years later, but nearly all the other people had disappeared. I asked him what happened.

"They were drug users mainly, so they either cleaned up which is doubtful, or died from overdoses, HIV or Hepatitis."

His first journey entailed him travelling to the north of England, then to Ireland and walking down the length of the country. He had savings from his time in Japan that he used, and he then travelled to France, staying for a while in Paris. He walked from Paris up to Holland and then to Germany. He walked down the Rhine and ended up in Switzerland. It was here he was sectioned again and sent back to the UK.

"The Doctors told me that I needed to go back and have some rest."

"When I returned to England I began to walk around the countryside for six years, strolling from Scotland to Wales to Brighton, then up to Norfolk and on to Northumbria."

"I must have done around five trips, walking across the UK."

I asked him if could remember how he felt. He said he couldn't remember much, just the cold. He recollected staring at the sea for days when he stayed in Brighton during the summer. He had money to buy vodka and this isolated him from his feelings. Chris had wandered around in a fugue sticking to canal paths. He wanted to see nature, and could expound on the different walks. During this period, when he was walking, he stated he spoke perhaps a dozen words to other people, such was his emotional shutdown. This highlighted the significant improvements he made within the hostel. He spoke more in his first session that he had in 12 years, he later recounted. I asked if he had any companionship whilst he was wandering around the UK. He said he occasionally said "Hello," when he recognised people. Intrigued, I asked him how he managed to recognise people when he was isolated. He stated there were around 200 people wandering around the UK, doing what he was doing. They would bump into each other and offer quick greetings, before going on their way. He obtained clothes from those dumped outside charity shops, washed in public toilets and sought warmth in public libraries. He had tried pubs but was often refused entrance. He also supplemented his income and warmed himself in bookies. He said he only gambled to get enough money to drink and often won rather than lost.

Chris did his wanderings for years, until turning up a bench in London in the middle of winter, frozen, unable to move. A member of the public rang the ambulance service and he was taken to hospital, where he had some of his toes amputated because of frost bite.

"The Doctors told me I needed to stop wandering around."

Chris began to readjust to a life in the hostel, living indoors for the first time in years, apart from when he was detained under the mental health acts. Whereas previously he had been isolated, now he was surrounded by 51 other men with

265

various psychological issues. Chris liked the hostel and made the most of the facilities.

As we began therapy, the whole process was akin to defrosting Chris's life and then watching him emotionally thaw. He began to recollect his life prior to wandering. Each week Chris remembered another fragment of his life in Japan in the late 1980's and the 1990's. Each week brought another revelation, as the session triggered memories. He had trained in the theatre initially, and then went to live in America where he toured across the country, before finally meeting a Japanese Geisha who asked him to come to Japan. Chris went over to Japan to stay with his Japanese girlfriend and worked in an upmarket company. He remembered being given special dispensation to work at this particular office. He made friends with other Japanese, learnt the language and took up skiing. He went to the top resorts and began to recount the memories.

Life in Japan however was difficult, as he was constantly reminded of his strangeness as a "gaiijin" This began to affect him, from the first months he lived there, as he could be sitting on a beach, walking in a park, queuing in a shop, waiting in lift when someone would casually walk up to him and call him a "gaiijin." This was a daily corrosive event that ate at his self esteem. It became ever more corrosive on his relationship. When he rented an apartment the landlord stipulated he had to have it fumigated when he left, because he would have difficulty in renting it out afterwards, because he was a gaiijin.

He described his next door neighbour as a devout nationalist who would drive into the centre of Tokyo with a loud hailer on his van, playing nationalist songs, wanting to bring back the Emperor and making anti foreigner statements. At the end of the day when he returned, he would bow but never speak, as they went into their respective houses. Chris began to relate the impact of the strangeness and how it affected him. He was caught between the culture of manners on the surface, and a deep hatred that lay underneath the politeness. His employers told him they were taking a gamble in employing him, and he had better be a model worker. It would reflect badly on him and the company if he let them down. They took him to Karaoke events, and all would be well, until a certain moment, when he would be politely asked to leave when "extras" were discussed, and attended to. The expectation being, that no proper Japanese woman would wish to be with a foreigner. This was made clear. This was an added pressure on the relationship between Chris and his wife.

She represented traditional Japan, paradoxically earning a living as someone who displayed a Japanese sense of high culture in her role, whilst married to a "gaiijin." She was trying to escape her role, whilst performing it.

At first he described trying to fight the endemic racism, by asking people why they were doing it. Then he tried to ignore it, eventually due to its pervasiveness it seeped into the background, or so he thought. He described shutting it off. Although he managed to shut it down, it only affected his conscious self. The daily interactions and ritual humiliations meant he was constantly faced with being seen as an outsider, and therefore outside the internal hierarchy. When Chris spoke Japanese people would smile and speak English instead. He was part of the "other" (Sartre 1943).

"When I spoke Japanese, they would feel embarrassed, so I would feel embarrassed," is how he related it.

He said they were embarrassed that a foreigner could learn the language and speak it fluently. It made them ill at ease. All of these interactions ate away at him, the constant bite into his self esteem, and it eventually shattered his marriage. His wife provided a certain timescale for its longevity, he recollected, when they first met. They divorced according to her calculation. He remembered trying to patch the marriage up towards the end. There were the long awkward silences, as they both sat there staring at each other. They were unable to communicate emotionally.

"In the end we literally had nothing to say to each other. I never saw or heard of her after that, a complete blank. It's not until I sat here and you asked me, that I even realised what had happened, that I had been married. I had forgotten all about it"

Spending a year trying to rebuild his self esteem he met another Japanese woman and married her. They lived happily, he recollects, as he continued with his teaching, but the stress of day to day life was getting to him. He would go to the English Club in Japan and there he saw the long term effects of how living in Japan affected other ex Pats.

"It was driving everyone crazy" he recalled, "All had their different ways, but no one was coping."

The marriage to the second Japanese woman ended his loneliness. Recollecting that he had married again, brought a stark realisation, as he could not remember ever becoming divorced. His initial recollection of the second marriage was hazy as each week we worked to sharpen his memory. As he gained his memories he became eager to discuss them in the sessions. We worked on rebuilding the positive memories of going out for walks, eating in restaurants and seeing shows to build a sense of momentum. Chris was a man who had been weighed down in a sea of negativity for years. Within this swamps he had now gradually risen to the surface to recount his life. Building on the positive memories bolstered his self esteem, and allowed him to retrieve more recollections of the past. It helped to build his identity within the present.

It was when he lost his job teaching that the money problems piled up. This is when he began to spiral downward, when he lost his structure.

"My wife tried everything to try and bring me out of it, but it was hopeless. I just surrendered to the meaningless of it all. I gave up, I no longer wanted it. I had already planned to return to Britain and I was already walking around the countryside in my head."

Whilst falling into the pit of despair he had created an escape route. Shifting from the high pressure world of Japan he would seek its negation, by casting off all responsibility, and walk around Britain alone. He planned to walk around for six months to gather his thoughts. This was when he pressed the ejector button, and went inside himself. He could not shake himself out of a stupor. He recollected walking around chatting to himself in the house, whilst his wife went to work to pay the rent.

His explained that his psychological health deteriorated to the extent, he eventually became inert. Eventually he was sent to a psychiatrist in Tokyo, his wife was worried what had happened to him. They told him

"You've spent too long in Japan and you need to go home."

Within a week, after spending time in a psychiatric institution, he was back in the UK. He had saved a considerable amount of money and could exist free of the State. He stayed with a relative for a few months to recuperate, and then went on his walking journey.

As we shifted to look at his personal history, I explored his early life. He described his parents as working hard. They moved from living in social housing to a large townhouse. They had sent him to an Independent School. This is where he stated, his isolation had begun. He did not adjust to his surroundings he recounted. Leaving school he worked for the local railway company and then went to college to study art. He remained blocked, around any further exploration of early events, but noting his considerable shift in talking about Japan, Chris was returning back to existing within the present.

Chris developed a structure rapidly. He was attending art classes three times per week and he was taking his anti depressant medication. He spoke to staff and was no longer shuttered. The decision was undertaken to move him out of the hostel. Chris was ready to engage with the wider world. He had created a structure, independent of the hostel. Over the months I worked with him, Chris went from frozen, to partially defrosted, to melting. He finally became connected to the world around him, laughing and telling jokes about his past. His self medication strategy had been an inward retreat. He had drunk heavily when he was homeless but stopped when his money had run out, as an act of will. He could exhibit remarkable control over his behaviour and then just let everything slide. He oscillated between two polarities. Finding a meaning to exist and inhabit the world, instead of shut it down was what he needed. The therapeutic work helped to uncover the past, and then create a meaning that he could finally inhabit.

Case History 27; Lost Childhood

Dennis was a mixed race man in his 50's from a West Country town. He was introduced to me by a project worker. The project worker was training to be a therapist and understood how therapy worked. Dennis was hesitant about talking initially. He wanted to meet in the open space of the garden, rather than the privacy of the counselling room. We met three times in the garden and I began to feel we needed to move to a safer space, because of the issues he was relating. When we met in the surgery he baulked.

"I don't like this Dean; it reminds me of the Children's Home I grew up in."

The first session was used to allay his fears and make it into a safe space. I highlighted that at least it was confidential and no one would disturb us. It entailed hard work to overcome the psychology of the hostel. It had a particular resonance for the men who inhabited it.

Dennis had recently split up from his girlfriend who was half his age. He had a deep sense of loss, because of how she had left him. They had both been using Crack, and this had initially bound them together. Dennis said he found it hard to relate to women because it entailed being emotionally open. He had been hurt in the past, and did not want to feel that pain again. However he had let his guard down and he had become emotionally involved and now he was filled with remorse at being so naive. He was expressing a volcanic anger towards her. He described the dynamics of the relationship, shifting from an initial, sexual loving relationship, even though they both used Crack, to one where anger dominated. Initially he felt they had many connections; being mixed race, being in care, living in a hostel, their mutual drug use and their physical attraction. Dennis spoke about this relationship as a crucial event connecting to his emotional world. As shifted beyond his "front" this became revealed as tortured, based upon childhood violence and early attachment severance.

There were considerable complications with his relationship, as she also sex worked to sustain her self-medication strategy. She was also involved in another relationship with an older woman, who was away at the time. Dennis expressed his jealousy at the continuation of this relationship and wanted her to break it off. He also wanted her to stop sex working, but this placed the onus on him to supply the finances to sustain both of their strategies. This also caused friction between them. He was in a quandary. He had been with his partner for six months, and his feelings had intensified, he became more consumed with desire. This led to increasingly violent rows as his need was driving her away. The escalating rows were brought to the attention of the hostel management, as they become more virulent. There was one serious incident where it was felt Dennis had to be moved away from the hostel. This devastated Dennis. He felt as though his world had collapsed, as he perceived his partner to be his last chance to build a life with a woman. Dennis was then sent to the hostel I worked at, brimming with anger, directed at the system, whilst feeling murderous towards his former partner. She had used the incident to become rehoused in a flat. Whereas he felt he had been punished by being sent to another homeless hostel full of men. She had been rewarded and he was sent back to the beginning. He expressed homicidal ideation. The first few sessions were based upon this surging anger, and my role was to let him express it in a safe environment. This is why he needed to be contained in a safe space. She had been provided with a secret address to stop Dennis from contacting her.

As he related his narrative, it appeared he had some basis for feeling aggrieved. She had claimed he had kidnapped her, and then held her against her will. The police were called and they arrested him. Charges were later dropped when CCTV footage revealed that during her "kidnapping" she had left the building and then returned later. Dennis said she went out to buy some Crack. He stated his anger flared when over her relationship with the older woman, and he stated he made some threats. The criminal charges were later dropped.

The resonances of this incident remained unresolved. Dennis was chronically angry, and his former partner was living with one eye looking over her shoulder. The outcome was unsatisfactory for both parties, as each was left aggrieved or fearful. In the sessions Dennis expressed violent revenge fantasies. This became exacerbated when she sent him a text that was aimed at deliberately wounding him. He already felt raw after she had reported him to the police and tried to press charges over the incident. Now she was mocking him about his past life. The situation was becoming critical. The text related to some deeply personal issues he had revealed to her, which she was now using to humiliate him.

"At least I know who my mum is. Do you know yours?"

Dennis related his mum was a white woman who lived in a West Country town. She had a tough early life, eventually becoming a carer for her mother. She eventually escaped from her family through becoming pregnant. Her Dad was a war hero who never adjusted to peace. He had a chronic alcohol problem after serving in Normandy and beyond in 1944. Returning back from the war he continued to self medicate and project his violence. She had eventually fled from his rages and met Dennis's dad, who was a student from Africa. She had two children with him and then his father disappeared. With no parental support and ostracised because of the colour of the babies in 1950's Britain, she went into sex working at the age of 28. To cope with the pressure she turned to alcohol, Dennis's mum died in her late thirties, having a child near enough every year until she died. All were taken into care by Social Services. Due to his mother's perceived fecklessness Dennis and his brother being put into a Children's Home, the other half brothers and sisters were split up and put into different homes. Dennis had a deep underlying hatred against women which he began to recognise in the counselling sessions. This violence was projected onto his partner. He also had a deep hatred of society because of how he had been treated. He had survived by shoplifting from an early age. He had ensured he stole something every day. I questioned him about its role in his life.

Dennis replied, "When I was in the Children's Home there was never enough to eat so the kids supplemented their diet by going out to the local allotments, supermarkets and corner shops to get hold of food. As kids we were always hungry. It became a way of life."

As part of their duties at the home they were expected to work. Dennis managed to obtain a job on a market stall at the week end, then do a milk round as a milkman's mate, undertaken every morning, before he went to school. The women who ran the Home used to take the money from him for safekeeping, saying they were putting it into a Bank Account for him. He said he knew that was not true. They were using it for themselves. They had all the children working, and by operating this child labour system they received a considerable extra income from their many charges. The school was seemingly run on an austerity budget, with money saved from turning down the heating and skimping on the meals. This took place in the 1960's. Punishment was also rife, in particular the cane and the slipper for any minor infringement. Dennis stated after a while, the violence lost its menace. He revealed that losing contact with his mum was a far worse psychological punishment than any physical beating. As the children grew older the punishments became more elaborate, such as standing on one leg for hours, or holding out your arms or standing still on a chair. The School used various stress positions to impose discipline.

I asked Dennis how this affected him.

"Toughened me up, no end Dean. I became a real horrible spiteful bastard. I had to, to survive. There was no other way. I was the smallest in the place and the most bullied at first. It was a question of either becoming a hard bastard or going under."

Sent to the local Secondary school, Dennis recounted, along with his brother, he was the only non white there. He faced daily racism. He coped by fighting back, then he gained a reputation as a hard man and this entailed he was respected.

"They kept coming, bigger and harder, but I was filled with so much rage, no one could touch me. It wasn't that I was the toughest; I was the one who did not care if I was hit the most, because I would get up and keep going. They would have to kill me. In the end they gave up and became my friends. It was easier all round."

As he was from the home there was also a sense of him being different. He said the worst thing about the school were the taunts he was subject to.

"Your maam don't love you."

"I used to run up to them and smash them in the face going, she does love me, she does. Of course, really, I knew they were right. She didn't."

"I used to tell people she's coming back to get me, but she never did and after a while I began to forget about her. I become institutionalised. The one person I had in my life was my brother and we used to get into trouble, backing each other up. This is what kept me going. If I hadn't had him then I don't know what would have happened."

"The women who ran the Home were cruel, now looking back, unnecessarily cruel in how they treated us. They would find ways to inflict all types of punishments on us, and then at the end of the night, we would have to go up to them and kiss them goodnight. What type of things were they thinking of? These were women."

We looked at their emotional coldness and its effect on him and his brother. There was no love in the Home, only discipline and punishment. As he grew older, Dennis began to rebel against the regime. One of his acts of rebellion was to steal from the women's purses at any opportunity. This also provided him with a sense of respect, because at least he was fighting back and not just being a victim. It was from these dynamics that he was propelled eventually into crime as a lifestyle. After leaving the home he became involved in various criminal acts. This ranged from running a brothel, to shoplifting and theft. Dennis had an underlying hatred of women that we worked upon. This is why he could run a brothel. He made an instant recognition on the sources where this arose from.

"I'm not proud of what I've done but I had to survive and there was nothing there for me, so I used the skills I had developed to get ahead."

He also related it back to his hatred of his mother, putting him in him the children's home, and the treatment he received from the women there.

"After I left the home I went to find her, but she was already dead. I went to the cemetery where she was buried. I spent hours looking at the gravestones but still could not see her name. I found the people who ran the cemetery and asked them where Mrs. Smith was buried. They pointed to an area where the poor people are laid. It was there I found her unmarked grave. There was no headstone, it was bare. I sat there for hours crying and cursing, swearing at her."

"Why? I asked her, did she did this to me? Why did she have me, just to put me in a children's home?" Then I left.

"Did you feel better?"

"I can't say either way really. It was just so sad, seeing her grave in the poor part of the cemetery, with no one bothering to mark her death. I can't say it made me feel better. To be honest, thinking about it now, it made me feel even worse, if that was possible."

These issues remain unresolved and were carried into his first marriage. Dennis had married quickly after leaving the care home.

"I fell in love and it was great at first," he recalled. "We used to go out and have fun. My wife's family were bonkers though."

He recollected going to meet her parents and her father standing at the top of the stairs naked, berating his daughter for being late for Xmas. They had been stuck on a train.

274

The father in law was screaming; "You're gonna get some of this next time you're late. He was pointing to his penis. I should have known then, that things were not right but we loved each other. I put it out of my head, and thought we could just make a go of it."

After the children were born, Dennis recalled the relationship dynamics changing. There was more emphasis on him to provide the family income and there were more strictures put in place to make him stay in. She did not want him going out without her, but then she wanted him to provide the family income. This did not seem to be a satisfactory relationship, according to Dennis. She spent more time with the baby than with him. Correspondingly he said his wife became possessive, and he became more anxious about his role, feeling not good enough, not knowing what to do. The baby was bringing up his childhood traumas. He became estranged from his partner, as he sought solace in going out and she would scream at him when he returned. The relationship deteriorated. Eventually it collapsed. Reflecting back, he realised they were too young and immature to have children. Both he and his partner were emerging from trauma, and neither knew how to resolve it. Both thought it could be transcended through loving each other, but it was not enough.

"What happened to your son?"

"Eventually he went into care. She could not cope with looking after him. After we split up she became more chaotic. She became a drug addict. I haven't spoken to her for years and I have few fond memories of her"

Dennis had sworn not to replicate his family dynamics but ended up repeating them. This was a source of deep shame as he described the anguish and torture of doing to his son, what was done to him. Describing himself as Mr. Flash in his youth, the first man to have a full length leather coat in 1972, he had become bedraggled as he became older. Years of being on the street after the relationship collapsed sent him into a spiral. His son had contacted him recently and he was full of both trepidation and joy. It transpired after an initial angry encounter, this was to be the catalyst for change.

When they first met, Dennis came away distraught. His son was extremely angry at what his father had done to him and poured out his resentment. Initially it was a false dawn.

"He's a very angry young man. I saw myself in him." Dennis reported after their first meeting. "I don't think I will be seeing him again however. It's just too difficult. He's also on drugs as well, and his girl friend is pregnant."

Initially when we met the whole family seemed enveloped in dread. Dennis spoke about his siblings. He had tried to contact them. His brother who he grew up with in the children's home died from HIV, and this had left him devastated, when he was in his early thirties. Another brother was sectioned in Broadmoor, he met a sister who was initially supportive and then became angry and ostracised him. As he met up with his step brothers and sisters, it became clear the family was drenched in trauma. Apart from the attachment severance, they were also the victims of racism and institutional violence.

We began to work on the precedents to his mothers collapse. We looked at her upbringing and what led to her self destruction. Dennis had undertaken a considerable amount of work on his family. He was able to piece together the fragments quickly. Her father was a violent bully who drank heavily. He had fought his way across Europe, after taking part in the Normandy landings. He never slept and would scream for hours about the war, and it appeared he suffered from Post Traumatic Stress. Meanwhile his mother had looked after her mother and father for years and never married. She was a family drudge who found a release. Then, Dennis revealed, she met this good looking African student and they had this relationship. That was when his older brother was born, and then afterwards she had me. This happened within two years. Society was not tolerant of women having relationships with Africans and so he disappeared. Dennis recounted he met him once, a tall man from Ghana.

"He was a nice man, quiet, considerate but to me he was a foreigner. I could not relate to him at all. I could see nothing of me in him at all, apart from my brown skin. After a first meeting we never contacted each other again"

Dennis searched for an identity, trying to connect with the different elements of his family structure, trying to build an attachment base, but everything appeared fragmented. As he spoke about the past he was also connected to the present. He was still intending to find his previous partner. His anger towards her had not abated. I spoke to the Hostel Management and they assured me she was in a safe place. Dennis would go out each day and scour the Methadone dispensing clinics to try and find either her, or a friend of hers. Eventually by chance he saw her on a bus whilst he was walking down the street. He chased after the bus but could not catch it. He knew he was on the right path. Tracking down her former friends, he stated he knew the Borough she lived in. After three months he saw her by chance and followed her home. Then he knew the address.

This was the moment of make or break in our therapeutic relationship. One session, Dennis revealed he had found her. We had reached a crisis point.

"What are you going to do?"

"What do you think I should do?"

"Write her a letter, telling her how you feel. It will be a shock and make you feel better."

"What, write a fucking letter, are you serious? I want to kill her."

"No you don't, otherwise you wouldn't be discussing it with me. You would have already acted."

Confidence in the bond we had developed was the key, and also I was aware of the relationship he had built with his son. This had ensured he had an emotional investment. After the first meeting with him, his son contacted him again and the next meeting was less angry as Dennis related his early life and trauma. Rather than keeping the masculine silence, Dennis broke the cycle of violence by revealing why he had rejected him. The anger had dissipated in the relationship. Now, through a reconciliation, father and son spoke to each other at least once a week by telephone, and Dennis expressed his love for him openly. If I reported him I would be the same as everyone else. If I did nothing them the girls life may be in danger. The fact he had come to me was also crucial. He was looking for advice on how to proceed.

We discussed the writing strategy over the hour, along with all the different scenarios, including violent revenge. We went through each of them and then I asked him to choose.

"I like the idea of writing. I've never done it before. It has more of an effect than a beating, it stays with you."

He was swayed by it. This way, she would also be forewarned that he knew where she lived. She could take the appropriate action. Meanwhile he could express himself in a letter defusing the situation and then gauge by the response on how to proceed. He wrote the letter in the session and together we were able to fashion something that displayed his hurt, without it creating any further problems for either party.

He received a response within a day.

"She wants to meet me."

"What are you going to do?"

"Yes I will meet her. The letter she wrote said she knew I would find her. She wants me to come round the flat and talk. She's also saying sorry."

They met and the anger flowed from Dennis, meanwhile she held her tongue. After he had finished, they had a cup of tea, a joint, and they began a process of reconciliation. She apologised for her spiteful behaviour and he used the techniques we had developed in counselling to try to understand her behaviour, rather than enact more violence. There was a brief reconciliation and then another component began to emerge. Dennis began to see his need for her company, building from the loneliness of his childhood.

Remarkably he forgave the cruelty of the women in the home, as we worked on why they behaved as they did. He recollected they had stated they were orphans themselves. He understood no one knew any better. Just as his son had gone into care, because he could not cope, they also had self medicated through power. He said he saw society as just self replicating its dynamics, and it was nothing personal, people were just locked into their own psychological states.

Their violence was not aimed at the badness in him, but what they saw in themselves. They just did not know any better. It was from this revelation; he began to see the patterns in his life. He saw clearly his role with his son. He saw the value of the contact he had with his son and how he needed to make amends, just as he wished his mother had made his life more comfortable. Dennis began to see himself as someone who could shape his life rather than seeing himself as a perpetual victim. This created a chain reaction as his son went into detox and rehab. This had a corresponding impact on Dennis

"Well if he can do it, so can I. You mentioned detox and rehab before Dean. What is it?"

I explained the process to him.

"So it's me getting in touch with that small wounded boy still inside me?"

It was at this juncture, I tackled Dennis on his shoplifting habit. Embittered by his past he still stole something every day. I reflected on the wider social interest and the impact on shopkeepers who were struggling to make a living, and as a type of harm reduction he told me he would limit himself to the occasional foray into the big supermarket chains. Eventually even this began to taper off, as we worked on his life purpose. When he had something to live for, the substance use and the shoplifting became redundant This is how Crime Reduction works, through working with people to perceive their better interests, then developing a meaning for living and enjoying their life.

Dennis made the leap without any prompting. He shed the layers in the counselling, returning for nine months after he had moved out of the hostel, until he went into detox and rehab. During this time he stripped off a great deal of his negative, emotional baggage. He also developed a hobby; he began to attend public speaking sessions and participated in group work. As we neared the end of our time together he broke down into huge waves of sobs, wracking his body.

"That poor kid. That poor fucking boy. What did they do to him? He never hurt anyone."

In hardening himself against the violence he had shut down the emotional connection between him and others. Opening himself up to his son, entailed him opening himself up to who he was when he was a child. Dennis later went on to rebuild himself after years of emotional violence.

Case History 28; Managerial Descent

James was a mid forty year old man who was transferred to the hostel after being asked to leave the previous one. He had been transferred because he had been involved in a fight. This had arisen over a dispute over a woman who lived in a mixed gender hostel. This led to him feeling aggrieved at being forced out. His partner was still housed in the hostel and now he was banned from going anywhere near her. One of the significant gender issues in the homeless sector are the large number of homeless men. Subsequently there are more male beds than women. Therefore it is easier to transfer men across hostels. There is also an unstated belief that women are more vulnerable when they are living on the street. They are more liable to be physically attacked and sexually assaulted. This issue becomes problematic, not because it is untrue, but because as these case histories show, men are also attacked physically and sexually, but it is part of their "masculinity" to keep quiet about its effects. This trauma becomes sublimated into anger and violence that becomes projected onto vulnerable women.

James attended therapy readily. He told me he would not be in the hostel for long. He felt he was not in the same position as the other men, because he had run his own business and had been a pub manager. He therefore believed he had a social stake in the world. Previously he had lived in a semi detached house with two cars, with two holidays abroad per year. All he needed to do, as he expressed himself to me, was snap himself out of it, phone a few contacts and then get back to work. It would happen as soon as he snapped his fingers. Therefore, he said, he would come and see me to pass the time, but any time soon, it would all come together, and he would be off. He had already spent nine months in the previous hostel, but he said, he had stayed there to comfort his girlfriend. He wanted to help her, stop her from using alcohol, that was why he had stayed. It was not because he was the same as everyone else.

James had a previous relationship with a woman who had been a childhood sweetheart. He had lived with her for around twenty years and they had a stable routine. They had a son, who he was still in contact with. It was after this relationship finished, that he descended into alcoholism. He never saw it as alcoholism however. He viewed himself as a heavy drinker, who could manage sobriety for days and then have a blast for a day or two.

James had always liked to drink, four pints of lager after work, but now he was drinking 1-2 litres of strong cider each day. When he drank his personality changed, and he began to fall over. He banged his face; he also became morbid, aggressive, melancholic, spiteful and stuck. It depended on his social circle as to how he presented. When he was sober he was very pleasant and courteous. The change was quiet marked, between his sober and alcoholic state, as he swayed between two polarities. James initially viewed himself as a binge drinker when he first attended the hostel. He informed me he never had a problem with alcohol until he was housed in this hostel. He blamed the environment and conditions, asking me why were there not more bans on alcohol and drug use in the hostel. The problem as I pointed out to him is that these men would not access the shelter if that was the case. This was a high needs wet hostel. There were dry hostels but this entailed working towards stability. This could not be enforced as a rule because it would be circumvented. It would then entail throwing people out before their problems could be worked upon. James could not connect to the fact he was part of this milieu. He perceived them as the "other" (Sartre 1943), when he was part of the milieu.

His binge drinking had become more frequent and the gaps between binges less and less. James represented one of those people in hostels who try to convince you they have been placed there due to a bureaucratic mix up, that it was all a mistake. Soon they will be out into the wider social world and everything will return to normal. They represent a substantial minority within the hostels, people still clinging onto their former status, unable to see where they are in the present. James had no idea why he drank so heavily.

James had social connections to get a flat and twice he was offered a move on, outside of normal rehousing procedures. He prevaricated about moving out, and twice he lost out. Eventually due to his drinking levels it was felt that offering him a flat was not a feasible option. James then became angry at the withdrawal of the offer, feeling no one had the right to judge him. The reason why he could not take the flat was because it was someone's birthday and what were you supposed to do on a birthday, but drink. It was not his fault that he was hung-over the next day and he forgot to attend the interview. Why could they not rearrange it, then the problem would be solved. The problem as he saw it, was that no one understood him and his predicament. He was not a drinker but he was being stigmatised as if he was one.

The real problem however, was that due to his previous status; he had failed to see what had happened to him. James was a different type of alcoholic, and although he had alcohol free days and he could keep sobriety for a period, his relapses were becoming more frequent. He blamed the hostel for this decline and saw his alcohol use as environment based. However his behaviour when he was drunk became more out of control. He still blamed it all on the hostel. It was being surrounded by 51 other people with chronic problems that affected him, he reported to me. If he was not in a hostel then he would not be drinking. Being around these other men with their problems was affecting him. He could take no personal responsibility. As I pointed out to him, there were men who did not drink or take drugs in the hostel. They were a minority, but they did exist.

As he drank, he lost his memory of what he did to whom, and when. He became involved in fights outside of the hostel with Eastern Europeans. His friend was badly beaten. James prided himself on being a South London man and no one could tell him what to do. James was trapped in a series of roles, which he could not visualise.

He hung onto his former status as a manager to separate himself from the others who were more bedraggled and unkempt. They had all been something once, other than how they appeared at the moment. Everyone had either been a father, son, manager, artist or fighter. No one was born homeless.

Hanging onto this self perception, helped James adjust to the hostel up to a point, after that it became a fantasy. This became more threadbare as time receded, and he was still reiterating the same lines. Then it became an unreal depiction of his personal reality. This hanging onto his former status was something we looked at. It helped him maintain his self esteem because he could hang onto the positive memories of exercising control in his life. However it was also a hindrance as it stopped him from gaining a sense of what was occurring in the present. He failed to register he was sliding downwards. This was a conundrum, as I did not want to dismantle his defence mechanisms. Usually the work focuses on trying to build self esteem, to retrieve some notion of being stable. With James a different solution was needed as he hung onto his social status, as he sank downwards into the abyss.

When he was drunk, James veered near suicidal ideation, and then working with him was a tightrope of managing his mood swings. Then the focus became based on bolstering his self esteem so he could begin some form of ascendance. James was adamant he did not need a detox or rehab because he only drank, but was not a drinker. All he needed to do was go to his Mum's dry out and he would be fine. He could then go back to his old job. He was still attached to his mother in his mid 40's, and this form of attachment was based on a dependency. He asked me to speak to his mother and she asked me to help him access a detox, as she could not cope when I explained the process. His mother, similar to the women in "Beaten into Violence" (Whittington 2007) provided care to her children. She had two boys and a daughter. The two boys would stay at her house to dry out from their alcohol and substance use. James had a fractured relationship with his brother. They were extremely close, but they also fought extensively. The fighting often became physical. James had been the protector of his younger brother and he had provided stability. I began to look at his past. His dad passed away when he was young and James lived with his brother, sister and mother. His mother met another man and remarried when he was 7 his brother was 5 and his sister was 3. The man began to enact his own disciplinarian systems in the house. James endured the violence until he was 14 when he returned to see the man beating his younger brother. James described the man punching and kicking his younger brother who was bleeding heavily. He described something in him just flipped. James pulled the man off, and then his 12 year old brother sprang on the man. Together they manhandled him out of the door, out of the flat, onto the balcony ledge and then threw him over. This was a drop of three storeys, as he recounted. Luckily for all concerned, there was a delivery van underneath full of cardboard boxes otherwise both of the boys would have been charged for manslaughter or murder. After this event James's mother, chose her children over her second husband. He was forced out of the house and did not press charges. The boys were left to live with their mother. I looked at the event with James, to see how it had affected him, the violence beforehand and his adjustment afterwards. He viewed the violence as normal, until I pointed out his actions said something else. He paused and thought. He saw it as a moral issue relevant to one particular juncture of time. He saw his brother being attacked and helped him. He could see no antecedents or perceive any effect. He was emotionally shut down, around these events. He could recount them but not inhabit them. He narrated them as if recounting story from a book, rather than a chapter from his own life.

It was in his adolescence James related he was raped by an older female relative. She came to his bed, aroused him, and then enticed him into sex. This occurred when he was 14. She later told him that if he ever mentioned it to anyone then she would tell them he had raped her. No one would believe him and he would go to prison as a rapist. James was terrified for years about being unmasked as a rapist. I worked with about the effects of the event and how it had shaped his self perception. The resonant effects of this account clearly had a traumatic impact upon him. As an adult he was confused about what had happened. The recollection was extremely traumatic for him as he was confused whether a woman could rape a boy. We worked through the myths of arousal, the impact of incest and the affect of the commands upon him. The internalisation of being labelled a rapist also became an issue. After he revealed it to me, he stated he would have to speak to his mother about what happened. We looked at the various consequences. It would still have an impact on the family, not as devastating as it would have been if it had been reported at the time.

He relayed the incident over a number of weeks, when he was sober and drunk. The account never varied highlighting its resonance effect upon his adult life. I worked with him on the after effects of keeping the secret for so many years. He eventually approached his mother about what had happened. His mother was supportive when he finally told her. She ostracised the relative.

James's behaviour and alcohol use improved for a few weeks and he began to focus on change, then he slipped backwards again into oblivion. James began to talk about his relationship with his former wife and her need for order which created conflict. His former wife was obsessive about neatness. She also had an issue with buying sale items from supermarkets to such an extent the house overflowed with "bargains." She was an addictive shopper. This became a source of tension as James worked six days a week for years whilst his wife amassed more things that were not needed. She also provided James with a great deal of emotional support and she provided the structure in the relationship. Without her, James realised, he was bereft of structure and he had collapsed.

He had married young and after 19 years, said he wanted to escape the confines of the marriage, and see if he could survive by himself. He still spoke to his ex wife. The answer to his question about whether he could cope was answered by subsequent events. Clearly he needed her structure. Without his former wife's organization, he relied on his elderly mother. After he was divorced, he had

284

found another partner in a pub. He described her as the complete opposite of his wife. She was fond of going out and socialising. She was the life and soul of the party. He thought he had found someone who he could live with. However after she drank, her personality changed from serene to violent. After a few months of having a relationship, she began to engineer fights in pubs between James and other men. He stated he stayed with her, thinking he could change her, so he hung on for months. Meanwhile she shredded his self esteem through constant criticism. It seemed she abhorred intimacy and used various strategies to undermine it.

When he left the relationship he was drinking heavily. He was trapped in trauma, where he could describe events and feel some effects, but unable to see any connections between them. He seemed oblivious to the violence inflicted on him as a child, and his later need for self medication.

What emerged within the therapy is that when he had imposed boundaries on himself such as work and marriage, he functioned within those parameters, as an ordinary member of the community. When these boundaries no longer existed, he became incoherent and unstable. He was unable to impose any limits by himself. He only functioned when limits were imposed upon him. The person he looked to assist him now was his elderly mother. She would sort him out, and make sure he stopped drinking he told me.

Receiving warnings from the hostel ensured he changed his behaviour for a period of time, because I discussed these warnings with him in the sessions. If he was evicted from the hostel, he only had the street to look forward to. This is when the full realisation of being homeless began to hit him. Talking about boundaries in the sessions reinforced the behavioural contours he needed to adhere to. These had to be imposed upon him, because he could not create any boundaries himself. Without work and marriage he was formless.

In trying to change his behaviour, James needed to see a reflection of himself. He could not make a self diagnosis. He asked me to write a letter to the DWP (Department of Work and Pensions) about his alcoholism and to assist him to keep his benefits. Clearly he was deluded, about returning back to work, as his alcohol use was beyond control. I showed him the letter I wrote detailing his self delusion.

I was unsure whether he accepted that he had a problem that needed addressing or was still in denial. James however did work towards stabilisation in his behaviour, if not his drinking. Eventually he was later transferred to yet another hostel to break up the alcohol group that had formed around him.

James eventually did make changes by becoming sober for a few months but then he relapsed, adamant that he did not need to detox. Still resistant to attending any structured support, the memories of management diminishing, he was appearing as a middle age man vacilitating, as time move onward. The problem he faced was surrendering his status, to accept the need to change. This was a considerable problem amongst men who had status and then lost it.

James was the example of a man trapped in his self image and he could not see what was happening in the present. It was an issue Bruno Bettelheim discussed in "The Informed Heart," (1980) the belief that hanging onto status is a bedrock, despite external events nullifying the position, people cling onto their rank. Meanwhile the social reality it was based upon had shifted irrevocably.

James explored his background in the sessions, the sibling rivalries and its effect, his role as a surrogate protector and father. He made some changes within the sessions but the behavioural impact of the warnings was a greater impetus. James did not have the same prison background as the other men, and he took the warnings seriously. The other men would have shrugged their shoulders, but he was genuinely worried. When he was transferred to the other hostel, he continued to drink and at the time of writing he was in his third year of living in hostels. He had weeks of sobriety and then he relapsed. He needed to adjust to his reality and seek an escape through attending detox and rehab, but he fought against it. This would entail he was in the same position as everyone else and that would entail a negation of his self belief. This was the conundrum he was caught within. He needed to surrender his status to move forward.

Case History 29; Non Prodigal Son

Ahmed was a Middle Eastern man in his mid forties. He was receiving support from the mental health team, taking various forms of medication to curtail his diagnosed schizophrenia. He had spent his life going in and out of prison,

286

for various small offences. He was an adept pickpocket and small time thief, who spent his money self medicating on Skunk, Crack Cocaine and Heroin. He also drank occasionally. Ahmed was also emotionally vulnerable, used by more determined people as a vehicle to sell their drugs. He was constantly being caught as a holding man, and then being given non custodial sentences because of his mental health status. He went to court on two occasions over the two years we worked together. On both occasions, he was asked to hold a weight of Cannabis, whilst it was being sold.

Ahmed was extremely anxious; initially he would only spend between 10 minutes in a session and then get up and leave. As we built up trust he spent an hour talking to me. As he trusted the process, the sessions became longer, and he revealed more about himself, stating he found it difficult to have faith in people. He had been let down considerably in the past by institutions and his family.

Relating his life, he provided an insight into the issues migrant communities faced when they came to the UK. His father was a successful businessman who had built a trade through working 16 hours per day, creating a fast food chain of 6 shops. This had enabled him to support his wife and several children. Ahmed described him as a strong man who ruled the family when he returned from work with an iron glove. Every one of the children was fearful of him. Ahmed spoke little of his mother, except to say she was dominated by her husband. His father would drink and carouse when he was not with the family. He also had numerous mistresses, and so Ahmed stated, he had several step brothers and sisters. This was his Dad's life; work and play.

Ahmed was the oldest son and he was expected to work in the business. Ahmed took his part in it from an early age. He would clean tables, replace cans and bottles when needed in the store cupboards. Ahmed never went into details of his early life and we kept away from a deeper exploration. There were certain no-go areas that we tacitly agreed to shy away from, as he needed to be supported within the present. He was another man who was extremely fragile. The main importance for Ahmed was trying to curtail his drug problem and dealing with the effects of his relationship with a woman who was not emotionally stable. They were in a co-dependent relationship and both triggered off events in each other. Ahmed had a strong need to build an attachment relationship, but his partner was violent. Ahmed could also be violent in response to her, but he was also trapped between feelings of care and fulfilling his emotional needs. She was half his age and he was worried that another opportunity to meet a woman may not arise, so he became desperate to keep hold of her. This linked to his low self esteem as he was lonely and felt the need to find someone to share his life with. At the same time, her outbursts were extreme. He described her picking up a glass cabinet and shattering it over his head in a rage. She also attacked him in the street verbally and physically. She also saw other men in casual relationships. Ahmed described one time when he went to see her and discovered her in bed with another man. He smashed her windows, he was arrested then remanded.

Ahmed also expressed ambivalence about the relationship, reflecting on whether he should be leaving her, or staying with her. This would dominate the sessions. My role was neutral, weighing up the pros and cons. The relationship was destructive, but he was growing within it. He would seemingly come to a decision to end the relationship and then he would immediately be pleading with her via text to meet him. This was the pattern for six months.

After he smashed the flat, she had a restraining order placed on him. She still however asked him to meet her, and they continued the relationship with him staying at her flat. She now had total power or a boundary placed over him, depending on how the relationship was viewed. If he upset her, she could phone the police and have him arrested. During the period before the trial both parties flouted the order continuously, to the point where he stayed with her, the night before the trial. At the trial she insisted the control order was reinstated for her own safety. The female judge perceived the complicated dynamics without any ideological blinkers. She refused the request, instead giving Ahmed a Conditional Discharge. Ahmed spoke about his feelings of betrayal, querying why anyone would want to reinstate the control order, when he had been staying with her for at least two nights per week for months. Walking out hand in hand, he said he was confused. Ahmed forgave her for these lapses, declaring his love to her in poems and songs written especially to eulogise his "beloved."

The relationships continued to see-saw and when he broke it off, she camped outside the hostel for three days. The police were called because of her behaviour, as she was shouting and screaming for him. It was clear she was vulnerable, but she was also capable of holding her own, as the neighbours called the police to ask for her removal. Ahmed finally relented to her pleas to see her again.

I worked with Ahmed to create a future, based upon his hobbies. Due to his mental health diagnosis he was on a high rate of DLA and was unlikely to hold down a full time job, due to the severity of his depression. He could act as a ruse for gangs, but there was no feasible job he could do. He was interested in the arts. I worked with him to attend College courses to develop his musical passion. Returning back to the hostel with his compositions, he would recite poetry and then put them to music. The staff supported him in this positive endeavour; they played his songs over the tannoy system. Ahmed had found a meaning and a rationale for his social expression. Having this as his dream, he began to curtail, if not cease his drug use.

Finally he ended the relationship with his partner. He had planned a celebration for her based on alcohol, cannabis and crack. I had questioned him on the soundness of his planning, reflecting on what had occurred previously. She had exploded towards the end of the evening and then called the police for the third time. The relationship had fragmented, as he stated he could take no more, as he expressed his loneliness and isolation. He revealed he had not felt so bad since he had been placed in the Children's Home. Ahmed stated that as a ten year old he had stolen some family objects, and to teach him a lesson his father had sent him away. He spent the next six years in a Children's Home. His father thought this would toughen him up, to take over the family business when he was ready. This was his way of making sure his son was obedient, when he finally emerged as an adult. Instead Ahmed emerged from the Children's Home an emotional wreck, from all of the bullying he endured. We only spoke about it briefly. After he left the home he embarked on a crime spree lasting nearly thirty years. Looking at this it became apparent Ahmed was involved in ongoing psychological revenge.

Ahmed never spoke fully about life in the children's home, but from his account there was a clear difference between the cheeky rule-challenging boy that went into the home, and the shattered adolescent that emerged. The father's businesses, for all his hard work were made obsolete by the changes in the catering business, and he had nothing to hand over to his son, when he retired. His hard work was all for nothing. He returned back to Lebanon, with his wife, whilst Ahmed stayed in the UK. Ahmed's punishment had been for nothing, other than to shatter him emotionally.

I worked with Ahmed for over two years, and eventually he pulled himself from being locked inside his fugue. Instead of looking within, he began to engage with the outer world. He never became drug free, but when he moved out he was able to maintain his flat and continue with his art career. Ahmed represented someone who was emotionally fragile and he needed to keep hold of some of the illusions he had created. These illusions provided him with a meaning. Taking them away, as discussed in supervision would only leave a great chasm, which he could topple into, with a deep sense of despair and then not climb out of again. Ahmed's personal transition was based on working through a set of internal propositions he devised, rather than dictating any external beliefs. I was careful during the period of turbulence with his partner, never to criticise her. Making one near critique incited Ahmed to surge with anger. Aware of any infringement on his autonomy, the complex dynamics were worked through each week. It would have been an easy temptation to say to him, the relationship should end, as it was a disaster, and that he needed to keep away. At the same time this would have reinforced his loneliness, linked to the feelings of "what if?" Ahmed needed to go through the process and be supported when he emerged the other side. As he looked back, he retrieved the good memories and reflected on the bad, stating he would not have wished to have surrendered so early; the whole process had helped him.

"I can use the feelings of hurt Dean and put that it into my art, nothing is wasted. I hope she finds what she is looking for."

Case History 30; I did it my Way

Dave was the archetypal self made man. He attended five sessions of therapy before deciding the hostel was not for him. He had been discharged from a mental health unit and was trapped in a thousand yard stare, as he took a variety of prescribed medications. He neither militated against the hostel, nor acknowledged its existence. He walked in and out of the door, as if trapped within other worlds. He was completely oblivious to the real world, or so it appeared, lacking any sense of grounding. A slight change occurred when he gained a pushbike, and he would disappear for the day. He cycled off to his drug dealer to buy his Heroin and Cocaine, as well as pick up his prescribed medication. This would obviously entail an ability, firstly to communicate, and secondly to acquire money to pay for the illicit substances. Dave could reach out into the world when required. Then he would wall himself up again. He lived in a self imposed cocoon.

I began to strike up a gradual conversation with him about the weather. We made small talk about the rain, cold, sun and ice. He began to engage gradually. Eventually after nine months he agreed to meet with me.

He recounted his life history as someone who had left school, worked hard and built up a series of businesses; car washing, waste disposal, recycling, second hand cars, collecting pallets, scrap metal. By the time he was twenty five, he had a Rolls Royce, a big house outside London, a wife and two children. He was a self made millionaire. He described his former life of holidays in the Seychelles, Barbados and Thailand, going out to restaurants to eat, because no one ever needed to cook, the children going to public schools.

"What happened?" I asked.

"Charlie. I started serving, thinking I could make even more money. I became greedy. Then I started taking it, doing grams of the stuff everyday with a big tray of it on the table. Help yourself type of thing, a bit like you eat fruit or something. People would just come round and hoover up some lines, and we'd watch a film, you know what I mean?"

He recounted his life when he began to start taking drugs. He said he felt bored and empty with his achievements. Once he had reached the top, he felt lonely and isolated. He had split from all of his former friends and lived in a big house with his wife and children. They were given everything they wanted, but it was never enough, and he began to resent the lifestyle. He had built his life on the acquisition of objects and money, believing this would liberate him from the effects of poverty. His life history detailed many of the issues Erich Fromm (1957) documented as conundrums in the "Art of Loving," the belief that objects can liberate and the passing of these objects as gifts, cements care and attachment. What became missing from his account was any mention of the emotional resonances between father, mother and children. It was also missing when he described his childhood.

Feeling left out of the family he had made, he revealed he had a series of affairs with other women, to take away the boredom. This gave him a feeling of power. Then he stated he was dialling up escort girls and arranging cocaine parties.

"Did you enjoy yourself?"

"Of course I fucking did, what type of question is that?"

"It's just that your habit was getting out of hand as if you were blocking something."

"Yes, you're right perhaps I was."

This double lifestyle went on for three years until it began to take an effect. He recounted how he began to become paranoid. He felt he was being watched and bugged. He would double back and have his house swept for any surveillance equipment. He no longer trusted his brothers or his father. He began to suspect his wife was cheating on him.

"I wouldn't have blamed her. I had pushed her and the kids away and I was awful to live with. They could not cope with me. The Coke was giving me delusions. I felt I was the most powerful man in the world and could do anything. I was only a local man who made some money. That's how mad I had become."

I began to explore his need to feel power, but Dave decided he did not want to explore this.

"Who wouldn't want to be a millionaire by the time they were 25, coming from a poor family?" was his response.

Dave had achieved a pinnacle of power, as a self made man. There were a minority of these men within the hostel. Dave was not the first. The desire to overturn the humiliation of poverty, and gain control was a strong desire. He had projected these desires as an individual need, his sole need. Money was deemed to rescue him from his poverty, but as he stated, when he acquired money it primarily provided him with the strategy to self medicate. The issues for Dave, he had identified were based on his observation, that money was never enough. He was never satisfied and this drive drove him onward to try and find meaning through sexual power. He recounted his illicit trysts in hotel rooms and the feelings it gave him of excitement and shame. Increasingly the effect of both wore off, and instead it provided him with a sense of dread. He recounted he could never understand why, as he felt he was entitled to the experiences. He then stated he had a strong sense of morality, despite outward appearances and this was the conflict he faced. It was this internal battle that raged when he returned home to his wife. This would be negated by taking more cocaine to obliterate the effects. This need to block out the impact of his behaviour became his "addiction."

He recounted other experiences, when he went on holiday he would become out of control, as he consumed both drugs and bodies. He was deported from two countries after being locked up, because of the danger he represented. Eventually his paranoia began to dominate everything, and in response his wife and children fled. Feeling betrayed he tried to commit suicide, and this triggered off a Section in a mental health ward. His immediate family took over his business empire which was still intact, his wife went into hiding and he was eventually sedated after six months. This had been twenty years ago. Since that time he had been in and out of hostels, sleeping on the streets, sleeping with friends, then arrested and put in prison.

After thawing in the therapy after five sessions he decided he no longer wanted to stay in the hostel, phoned a former friend and left to go and stay with him. It was only a short term solution, as six months later I saw him on the street. He was sitting on a concrete bollard staring into the distance. I stopped and broke his reverie and had a chat with him for quarter of an hour. He recognised me and that was significant. He had been sleeping with friends, taking drugs, but his health had deteriorated. They had eventually asked him to leave and he was back on the street. He wanted to come back to the hostel.

Case History 31; Detox Explosion

Shaun came to the hostel from the streets. He was picked up by the outreach team and placed in an initial rolling shelter. He was a northern man in his 40's befuddled with drink. He could hardly remember where he was, and constantly became lost in the hostel corridors. He had to be shown back to his room and then taken to the dining room with a personal escort. Staff expressed severe concerns that his memory lapse was organic, and that he needed long term residential care.

Shaun had a variety of modes or roles he adopted; camp flamboyant, hard man and volcanic fury. All were related to the levels of alcohol he had taken, and who he was talking to. They were social roles. When he spoke to me for example, because he developed an investment, I could pull him out of his volcanic fury mode within a second. However the problem remained for the other workers, who were on the receiving end of his fury. They did not have the same connections and his wrath would be uncontrollable.

Shaun was open about his life story with me from when we first met. Growing up with his sisters he was the eldest boy. He had both a mother and father. His father drank heavily and attacked his mother constantly. Shaun recollected the levels of violence being horrific, with his mother being beaten to a bloody mess, her head battered against a wall with blood pouring from her nose and mouth. He related he had to constantly run out of the house in his underwear, from the age of 5 onwards to get to the public phone to call the police. His Dad would be arrested, but his mother would never press charges. He recounted he always felt let down by her inability to prosecute him. Instead she would take the children and live in Women's Refuges. Shaun described the dynamics reoccurring for 15 years until he finally punched his Dad out, beating him to the ground. From his description it appeared his father was a paranoiac who had bullied his family relentlessly during his childhood, severing all forms of attachment and replacing it with fear, fright and then ultimately fights. Shaun described living in fear and this affected his body as he was often incontinent throughout his childhood.

Shaun had gained revenge for the levels of aggression that was showered onto the family through the power of his body, thereby ending the domestic violence. This did not end its affects, as it is had layered within him, as memories, the stings of humiliation (Whittington 2007). Shaun was traumatised through witnessing and enduring such high levels of violence. It lay as various stressors within the body, and we looked at its latent impact on him and his current levels of drinking. I worked with him to validate and externalise the levels of violence he had endured, as he spoke of witnessing his mother being dragged *naked from room to room, having her head smashed against walls and then kicked unconscious.*

Social Services had not intervened. This was the late 1960's and 1970's, where there was a limited understanding of these family dynamics. Meanwhile his mother and siblings moved around the North of England, Scotland and Wales to escape. Each time their father found them, pleading that he was going to change, and that they should return. For two weeks or so, he would be the model father, and then he would start drinking. Then the cycle of violence would be re-enacted. Shaun had undertaken little schooling, as a result of the constant moving, but remarkably he could read and write. Literacy was a big issue in the hostel.

Shaun had a nihilistic attitude to his life and was engaged in a slow suicide. There was no point and no meaning, so what the fuck? This was his attitude. He would attend the counselling each week, and then shrug his shoulders.

"I am still going to drink. Thanks for the talk, thanks for your time. It's been a pleasure talking to you."

Shaun had defined views on race and was heavily racist. I would explore his meanings with him using Socratic Questioning, looking at how judgements affected people, and their effects. He shifted from virulent hatred, to ambivalence, making friends with some of the black residents in the hostel. When he drank, I could see elements of his father emerging, as his anger emerged as volcanic, then he would launch into racist tirades. The other residents viewed it as a mental health issue, and provided space for him. This was how they developed their social interest.

When questioned by the management, he would claim he was not racist, but just going for a weak spot in someone's armour. This was the residue of his father. The night staff team who were black, knew how to deal with him when he started shouting abuse, they had a bag of sweets ready under the counter. When he began to scream abuse, they would offer him a sweet, and he would stop mid sentence, say thank you and then go about his business, as if nothing had happened. Shaun could switch from volcanic anger to politeness, within a second. As I knew him well, I could deflect his anger with humour. I found him berating a female member of staff, about the lack of hot water, screaming abuse at her. I asked him to stop bullying a woman and show me the problem. I turned on the tap, he said did not work. It had an air blockage. It did not pour for a second and then it gushed out a torrent of water. Shaun stood back amazed at the "synchronicity" of the event. I spoke with him about needing to apologise for his tirade. He returned back to the counter to offer his apologies.

Shaun had a charge sheet, that listed over 400 offences, ranging from breach of the peace, theft, domestic violence to wounding. He recounted, that he had been arrested as an adolescent and adult in his home area, so often, he was on first name terms with the local police. He recalled an incident where a local officer took him to the pub to talk about the effects of his bereavement, as he had no one else to talk to; the nearest person in his life was Shaun because he arrested him so often. Shaun had empathy underneath the vast aura of violence that emanated from his drunkenness. This was the paradox in his character.

Replicating his father's anger as an adult, I worked with him to try and locate the various sources to help limit the outbursts. Shaun recounted the impact of his early life, and how he had been bullied by his Dad, but unlike the other men I had worked with, he still had an idealised image of him. Shaun was trapped within these two competing images. The first was a man who could express remorse, and then there was the man who vandalised his family. Shaun at some point had lived with his father, after his mother had died. They had bonded in drinking together. Shaun described his Dad as screaming for his wife in the middle of the night, when he was asleep, after she died. She still haunted his dreams.

"He never got over her. I would be in the same house as he was, he was screaming in a nightmare."

She had died in her early 40's from Alzheimer's disease. Shaun described the disease as resulting from the trauma she had endured when she had been married. The constant beatings around the head were the real cause of her death. Although described as Alzheimer's he knew the real reason.

"Who is going to say anything different to the Doctors? No you got your diagnosis wrong. It's my father being a bastard. We knew what caused it. That was enough."

Encouraged by his sisters to go and see her at the hospice, Shaun had tried to ignore her decline by drinking it away. Eventually he relented and travelled to be near her for four months. He described the shock when he met her. She did not recognise him. She just stared at him without recognition. He went back each day thinking it would change, that she would get better and say something. He kept going every day for four months but with no change. This had a devastating impact upon him. Describing it as heartbreaking to see her retreat and not be able to connect to the world around her and to him. Each day brought more despair, and as it continued, he became enveloped in a sense of dread, as she steadily deteriorated. Meanwhile, because of his accent he was getting into fights with local men.

"They didn't like northerners there, and they made it clear, but I had to stay there because of my Mam."

After four months he felt he could not cope with the emotional and physical violence and he left the town. Leaving his mother gazing into the distance, he stopped working and began drinking, living on the streets consumed with depression. He had succumbed to a way of life that would become his norm for the next ten years apart from short stays with his Dad, friends and the occasional detox.

Shaun had developed a reputation in his local area as the "nutter." When arrested he had no boundaries around his behaviour. The police showed him CCTV pictures of him urinating through the door of Greggs Bakery. He described it as humiliating, as if he was watching somebody impersonating him. He knew it was him. Trying to cut down his alcohol use only brought greater conflagrations when he returned to drinking. Shaun related one episode when he stopped for three months and felt secure. Then he asked his friend to come and see him along with his girlfriend at his new place. He had a flat and a job.

Feeling happy they were coming the next day, he went out to celebrate, and bought two bottles of wine for them when they arrived. He thought he would remain teetotal. At 7pm he opened a bottle and took a sip, by ten he had drank both bottles. He stumbled out to a garage and bought two more. When they turned up at 10am, still drunk he stormed down the stairs, punched his friend in face and kicked his girlfriend hard between the legs. Then he stormed

297

around the town fighting anyone that walked in his way, until he was finally arrested and imprisoned by the police. In the space of 24 hours he had lost his girlfriend, best friend, job and flat. Finally taken to court he was given an ASBO and not allowed to return to the town. Reflecting on this account, he spoke about transferring his feelings onto others. He felt guilty in relapsing, and then blamed his girlfriend and friend for his drinking binge. He attacked them because he felt it was their fault. If they had not come to see him, he would have remained sober. He was trapped in a double bind, emotionally frozen, unable to articulate or make sense of his feelings. He then displaced these feelings onto others. This entailed him not taking responsibility for his actions.

He described having a number of relationships and had five children. There were glimpses at the hostel, that he could if he concentrated he could make connections with others. It was heavily disguised under his bravura.

Alternating between charm and anger, Shaun began to be grounded in the hostel. The next stage was to work towards putting some boundaries around his drinking. Shaun did not want to go to a detox. It appeared he had briefly attended a detox for a few hours, just before he accessed the hostel. Staying for an hour, he had walked out to buy a beer at the off licence. Shaun maintained he could come off alcohol by himself. This did not appear to be a viable option.

I became more directive in speaking to him, about his need to gain support. Shaun felt he was stronger, and said if he was going to do it, it was going to be done his way, or not at all. The crux came when a relative contacted him. This was a significant event, because Shaun was isolated within the hostel. He had few friends, as his racial outbursts were alienating everyone. Although they tolerated him, it was only because he was clearly not well. He had numerous warnings from the management about his vitriol, and if he continued he would be put out on the streets. These boundaries were needed, to safeguard the staff and were used as a last resort as a form of social interest. If the abuse became too virulent, then the staff could phone the police and ask for the person to be arrested. This happened on a few occasions.

Shaun made contact with a member of his family and spoke with them every day. He stopped drinking and I became apprehensive, reflecting on what happened previously. Meanwhile, a different man emerged altogether. He was polite, cheerful, respectful and pleasant to talk to. This was noted by everyone. He remembered everyone's name and took part in the world, instead of shying away from it. I was alarmed because of his sudden cessation. My concern was he would explode, after the relative had left. I last saw him on a Tuesday; the relative was due to meet him on the Saturday. On the Friday before they met he exploded. It was a dramatic outburst that entailed the police being called. The whole situation could have been doused if there was a therapist on hand to work with him about his expectations for the following day. Instead Shaun had wobbled and returned back to drinking.

Shaun had internalised many of the characteristics he had described as belonging to his father. A day before he was due to meet his relative Shaun detonated. He had relapsed from the fear of making contact. The police were called to remove him as his racism was so extreme, staff pressed charges. The police held him on remand. Eventually he was given bail, he returned to amass his possessions which he collected, then threw them across the street and walked away. Shaun had failed again. He took nothing apart from the clothes he wore with him.

Shaun was brimming with anger, that could only be contained within a long term rehab, and he needed to work towards it in stages. Therapy was the main support. He needed ongoing sustained help, to meet his needs during this brief window of opportunity. It needed a cohesive strategy from a group based on the ground who knew his personal dynamics, as every other agency that interacted with him failed to make an impact. The bureaucratic tiers would be an anathema to Shaun as he railed against anything perceived as having authority.

Alternatively left to himself he could not contain his emotions and they burst as a bombshell within the hostel. His anger detonated and fragmented everything around him. He returned to the streets, alone. The other residents applauded the management's decision as they were also upset over his behaviour. Shaun had pushed everyone away because he did not feel good enough. He had become his father.

Case History 32; A Great Unsaid

Frank was another man from the north who had moved to London and lived on the streets for months. In between sofa surfing he was picked up, finally, by the Outreach Team, and brought into the hostel. He was in his late thirties and had been technically homeless for years, living in and out of hostels, streets and couches. Frank had a skilled trade, previously living with his parents, before moving in with his sister and then finally becoming homeless. It transpired he had an uneasy relationship with his mother, during his childhood, before getting a job. It took several sessions and months of work, before he disclosed this. Frank was continuously drunk and sceptical of the counselling process, one of the few men who attended who was gently disruptive. He had been estranged from his father and sister, nine years previously after an argument in his family, where his Dad had backed his sister. He felt aggrieved over this and had not spoken to his family since, drifting onto the street. This had finally occurred after working in the middle of England; he had missed his train stop and awoke in London. He had no money to get to work, and feeling he was going to be dismissed, he got off the train, jumped the barrier and went to stay with friends in London. Signing on, he constantly moved around, until he ran out of friends, then he began to sleep on the streets. He developed an entrenched alcohol habit which helped him forget his problems. The stigma of his position stopped him from contacting his family. Time move onward and he lost connection with the mainstream world. I worked with him for several months, to ascertain what his issues were. Frank remained unclear and elusive, sometimes wanting to speak and other times he was shuttered. As he began to speak about his life, it emerged his father had moved abroad after divorcing his mother. Frank and his sister remained behind in the UK. They had supported each other initially, but Frank's binge drinking and then turning up late, when she was looking after her baby created dynamics in the house. They had an argument, and she told him that he needed to go and find somewhere else. This was a catalyst for his self destruction. He had been working, returning back to his local town at the weekends, where he would become inebriated and then stumble back to his sisters flat. She would rent a room out for him over the week-end. Then he would return to work during the week, and then live on site. After she told him, he needed to live somewhere else for his weekends; he never spoke to her for years. She could not cope with his needs, and he felt the last attachment bond being severed. She had chosen her baby over him.

There was a dynamic of unemotional attachment between Frank and his mother that was unstated. Frank did not want to talk about the impact of the divorce, saying it had no effect. This appeared to be a denial and I had to work carefully around it. It had been the catalyst for his descent. It appeared pivotal, but he denied any connection between his parents splitting and his alcohol use. His alcohol use was high, drinking 6-8 cans of cider, sometimes more, as he was locked into a hostel drinking circle.

Frank never caused any problems around the hostel, apart from swaying side to side and needing to be escorted to his room. When he joined the drinking groups, he never became involved in fights or arguments.

Exploring his early life, Frank said he survived school by playing the class clown, a role he had kept up into his adult life, as he could take nothing seriously. Emerging within the sessions and repeated consistently, were the stated bonds between his father and sister. I began to perceive his predicament being based more upon miscommunication, rather than malevolence. Although he never spoke about his mother, the bonds between his sister, father and himself appeared strong. It struck me; Frank could reinstate communication with them, if he could shift beyond being hurt and drunk. This had worked with other residents, and it needed to be undertaken carefully. Far from being ideal support units, families were repeatedly the source of considerable pain. Treading carefully, and taking readings of the situation, I gained a picture of someone isolated though pride and being wounded.

Reflecting on working class values, and the communal spirit of certain areas (Wilmot and Young 1969), I asked Frank if he still had any friends where he grew up. He remembered the telephone number of a friend from nine years previously. I asked him to go and get it. Frank was reasonably sober, and we had developed a window of opportunity to make a change. Frank returned and shakily dialled the number and it was an answer machine. He panicked and garbled a message that was unintelligible. He was not used to speaking to answer machines. I let him finish, and then rehearsed with him what he needed to say. We wrote an outline on a piece of paper. I provided him with the phone number of the hostel, so he could leave a contact address. Frank began to get cold feet, stating he was unsure if his friend still lived there. So I said to him to leave his full name, Frank Smith and the hostel number, letting them know who he was and why he was calling. He began to retreat saying,

"What is the point?"

We worked it through again as I asked him to rehearse the address and he rang again. Frank again garbled his message quickly. I pointed out to him he would need to slow down, take some deep breaths and speak the number slowly. This was a huge moment for Frank, and I knew we stood on a cusp. I was aware of the steps he was taking to break out of his isolation. Frank rang again and left a message. He did it perfectly, speaking slowly and leaving the number.

Nothing happened for two weeks and then a seismic force gathered momentum. His friend from nine years previously, rang the hostel to speak to him. Frank was overjoyed. It was the friend's mother, who had taken the message, and relayed it to her son. He had moved out of the area and lived far away. He had, through his contacts spoke with Frank's sister. She then contacted his father. Frank's Dad flew from his home abroad, to meet up with his daughter. They rang the hostel, wanting to know if it was OK for them to contact Frank. Frank's isolation was melting, as he became euphoric. So began the painful healing of a family reunion. Within two weeks his sister and father arrived in London. They stayed at a hotel and Frank showed them around the capital. Within a month they had found some accommodation for him and then took him back to live with them. Frank contacted the hostel a few months later to let everyone know he was doing well. He had returned back to work. Attachment and knowledge of communities (Wilmot and Young 1969) and the notion of Social Interest (Adler 1956) had created a catalyst for change in Frank's life. He escaped the hostel and homeless worlds through the application of this knowledge. This was his catalyst for change.

Case History 33; Rejection as a Way of Life

Carl was a man in his mid forties who had been in a revolving door with the hostels, homelessness and prison. He had recently come out of rehab and detox. He had relapsed after being clean for a year, returning back to being homeless in London. Finally he was found by the Outreach Team. He had maintained stability for a significant period and he had found a purpose in becoming involved in Green politics.

Recounting his life he detailed his childhood as a loss he had endured. He was placed in a Children's Home by the Social Services because his mother could not cope. She was having a breakdown, a single parent in a Catholic community in the 1960's. She faced social stigma, with a child born out of wedlock and could not look after him. Carl related a litany of sexual and physical cruelties inflicted, on him as he spent 11 years in "care," from 5 until 16. I asked if him if he worked on its psychological impact in the rehab. He replied he had done some work on how it had affected him. At first he had denied any effects, but had seen its legacy reflected in the lives of other group members, many of whom were also survivors. This helped him realise how the abuse had affected him physically, emotionally and sexually. Locking himself down emotionally, he had stopped himself from forming any deep emotional relationships. Connections to other people were deemed a source of emotional pain. He could not cope with being hurt again. Heroin use had helped to seal it all off. We explored the role of his self medication strategy, and how it had helped him cope with emotional pain.

We worked together to piece together the fragments of his life. He was open to self analysis as he had undertaken months of group work. I asked him what aspect of the previous therapy had helped and why? I wanted to know what had gone right. He replied it had helped him to gain an understanding how he had been shaped, its effects and what he needed to do to change. The group work in rehab was difficult, because everyone was wary of each other. It was only later, he felt comfortable to talk about the impact of the care home and the humiliations and sexual violence. He also expressed his rage at his mother, for leaving him alone to be attacked by strangers.

"What kind of mother would do that? To have a kid and then just abandon it."

It was this question that haunted him.

He had children from a first relationship which had foundered on his drug use. He used drugs from the age of 17, a year after he came out of the home. After the collapse of this relationship he descended to the street where he lived for years.

After rehab he formed a second relationship and this produced a challenge. He wanted to re-enact his sexual experiences to gain an understanding of what happened to him in the home. This alienated his partner. She was also recovering from trauma. In retrospect, he realised he should have been more understanding, but was wrapped up in his own world, gradually emerging after years of torture. This tension drove them apart, and Carl began to realise he would never keep a relationship if he was continuously haunted by the memories of the abuse. As the relationship began to fracture, all his fears began to rise, as he had no tools to repair it. It was another severance attachment loss. He fell into despair as it unravelled and was desperate to make amends.

When they broke up, the effect was therefore cataclysmic on Carl. He began to follow his former partner around and plead with her. She ended up taking out a control order on him, and he was banned from the locality. He returned to London and relapsed, he was back on the street. He felt a failure, as he had left the rehab found a job, a partner, become involved in a cause he felt worthwhile, then everything crumbled. At first he felt it was the partner who was at fault, but after a period of time, he realised he was still trapped by the past.

"It's like being trapped in a fucking dungeon. That's what the past is like. There's no fucking way out."

Despite his pessimism the sessions allowed Carl to visualise what he needed to achieve as the rehabs had helped him to validate the past. What he needed to do was transform himself. Carl realised he was still vulnerable to the effects of the past and this was impacting upon the present.

After having a long session on a Tuesday where he spoke about his pain, I returned back to work six days later and everything had changed. He had decided during the intervening period he would no longer speak to any member of the hostel staff. The catalyst was being offered a place on a Diamorphine programme, instead of taking Methadone. He attended on time, but there was some bureaucratic confusion. The receptionist had spoken to him brusquely, he became angry and then walked out. This was the trigger point, as all the previous work unravelled. Carl had minimal trust in bureaucratic procedures, being the recipient of them in the Children's Home. As he related to a member of staff later;

"I suddenly realised I was vulnerable again, people were taking control over my life and I didn't like it. It brought it all back."

This continued for weeks and he became increasingly angry and hostile. Eventually he broke the boundaries of the hostel in a very significant way. He was asked to leave. Like a footballer who had just broken an opponent's leg, he was already leaving the field before the red card was issued. He had his bags packed when he met with the management and was given the ultimatum. He shook the Managers hand and left.

Carl continued to hang around outside the hostel with the other residents. It appeared he had pressed the zero option button, marked self destruction. He continued to be belligerent and try to make demands on staff. However he was excluded from the hostel again, now as a visitor. Remarkably as he surveyed his status, he made a decision later revealed to one of the outreach workers.

"He said he woke up one day in one of the parks and was surrounded by flowers and remembered the good times he had, and said he wanted to be part of it."

Within a week he had booked himself into a dry hostel was attending a Day Programme, then within three weeks he worked to detox, finally gaining Community Care Funding and appeared focused and ready to resurface. At some point during this journey he relapsed. It must have been the last strand that held him to this world because after this he committed suicide.

Case History 34; Man Who Fell to Earth

Theo originally had travelled to the UK from a war torn North African Country. This country had been at war for years and had latterly become a one party state. Theo had fled from his country after being imprisoned for his religious beliefs. He belonged to a radical protestant sect that was not tolerated by the regime. He spent 18 months in gaol, before he escaped from his country. He described how it took place, bribing the guards, travelling in the back of trucks, the fear and the loneliness, basing his life on trusting other people, unsure of whether they were going to look after him. Then there was the wrench of leaving his family behind, his mother, father, wife and child. It was into the unknown he reached.

In the therapy sessions Theo was terrified by the hostel conditions. He felt trapped in coming to Britain and was caught between a numbers of competing ideals. He felt a wrench in leaving his country, as both his parents were still alive, living with his brothers and sisters. He could never return to his country, because he had fled from prison. If he returned back there, he would be put back into a cell, or perhaps shot.

He spoke about his turmoil, about his wife and child trapped and penniless, relying on him to send money to them. He had escaped to the Promised Land, where freedom and money showered onto those who arrived on the shores. His wife lived in another African country, also fleeing from arrest, existing in a refugee camp. Theo expressed his despair at the separation and his inability to care for his wife, as this was a cultural and familial expectation. The hostel entrapped him, because he was desperate to get a job. He wanted to work, but the weekly fees of £220 stopped him from applying for work. He needed to send money back to his wife and child, to support them. There were numerous problems with his benefits, because of his nationality. This pressure coupled with requests from his family and his wife asking for money entailed the pressure mounted upon him. They imagined he was living a life of luxury, compared to them. He revealed he could not tell them his reality, because they would look down upon him, as they had supported him to escape in many different ways. Now he had arrived at his destination, it was felt he should support them, but he found it difficult to obtain a job. His immigration status was still in the balance. He had no benefits, and was isolated in a homeless hostel, marooned in cultures he had no connection to. He had never seen Heroin and Cocaine before, although he occasionally drank. He was in constant contact with his wife, because he had sent her a mobile phone, so she could text him. It was this form of contact that had put him under pressure.

He had a friendship network, a connection with other men, who had also fled his country. This was his cultural attachment, and provided him with a secure base. They had shared meanings, culture and history, they could all relate with each other, up to a point. Theo could not relate his secret fears to them. This is why he accessed the therapy. I asked him what they spoke about.

"The guys talk about the regime, and one day they would like to go back, how they would do this and do that. The thing is it's not feasible. No one is going to be able to go back in any hurry. Our country is a mess. It's going to remain

that way. We can work here for some money and send it back. That's the only way we can rebuild it."

These social connections helped to feed him. Theo was not used to eating the type of food offered at the hostel, which varied from chicken curry to beef burgers to stews. He said he would rather starve than eat it. He was also from a middle class family in his own culture, and had family support. He would not fit into any of the groups that had formed in the hostel as he was not a substance user nor had mental health problems.

He did however suffer from PTSD, as he related the prison conditions, detailing the beatings and the deaths. He had been incarcerated in a large holding cell, with many other prisoners. Relatives brought in food, and those without support, died from illness and disease. His sleeping pattern was shallow, as he constantly jumped out of his sleep with alarm, at the memories of his months in this cell. He was terrified of people walking into his room, and jolted with distress if anyone knocked on the door. He slept 1-2 hours per night, and was constantly startled by the hostel noise. Theo suffered from a lack of sleep as a result, and he was in a constant fugue, that he felt he could not shake off. I worked with him on his sleeping pattern, as we looked at the dreams that startled him. They all related to being arrested and put behind a door then banging to get out. I worked with him to find the meaning. On the surface it appeared obvious, directly related to events. He began to talk about his life in his country before the arrest as an imprisonment. He felt suffocated which is why he joined the religious group. There was no room for any individuality, as everywhere people were watched and reported upon. He spoke about Christianity, as reverting to its earlier state as it had flourished under the Romans, as a secret society. It provided a meaning and purpose to people who had very little freedom. This was the prison he had escaped from, the prison of everyday life. He had been banging to be released from his life enacted as a prison.

He was terrified of staying in the hostel, as he felt threatened by the other men. At least in the holding cell he knew the contours of the culture. In the hostel, everything felt alien. Although anchored by an outside peer group, he spoke about the tensions this caused, as they constantly spoke about home. This raised his anxiety, as he felt helpless but could not reveal it. Although the shared food and camaraderie created a sense of warmth, he was reminded why he had escaped, and this created some turmoil within him. Theo felt if he stayed with them too long, he would become despondent, and would not be able to break out of his situation.

He resolved to get a job, and he found one. It was a delivery job. This occurred after his Home Office papers arrived. This meant he would be paying the high weekly rent costs. He said he needed to be doing something, as he felt useless. His lack of sleep created problems, as he could not concentrate, and after two weeks he crashed the van, not seriously, but enough to cause some damage. He was sacked. Realising he needed to put his energies into finding a place to live, I worked with him so he went to see the rehousing worker.

Theo was under constant pressure, as his wife and child in the refugee camp, wanted him to bring them to the UK. They had no marriage papers, because they belonged to an illicit religion. It was a Catch 22. He would phone them, and his wife would write or text, and it was always the same conversation. Theo could not help them, and felt frustrated so he stopped telephoning and changed his number. This added to his stress and his sleep became even shallower.

The sessions with Theo were primarily practical based, in helping him to understand the rules of British bureaucracy, a conduit to allows him to speak about the various binds he was involved in, and to assist him to develop his future vision.

This took place over 8 months when Theo finally moved out to a one roomed flat. He had begun to put in operation his vision, of getting a place to live, find a job and then bring his wife over to the UK. I had worked with him to write to his wife, to let her know his problems, and finally be open about his situation. I explained to him, she will find out when she eventually arrives, so why not let her know the truth beforehand. This relieved the pressure on him. He let them know that it was not easy in the UK that life was difficult, and this released him from keeping up a pretence.

Being honest, provided a clearer understanding of the challenges he was facing. Theo had kept quiet about his situation with his family. It looked as if he had abandoned them, after they had sacrificed themselves. Theo as the eldest male was also expected to support his blood family. This would have jeopardised his Home Office Application, if discovered. He had come to the UK illegally, but asked for political asylum on the basis of religious persecution.

I worked with him around his religious beliefs, and how he had been attracted to this Protestant sect. It had arisen from American missionaries who offered an alternative to the other religions. The people were genuinely interested in him, so he attended their services. The illicit ceremonies organised underground due to the persecution, created camaraderie and with it, a sense of freedom. Now he was in the UK, he had discovered another form of freedom. He felt stuck between his dreams and reality. Theo needed to adjust to reality, otherwise he was in danger of collapsing under the pressures of expectation.

In the UK, he was supported by the religion, as they provided camaraderie in the church. This was another secure base he had created. Although his sense of liberation had been blunted by his UK experiences, he preferred to be here, than in his own country, because of the freedom from observation. When the situation was calmer, and not so paranoid, he planned to return. In the meantime, he wanted to rebuild his life, as he was still young. He left the hostel, and I never saw him again. Theo epitomised the belief in the developing world that if only they escaped their local situation their problems will be resolved. When he arrived here, his dreams were shattered, and he was in a dangerous position. If he revealed the reality, he would not be believed, as there was a huge investment by people to idealise the escape route and to uphold the picture of the UK as a paradise. It was an illusion that was shared and kept intact by other refugees, who also did not want to reveal the reality. Theo was trapped in various expectations as a result. I worked with him to reveal some of the truth about his monetary situation and the Home Office bureaucratic process. It was through breaking the news gently, and asking his wife for support, he began to make the connections to sustain him, rather than uphold a masculine silence. This was creating the stress that was choking him and we learnt together how to release it.

Case History 35; Man in a Lizards Skin

Alex was from the north and had come to London after studying printing, design and technology at a London institution. He had lived by himself for thirty years, and played in various bands, hoping to be successful, but financial success had never materialised. When he came into the hostel, he suffered from extensive nervousness, which externalised itself in the worst case of psoriasis I have ever seen. It reminded me of a dead Xmas tree, shedding its needles after the New Year. Every time he stood up the skin cascaded. The staff team were concerned for their safety, feeling it may be contagious. When he stood at the front counter he left a fine spray of white skin powder on the varnish, as his skin dropped off.

I highlighted it was the representation of his internal malaise, and pointed out it was a psychological issue, in the staff team meetings, as much as it was a physical problem. It was clear he would need hospital treatment to clear up the effects. I felt he would also need some therapeutic support to ascertain what the psychological issues were. However Alex had other ideas, and he declined to go to hospital, or attend any support sessions within or outside the hostel. Instead he steadily drank himself into an abyss. His lifestyle had impacted upon his immune system, and his skin condition occurred as a result of his general depression. His self medication strategy was keeping everyone at arm's length, then drinking alcohol and smoking Crack, as it appeared to lift him out of his internal morass, for the times he was inebriated. The problems that Alex faced arose from keeping this ongoing strategy intact. He needed to keep it up every day. He was negating the impact it had on his body, by self medicating away the effects of what he was doing. He had built a fantasy world, in pretending it did not exist. He was trapped within a never ending circle. Unless someone could break in and show him another reality, he would be incarcerated within a prison of his internal psychology and an externally deteriorating body.

I developed a rapport with Alex through talking about old punk rock bands of the 70's and 80's, as well as famous design movements. Steering clear of lectures on drugs and his body, allowed him to develop a rapport based on mutual interests. Reminiscence was again crucial, as it created a resonance, a shared connection to a time he was not trapped within his current state. This triggered off memories for Alex, and he came to attend therapy of his own accord. It was from the reminiscence; I was able to build the therapy within the shared talk.

He would come and ask me my opinion about art events, and it was through building up this rapport, we created trust. This was further strengthened, when I worked on a small art project at the hostel, and he joined in. This highlights the significance of art for creating batons of trust.

I firstly worked with Alex to try and stabilise his medical condition, as he was both aware of his psoriasis and had also blocked out its effects. He showed me his body, and the layers of skin, lying on top of each other in the process of shedding, were abhorrent. In between his layers of shedding skin were raw, red, cracks that ran through his torso and limbs like rivers. It looked like a version of hell, as he was caught between scratching, because of the itchiness, and screaming, because of the pain caused by touching these sores. This ensured that he had minimal sleep, as he was constantly tortured, by the double effect.

Exploring his drug use, the Crack and Alcohol helped him to escape from his body, as he could exist beyond it, in the moments he was intoxicated. We would undertake around 30 minutes of therapy in the initial stages, before he would direct the topic away from him, back onto music. I let him direct the sessions, as this provided him with some control, something that he did not have in his everyday world, as even his body seemingly conspired against him. He rarely complied with any of the hostels directives, and was always subject to being asked to tidy his room, which he never did. I managed to work with him to do this, not by ordering him, but by suggesting it would be better for his health.

As he spoke, he began to talk about the conflict he had with his father, who was a strong powerful, successful, man, who left the family when he was young. His mother became pregnant when she was 15, and his father stayed with her for two years, until his younger brother was born, and then he left. Alex stated his mother hated him from the moment he was born. He stated his father had seemingly trapped her into having children when she was young, and she took out her resentment against him. The dynamics of the family was explored, using the concepts of Adler's (1956) Birth Order, as Alex was the eldest he was treated differently to his brother. The two had divergent career paths, with the younger brother going on to have a successful professional career. Alex was stuck in the doldrums. Alex stated he was jealous of the affection his brother received from his mother, whilst he felt he always had to fend for himself.

I returned back to Renee Spitz (1965) as he mentioned psoriasis in the index, and he noted it arose from an early rejection experience and so I explored this with Alex. It was an issue he reflected upon, and it helped him to think about his body instead of rejecting it. When he began to notice his body instead of ignoring it, we made some headway as within a week he attended hospital for inpatient treatment. Renee Spitz (1965) provided a catalyst for change.

Attending treatment entailed some very challenging moments, as Alex was extremely worried about surrendering himself to the hospital. The hospital rang the hostel to complain about his attitude, and behaviour, stating they were thinking about discharging him early, as they could not put up with his anger outbursts. The hostel staff visited Alex, to calm him, and he completed treatment. Returning to the hostel, we made significant headway, about these feelings he held towards his mother and father, stemming from childhood. There was the pain of rejection and his imbibing of her critical commands "Oh you'll never be good enough." "You are just like your father." Seemingly innocuous at the time, but when injected with spite, these had a devastating impact upon him. When his brother was born he felt left out of the family relationship even at such a young age. He did well at school however and attended the local Grammar School, but as he described his experience it was obvious he became a loner, and was extensively bullied.

This is why he said, he moved to London, to get away from his area, as he could not stand its small mindedness. After his degree, he drifted for years, hardly holding down a job, or a relationship. He played music, lived in Bohemian circles, until he found himself with an entrenched drug and alcohol habit, and nowhere to live. All the sexual relationships he had formed over the years were for small periods of time, as we explored his relationship to women. Alex had drifted through the years, into an early middle age, with no purpose. Alex realistically needed to go to an inpatient detox, and then to a rehab, but was adamant he did not want to follow society's rules. Another part of him realised, he had made a mess of his life and he needed to find some solace. Facing up to this, finally confronting it, was hugely problematic, as it entailed looking into a void. These were the elements that vied for supremacy within the counselling sessions.

The stay in hospital, and the therapeutic work cured the skin disease. Alex began to define a purpose, as he began to reflect on going back to study design as a hobby. His attachment relationships were poor, although he had made some connection with his father years later. This was fraught with difficulties, and we looked at how we could work through some of the underlying dynamics. It appeared to be one attachment relationship that could be built upon. He still however projected a sense of alienation, and confronted female staff, an issue we looked at within the therapy. His relationship with women was dominated by the presence of his mother and the emotional violence she enacted upon him, when he was growing up. He now transferred this onto all women he came into contact with, pushing them away. This impacted on his self esteem, as he never felt good enough, entailing him to self medicate. He was trapped in various Langian "Knots," (1972) that needed careful unravelling. This was my role in working with him, using Socratic questioning to try and work with him to see how he had constructed his various view points on the world, and how these were constraining him. Underneath his front of nonchalance, he craved attachment, but was trapped, as he felt that when he connected he would be vulnerable. This would make him open to being hurt again, just as he was in childhood. This took careful coaxing, and highlights the complexities of the dilemmas these men face in building self esteem, and designing a purpose. Their lives exist in layers that need to be gently explored, so they can gain the tools to finally transform. Alex ideally needed a peer group where he could act more naturally and then develop a more relaxed, at ease, authentic self, without displaying his shell of haughtiness. He also needed to ensure he did not become submerged within the group. His hobbies were a potential vehicle out of his morass.

Alex managed to connect with the world and work upon his skin problem. This cleared up after he went to hospital. We also worked on him trying to enhance his skills as he was a trained artist and drummer. These were the bases for him to rebuild. A structural problem then emerged for him as the government cuts slashed all of the support mechanisms that would have built the psychological ladder to allow him to escape. Alex represents one of the many men psychologically marooned in the twilight worlds of homelessness with nowhere to go.

Epitaph

The Case Studies highlight the range of problems that arise within the homeless field, and the depth and scale of the problems people face in climbing out of the labyrinths of despair. These were a selection of the men that I worked with, during a four year period. I undertook 1807 hourly therapeutic sessions with 119 men. The issues they face are not just whether they can sustain a tenancy. The basis of all the problems these men faced related to the levels of trauma within their childhoods carried into adulthood. Self Medication had entailed them no longer connecting to the mainstream world, and then developing various strategies of withdrawal. For many of them, it required finding a meaning to live, and this was my role in working with them to create it. This was entailed bouncing ideas off my supervisors, having my reality being validated, talking to the management to push the envelope. Trauma needed to be elevated as a precursor of many of the problem these men faced. Previously it had existed, but it was buried under a blanket of institutional amnesia.

These case histories are the emotional foundations, resonating with the other case histories detailed in "Beaten into Violence," (2007) that show the substance use/homelessness and mental health fields need to change direction. They need to become effective. These hidden emotional worlds are the foundations upon which the substances use, homeless and mental health services exist. Ignoring these emotional realities will not mean they will go away, it just means they will continue to be ignored.

CHAPTER 6
SMALL IS NOT ONLY BEAUTIFUL BUT ALSO PSYCHOLOGICALLY EFFECTIVE

In 2011, Julian Le Grand and his teams of autonomous social workers, replicated the Orexis model of 1997, and the spokes in the wheel have turned around. Praxis finally is emerging as the new ideology. The issues delineated in the previous chapters highlight the constrictions on delivering PIE's, burdened with bureaucracies. The fundamental problem is their grip on the work (Weber 1992).

Instead of this "Control and Command," (Seddon 2003) team formations should be delivering the work. These would be smaller, more efficient, and more autonomous. They will aim to regenerate people, based on building a sense of purpose, derived from the ideas of Individual Psychology. This will build on Adler (1956) and Frankl (1952, 1959). These will aim to create holistic interventions based on client need, and this will move beyond the narrow focus of CBT (Beck 1990) and Systemic Family Therapy. Psychological Social regeneration necessarily incorporates all philosophic modules, and on the basis of Praxis, it sees what works.

The aim is to deliver social change, so these teams can also be adapted for outreach work. Firstly hierarchies need to be abolished, and psychological changes need to begin at the top, then cascade downwards, following a GP Practice model (Le Grand 2011).

To begin the change, all organisations should be asked to undertake an audit, to ascertain what blockages exist in the process of psychological regenerative change. This will provide the impetus to bring about the transformation that is needed in the sector.

All current Social Care practices will need to reflect on their remit.

How does my service, organisation regenerate people?

How does my service work to block social regeneration?

Within the homeless sphere, the change in terminology to social regeneration entails a change in perception. Once perception changes and people perceive the issue differently, then they can be guided to the solution. Teams of highly trained therapists, who can build a purpose, need to take over the running of the hostels along with Practice Managers who understand the dynamics. They operate the day to day running and the admin. These staff who keep the place operational. This means however, moving beyond the IAPT Stepped Care model. This would not work with the homeless population, as they would just turn their backs to the machine grind of this module. The therapy has to engage with them, rather than they engage with the therapy.

Addiction needs to be renamed self medication. A hostel should become a place of recovery. Food would be nutrition. Therapy would involve defining a purpose. Rehousing would be a celebrated end point for all the residents to move onto, after a therapeutic journey. This entails a transformation of people.

Practitioners should be actively encouraged to formulate new ideas from their teams, and should be rewarded for innovation. Ideally, instead of power being in the hands of the commissioner, power will be handed to the practitioner. It should be in the hands of those who regenerate people. Management systems within teams would copy the GP management model and be congruent with the work practices they inculcate. Flatter, leaner, structures, that deliver real forms of change, would replace the top-down, bureaucratic, management systems, where currently all the financial resources are consumed. Creativity would be rewarded. Old components stifling change still exist, because change is perceived as a threat. New modes of delivery challenge old forms of thinking. Bureaucracies work to ensure they exist at the expense of service delivery. These are the antagonists of psychologically informed thinking. The key players within this new type of service delivery are practitioners.

Practitioners in the meantime will need to raise their skill levels. They are not going to be rewarded by dispensing methadone, needles, kindly homilies and brief therapy. Those modes do not deliver transformation. The new practitioners are going to be those who are psychologically and socially literate, who engage with people in transformative change. These are going to be the new cadres, the new elites.

Those who wish to embark on this new direction need to obtain the skills to work at the coal face. Within PIE's, the ideas of entrapment still exist, the old ideologies of management sitting above practitioners, directing events needs to be transformed.

Informed practice needs to be managed differently; many of the normal rules around work practice surrounding targets need to be dispensed with. Ideas and innovation do not arise from strictures, admonitions and targets, set by bureaucracies who are not immersed in the work. These dull the imagination, and prohibit new forms of work from evolving. These represent the old alienated work practices marking the 20th and the beginning of the 21st centuries, where people are not paid to think, only to enact. Bazalgette and Brunel were not constrained by targets, only by their imagination. These were the 19th Century pioneers, the new creators need to emulate.

Practice Managers would no longer manage, but act as psychological catalysts and be problem solvers. They will assist in completing the overall mission, tasked with resolution. This would provide a sense of meaning and purpose to the work. Power will be devolved to decision making practitioners, with a series of awards and accolades built into the system, as recompense. Work practices will become psychologically informed, and create the conditions within the marginal environments to facilitate emotional growth, drawing on the conceptual language of Claude Steiner

(2003). Emotional Intelligence has its grades of awareness, and this informs the new elites.

Resistances to these transformative messages will occur, as it disrupts the linearity of the old work practices. However the transformation needs to be complete as the large unwieldy charities/businesses need to be carefully reformulated. At present the tendering has required resources being directed away from front line service delivery (Craig 2008). Too many bureaucratic tiers eat up precious resources and these tiers are unaccountable. Creating smaller units allows local communities to gain oversight over their facilities. Local voluntary management committees who have free training in psychologically informed environments could manage these units. The effects need to be transmitted far and wide.

The psychologically informed team will cut through a swathe of red tape blocking regeneration as the older top down models will no longer be needed. Commissioners, NHS drug services, huge bureaucratic charity structures and social service funding panels will no longer be needed. This money can be reinvested in front line services. Funding instead can be devolved to GP budgets, where a specialist GP would sit on the management committee along with qualified practitioners, residents and service users. The management committee would act as a balance between professional and local needs. Creating a therapeutic milieu should be the vision of a PIE (Johnson and Haigh 2010), locally organised. Management committees should be composed of local people with a social stake in social regeneration. Recruitment to paid posts should be from a nationally recognised body such as the FDAP (Federation Drug and Alcohol Practitioners) who should be provided with the oversight of professional registration of the new cadres. This would prohibit the nepotism of the early 90's, and provide a cadre of people who are psychologically aware, similar to the professional ethos of GP's.

The therapeutic process is the crux of the service. For effective work there also needs to be a series of collective and ancillary services that collectively make the first impact in the way these are delivered. The team work involved in creating a psychologically informed environment is akin to Junger's (1920) notion of the shock troops of World War One, an elite trained unit. These units act as a vanguard to cut through the barbed wire entanglements and then works in the trenches to overturn institutional malaise. This elitism would be reflected in status, pay, conditions and prestige. No longer would work with the marginalised, perceived as a poor relation. This type of work needs to be equated as social regeneration, rather than dumping grounds for societies problems. As the conditions are raised, so are the expectations. These services need to deliver in line with a raised morale. The savings made from cutting back on bureaucracy and the tendering process can be used to bolster the pay and conditions of front line workers, ensuring their training and ethos is in line with other professional bodies.

The major difference being Junger's (1920) shock troops were aimed at destroying life. Emotional shock troops are the reverse of this shadow, militaristic paeans to hard masculinities, these workers are an elite engaged in saving lives. The hostels and later local communities would be transformed. Hostels would shift from places of housing management to places of rehabilitation for returning back to mainstream life. This would be the crucial difference. They would support people to access detox and rehab to escape the rigours of their local area. The hostel instead would change from its remit of being a repository for placing troubled people, instead transformed into supporting people with trauma to overcome their previous lifestyle. The psychological shift in mission statement would transform the élan of the social environment. This same model could be used to psychologically regenerate housing estates, and liberate the vast reservoirs of human potential. If headway can be made with people who exist at the margins of society, imagine what could be achieved with people who have a minimal social stake?

These teams would be comprised of the core therapists, trained in psychotherapy, people skilled in substance use issues, those skilled with counselling training having attached skills such as literacy, welfare rights/budgeting, hobbies/skills/training/education, housing, substance use, nutrition, homeopath/alternate therapies, First Contact Worker, Administrator and Practice Manager. The pathways to being rehoused would follow the rehab model, where people work through a route of their choice. This would involve literacy improvement, development of a hobby, education or job training, and working towards either maintenance/control, abstinence of substance use. The welfare rights support would also assist with the management of personal budgeting, building from the chaos to structure. For those in severe trauma, who need outside medication, then support from psychiatric services would entail a joint partnership. Although the focus is on therapy, the various forms of self medication for trauma still need partnership working.

The team strategy would be built on mapping progress. This naturally flows from the work of the therapist, who engages the clients, and acts as the referral point for the other services. The therapist operates as a fulcrum, and catalyst for change. The therapist creates the care plan, along with the other team members. Each contributes, but unlike the case conferences detailed above, there is a chair and someone who conducts the orchestra. As people connect to the therapy, this provides the introductions to the other components of the team. This would not prohibit other members from working on individual components first, if the residents approached them for support. This is their choice but it needs co-ordination and flexibility. The onus would be on the therapist to make the referrals to the other team members and build the infrastructure, as well as accepting referrals from other team members.

These other workers would develop the holistic version of the care plan, to create a wider vision for the resident/client. Whereas now the events are sometimes enacted as diversionary, they will be enacted as components of psychological change. This may vary from shifting the mood of the building, to helping people to create new social enterprises.

The substance use worker should work directly with a local GP practice in a form of shared care arrangement with the residents, to work out their scripts. This would circumnavigate the bureaucracy of referring to an outside treatment agency. They could work in joint partnership around health and the components that link to trauma, stress and health; Epilepsy, DVT, Hep C, HIV and TB. Accompanying clients to their appointments and thinking laterally would be the nature of the brief. The aim would be to develop a close rapport with a GP surgery, developing specialist interests and personalised care with the client group, to overcome the stigma of marginalisation. This was the successful strategy of Orexis in Deptford. GP's become allies of the process and embarked upon the discovery. It would halt Rickie's need to keep calling ambulances for company, as he would be embedded within a supportive care system. There would be no need for a shared care co-ordinator, the model at Orexis involve close co-operation.

Making the substance use therapeutic/treatment in-house, entails residents accessing Methadone stabilisation treatment quickly, its effects monitored closely, along with the on-top use. This details any psychological issues that need to be resolved if someone's use goes up. More importantly they will be working on a therapeutic programme of change. The access to detox and rehab is managed as a team. The in house decision is made alongside with the client, as part of their overall care plant. The other options such as being rehoused locally are also explored as part of this care plan.

Clients are placed at the forefront of their recovery, and they dictate the pace. This model is based on client empowerment, to overturn the vicissitudes of the past where their voices were negated. Hostels should be seen as ladders out of mire. Issues which militate against a psychologically informed environment, those relating to the local conditions and the quality of the local support infrastructure, should be held up for scrutiny. Local councillors should work to dismantle any obstacles to psycho-social regeneration. This model requires extensive partnerships from other practitioners and a political will power.

In some of the London Boroughs I have worked in, the ability to send people to detox and rehab was greatly thwarted by the limits and hurdles placed on spending resources on treatment.

A significant change occurred when Virginia Bottomley introduced the legislation around Community Care in the early 90's. Where previously Housing Benefit had provided the payments, this was now the remit of Social Services. They are asked to contribute from their budgets. This entails care being rationed. Panels were introduced to ascertain criteria for placing people in residential treatment. These panels use considerable resources (Craig 2008) and have become heavily gatekeeped. Substance Workers are in effect rescrutinised by Community Care Commissioners whilst the purse strings are held by Social Services. This can easily be streamlined into a more effective system, and the money given to the professional treatment practitioners. The therapeutic team need to make these decisions, as they are the people on the ground who understands the client. They can operate within budgets.

The nutritionist would work with the clients on their diet, along with the internal catering staff, helping people to plan and monitor their health. The worker would also help with meal planning, cooking and the buying of food, along with health food days, enticing people to come and provide food to the clients. She/he would also encourage them to cook shop and clean. Nutrition will take a more forward position. This is essential to health, and cooking is part of the therapeutic milieu, along with hygiene. This was undertaken in the hostel, but within a therapeutic team, it needs greater emphasis, as nutrition is the basis of psychological health.

The welfare rights worker would assist the clients with their claims, accompanying them to their medical examinations, work out their training/educational needs, plus assist them to achieve their long term aims. This would involve accessing the other agencies for support around jobs and training. Budgeting and planning ahead are also crucial, even for people trapped in a substance use habit. Working with people in the throes of their crisis entails they can build trust and confidence in the service. The Welfare Rights Worker is key to building community confidence in the service delivery. The workers would be working amongst the residents, rather than operating from behind a screen. Visibility is the key. This was the template at the hostel and it worked. This should be used in the new environment. The homeless men were keen to work, and meaningful placements in voluntary work will provide them confidence and self esteem. They will also have a purpose. The Welfare Rights worker can engage and then begin the therapeutic process.

Literacy, along with a therapeutic intervention is crucial, as this underpins people's ability to engage with the outside world, access training, boosts internal confidence and self esteem, thereby opening up life chances. This needs to be undertaken in one to one sessions. When not undertaking the one to one work, they need to be amongst the residents, building up their self esteem through conversation, and using their lateral knowledge to enhance literacy. This would involve newspaper discussion groups, formal or informal to Scrabble sessions. It would also entail the use of other innovations such as a newsletter, building a library, word games.

Literacy therefore needs to be perceived as an emotional issue. As Jay's case highlights, he used it as a way of shutting out the world, because the real world was deemed problematic, a source of emotional pain. The pedagogy of school reinforced his alienation. His inability to read, became embedded though disruption. This created a masculine identity, based upon overturning rules and procedures. More discipline was enacted to try and control him, and a greater resistance was engendered.

The task of a literacy worker is to unpick the various strategies of refusal Jay constructed. This would assist him to enhance confidence, to act upon the world, rather than retreat from it. Literacy, linked to passing a driving theory test, could later be used to read Shakespeare. It has to first create a purpose. This provides a concrete visualisation for reading. Literacy is low within this client group not because people have damaged brains, but because they are psychologically traumatised. This has occurred at an early age, and was not picked up by the school. Schools were not psychologically informed environments. Their mission statements traditionally have centred on the need to impart learning to empty vessels, coupled with the notion of discipline and control. The teachers were not exposed to psychologically informed practices in their training, and as a result, those who have gone into the profession have not built relational bridges.

There have not been many links made between low educational achievement and emotional trauma. It is apparent in these case histories; these men endured significant traumatic experiences as children that were missed by teachers. The use of discipline, imposed upon people, challenged by Skinner and Behaviourism, but continued to be used to regulate young people. Illiteracy, derived from an inability to concentrate, is linked to trauma, but it lacks in depth research between post traumatic stress and lack of concentration in children. This highlights how research has been constructed to ignore the effects of trauma. The social psychological regeneration of people will necessarily unpick those belief systems, and then provide transformation. This will provide the evidence to influence mainstream education.

Hobbies and Events are crucial, as many of the residents had a former interest in reading, art, theatre, sports and other artistic forms. These need to be carefully nurtured, through guiding people to access outside courses, or create new internal events. Having someone to talk to, when travelling to an event and making the introductions, is crucial to creating self confidence with other organisations. This is the baton of trust. Working alongside clients, to build trust and relationships with outside agencies, is crucial for their emotional growth and move on. When people leave the hostel, having a hobby dissolves the sense of isolation many people experience. They can find a peer group of like minded people, away from the substance use/homeless milieu. These workers would be operating within the hostel, rather than residing in an office, and they can also create a local newsletter/magazine/Ezine to circulate the work of the residents. These workers would work with outside organisations to undertake workshops, and build up the vibrancy of the therapeutic space. Thinking laterally is crucial to the success. The therapeutic space can be utilised as an arts space, workshop or group work, as initiated at Orexis with the Young Vic.

The First Contact Worker is the important face of the project, and sets the psychological tone. They need to adapt to various crises as well as answer the telephone and welcome the visitors. They are also the repository of knowledge, having direct contact with the residents on a daily basis. Building up a store of local knowledge of services and having an understanding of the psychological dynamics within the organisation, they are a crucial underpinning.

Local folk knowledge is crucial to providing a consistent service, and this can only be undertaken with continuity, having the same person on the front desk. They control the flow of information, develop a local knowledge of services, create rapport with the clients/residents and gauge the emotional temperature of the client/residents and provide reassurance. The First Contact Worker, the person at the front desk is the human interface between the agency and the client. They establish the psychological scene. Their brusqueness can create a template that ripples throughout the organisation. Their ability to welcome and defuse tension is crucial to creating a supportive psychological environment. They are more important than signs, decor and furniture, because they make the emotional connection. The furniture and decor is secondary to this welcoming and general putting at ease. A First contact worker is not a receptionist, but the organisational totem. They emanate the organisational ethos.

Cleaners and cooks are also part of the therapeutic milieu. They carry a repository of knowledge as the clients/residents talk to them about their ongoing problems. The ancillary staff team are so often overlooked, but they are crucial to the delivery of a therapeutic environment. They can sign post people for help as they reveal in informal exchanges their problems. They can offer the baton of trust to individual workers, through their informal networks and need to be incorporated into the therapeutic milieu as part of the team.

The Practice Manager role is another crucial role. He/She undertakes the major decisions around client behaviour as the person who manages the hostel. Separate, but inter-connected to the therapeutic environment they enact the key decisions on policing. They are an arbiter in the various disputes, overseeing the support staff, thereby ensuring the smooth running of the organisation. This is a key integral post, as this person creates the aims of the collective and brings it altogether. They outline the composition of the work; arrange the staff structures, training needs, and work around any staffing issues. They utilise the use of space, budgeting, booking in residents, interview, induction, dealing with income and expenditure. They work along with the administrator, thereby ensuring the function of the organisation is maintained in terms of IT equipment, processes for protocols, audits and government legislation. This frees up the front line workers to deliver.

The Administrator works alongside the Practice Manager to implement processes, collates the audit figures, works to balance the books, ensures the wages are paid; funding is received, and produces reports, all working alongside the main central staff. They can also fill in for the First Contact Worker and deputise for the Practice Manager Role during sickness or holidays. They constitute the organisational backbone.

Four therapeutic project workers would be needed to cover the shifts in a hostel. Their main role would be to support any activities and ensure the smooth running of the organisation over a 24 hour period. In particular they would resolve the issue of hostel noise and provide emergency crisis intervention, as many of the men have difficulties in sleeping.

The project could also take trainee therapists and counsellors to work on front line services to bolster the face to face work. If there are personality projections, then clients have a choice.

In summary the PIE (Johnson and Haigh 2010) is more than employing a therapist, it is a revolution in care delivery, entailing a new service design. The therapist cannot work in isolation, as many of the issues need practical intervention. Literacy, the development of hostel living issues, court/ probation, nutrition, psychiatric medication, substance use, housing, DWP/Job Centre/Housing Benefit issues, Jobs/Training/Employment all need to be addressed independently of therapy. They also need a therapeutic input. The practical needs are considerable, as people need to be accompanied to their appointments and supported. The case histories highlight that when people follow on from the therapeutic intervention, they find a meaning to interact with the wider society. Workers skilled in benefit advice and understanding the DWP labyrinth, are absolutely crucial.

This was the format funded by the GP's in Deptford, Lewisham in 1997 when they looked forward into the future. At the time we had not established hard and fast guide lines. The conceptual language for what we were involved within, had yet to be invented. The idea of joint partnership, self medication, trauma, working on masculinities, thereby regenerating people and building social infrastructure were not expressly articulated. At the time we were engaged in trying to find forms of truth, based on intuition, rather than previous research. This was to be innovative, as the drugs agency and the GP's pushed ahead to make huge advances. These were undermined by the local council bureaucracy. This was left behind and became destructive. The only true knowledge resides in the practitioners. These are the people who need to forge the future, and release the potential of those who have existed for too many years entrapped.

BIBLIOGRAPHY

Adler, A. (1927). "Understanding Human Nature." Oxford: Oneworld (reprinted 1992).

Adler, A. (1931). "Social Interest," Oxford: Oneworld Publications (reprinted 2010).

Adler, A. (2004). "Adler Speaks, The Lectures of Alfred Adler," Lincoln USA: iUniverse.

Adler, A. (1956). "Individual Psychology," New York: Harper. (reprinted 1964).

Algren, N. (1949). "Man with the Golden Arm," London: Pan Books (reprinted 1990).

Arendt, H. (1958). "The Human Condition," Chicago USA: Chicago University Press.

Baran, P. and Sweezy, P (1989). "Monopoly Capital: An Essay on the American Economic and Social Order" http://monthlyreview.org/ contact: Monthly Review Press.

Barton Evans, F. (1996). "Harry Stack Sullivan," Sussex: Routledge (reprinted 2006).

Beck, A.T. and Freeman, A. (1990). "Cognitive Therapy of Personality Disorders," New York: Guildford Press.

Becker, H. (1963). "Outsiders." New York: Free Press (reprinted 1993).

Berne, E. (1964). "Games People Play," London: Penguin. (reprinted 2010).

Berne, E. (1961). "Transactional Analysis in Psychotherapy," New York: Grove Press (reprinted 2009).

Bettelheim, B. (1960) "The Informed Heart" London: Penguin (reprinted 1986).

Blum, D. (2002). "Love at Goon Park, Harry Harlow and the Science of Affection," Jackson TN: Perseus Books.

Bourdieu, P. (1984). "Distinction," Sussex: Routledge (reprinted 2010).

Bowlby, J. (1969). "Attachment and Loss," Attachment. London: Pimlico (reprinted 1997).

Bowlby, J. (1973). "Attachment and Loss, Separation Anger and Anxiety," London: Pimlico (reprinted 1998).

Bowlby, J. (1980). "Attachment and Loss, Sadness and Depression," London: Pimlico (reprinted 1998).

Bowlby, J. (1988). "A Secure Base," Sussex: Routledge (reprinted 2009).

Brady, K. T., Dansky, B. S., Back, S. E., Foa, E. B., & Carroll, K. M. (2001). Exposure therapy in the treatment of PTSD among cocaine-dependent individuals: preliminary findings. *Journal of Substance Abuse Treatment, 21*, 47-54.

Braverman H. (1974). "Labor and monopoly capital," New York: Monthly Review.

Burroughs, W. (1977). "Junky," London: Penguin.

Carpenter L. (2009) "Once were warriors," www.guardian.co.uk/lifeandstyle/2009/feb/01/post-traumatic-stress-disorder Accessed 16th September 2011

Celine, F. (2008). "Semmelweiss, A Fictional Biography," London: Atlas Press.

Chomsky, N. (1996). "Power and Prospects," London: Pluto Press.

Cloward and Ohlin (1966). "Delinquency and Opportunity," New York: Free Press.

Collins M and Phillips J (2003) "Disempowerment and Disconnection—Trauma and Homelessness Report" published by Glasgow Homelessness Network

Connell, R. (1995). "Masculinities," Cambridge: Polity Press.

Craig, D. (2008). "Squandered," London: Constable.

De Beauvoir, S. (1949). "The Second Sex" London: Vintage Classics (reprinted 1997).

De Zulueta, F. (1993). "From Pain to Violence," London: Whurr Publishers (reprinted 1996).

Deleuze, G. and Guattari, F. (1972). "Anti Oedipus," Minneapolis: Minnesota Press (reprinted 1992)

Deleuze, G. and Guattari F. (1980). "A Thousand Plateaus," London: Athlone Press (reprinted 1999).

Evans, K. & Sullivan, J. M. (1995). "Treating addicted survivors of trauma." New York: Guilford Press.

Fanon, F. (1952). "Black Skin, White Masks," London: Pluto Press (reprinted 1958).

Fanon, F. (1965). Wretched of the Earth," London New York: Grove Press (reprinted 2004).

Fenichel O. (1945). "The Psychoanalytic theory of neurosis," New York: Norton, New York (reprinted 1972).

Fielding L (2011). "To Live Outside the Law: Caught by Operation Julie, Britain's Biggest Drugs Bust," London: Serpents Tail.

Foucault, M (1977). "Discipline and Punish," London: Penguin (reprinted 1991).

Foucault M. (1972). "The Archaeology of Knowledge," Sussex: Routledge (reprinted 1995)

Foucault, M. (1998). "The History of Sexuality: The Will to Knowledge:" London: Penguin.

Frankl V. (1952). "The Doctor and the Soul," London: Souvenir Press (reprinted 2010).

Frankl, V. (1959). "Man's Search for Meaning," New York: Simon and Schuster (reprinted 1985).

Free B. "Silence, Secrecy, and Shame Lead to Trauma," www.nmoi.org/articles/SilenceSecrecyShame.html Accessed September 9th 2011

Fromm, E. (1957). "The Art of Loving," London; Thorsons (reprinted 1995).

Fromm, E. (1955). "The Sane Society" Sussex; Routledge (reprinted 2001)

Gerth, H. and Wright Mills, C. (1953). "Character and Social Structure: The Psychology of Social Institutions," Orlando Florida: Harcourt Brace and Jovanovich.

Gilligan, C. Ward, J. Taylor, J. (1988). "Mapping the Moral Domain," Cambridge Ma: Harvard University Press.

Gilligan, C. (1990a). "In a Different Voice: Psychological Theory and Women's Development," Cambridge Ma: Harvard University Press.

Gilligan, C. Lyons, P. Hanmet, T. (1990b). "Making Connections," Cambridge Ma: Harvard University Press.

Gilligan, J. (2000). "Violence-Reflections on our Deadliest Epidemic," London: JKP

Goffman, E. (1959). "The Presentation of the Self in Everyday Life," London: Penguin (reprinted 1990).

Goffman, E. (1961). "Asylums," London: Penguin (reprinted 1991).

Goffman, E. (1963). "Stigma," London: Penguin (reprinted 1990).

Goodman L, Harvey M. (1991) "Homelessness as psychological trauma. Broadening perspectives." No;46(11):1219-25

Halpern, D. (2004). "Social Capital." Cambridge: Polity Press.

Halpern, D. (2009). "The Hidden Wealth of Nations" Cambridge: Polity Press.

Hare, R. (1999). "Without Conscience," New York: Guildford Press.

Harrison, J. (1986). "Love Your Disease, its Making You Healthy," NSW Australia: Angus and Robertson.

Herman, J. (1992). "Trauma and recovery: The Aftermath of Violence—from Domestic Abuse to Political Terror." New York: Basic Books.

Heuer, G (Editor) (2011). "Sexual Revolutions," Sussex: Routledge.

Hough M. (1996) "Drugs Misuse and the criminal justice system: a review of the the Literature."

www.drugslibrary.stir.ac.uk/documents/houghdrugscrime.pdf   Accessed 14th September 2011

House of Commons (2002) "Hansard Debates for 8 Mar 2002 (pt 6)" www. publications.parliament.uk/pa/cm200102/cmhansrd/vo020308/ debtext/20308-06.htm Accessed September 12th 2011

Illich, I. (1977). "Disabling Professions," London Marion Boyars (reprinted 2010).

Johnson, R. & Haigh, J. (2010). "Mental Health and Social Inclusion," Social psychiatry and Social Policy for the 21st Century: new concepts for new needs. Part One—'the psychologically informed environment' Article

Jung, C.(1964). "Man and his Symbols," London; Aldous Books.

Junger, E. (1920). "Storm of Steel," London; Penguin Classic (reprinted 2004).

Kamlesh, P. and Wibberley C. (2002). "Young Asians and Drug Use," Journal of Child Health Care, March vol.6 no, 1 51-59

Khantzian E. (1985) "The self-medication hypothesis of addictive disorders."American Journal of Psychiatry, 142(11): 1259-1264

Khantzian, E., & Murphy, S. (1995). "Self medication disorder; application of ego psychology to the treatment of substance use." In: A. Washton (Ed.), Psychotherapy and Substance Use (Chapter 8). New York: Guilford Press.

Khantzian, E. (1999). "Treating Addiction as a Human Process," Lanham MD: Jason Aaronson.

Khantzian, E. and Albanese M (2010). "Understanding Addiction as Self Medication," New Delhi, India: Good Times Books.

Kierkegaard, S. (1844). "The Concept of Dread" New Jersey, USA: Princeton University Press (reprinted 1964).

Kuhl, S. (1992). "The Nazi Connection: Eugenics, American Racism, and German National Socialism," Oxford: OUP.

Kuhn, T. (1996). "The Structure of Scientific Revolutions," Chicago: University of Chicago Press.

Laing, R. D. (1971). "Knots," Harmondsworth Middx: Penguin.

Laing, R.D (1967). "The Politics of Experience and The Bird of Paradise," London: Penguin (reprinted in 1990).

Laing, R.D. (1960). "The Divided Self." London: Penguin (reprinted 1990)

Laing R.D (1961). first published 1961 "Self and Others," London: Penguin (reprinted 1990)

Laing R. D. (1964). "Sanity Madness and the Family," London: Penguin (reprinted in 1990)

Landsberger, H. A. (1961). "Hawthorne Revisited," Ithaca New York: Cornell University Press.

Leadbeater C. (1996) "The Rise of the Social Entrepreneur," UK; Demos,

Le Grand J. (2006). "Motivation, Agency, and Public Policy: Of Knights and Knaves, Pawns and Queens," Oxford: OUP

Le Grand J. (2006) "A Better Class of Choice," www.publicfinance.co.uk/features/2006/a-better-class-of-choice-by-julian-le-grand/ accessed September 12th 2011

Le Grand, J. (2007). "The Other Invisible Hand, Delivering Public Services through Choice," New Jersey, USA; Princeton University Press.

Lerner, P. (2003). "Male Hysteria," Ithaca, New York: Cornell University Press.

Lewisham Strategic Partnership (2011) "Integrated Offender Management," 2011/2012www.lewishamstrategicpartnership.org.uk/ docs/SLP%20Marc . . . Accessed 12th September 2011

Lister E. (1982). Forced Silence: A neglected dimension of trauma. The American Journal of Psychiatry, Vol 139(7), Jul 1982, 872-876

Lynch, D. (1980). "The Elephant Man," Film DVD (reissued in 2001).

Lyotard, F. (1992). "The Post Modern Condition," Manchester: Manchester University Press.

March, W. (1997). "The Bad Seed" New Jersey, USA: The Ecco Press.

Marcuse, A. (1972). "A Study on Authority," translated by De Bres, London Verso (reprinted 2008).

Marsden, J. and Farrell, M. (2007). Tops Form, London; DOH

Maslow, A. (1968). "Towards a Psychology of Being, Radford, Va: Wilder publications (reprinted 2011)

McDonagh, T. (2011). "Tackling homelessness and exclusion: Understanding complex lives," UK; Joseph Rowntree Trust

Miller, A. (1991). "Banished Knowledge," London: Virago (reprinted 2006).

Miller, A. (2005). "The Body Never Lies," New York: Norton.

Miller, A. (1987). "For your own good, Roots of Violence in Childrearing," London: Virago.

Miller, A. (1985). "Thou Shalt Not Be Aware," London: Pluto Press.

Miller, A. (1990). "The Untouched Key," London: Virago.

Miller A. (2001). "The Truth Will Set You Free," New York: Basic Books.

Miller A. (1987). "The Drama of Being a Child," London: Virago

Moncrieff, J. D., Drummond, D. C., Candy, B., Checinski, K., & Farmer, R. (1996). Sexual abuse in people with alcohol problems: A study of prevalence of sexual abuse and its relationship to drinking behavior. *British Journal of Psychiatry, 169*, 355-360.

Motz, A. (2008). "The Psychology of Female Violence," Sussex: Routledge.

Najavits, L. M. (2002). *Seeking safety: A treatment manual for PTSD and substance abuse.* New York: Guilford Press.

NIDA (2011) Understanding Drug Abuse and Addiction http://www.drugabuse.gov/infofacts/understand.html Accessed September 20th 2011

Nietzsche, F. (1878). "Human All Too Human," Cambridge: Cambridge University Press (reprinted 1996).

Nietzsche, F. (1881). "Daybreak," Cambridge: Cambridge University Press (reprinted 1997).

Nietzsche, F. (1882). "The Gay Science," London: Random House (reprinted 1991).

Nietzsche, F. (1886). "Beyond Good and Evil" Cambridge: Cambridge University Press (reprinted 1991).

Nietzsche, F. (1888). "Ecce Homo," London: Penguin Classics (reprinted 2004)

Nietzsche, F. (1895). "Twilight of the Idols/The Antichrist," London: Penguin (reprinted 1990).

Nietzsche, F. (1968). "Will to Power," Translated by W Kaufman and R Hollingdale, New York, Vintage Books (reprinted 1973).

Nietzsche F. (1954). "The Portable Nietzsche;" Translated by Walter Kaufman, USA; Penguin Classics, (reprinted 1994).

NTA (2006) "Models of Care for Adult Drug Misusers" www.nta.nhs.uk/uploads/nta_modelsofcare_update_2006_moc3.pdf

Office of Science and Technology (2011) "Drugs Futures 2025 The Scenarios," www.bis.gov.uk/files/file15418.pdf Accessed September 11th 2011

O' Hare, Drucker, Newcombe, Mathews, Buning (1992). "The Reduction of Drug Related Harm," Sussex: Routledge.

Orwell, G. (1933). "Down and Out in Paris and London," London: Penguin (reprinted 2001).

Painter J, Riley-Buckley D and Whittington D (2000). Practical Considerations, Making Women's Services Available, 15: 18-20

Passolini (1967). "Oedipus Rex," DVD.

Pearce, J. and Pezzot-Pearce, T. (2006). "Psychotherapy of Abused and Neglected Children," New York: Guildford Press

Pinker, S. (2003). "The Blank Slate," London: Penguin.

Plummer J (2006) "Businesses and Charities are very similar these days," www.guardian.co.uk/society/2006/nov/08/charities.voluntarysector Accessed 9th September 2011

Rank, O. (1936). "Truth and Reality," London New York: Norton (reprinted 1978).

Rank, O. (1932). "Art and the Artist," London New York: Norton (reprinted 1989).

Rank, O. (1952). "The Trauma of Birth," Connecticut: Martino Publishing (reprinted 2010).

Reich, W. (1933). "Character Analysis," New York: Farrar, Strauss and Giroux (reprinted 1990).

Reich, W. (1946). "The Mass Psychology of Fascism," London: Souvenir Press (reprinted 1997).

Rice, C., Mohr, C. D., Del Boca, F. K., Mattson, M. E., Young, L., Brady, K. T., Brady, K., Nickless, C. (2001). Self-reports of physical, sexual and emotional abuse in alcoholism treatment sample. *Journal of Studies on Alcohol, 61,* 114-123

Rogers, C. (1969). "Freedom to Learn," New Jersey: Prentice Hall (reprinted 1994).

Rogers, C. (1961). "On Becoming a Person," London: Constable (reprinted 2004).

Sartre, J. P (2001). "Sketch for a Theory of Emotions," Sussex: Routledge.

Sartre, J. P (1943). "Being and Nothingness," Sussex: Routledge (reprinted 2003).

Schaffer, H. and Stimmel, B. (1984). "Addictive Behaviours," Sussex: Routledge.

Schaler, J. (1999). "Addiction is a Choice" Chicago, Illinois: Open Court Publishing.

Seddon, J. (2008). "Systems Thinking in the Public Sector," Axminster Devon: Triarchy Press.

Seidler, V. (2005). "Transforming Masculinities," Sussex: Routledge.

Selby, H. (1978). "Requiem for a Dream," London: Maryon Boyars (republished 2003).

Shiner M (2011). "Youth Justice Handbook; Theory, Policy and Practice," by T. Taylor, R. Earle and D R. Hester (Cullompton: Willan Publishing/The Open University, 2010 review in Brit. J. Criminol. (2011) 51, 459-472

Society of St. James (2011) "Drug Rehabilitation Requirement," www.ssj.org.uk/addiction-services/drr.html Accessed 12th September 2011

Spitz, R. (1965). "The First Year of Life" New York: International Universities Press.

Stack Sullivan, H. (1953). "Interpersonal Theory and Psychotherapy," New York: Norton.

Stack Sullivan, H. (1970). "The Psychiatric Interview," New York: Norton.

Stack Sullivan H. (1974). "Schizophrenia as a Human Process," New York: Norton.

Steiner, C. (1974). "Games Alcoholics Play," New York: Ballantyne Books.

Steiner, C. (2003). "Emotional Literacy, Intelligence with a Heart," California: Personhood Press.

Stirner, M. (1844). "The Ego and It Own," London: Rebel Press. (reprinted 1982)

Stout, M. (2007). "The Sociopath Next Door," New York: Broadway Books.

Taylor, F.W. (1911). "The Principles of Scientific Management," US: Dover Publications (reprinted 1998).

Third Sector (2011)." Interview with Julian Le Grand," www.thirdsector. co.uk/news/Article/1075751/Interview-Julian-Le-Grand/2011 Accessed 16th September 2011

University of Utah (2011) "Genetics is an important factor in Addiction." http://learn.genetics.utah.edu/content/addiction/genetics/ Accessed September 12th 2011

Vickers J. (2008) "Lou Salome: A Biography of the Woman who Inspired Freud, Nietzsche and Rilke," Jefferson, NC: McFarland & Co Inc.

Wand, McCaul, Yang, Reynolds, Gotjen, Lee and Ali (2002). "The Mu Opioid Receptor Gene Polymorphism (A118G) Alters HPA Axis Activation Induced by Narcotic Blockade" in Neuropsychopharmacology (2002) 26 106-114

Washton A. Editor (1997). "Psychotherapy and Substance Abuse," New York: Guildford Press.

Waterhouse R (Hon), Margaret Clough, Morris le Fleming DL (2000) "Lost in care, report of the tribunal of inquiry into the abuse of children in care in the former county council areas of Gwynedd and Clwyd since 1974" published by Crown Copyright, UK

Weber, M. (1978). "Economy and Society," Berkley California: University of California Press (reprinted 1992).

Whittington, D. (2007a). "Beaten into Violence," Milton Keynes: Authorhouse.

Whittington, D. (2007b). "Harrison Narcotics Act; Encyclopaedia of Drugs, Alcohol & Addictive Behaviour," USA: Macmillan

Whittington, D. (2011). "Wrenching Open the Doors of Perception," Attachment Journal March 2011, London: Karnac.

Willis, P. (1978). "Learning to Labour," Aldershot: Ashgate Publishing (reprinted 2000).

Wilmot, P. and Young M., (1969). "Family and Kinship in the East End," London: Penguin.

Winnicott, D. (1964)." The Child, the Family and the Outside World," London: Penguin (reprinted 1991).

Winnicott, D. (1965). "The Family and Individual Development," Sussex: Routledge (reprinted 1995).

Wright Mills, C. (1999). "The Power Elite," Oxford: OUP.

Yalom, I. (1991). "Loves Executioner," London: Penguin.